Mackey, 1994.

DARLING LOOSY

ALSO BY ELIZABETH LONGFORD

Jameson's Raid
Victoria R.I.
Wellington: Years of the Sword
Wellington: Pillar of State
Byron
Byron's Greece
The Royal House of Windsor
Louisa Lady in Waiting
A Pilgrimage of Passion:
The Life of Wilfrid Scawen Blunt
The Queen Mother
Eminent Victorian Women
Elizabeth R
The Pebbled Shore: Memoirs
The Oxford Book of Royal Anecdotes

Letters to Princess Louise

1856–1939

Edited by

ELIZABETH LONGFORD

WEIDENFELD & NICOLSON
LONDON

Copyright © Selection, editorial matter and Introduction

Elizabeth Longford 1991

First published in Great Britain by
George Weidenfeld & Nicolson Limited
91 Clapham High Street, London SW4 7TA

All rights reserved. No part of this publication may be reproduced, stored in a retrieval system, or transmitted, in any form or by any means, electronic, mechanical, photocopying, recording or otherwise, without the prior permission of the copyright owners.

ISBN 0 297 81179 7

Printed in Great Britain by Butler & Tanner Ltd,
Frome and London

For Frank and Flora

CONTENTS

ILLUSTRATIONS

(Unless otherwise stated, the photographs are taken from the Royal Archives, Windsor Castle, copyright reserved, and are reproduced by gracious permission of Her Majesty The Queen.)

Between pages 118 and 119

Between pages 182 and 183

NOTES ON THIS EDITION OF *DARLING LOOSY*

All the letters that follow are collected in the Royal Archives. The collection may have been larger at the time of Princess Louise's death because the Royal Librarian, who at the time was Sir Owen Morshead, refers in a note to the Princess's collection being eventually 'dispersed'. This may have happened. Almost all the letters are *to* Princess Louise and very few *from* her. Only a handful, for instance, out of the many hundreds of letters that she wrote to her mother Queen Victoria are in this collection; nor are the missing letters anywhere else in the Archives. It looks as if the vast majority were destroyed.

The letters printed below are a selection: nearly 450 letters or extracts (including a few verses) out of a total of some 2,000. Most of them are filed under the archival reference of 'A17', followed by the appropriate number. In order to save unnecessary repetition, all references here that contain only numbers will be found under A17 in the Archives. All other references contain letters as well as numbers, e.g. A15.

The original spelling and punctuation have been followed except where clarity or appearance invited amendment, particularly in the case of Queen Victoria's famous abbreviations, and all ampersands.

EDITOR'S ACKNOWLEDGMENTS

First I must thank Her Majesty The Queen for graciously allowing this collection of Princess Louise's letters to be published, with the necessary captions and explanations. HRH the Princess Margaret, Countess of Snowdon, has been good enough to give me the benefit of her knowledge of Kensington Palace and its relevant apartments, and I am deeply grateful to Her Royal Highness and her staff.

I am most grateful to Oliver Everett, the Royal Librarian, for his kindness and encouragement, and to his staff at the Archives for their absolutely indispensable help. Without their ability to explain allusions, and their knowledge, wisdom and almost magical powers with scarcely legible handwriting, too many of the letters would have remained as tantalizing enigmas or just plain mistakes; for example, they once saved me from transcribing 'diet chart' as 'deck chair'. (Any remaining mistakes are my own.) Incidentally, the first typewritten letter in this collection came from the Crown Princess of Sweden in 1916.

I am especially indebted to Elizabeth Cuthbert, then to her successor as Registrar Sheila de Bellaigue, with her masterly interpretation of German expressions, and to Pam Clark. I should like to thank all the staff for making me so welcome during the lunch break in the romantic Round Tower – an informal social event that I shall always remember with nostalgic pleasure. I am also glad to have seen them making the most of their new temporary home, the giant Portacabin where they succeed miraculously in being as helpful as ever.

Many friends old and new have given me insights and information for which I am in their debt. Elizabeth, Duchess of Hamilton, has found time amidst her own work on the Carlyles to put me in the picture as regards Princess Louise's Scottish background through her marriage. I thank the Earl and Countess of Selkirk for advice on family records; the Earl Cawdor, the Duke of Argyll and Lady Adeane for their kindness. Jean Babington-Smith has been extremely illuminating on the family life that circled around Lord Lorne, 9th Duke of Argyll, his brothers, sisters, nieces and nephews. Miss Flora Stewart kindly told me her memories of the Princess in Scotland. For other memories and stories I thank Patience Thesiger, Mrs Duckworth, Brigadier G. L. D. Duckworth, my friend Philip Ziegler, Nicholas Locock and the Revd T. McLean Wilson.

I can never thank Sandra Gwyn enough for the serendipitous discoveries she made for me in the London Library when I was immobilized, and for opening windows for me on the Canadian scene through her personal knowledge and prize-winning book, *The Private Capital*. I am extremely grateful to Robert M. Stamp (*Royal Rebels*) for his Canadian expertise and for answering my enquiries. I have found three other highly recommended Canadian authors most useful: R. H. Hubbard (*Rideau Hall*), W. Stewart MacNutt (*Days of Lorne*) and the reprehensible but enlightening J. T. McAdam, whose pseudonym was Captain Mac. I would like to thank the staff of the National Archives of Canada most warmly for their unstinted and essential help, especially Brian Murphy and Dale Cameron; Gwynneth Evans of the National Library; and C. C. J. Bond.

I have gained a great deal from talking to my friend the writer Hugo Vickers, and from the biography by Hannah Pakula (*Queen of Roumania*) and the researches of Dr Joan Huffman. All have been most helpful. My old friend A. L. Rowse was kind enough to summarize for me his very interesting views on the Marquess of Lorne's character. My friend Nina Epton (*Queen Victoria and Her Children*) answered my many questions both in discussion and writing.

No study of the letters to Princess Louise could proceed without constant recourse to Jehanne Wake's splendid biography: *Princess Louise – Queen Victoria's Unconventional Daughter*. I read it before publication with great enjoyment and have found it invaluable since. Among the classics I need hardly mention *Queen Victoria's Letters and Journals,* the mother-and-child series edited by Roger Fulford (*Dearest Child, Dearest Mama, Darling Child*), the concluding *Beloved and Darling Child* edited by Agatha Ramm, and *Letters to a Granddaughter* edited by Richard Hough. If this were a regular bibliography I would certainly record my debt to many other books of general and special interest, notably Richard Ellman's *Oscar Wilde* and James Lees-Milne's *The Enigmatic Edwardian.*

My thanks are due as always to the staff of the London Library and of the public libraries of Kensington and Chelsea. I would also like to thank Nigel Arch, curator of Kensington Palace; Mrs E. Nixon of Westminster Abbey Library; the biographical information service of the British Library; the Librarian of the Royal Academy; Steven Tomlinson of the Bodleian Library; Susan Cross of the Fawcett Library; R. N. Smart of the Library of St Andrews University; and *The Times*' archives.

On the artistic side of Princess Louise's career I must thank Geraldine Norman for putting me on to a rich vein of research, through Geoffrey Munn and Jeremy Maas who were both extraordinarily helpful. I benefited greatly from *Artists' Jewellery* by Charlotte Gere and Geoffrey Munn and from *The Victorian Art World in Photographs* by Jeremy Maas. Jane Roberts' *Royal Artists* was highly relevant, as was Mark Stocker's *Life and Work of Sir Joseph Edgar Boehm*. I would also like to thank Joanna Banham, curator of Leighton House, Shirley Nicholson and Nan Chapman.

For illustrations I am extremely grateful to HRH the Prince and Princess Michael of Kent for their generosity and the great trouble taken with photographs. I owe sincere thanks to Frances Dimond, curator of the Photograph Collection in the Royal Archives; to my friend Sophie Baker; to the Rev. S. D. Cleaver of St Mildred's Church, Whippingham; and to my daughter Judith and grandchildren Miranda and Arthur for photographing some of Princess Louise's sculpture. I so much appreciate the kindness of Christopher Newall in allowing me to use the beautiful portrait of Princess Louise for the jacket; and of the Princess von Coburg-Gotha and Mr Simon Reynolds for the photograph of the unusual W. B. Richmond portrait.

Linda Osband has been a most heartening editor (not for the first time) and I have warmly welcomed the suggestions of Christopher Falkus. I thank George Weidenfeld for his interest and support over so many years. Michael Shaw has been as usual the perfect agent. My secretary Agnes Fenner has typed and retyped a complicated manuscript with undiminished zeal. Lastly I express my gratitude yet again to my family for sophisticated advice, with special thanks to my granddaughter Flora – whose path to Windsor has happily crossed mine – and to Frank for reading and greatly improving the Introduction.

Elizabeth Longford
Bernhurst 1991

INTRODUCTION

I

1848–78

All letters were private, according to the nineteenth-century code, but royal letters more private still. So when a member of the royal household sold to a man in Paris a letter written by Queen Victoria to Lord Melbourne, there was fierce indignation. 'I can't understand his doing such a thing, I am not astonished at Georgie [George V] being annoyed,' wrote Prince Arthur, Duke of Connaught, to his sister Princess Louise. 'There is a perfect craze for memoirs at the present moment [1923] and people will go any lengths to satisfy this.'

Today Prince Arthur would be scandalized to discover how far the craze has gone. Royal letters are now recognized as important sources of history, and as such have already been published in their thousands with the willing co-operation of the monarch of the day. From published letters has developed understanding of the royal family and, through them, knowledge of other families living in Britain at the same time. Not only because it is 'royal', but also because it is so well documented, this particular family becomes of consuming interest to historians and general readers alike. The collection and preservation of their letters – both to and from – is one of the activities for which we cannot be too grateful.

In the following pages a selection of the letters written to Princess Louise and filed in the Royal Archives, Windsor Castle, is published, almost all for the first time. The life story of the Princess, as it emerges from the vividly expressed hopes, frustrations, affections and jealousies of her mother, sisters, brothers, husband, relations and friends, is a fascinating replica of much that was going on around her. We see in particular a royal illustration of George Bernard Shaw's epigram: 'Home is the girl's prison.'

Even if the Princess's cage was a golden one, her efforts to escape from it were just as determined as those of other less favoured prisoners. What makes this particular life so interesting is that she realized exactly what was happening and resolved to change it, but without breaking the royal mould into which she had been born.

The year of her birth, 1848, was a significant one for Europe and for the breaking of many patterns. In this Year of Revolutions, the continent was swept by violent political changes; the French throne collapsed and even Britain's political reformers, the Chartists, were momentarily thought to have a chance of success.

Six months after her birth, a domestic mould was broken in the Princess's own family. Her Hanoverian ancestors had hardly ever visited so remote and wild a realm as Scotland, let alone lived there, but in 1848 her family made their first stay at Balmoral – to Queen Victoria and Prince Albert such a joy, to most of their children after Albert's death such a bore.

Also in 1848 John Ruskin married Effie Gray, both of whom were to play a part in Louise's life. The marriage was annulled in 1855 and Effie, having married the painter Sir John Millais, was ostracized by Queen Victoria. When Millais was dying, Louise asked him if there was anything the Queen could do for him. 'Yes, let her receive my wife.' The Queen did so, presumably at a Drawing Room, as there is no official record of a private audience.

It was also in Louise's birth year that the young artists, Millais and Holman Hunt, watched the demonstrating Chartists and decided to found an idealistic movement of their own, the Pre-Raphaelite Brotherhood. Louise was to be influenced by this and other new movements in the arts.

The Prince Consort himself, Louise's father, made a gesture towards the new thinking by proposing to the Liberal Prime Minister, Lord John Russell, the creation of life peers. Russell was not ready for such a controversial act. Many years later, however, Louise was to support the idea in order to curb the power of the House of Lords to kill Irish Home Rule.

Queen Victoria gave birth to her sixth child and fourth daughter at 8 a.m. on 18 March. She was named Louise after Albert's late mother, Caroline after his step-grandmother, Caroline Amalia of Saxe-Gotha, and Alberta after himself. Neither parent was in good fettle at the time, Albert because of the international situation on top of the death of his step-grandmother in February, which had left him distressingly 'sad and pale'. A few weeks before Louise's birth he had wailed to his stepmother in Coburg, 'What dismal times are these!' When his baby daughter arrived, his main feeling was of relief that Victoria's exceptionally long labour was over. Her suffering, she said, was an experience she would never forget. Both of them would have preferred another boy.

However, the Queen bravely interpreted the excitements in Europe as somehow good omens for their child. 'Something peculiar', she wrote, was sure to be what this child turned out. They did indeed get the 'peculiarities', but did not foresee the talent. She was to become an artist.

Eager to show off their French, Louise's clever elder sisters christened her 'La Nouvelle', though this was quickly changed to something more cosy, 'Loo Loo'. The newcomer was a beautiful baby according to the children's governess, Lady Lyttelton: 'Extremely fair with white satin hair; large long blue eyes and regular features: a most perfect form from head to foot.' Beauty was to be one of her special gifts in a royal family not noted for it, at least till the coming of the lovely Princess of Wales, Alexandra (Alix) of Denmark, in 1862. For a genuinely loving mother, Queen Victoria was extraordinarily tactless in pointing out her children's faults to each other. Louise would be told that Vicky, the eldest of the family and Crown Princess of Prussia, had put on weight, while Alice, the next sister and Grand Duchess of Hesse-Darmstadt, was unbecomingly thin and drawn. At a fancy-dress ball the third sister, Helena, aged seventeen, was described to Vicky as spoilt by her heavy features whereas Louise, aged eleven, looked particularly pretty. Vicky heard that Louise at twenty was much more 'distinguished looking' than Alice, whose haggardness made her 'total want of chin so very apparent'. Whatever her faults, Louise always managed to appear 'exquisite'. Though even there the Queen found one exception. In May 1862 the youngest sister, Beatrice, 'Dear Baby', was 'the bright spot in this dead home', while 'Poor Louise has an awful stye on her eye.' The Queen made up to the sufferer by presenting her with a book of her favourite, turgid German hymns, compiled in memory of Albert: 'To dear Louise from her brokenhearted & affectionate Mama V. R. Balmoral May 1862.'

Brains, however, were the undoubted possession of Louise's sisters Vicky and Alice, though not thought to be outstanding in Louise herself. Indeed, the young Louise suffered from the usual deprivations connected with the middle position in a large family. For instance, when the Queen went abroad, Louise would be left behind at Osborne, their home on the Isle of Wight, because she was both 'too young and too old' for the expedition. As a result she lacked self-confidence and was in turn under-estimated. She reacted sometimes with exuberant enthusiasm, as when Vicky's first-born son William arrived and Louise shouted that they were no longer mere royal children, 'we are uncles and aunts'. At other times she reacted with sharp criticism. The array of family Christmas trees at

Windsor drew from her the pert remark in excellent French, 'Vraiment, c'est un peu trop extravagant.' Or, in her teens, she would treat court ceremony with a lack of seriousness. 'I shall be so pleased to see you at Court', she wrote to her friend Louisa Bowater in 1866, 'and will try and behave very well when you pass [to curtsy to the Queen] because I have always had an inclination to laugh when I see anyone I know.' She also suffered at this stage from headaches, which could be put down to the tensions of a teenager or to the after-effects of tubercular meningitis in 1864.

It was this same friend, Miss Bowater, who was the confidante of Louise's melancholy moods. 'I feel low and sad, and sit in my room and cry,' she wrote to Louisa on 20 July 1866. 'I cannot write and tell you why, there are so many things ought not to be as they are.... I am expected to agree with them and yet I cannot, when I know a thing to be wrong.' This was probably a reference to the Queen's unpopular seclusion, for at that date, 1866, Victoria was accusing her daughter Alice of sowing pernicious seeds on this subject in Louise. Five months later the depression seems to have been typical teenage wretchedness, inexplicable and incommunicable: 'I am often sad, but I never let others see that I am.'

The expression of her self-depreciation had reached its peak when her father died suddenly of typhoid on 14 December 1861. In her misery the crushed thirteen year old cried out: 'Oh! why did not God take me. I am so stupid and useless.' But her art came to her rescue as so often. She expressed her sympathy in a poetic drawing of her mother asleep and dreaming of being reunited with Albert.

Prince Albert had in fact been one of her mainstays. Perhaps he realized that her nose might be put out of joint by the arrival of two more brothers, Arthur and Leopold, two years and five years respectively after Louise's birth. (There were already two brothers, the Prince of Wales and Prince Alfred – 'Affie' – above her.) It was the five-year-old Louise's hand that Albert held at Prince Leopold's christening, and Louise whom he led forward at the head of the procession. At ten she was writing to him, 'My dear Papa, How long it seems that you are away [on a visit to Germany], I long very much to see you again.' While her father was alive she could look forward to the usual gaieties of royal children, all of which ceased after his death: children's balls, fancy-dress parties, *tableaux vivants*. But it was perhaps no accident that when the first six children performed a *tableau* of Thompson's *Seasons,* the two least appreciated children in the family – Bertie, the disappointing eldest son, and Louise – were relegated to the joint part of 'Winter'. As Albert's health began to fail, even he became more critical of her moods, though Louise never ceased to present him with charming little letters, essays and hand-painted cards framed in paper lace.

Fortunately, she could not know how completely Prince Arthur, the brother next to her, born on 1 May 1850, had superseded her in their mother's affections. When she was ten, her mother wrote to her father of little Prince Arthur: 'This Child is *dearer* than any of the others put together. . . .' Louise was picked out to Vicky as being 'very naughty and backward though improved and very pretty and affectionate'. Meanwhile, another source of jealousy had arisen at about the same time, with the birth of Princess Beatrice in 1857, the Queen's youngest, precious 'Baby'. Louise began having night terrors.

While Louise, Arthur and Leopold were entering their later childhood, they formed a solid trio of family support that was to help all three of them through the years of normal youthful rebellion. As these letters so strikingly show, Queen Victoria not only felt that defiance of one's parent was an unacceptable 'modern' invention, but that if one's parent happened also to be the sovereign, rebellion amounted to *lèse majesté*.

Louise emerges as happy to play the part of elder sister to the two boys, who are struggling to find their own feet: Arthur through army discipline, Leopold in opposition to the cotton-wooling meted out to him as an accident-prone haemophiliac.

Louise's own status in the family improved remarkably owing to the marriages of her sisters, whose places she eventually took as the eldest daughter at home. Family weddings were among the few occasions when the mournful Queen allowed some faint semblance of rejoicing. As a bridesmaid to Alice, Bertie and Helena, Louise had the added satisfaction of being in the limelight. It was noted that at Bertie's wedding, Louise was the only one of the five sisters not to shed a tear. Why should she? For one thing, she was wearing the fine pearl necklace belonging to Prince Albert's mother that he had always meant for her.

Her longing for recognition yet fear of a snub led her into many situations that earned her a reputation for both pushiness and extreme shyness. She surprised a visitor to Balmoral in 1858 by suddenly coming forward to shake hands with him – needless to say, to his great delight. When the friendly Princess Alexandra first arrived in England, Louise, to the Queen's considerable astonishment, was not pushy but kept 'quietly, and without grumbling, in her own place'. 'She is so happy to be a little made of,' explained the lady-in-waiting, Lady Augusta Bruce.

To her own great advantage, Louise was gradually to become an intermediary between her two closest brothers and 'dearest Mama'; not unsympathetic to their criticisms of parental discipline, but sincerely able to put Mama's point of view. This she did with extreme loyalty. Even the great Bertie used Louise as an intermediary. She must explain, for instance, that he had not written to Mama because he had nothing to say, 'and I hate writing about "la pluie et le beau temps"'. It is a tribute to both mother and children that however unwisely Queen Victoria treated some of them after Albert's death, she never lost their affection. The continual reiteration of the adjective 'dear' whenever Mama's name is mentioned in the letters sounds artificial, even hypocritical to modern ears. No doubt it was a phrase that had been dinned into the children's heads by royal governesses and tutors when the art of letter-writing was being taught. Nevertheless, the word 'dear' remained something of a genuine talisman. Their duty was to love Mama, and they did love her. Even when she was manifestly not behaving as a Queen should – trying to get out of holding a Drawing Room or of opening Parliament – she must be argued with gently; and not argued with at all when it turned out, to their combined consternation, that dear Mama was really ill.

The improvement in Louise's status was most marked after the sister immediately above her, Princess Helena, was married off to Prince Christian of Schleswig-Holstein in 1866. Apart from everything else, the wedding gave Louise the opportunity to produce her most masterly witticism. What should she give Helena for a wedding present? asked Vicky, the Crown Princess of Prussia. 'Bismarck's head on a charger,' suggested Louise, displaying the nerve to tease her eldest sister and also a keen understanding of what the rest of Europe felt about Prussia's 'Iron Chancellor'.

After Alice's marriage in 1862 to Prince Louis of Hesse-Darmstadt, Helena, always known in the family by the German diminutive, Lenchen, had become their mother's favoured companion-secretary. Intelligent and popular because of her good nature (but with no enviable good looks – she ate too much), Lenchen none the less stirred Louise's jealousy. This among other things had helped to develop the vein of sadness in Louise's otherwise lively character. Then in the 1860s two things happened to release her spirits: the coming of Alix and the departure of Lenchen.

Louise's sister-in-law Alix, who had married her eldest brother Bertie when Louise was a pretty girl of fifteen, definitely ganged up with her against Lenchen, Christian and his foreign relations. International political differences over the Schleswig-Holstein affair were originally at the bottom of Alix's hostility. However, there is no doubt that Alix personally preferred the enchanting Louise to her sensible but less obviously attractive sister. The letters contain a series of sly digs at Prince and Princess Christian by Alix; and though we do not know Louise's answers, we must assume that Alix's jokes amused her. In any case it was fun to be taken into the Princess of Wales's confidence, against a hitherto superior elder sister.

The letters make it clear that all through her teens Louise was yearning for the gaiety of parties, perhaps at Marlborough House (the Wales's London home), or the other great houses frequented by her girl friends like Louisa Bowater and the Grey sisters, daughters of General Grey, the Queen's Private Secretary. In contrast to their seemingly liberated lives was the arid and strictly regimented existence she was forced to lead between her mother's four melancholy homes: Windsor, Buckingham Palace, Balmoral and Osborne. The year after their father's death, Vicky had visited Osborne and written it off as nothing but a 'vault'. How Louise longed to share her brother Arthur's good fortune and actually see Venice! Instead, throughout the whole autumn of 1864 she was shut up at Balmoral struck down by tubercular meningitis, and consoled by a mother who recognized her artistic talent 'despite her difficulties'.

With Lenchen's marriage Louise's horizons suddenly expanded and even lightened somewhat. The Queen got her made a godmother to Vicky's new baby as she felt 'inferior'. It was Queen Victoria's rule that she must have an unmarried daughter to take her dictation and to perform the countless jobs of a royal social secretary. Louise found herself in a position of relative power; and though her kingdom was still a gloomy one, it was better that way than to have no responsibilities at all.

Not that the Queen thought that Louise was at present anything but a poor substitute for the reliable Lenchen. Just as she had regarded Louise as immature physically at twelve – 'poor Louise's birthday, she will be twelve and is in fact only 6!' (letter to Vicky, 17 March 1860), so different from her well-developed sisters – she saw her as backward mentally, at least not 'clever' like the others, and at eighteen 'very indiscreet and, from that, making mischief very frequently'.

Nor was looking after the Queen a bed of roses, especially when that bed was on board a night train. Queen Victoria was later to inform a granddaughter, Princess Moretta of Prussia, that from 1866 to 1870 Louise always slept in her mother's carriage on long journeys. Moretta, who had taken on that privilege in the 1890s, patiently endured the chopping and changing of bed-clothes, opening and shutting of windows, switching on and off of lights, and calling for drinks until the hours of sleep were reduced to three.

Abroad it would fall to Louise to liven up the royal party. In Lucerne, for instance, an argument as to whether William Tell had been a myth was settled by someone saying that 114 people who knew him had built him a Tell Chapel. Louise chipped in: 'The historian Froude says that those 114 people are as much myths as Tell!'

Louise's new position with her mother automatically meant that she wielded increased influence with all her brothers and sisters, whose letters in turn brought new interest into the dreary atmosphere of her fatherless Victorian home. She was always getting little notes asking her to do this or that job for a sister abroad or a brother in one of the services. A recurrent task for Louise was dealing with birthday and Christmas presents for absent siblings. It was never easy to think of something new for members of a family who admittedly had 'everything' – except, in Louise's own case, freedom and opportunity. But Louise's good taste and availability made her the one they all turned to. Alix did not want to trouble Mama about a court train for Princess Mary Adelaide, so she troubled Louise instead. They all relied on her for family news over and above the steady stream of letters they received from their mother and to which they were often expected to reply by return.

Affie at sea or Arthur with his regiment were usually hungry for family photographs. Arthur was a special favourite. He got a pair of gaiters as a present in 1864 made by Louise, as well as photographs, and was always welcome at Osborne. The year before he had received a more cheerful letter than usual. 'I look forward to your coming very much. I do not feel quite as dull as I expected.' But now the other visitors were leaving and Louise longed for her closest brother. Two years later she was designing a monogram for his tutor, Major Elphinstone. In 1867 she was choosing Arthur's birthday and Christmas presents for Mama, Alix and Bertie ('£1 to £3'), and he was sending her a sketch of a Highland officer in return for hers of Mount Lochnagar. 'I thought it would please you,' he wrote – one of the many hints that Arthur was Louise's confidant over youthful affairs of the heart.

Not that Arthur was always sympathetic to her moods. He could write rather brusquely: 'I am sorry that you should feel yourself so lonely, but I have no doubt that you will soon get accustomed to it.'

Towards Leopold she was both companionable and protective. Apart from his haemophilia and a chronically bad knee connected with it, he was highly strung and often got fits of the giggles during the sombre family meals, having to be carried out of the room. Louise disapproved of this treatment since it 'hurts his feelings'.

When Vicky's small son Sigismund died of meningitis, it was Louise who was called upon to get a miniature of him done from a photograph. And what a chore it proved to be. Vicky was difficult to please. Not only did it have to be a perfect likeness, but the price had to be exactly right as well. Louise's patience was phenomenal. One is surprised that she did not break off the correspondence with a request to the Princess Royal of Britain and future German Empress to stop haggling over a few pounds.

The truth is that Louise enjoyed her endless jobs, partly because they gave her a much needed sense of importance, and partly because so many of them involved the arts.

Louise's artistic life was at the bottom of all her happiness and many of her frustrations. The trouble was that almost the whole royal family could claim to be artistic, if it was only going out with a sketchbook. So it took some time for Louise's parents to realize that she was 'peculiar' in the sense of requiring special instruction. Since both Victoria and Albert were themselves extremely proficient, Albert at drawing and etching, Victoria with her paint-brush, they took it for granted that all their children would have similar interests. And they were right. Vicky exhibited in the Berlin Academy. Affie illustrated his midshipman's log-book with sketches. Alice copied *Jonah* from the Royal Collection. Arthur, as a boy, looked forward to sketching expeditions with Louise. Beatrice exhibited in the Water-colour Society. Leopold was so genuinely fascinated by the liberty associated with the arts' world that when he finally got himself to Oxford University he was able to introduce his favourite sister as a visitor to a dazzling artistic and literary coterie, which included John Ruskin and Dean Liddell, father of 'Alice'. Oxford was a wonderland for the royal brother and sister. But this was for the future.

At first, Louise's training had been no more specialized than that of her other siblings. There was William Leitch to teach her and Arthur drawing as children, and Edward Corbould to fire her imagination with something a little different from traditional copying. He taught Louise to draw the things she saw around her. That meant carrying a sketchbook with her wherever she went. When court events began to seem 'un peu trop extravagant' or tedious, she would get out her pencil and pad and while away the boredom of pointless protocol. She owed much to Corbould, a real friend. When she was about to be married she sent him a letter that contained a revealing passage:

> You have been one of my few true friends that I have looked up to all my life, and from whom I have always had encouragement and sympathy, and from whom I have learnt much besides art, though art was the foundation of all things.

Once more Louise was covertly expressing her bitterness at not having been given more encouragement by her family to strike out on her own.

One obstacle to Louise's artistic education still remained: Queen Victoria's ingrained opposition to professionalism. It was all very well for beloved Papa to visit the studios of famous painters and point out possible additions and improvements with his gold pencil or toothpick – an extra casket to be introduced by Winterhalter into his painting of the baby Prince Arthur and Wellington; an added cloud recommended to Heinrich von Angeli – but it would be fatal for any of their children to become anything but amateurs. Apart from the somewhat 'dangerous' attraction of *Künstler* (artists), what could the Queen's children do with their works of art if they were foolish enough to branch out into oils? Let them remain in the safe realm of watercolours, as the Queen herself virtually did. After all, you could always make your watercolours into charming albums. What could you do with large canvases? The Queen never dreamed of exhibiting. Her aim was not to train up artists in the home, but to develop national taste. Albert believed that royalty must be patrons, able to choose and display collections properly.

Louise did not want to advise but to create. In any case she seemed to have chosen the most awkward art form of all as her speciality. Sculpture, with its heavy masses of material, was considered fit only for men, and rough, craggy males at that. And you had to have a proper studio to work in – it was no good bringing out your clay in a corner of the Queen's drawing room, as you could with your sketchbook. It is possible that Louise's studio at Osborne House – her main one – had something to do with her choice of sculpture. To have a studio of one's own was halfway to independence.

Once it was admitted that the fifteen-year-old Louise needed special provisions for her 'peculiar' artistic choice, she was given the very best as far as private instructors went. Mary Thornycroft, her first teacher of modelling, was both the daughter of a sculptor, John Francis, and the wife of a sculptor, Thomas Thornycroft. Her husband was responsible for the striking bronze group at Westminster Bridge of the Warrior Queen Boadicea and her two daughters in their chariot. Whether or not Mary found the Victorian Queen and her daughters a little too like their tumultuous predecessors, Mary left her royal employment while Louise still required instruction. Mary probably wished to get on with her own work for she was to exhibit in the Royal Academy. Even Mary was not always considered completely respectable. When she sculpted young Prince Alfred, a teetotaller spotted a bunch of grapes in his hand. Disapproval was expressed, though in view of poor Affie's vinous future, it may have been a case of Mary's second sight. (Louise was a believer in second sight, particularly after she married her Highland chieftain, who not only had second sight but also, as a young man, the power to make a table 'rush about'. However, as Nina Epton writes in *Queen Victoria and Her Children*, 'It was not strong enough to warn him that his marriage to Louise would not be a success.')

The procedure in regard to Louise's work with Mary Thornycroft had been advantageous to both. Louise would model in clay the bust of her mother or one of her brothers, and Mary would carve the bust for various sums of money, usually about £50 to £75. The letters in this collection show how thrilled Louise was when she modelled and completed something unaided, such as the bust of Lady Churchill in 1866. 'I am pleased with it,' she wrote, 'as I took great pains, and did it all alone.'

It may have been the intelligent Mary Thornycroft who put Louise up to the daring plan of asking Mama's permission to study modelling at the National Art Training School in Kensington instead of remaining an amateur for ever. Louise began attending, sporadically, in 1868. But however unsystematic were her studies (she was still a royal princess with competing duties), she was at least the first princess to go to a public school. Six years later, when Louise was married, Vicky was again encouraging her:

> Potsdam. 21 November 1874.
>
> ... I am so glad you are enjoying your time at Inveraray, and that you have been drawing. Why do you not attend a class in the Kensington School of Art when you are in London? I do so at Berlin ... and I think one gets on best by following a very systematic course, because it is the technical part in which all amateurs are so deficient.

At the National Art Training School in 1868 Louise met not only many clever and attractive contemporaries, but also worked under her next instructor, Joseph Edgar Boehm, her mother's sculptor-in-ordinary. Famous for being the exponent of the so-called 'New Sculpture', Boehm was curly-haired, blue-eyed, urbane – and Hungarian. As a foreigner he possessed that touch of the exotic which the young Victoria had found so attractive when she had been the same age as her daughter Louise was now, recognizing it in herself as a taste for the '*outré*'. Louise, like many an art student, fell under her master's spell.

Another of Boehm's famous pupils was the agreeable, shy, plump Sir Alfred Gilbert, the sculptor of Eros in Piccadilly Circus. He too became Louise's friend and remained so until his death in 1934. Gilbert's fame, however, was happier than his master's. Boehm had the misfortune to do the busts of the Queen's favourite ghillie, John Brown, all but one of which was smashed up by order of Edward VII when he came to the throne. He loathed Brown. There is a letter in the collection from Bertie to Louise asking, 'What did *the brute* say to you?' No reason exists to think that Louise liked Brown any better than Bertie did. But characteristically on the first anniversary of Brown's death she was ready to pity and indulge her mother's infatuation by sending her a spontaneous letter of sympathy.

As an innovator, Boehm was mocked by *Punch*; the *Saturday Review*, reported Prince Leopold in 1870, 'sits on Mr. Boehm frightfully'. However, twelve years later Boehm was elected to the Royal Academy and *Punch* showed him riding a horse labelled R.A. above the flattering caption, 'THE HORSE AND HIS MASTER: OR, THE RECENTLY ELECTED SCULPTOR ON HIS NEW R.A-BIAN STEED'. The worst things said about Boehm were, first, that he had made passes at his pupil Princess Louise while working at Balmoral Castle for the Queen and, second, that he had seduced her when she had become an unsatisfied married woman.

On the first accusation, there was probably a good deal of what Prince Arthur, when writing to his sister, often dared to call 'fun'. Louise was twenty and still kept on a tight rein in her mother's depressing homes. When she got the chance, her instinct was to flirt. Her beauty was particularly attractive to men at this period – fair or 'blond cendré' hair, a flawless complexion, wide-apart blue eyes, moderate height, a good figure and small, pretty hands and feet. A story, repeated by many writers, has it that in 1868 Queen Victoria set about finding a husband for Louise because of her misbehaviour with Boehm. There is no evidence for anything so drastic. Nevertheless, one sentence in these letters may indicate that the Queen had put a stop to Louise's unchaperoned sessions with her sculptor instructor. On 5 February 1868 Prince Arthur wrote to Princess Louise: 'What a nuisance that Bauerlein had to sit in the room with you, I was afraid it would come to that.' (Fraulein Bauer was the German governess.)

On the second, more serious charge, one or two letters from Boehm to Louise in this collection suggest a warm relationship but one entirely devoid of extra-marital passion. When Louise first knew him, he was married with a young family. She herself later did a portrait of his wife who died before him, which his son was to receive as a present from the Princess after Boehm himself died in dramatic circumstances (described on page 60). Either the two Boehms and Princess Louise were the most extraordinarily insensitive hypocrites, or there was no truth in the legend.

Meanwhile, the twenty-year-old Louise was learning the facts of life, in two senses, for the first time in art school. She was working with a vast majority of ordinary people, royalty being in a minority of one. She became friends with many of her fellow students, particularly the Montalba sisters. Henrietta Montalba and her sisters were to become successful artists. After she married, Louise invited Henrietta to stay at her country house in Kent. Prince Arthur, who happened to be there, was much taken with this Kensington student and asked his sister to take him to the South Kensington School one day: 'I should like to see what she is doing....'

If Louise had taken her brother to an art school, he would have found life classes and also an 'Antique Room' full of naked male and female casts. Female and male students would be drawing them, but all more than adequately clothed: the women in flowing gowns and cloaks down to the ground, many of them working in hats. The most famous private art school was Heatherley's, run by an eccentric character in a gaberdine with a long white beard, who would offer students drawing-pins stored in the soles of his boots and whose wife was in favour of votes for women. In contrast, her successor, Mrs Mary Crompton, married to Heatherley's nephew John Crompton, was known to the students as 'Little Mummy'. It all sounded quite harmless, unlike the picture of 'dangerous artists' that Queen Victoria had once drawn for her daughters. Among Heatherley's students had been Louise's friends Boehm and Gilbert and her future 'Olympian' friend Sir Edward Poynter, though not Louise.

Despite Louise's attendance at the National Art Training School, a thoroughly professional institution, she rightly considered that her education and training as a sculptor had been inadequate. Years later when addressing the Girls' Public Day Schools Trust, of which she was a patron, she was to inveigh against an inflexible educational system that tried to mould all children into the same pattern. 'I know, because I suffered from it,' she said. Her art school career had been too little and too late. Constantly interrupted by her mother's requirements, she had to catch up on human anatomy when other students were already well ahead. Hence her early sculptures of horses, familiar to her through her joy in riding. Much later would come modelling from the nude.

Queen Victoria once wrote to Louise describing a present she had received – a beautiful and intricate *skull* from Landseer. How marvellous were the works of our Creator, the Queen rhapsodized, human anatomy among them! The Queen, however, was thinking only of the parts of our anatomy that were normally visible. Unlike her daughter Alice, she did not feel that she herself or Louise were called upon to admire the more arcane of the Creator's handiwork. As late as 1885 an academician named J. C. Horsley attacked the use of nude models in a speech to the Church Congress. Nicknamed thereafter 'Clothes Horsley', he was further lampooned by the modernist painter, Louise's friend James McNeill Whistler, in the slogan, '*Horsley soit qui mal y pense.*'

Whether or not it was the influence of Boehm and art school, Queen Victoria began to think that her fourth daughter needed a husband, though she was far from wanting to lose Louise's companionship and services. Instead of the endles references to 'poor', 'indiscreet' Louise of the old days, she was now a reformed character in the Queen's eyes: 'She is (and who would some years ago have thought it?) a clever, dear girl with a fine strong character, unselfish and affectionate.'

Louise's 'peculiar' temperament, however, still showed itself in bursts of excitement interspersed with moodiness. If falling in love had anything to do with these symptoms, her girlhood idol was more likely to have been her brother Leopold's instructor and later governor, the Rev. Robinson (Robin) Duckworth, DD, CVO, than her own instructor Boehm. Louise's biographer, Jehanne Wake, describes Duckworth sympathetically: 'At thirty-three, he was an extremely handsome, charismatic man.' Born in December 1834, he possessed dark good looks, an encouraging manner and a fine singing voice, which Louise and Sybil Grey loved to accompany on the piano or join with in songs at Osborne. One must not underrate the erotic delights of singing together in otherwise stiff Victorian social life. Robin was the 'Duck' in *Alice* and belonged to the brilliant Christ Church set that Prince Leopold was later to admire so much. He had taken a first in Greats and went on to become a Canon of Westminster, with a stained-glass window by his great-nephew Francis Skeat unveiled in his memory on 9 May 1988 in the Dark Cloister. Yet Queen Victoria apparently dismissed him from her household in 1870, only three years after his appointment to Prince Leopold, and replaced him with a governor who was also a doctor. Wake believes it may have been because of Princess Louise's 'crush' on him.

This explanation for the Queen's sudden action – which, incidentally, made Leopold miserable – will not hold water. Far from being removed from the ambience of the royal family, Duckworth maintained his popularity as an instructor to the younger generation. He took over as tutor to the Wales children when their own tutor, Canon Dalton, was absent in August 1874; but much more significant, he appears to have begun giving Princess Beatrice religious instruction in December 1870 and prepared her for confirmation in 1874. Remembering that it was the Queen's burning hope to protect her beloved 'Baby' from all thoughts of love and marriage, one can hardly imagine that Queen Victoria would have thrown the supposedly 'dangerous' Duckworth at Beatrice's head four months after he had been dragged away from Leopold and Louise.

Moreover, there is further evidence in a contrary direction. When the Queen's daughter Vicky and the Queen's half-sister Feodore both wrote regretting Leopold's loss of so trusted a friend as Duckworth, neither suggested that Louise's 'crush' on Duckworth had anything to do with it, but assumed that the need for a doctor/governor was all-important. And Vicky and Feodore, as the Queen's most intimate correspondents, would surely have known about the real reason for Duckworth's removal, had it concerned Louise. Prince Leopold himself attributed the change in governors to his own ill-health – with just a dig at the hated Brown brothers, Archie and John. He wrote to George Stirling, his former governor, in April 1870: 'Mr Duckworth is going to leave me, but ***not*** of ***his own*** accord, and, like you [see *Letters*] on account of my ***health,*** and to make place for an odious medical student, [adding] the brothers Brown have caused it no doubt' (Add. A30/350).

Furthermore, that frankest of writers, General Sir Henry Ponsonby (the Queen's Private Secretary), described to his wife how Duckworth was very 'low' about leaving, on Prince Leopold's account, but glad to have a living in London. There was no mention of Louise. Indeed, Duckworth was to be one of Queen Victoria's favoured chaplains, continuing to preach to her. Altogether he remained *persona grata.* None of this fits with the picture of a dangerous royal cradle-snatcher – Robin being over thirty-six in April 1870 and Louise just twenty-two.

The Queen carried out her intention and the day of final parting came on 13 August 1870. The sorrowful Leopold and Louise presented Duckworth with a farewell present in the form of a heavy gold ring designed by Louise and set flush with stones: lapis lazuli, ruby, diamond, lapis lazuli in that order. The initials of the stones stand for *L*eopold, *R*obinson, *D*uckworth, *L*ouise; the inscription inside the ring reads 'Forget us not, Le Lo '67' – the date 1867 marking the beginning of Duckworth's three-year period as governor when the trio's friendship became so firm. Louise also presented him with a gold signet ring containing a lock of her hair, while Leopold gave him a Prayer Book/Psalter/Hymnal in a thick leather binding in 'affectionate and grateful remembrance' of his confirmation on 30 January 1869.

Perhaps because of these presents, added to the unexpectedness of Duckworth's departure, an almost certainly baseless rumour spread that Louise had an illegitimate child by him. According to one story, Queen Victoria implored the Duke of Argyll to allow his son Lorne to marry Louise in order to rescue the Princess from her predicament. The child, it was said, died in Canada.

One undoubted fact is that Vicky suggested German suitors for Louise in 1867; the Queen was shocked – 'much too young'.

It was probably Louise's very natural capacity for falling for any handsome young man in her entourage – general flirtatiousness rather than particular affairs – that was beginning to attract attention, and even to create the kind of gossip already mentioned. A curious example has come to light in the last few years. It must be said at once that there is no record of this or of the above story in the Royal Archives.

When Louise was nineteen (still the fatal year 1867!), Queen Victoria's former gynaecologist, Sir Charles Locock, was living on the Isle of Wight not far from Osborne House. His wife had died that summer and, in his loneliness, he liked to have one or other of his sons to stay with him. This went on through the autumn. Then, on 22 December, he wrote to a lifelong friend, Dr Kerr, with whom he was in the habit of exchanging generous gifts at Christmas (a barrel of oysters for a turkey): 'In another fortnight I cannot have any of them [his sons] to remain with me, and I am going abroad for a change with one of my nieces . . . and I do not wish to be back in London till after Easter.' A strong tradition in the Locock family now takes a hand.

Shortly after the writing of that letter, Sir Charles is believed to have delivered somebody's illegitimate baby son, Henry Locock, who was legally adopted (a fact) by Sir Charles's third son Frederick. Frederick was to die in Canada in 1907. The date of the baby's birth was about 30 December 1867, though there is no birth certificate. Baby Henry Locock was to have six children and many descendants. One of his grandsons, Nicholas Locock, is firmly of the opinion that his grandfather was the natural child of Princess Louise by one of Queen Victoria's courtiers, an officer whose offence earned his dismissal and caused the Queen to remark that one should never have officers in a court.

The idea that the childless Princess in fact has great-great-grandchildren living in southern England to this day would not be altogether unwelcome. If she had indeed been pregnant, Sir Charles Locock, a resident of the island, would have been the obvious doctor for the confinement. Known personally to the Queen for twenty-seven years (since Vicky's birth in 1840), he was absolutely reliable and providentially possessed of a son of his own available to do Her Majesty the favour of adopting her grandson. Henry Locock told all his children that Princess Louise was his mother, letting him play with other royal children including the future Kaiser, and that she mounted his portrait (taken by the royal photographer Jabez Hughes) on a card she herself had painted with flowers and leaves. The Princess was indeed addicted to decorating photographs in this way. Nevertheless, there are grave objections to this story.

That August, when she would have been five months' pregnant, she was having 'fun' on a yacht, with one of its officers, Captain Rideout. A fortnight later her brother Arthur was looking forward to 'long expeditions' with her at Balmoral. Most of November seems to have been occupied by Louise (now in her eighth month!) reluctantly entertaining one of the Schleswig-Holsteins, whom she did not get rid of until early December, as a letter from the Princess of Wales shows. It is hardly likely that Louise would have been made to act as hostess, 'dancing the perpetual jig' (Alix) in the last weeks of a secret pregnancy; nor that the Queen would have written screeds about Leopold's illness, as she did, to a daughter who herself was about to be (in Victorian language) 'taken ill'. Of course more revealing letters could have been destroyed. How, on the other hand, could the Princess have concealed her condition from the usual family parties and omnipresent courtiers? True, skirts were full and shawls worn. But Louise had always had a willowy figure, unlike her sisters Vicky and Lenchen, both of whom would have stood a better chance of getting away with it.

The conclusion must be that, difficult as it is to prove a negative, Louise is extremely unlikely to have been the mother of Henry Locock. Even Sir Charles's suggestive letter to his friend is susceptible of more than one interpretation. Sir Charles may indeed have been unable to have his sons to stay and have left home because of something unusual that had been happening there. On the other hand, Sir Charles's sons may have been unable to visit him for their own reasons, thus causing the lonely widower's departure. If there is a connection with the court at all, it seems more probable that some well-born young lady, known to Queen Victoria and pitied by her, was the mother of the Locock baby.

The most harassing and humiliating period of Louise's long life has now been reached. Here we have a girl just out of her teens whose emotions are still highly inflammable and not yet under control. She has had very little 'fun' since she was thirteen. Now she is beginning to have some. She is much admired. 'If I were a young man', said Edwin Landseer, the painter, 'I should not rest until that lovely girl had promised to marry me.' Suddenly she is required to examine her feelings seriously and ask herself the impossible question: who out of a limited number of young gentlemen does she love enough to live with exclusively for – well, it could have been seventy years if the chosen 'he' had lived as long as she did?

Queen Victoria's favoured candidates – and what Victorian mama did not have a hand in her daughter's alleged choice, the royal hand being that much heavier just because it was royal – must pass four tests: a clean sheet morally; willingness to make his home in Britain, thus ruling out most foreign princes; pedigree and wealth to maintain Louise in the state to which she was accustomed; and the ability to inspire affection (though not necessarily passion) in the prospective bride. Most Victorian mamas would have thought these conditions perfectly reasonable if applied to their own families, *mutatis mutandis*. As for the absence of passion, Queen Victoria positively disliked an engagement that involved kissing, being under the lifelong impression that the love of herself and Albert never could, should or would be repeated in this world. Other people's kissing was totally unnecessary.

All the same there was humiliation for Louise. Before the idea of a foreign prince was finally rejected, she was made to inspect German candidates under Vicky's wing: they disliked her English independence, she disliked their Teutonic arrogance. The main controversy was over Prince Albert of Prussia, known as Abbat, who was the favourite of Vicky, Alice and Affie, but was turned down by Louise without even a single sighting, despite his eagerness and wealth. The letters echo the long family argument over Abbat.

It is possible that Serge of Leuchtenberg, son of the late Duke of Leuchtenberg and the Grand Duchess Marie, daughter of Tsar Nicholas I, was also brought to Osborne by his mother to reconnoitre Princess Louise. Queen Victoria found Marie 'most amiable' and 'still very handsome', while her son Serge was 'good-looking and very pleasing but very delicate'. Sure enough Serge died young. If that marriage had come off, a connection between Napoleon and the royal family would have been set up, as Serge's grandfather was Eugène de Beauharnais, Napoleon's stepson.

On Louise's behalf, the Queen's favourite minister among the ruling Liberals, Lord Granville ('handsome, simple and unaffected'), acted as a kind of exalted gossip columnist reporting the results of his social researches to his sovereign instead of to a newspaper editor. One day Granville would report to the ladies at Windsor that Barkis was willing and Barkis was rich; the next that Barkis already had his eye on somebody else and in any case his rolling acres were loaded with debt. Worse than all such disappointments was the family animosity that the question of Louise's marriage unleashed. Her mother was a doughty warrior with the pen. But so was her sister Vicky. Bertie and Affie could both write their hurtful letters. And all were on different sides in the great marriage stakes. Many of Louise's siblings had in times past called her (and would again call her) their favourite sister – Vicky, Bertie, Affie, Arthur and young Leopold. Now she seemed to cause them nothing but anxiety. Only the two youngest boys had no axes to grind and Leo, dear boy, would just scream with laughter at every family row.

The impression of Queen Victoria's brilliance in keeping before the eyes of the world a picture of flawless family unity and togetherness must be enhanced by these quarrelsome letters – and they, of course, were only a small proportion of the paper ammunition flying between Europe and Britain. However, if Louise could have known of the way her niece Princess Marie (Missy) of Edinburgh, for instance, would be traded by her mother (Affie's wife) in the cause of political prejudice and family revenge, she might have felt that she herself had got off lightly after all;

not forgetting the fact that Queen Missy herself (Queen of Roumania) was ruthlessly to marry off her own daughters for reasons totally unconnected with love, and in a Europe far less friendly to royalty than Queen Victoria's.

The umbrage taken in some of these letters is not unamusing, couched as it usually is in language of impeccable politeness. Even the Prince of Wales was not above showing his jealousy of young brother Arthur, who preferred watching a boat-race to staying with the Waleses at Sandringham. He complained of course to Louise. The letters show the Victorian royal family as very like any other family after all. One may doubt, however, whether there was another family that disliked their parents' favourite home as much as the young royal children hated Balmoral. It comes through here with surprising persistence, partly because so many of the letters were written by the younger members of the tribe, unlike those published between the Queen and her eldest daughter. Three 'Bs' seem to have caused most of the holiday grumbling, all interconnected: boredom, bleakness and Brown.

To return to the match-making: Queen Victoria's second research assistant was the Rev. Gerald Wellesley, Dean of Windsor, her royal conscience as opposed to her royal encyclopaedia (Granville). The letters give many of the names on various starred lists, but not all of them. The Waleses, for instance, thought Princess Alexandra's brother would be nice for Louise and the Danish press announced that the Princess Louise was engaged to the Crown Prince, only to be put in its place by *The Times*. Crown Prince William of Orange had been suggested early on, though promptly turned down by the Princess herself.

After all the possible princes had had their names struck off the Queen's lists for one reason or another, the choice was deliberately widened to include commoners. The introduction of commoners of course widened the family arguments as well as widening Louise's choice. The Prince of Wales in particular took months if not years to accept the idea of a commoner for a brother-in-law. In the same mood of implacable opposition, the diehard Cambridges, whose daughter Princess Mary Adelaide had been made to marry a penniless Teck prince rather than a commoner, had produced an eleventh-hour German candidate, their relative Adolphus of Mecklenburg-Strelitz. The Queen, 'most indignant', obliterated this 'preposterous and impertinent notion' before Adolphus' name had even got on to a list.

The world of 'commoners' (which at first meant the upper crust of the peerage, but was later extended to include those of lesser rank but greater wealth) presented Louise with personal problems. She knew no marriageable 'commoners' to speak of, never being allowed to dine out except now and then with the Waleses. Pathetically in 1870 she was telling Colonel Elphinstone that to make a decision without love was impossible. Beyond this, there was another limiting factor. The world of intellectuals that she had begun to frequent was all of one kind: the Liberal Greys and the Liberal Stanleys. There was the Hon. Arthur Stanley, Dean of Westminster. Married to a former popular lady-in-waiting, Lady Augusta Bruce, Dean Stanley would have been a more useful judge than Lord Granville or Dean Wellesley of what would suit Louise. His quick, eager manner reflected an equally alert mind. The Stanleys gave hand-picked cultural tea parties which both the Queen and Louise occasionally attended. Here Robert Browning and Thomas Carlyle were presented to Louise, Carlyle praising her as 'decidedly a very pretty young lady, and clever too as I found out in talking to her afterwards'. It was probably this meeting that inspired Louise to ask her brother Leopold for *Frederick the Great* and *The French Revolution* as birthday or Christmas presents. Louise's teacher Boehm was to sculpt Carlyle in bronze, the fine memorial statue standing today on Chelsea Embankment, close to Carlyle's old home in Upper Cheyne Row. Louise may have had some hand in getting Boehm chosen.

Through General Grey and his family, Louise met a most influential social reformer, the Greys' cousin Mrs Josephine Butler. Part of a long serious letter from Louise to Mrs Butler is in the possession of St Andrews University. Extracts such as the following show clearly that Louise would never have considered marrying an empty-headed lordling, far less an arch-Tory, like her sister Lenchen's husband. In March 1869 Louise had received a request for support from Josephine Butler in her work for women including women's suffrage. The Princess replied from Windsor Castle on the 27th: 'It has been with great interest, and pleasure, that I received your letter. I *do* take great interest in the happiness, and wellbeing of women, and long to do everything that I can to promote all efforts in that direction.' Louise then went on to discuss Josephine Butler's idea of starting up an International Review dealing with women's affairs. Unfortunately the next part of the Princess's letter is missing, but when it resumes Louise is discussing the name for the magazine:

> [If] I may say so, do not put anything about women in the title, as I think all appearance of exclusiveness should be avoided, as it is after all only with the cooperation of the cleverest men that we can hope to succeed. If the title of the Review suggests that subjects concerning women are alone treated many may turn away from it, who if they saw the question calmly discussed in an impartial way, would arrive at a true and just opinion. My reason for saying this,

> that I know the subject of women's rights, interests etc. has become so tedious to the eyes of so many, whose support it would be an advantage to gain.

The letters show Leopold also full of admiration for Josephine Butler's beauty, though he took his family's line on her work for 'fallen women' – disapproval. Even after she was married Louise was made to send back a book that Mrs Butler had written and presented to her, *Women's Work and Women's Culture,* which included the sex problem. However, Louise had already managed to meet another advanced woman, the pioneer woman doctor Elizabeth Garrett, through the Butlers and Stanleys, and called on her in London. Don't tell the Queen, Louise cautioned her; but of course Mama found out (Louise could not move around unaccompanied) and was duly enraged. Here was her daughter mixing with women who openly supported the royal *bête noire*: female suffrage.

Nevertheless, the Princess had personal experience of the growing need for women's emancipation. In May 1870 she opened the Inner Temple's New Hall on behalf of the Queen. Commenting on her grace and self-possession, *The Times* added that the legal profession was 'still ungallant enough' not to admit women as honorary benchers. Prince Christian, her escort, absurdly received the honour while Louise did the work. On the arts side, Louise and her professional friends had to wait until 1882 for Frederic Leighton, another 'Olympian' President of the Royal Academy, to admit women as members.

In her long letter to Mrs Butler, Louise gave her opinion of a letter that she had received from Elizabeth Garrett and was forwarding to Josephine Butler:

> I send you a letter from Miss Garrett on her successful examination at Paris [for a medical degree – the British medical profession still kept women out], I thought it might interest you to read it.
>
> I went to see her before she started, it was a great pleasure to find her so enthusiastic in her work, with liberal high min[d]ed[ness], she is one of those who *can* prove how much women can learn, if they put their whole heart, and soul, in what they are about.
>
> Louise

Louise longed to put her whole heart and soul into her sculpting, but for a royal princess such total commitment was impossible.

Throughout 1869 and 1870 Queen Victoria's chosen candidates for marriage with Louise turned up and vanished from Windsor and Balmoral, as stiff and unreal as figures in a medieval tapestry. The two whom Louise at first fancied, Lord Lansdowne and Lord Cowper, turned out to be already engaged. Louise was understandably annoyed. Lord Granville's detective work had been sadly inefficient. Lord Rosebery was at one time in the running, but was said to have been put off by the 'odious birch wine' served at Balmoral. One press rumour said that Louise was taking the veil, as the bride of Christ, since she was not allowed to be the bride of her beloved clergyman (Duckworth). Another titled young visitor was Lord Stafford. They had one thing in common – all four were Liberals. At least Lord Granville got that right.

Running through this increasingly drab tapestry was one golden thread that appeared, disappeared and reappeared, seeming to make the pattern worthwhile: the young Marquess of Lorne, eldest son of the 8th Duke of Argyll.

John Douglas Sutherland Campbell, Marquess of Lorne, known at first as Ian to his devoted parents and admiring siblings, was born on 6 May 1845 and was therefore nearly three years older than Louise. Queen Victoria had kissed him at the age of two, when she and Prince Albert stayed at Inveraray Castle, his parents' West Highland home and the Campbells' main seat. Little Ian had refused to kiss the hand of Vicky, the five-year-old Princess Royal. The question now was whether he would kiss the Queen's fourth daughter instead.

At twenty-four Lorne was certainly rather more like a fairy-tale suitor than some of the others. (He was now universally known as Lorne by family and friends, and will continue to be called by this name throughout this book, even after he has become Duke of Argyll.) Prospective head of the great Campbell clan with the romantic title of Mac Cailein Mor, he was well built though not tall, his features were good and he had thick yellow hair and the blazing blue Campbell eyes. He was a Liberal MP and had travelled in the United States and Europe, including Italy. As a true Liberal, he was anti-slavery in America, and in Italy he narrowly escaped capture along with his hero Garibaldi. His grandmother, the Duchess of Sutherland, served as both Queen Victoria's Mistress of the Robes and Garibaldi's sponsor and hostess in England, two roles that were only just not incompatible – the Queen detested Garibaldi, but accepted the situation. Many stately homes were open to Lorne, from Dunrobin Castle and Inveraray in Scotland to Argyll Lodge and Chiswick House in London (though Queen Victoria was to be deeply disappointed in the extent of his hereditary wealth). He had known Buckingham Palace and Windsor Castle since childhood, remembering being carried back to the Palace from the garden in Prince Albert's arms after having been felled by a heavy skipping-rope. He remembered also attending Castle balls as an Eton schoolboy. Ian, his brother Archie and his young uncle, Lord Ronald Gower, were among the favoured children invited to play with the royal boys, while their sisters played with the girls. When Louise was a year old, the four-year-old Lorne was one of the children dancing at Buckingham Palace – or rather, as the Queen put it, 'hopping about'.

Best of all, Lorne shared Louise's interest in the arts, being himself a writer all his life. His humour was active but unsubtle. He would send Louise what he called 'funny stories' by post and when he came to write the *Life* of Queen Victoria, he filled the early years with long-forgotten stories culled from Princess Victoria's first teacher, the Rev. George Davys; for instance, when asked by Queen Adelaide what she would like to do on a visit, the Princess replied, 'Clean the windows.'

Lorne was also something of a poet. Indeed the Queen was to ask herself wryly whether marrying a poet was the best way to cure her Bohemian daughter. The Queen was right. Through Lorne's influence Louise was happily to extend her circle of artists, many of them a good deal more Bohemian than she was.

At St Andrews University Lorne was a strong feminist. In barracking the dons who barred women from attending their lectures, among them Miss Jex-Blake, a future Principal of Lady Margaret Hall, Oxford, Lorne wrote:

> And youth's best instincts we obeyed
>   In hooting our professors,
> When they barred out each learned maid,
>   And us her intercessors.

Perhaps there was already one visible gap in Lorne's otherwise attractive qualities. Was he decisive? Was he ambitious? As a man, he was of course far better educated than Louise. But he had failed to stick out his degree course at Cambridge, disliking classics and preferring to seek adventure abroad, interrupted by some desultory study at Berlin. He had wanted to be a soldier, but was foiled by his family. Less serious than his scholarly, scientific father, he was relaxed where his father was 'fizzing'. He had the makings of an aesthete, or at least of a dilettante, not of a statesman.

The courtship of Lorne and Louise began like Louise's own life, under a revolutionary cloud. The Franco-Prussian War, resulting in the French Commune and the fall of Napoleon III, broke out in 1870. This of course meant that the family rows over Louise's continental suitors were revived in the form of French or German partisanship within the royal family itself. Some violently pro-German verses found among Louise's papers may mean that Vicky and Alice were trying to convert her to their side.

The war-song, entitled 'Hurrah, Germania!', was said to be as popular as Becker's 'Watch on the Rhine':

Hurrah! thou lady proud and fair,
Hurrah! Germania mine!
What fire is in thine eye as there
Thou bendest o'er the Rhine!

Negotiations between Queen Victoria and the Argylls on behalf of Louise and Lorne had opened strongly in 1869, only to run into the sand. Louise, having talked to Lorne for a few minutes at Argyll Lodge, liked him very much, but considered him too clever for her. She preferred to wait. Next time she was to find him too young for her. She met him again at Balmoral, but, in her eagerness not to lead him on, was off-putting. She respected him, but could not '*like*' him enough. Lorne was ready to have a go, but not to be kept too long in suspense. (This had been precisely Prince Albert's reaction when first courting Victoria.)

The Queen, who had started by finding Louise '*difficile*', quickly changed tactics and joined an unlikely combination of Louise and Lenchen against an early marriage. Lenchen pointed out to dear Mama that, without Louise's services in the home, the Queen would either have to rely on the immature Beatrice or would need to recall Lenchen herself – a solution that Lenchen, already occupied with husband and children, was devoutly hoping to avoid. Lorne, though deprived of the walk-over that he had been led to expect, was now generously prepared to leave it to 'the Supreme' – meaning God not Queen Victoria. It must be admitted that if an arranged marriage for Louise was really necessary, there was no excuse for a prologue of such ineffable bungling.

For a large part of 1870 Louise was back in the pool, considering candidates and being considered by them, but with the fresh blow that her confidant, General Grey, had died in April.

In July Gladstone, the Liberal Prime Minister, himself took a hand. Both Louise and Lorne were invited to one of the Gladstones' socially important garden parties, where Louise could not help noticing how superior Lorne was to her mother's present list of 'seconds'. Events moved forward. When at the end of September Lorne visited Balmoral again, Louise was impressed by his dinner-table conversation and burst out crying when she heard he was only to stay for three days. 'It is too hard.' The Queen liked everything about him except his ugly nasal voice – a relic of his cricketing days at Eton when his nose had been broken. Invited to prolong his visit beyond the weekend, Lorne felt that 'the Supreme' had spoken at last. He proposed to Louise on 3 October on a hillside above the romantic dark waters of the Dhu Loch. Louise accepted him. The Queen was delighted even though Lorne had not told her beforehand what he intended to do – a touch of spontaneity for once. Three weeks later the Queen was quoting Louise's marriage to Vicky as 'the most popular act of my reign'.

Years later, however, the Queen was to confide in Vicky that playing the royal marriage market was no pleasure. After warning Vicky in 1889 against trying to marry off her daughter Moretta and '*getting refusals*', she added: 'I had something of that kind to go through with Louise and Leopold and it was very painful.' *

There was more than one contretemps between the engagement and its public announcement on 14 October. The household was not told until the 10th, though Ponsonby noted how 'moody' and 'absent-minded' Lorne was on the 5th. 'I don't know what it all means.' No one had remembered to warn the Waleses, who were dead against Lorne's candidature. However, Brown quickly sent the unwelcome message by ghillie over the mountains to Dunrobin, where Bertie and Alix were staying with the Sutherlands, Lorne's maternal relatives. The Prince of Wales's unfavourable reaction comes over clearly in the letters.

According to Ponsonby, who had succeeded Grey as Private Secretary to the Queen, there were two more family 'rows' before the wedding, not to mention the unenthusiastic feelings of the anti-commoner party. One area of awkwardness was called by Ponsonby the 'Familiarity Row'. It was caused by the Queen's impression that both Lorne and his father were taking advantage of their novel, exalted position to go beyond protocol. Lorne, for instance, dared to address his betrothed in letters as 'Dearest Louise' instead of 'Dearest *Princess* Louise' – the title being essential until after marriage. Moreover, he began by writing to the Queen as 'Dearest Mama', instead of 'Dearest *Madam* and Mama'. Ponsonby noted that he sat in church in the pew with the Queen, 'at which, of course, we courtiers stood aghast'.

The other trouble area was known by Ponsonby as the 'Great Knee Row' – a family dispute so prolonged that Leopold was in permanent fits of laughter, whereas John Brown seriously thought of settling down as a married man to get away from it all. When riding on horseback with Lorne across the Scottish hills on 15 October, Louise sprained her knee. It was over a month before the Queen – secretly pleased to be legitimately stuck at Balmoral and saved from meeting the Waleses after all the unpleasantness – would allow the frustrated Princess and court to travel south. If they had been travelling *to* Balmoral, said Louise bitingly, her mother would have packed her into a train at once. It was several more days before she was allowed to be reunited with Lorne. The letters make all this unpleasantness abundantly clear. Nevertheless, Louise was happy.

* Quoted in A. Ramm (ed.), *Beloved and Darling Child* (1990).

According to her biographer, she proudly told her old nurse that she was going to marry no German prince but the '*cleverest* and *best*' young British nobleman of the day. Lorne was her perfect 'Arthurian Knight'.

The Queen seems to have put off the wedding date as long as possible with the excuse of Louise's health – to 21 March 1871. Meanwhile, there were the expected minor difficulties to cope with. Some members of the British aristocracy objected to the marriage because it would diminish royalty. Contrariwise, others objected because it would introduce royal etiquette and protocol into a family (the Argylls) that had hitherto been free from it. *The Times*, however, congratulated the Queen on her courage – she was allowing something that had not happened for over 350 years: the marriage of a royal princess to a commoner (Henry VII's daughter Mary to the Duke of Suffolk) – while the Princess herself was showing something better than 'mere sympathy' with ordinary people by marrying one of them. *The Times* called all this so surprising as to be 'revolutionary'.

The Liberal Lord Granville, surprisingly, regretted Lorne was not a Tory, as the marriage looked like 'a Whig job'. However, he told the Queen, 'The nation is Liberal, Your Majesty, and I believe Princess Louise sympathises with such ideas when not exaggerated but there is no other member of the Royal Family who does.'

The Ponsonbys wrote off all the German candidates under the rude generic title of 'Seidlitz Stinkingers' – Seidlitz powder being an ever-present and horrible Victorian aperient.

Though the King of Prussia expressed deep anger, Lorne remained unshaken. 'My forefathers were kings', he told Queen Victoria, 'when the Hohenzollerns were parvenus.' Bertie was particularly annoyed about Louise's suggested new title, which the Duke of Argyll wished to be simply Lady Lorne. A compromise (that did not actually satisfy Bertie) was finally reached by which she became HRH Princess Louise, Marchioness of Lorne. Whereas the Duke of Argyll wanted to 'lower' his daughter-in-law to Lorne's level, Queen Victoria wished to 'raise' her son-in-law: if Lorne would consent to accept a royal dukedom, many problems would be solved. However, both Argyll and Lorne stoutly refused. This battle was to be fought over and over again in the coming years, as the letters show.

Louise had her own sticking-point. She was utterly opposed to any trace of Balmoral and the hated Brown being brought into her future home. She would insist on footmen not ghillies attending her. '*Footmen*, mind,' she told Ponsonby. 'I don't want an absurd man in a kilt following me about everywhere and I want to choose the men at once or I shall have some others thrust upon me.' (Brown's brothers?) The letters show the Queen trying to thrust an 'absurd man in a kilt' upon Lorne instead.

As the wedding date drew near, contradictory accounts of the bridal pair's feelings for each other were on record. Lorne was said to be 'desperately in love', though he told one of his Campbell aunts that he felt 'rather sad as I turn from independence to – we know what!' Louise was not in love at all, thought Bertie and various members of the court; while the Queen decided her daughter's love was just right, neither 'desperate' nor totally wanting. Her drawing at least seemed happily inspired. She did two small heads at Balmoral, which Ponsonby thought 'very good – and there can't have been any help here'.

One last danger zone had to be entered by the Queen and Louise before they could reach the safe 'haven' of the wedding – 'haven' being a favourite metaphor for marriage among Victorian ladies. This was the royal request to Parliament for Louise's dowry.

Fortunately, Gladstone was a strong royalist. After a few minor alarms of radical opposition, the usual sum of £30,000 for a royal daughter's marriage, plus £6,000 annuity, was voted with virtually unanimous consent. Only one MP went into the No lobby, and he was the high-minded Liberal Postmaster-General, Henry Fawcett. The fact that he was blind and also a personal friend of Lorne's was somehow seen to soften the rough edges of his behaviour. Lorne even hinted half-humorously, in his *Life of Queen Victoria* (1901), that his blind friend walked into the wrong lobby by mistake! Two other Liberal MPs, Sir Charles Dilke and P. A. Taylor, were also opposed to the dowry, but their hostile activity was necessarily limited to being tellers. And 'an invidious and irrational demonstration' in support of Dilke by his Birmingham constituents was dealt with thunderously by *The Times*:

> Is it meant to express a popular objection to the match itself? On the contrary, the match, exceptional as it certainly is in character, is of a kind to commend itself especially to popular sentiment. The daughter of the Queen, with her mother's full consent, descends from the charmed heights of Royalty and marries a subject. What can the most advanced Liberal object to in that? For once the money will not even be spent out of the country, but will be kept at home and spent among the people.

The marriage was in truth extremely popular.

The letters to Louise give a vivid picture of the Queen's and her Ministers' anxieties over the dowry happily laid to rest by the result. Undoubtedly Louise's gender and her personal popularity for marrying a British commoner instead of a 'German beggar' had something to do with the very favourable vote. Fifty-three MPs were to vote against her brother Arthur's £6,000 annuity.

With hindsight we can see that Louise was lucky to get away so easily with such a satisfactory verdict. Republicanism was probably stronger at this date than at any other time since the years before Queen Victoria's accession. The general public was beginning to see the Queen's present seclusion not as ill-health but as sheer neglect of her duty; her family and court already saw it in this light, General Grey quoting Louise as saying that her mother was 'wonderfully well'. The royal seclusion might well have become totally unacceptable but for two providential events – providential, that is, from the monarchists' point of view.

In the late summer of 1871 Queen Victoria was taken seriously ill with septicaemia and in the late autumn of that same year her eldest son, the Prince of Wales, nearly died of typhoid. Once the heir to the throne fell under the shadow of death, the British people thought only of prayers for his recovery. Republicanism was again felt to be the prerogative of tasteless windbags. It faded away without any evil effect, like the bad smell in some of the rooms at Sandringham where the sick Prince of Wales lay in delirium, a menace that turned out to be nothing but a gas leak.

As a result of the Queen's returning popularity, due also to her gender and venerable age, she was never made to grasp the nettle of her public appearances. Her children, however, went on trying. Ponsonby wrote to a cousin during the Queen's last decade: 'Princess B[eatrice] seems to think it possible that H.M. would go to one Drawing Room. But H.M. in sad and mournful tones said to me she was damned if she would.'

Meanwhile, Louise's prospective marriage evoked two or three moments that would have appealed to her keen sense of the ridiculous. A letter of congratulation to the Queen rejoiced that Louise's presence in London as an MP's wife would discourage 'the profligacy which flourished there in a gay, thoughtless, lascivious society'. She and Lorne were toasted at the Scottish Corporation Festival in London on Christmas Eve 1870, Louise being described as 'one of the fairest and most accomplished of maidens even though she was a Princess (Applause)'.

A more consciously humorous approach could be relied on from *Punch*. In a piece on 'The Royal Marriage' of 22 October 1870, *Punch* reported: 'It was whispered in well-informed circles (long before the truth was known) that the PRINCESS LOUISE was to be married to a Bishop. This, of course, is soon cleared up: it was the mention of *Lorne* that led to the mistake.' Apart from a play on the words 'lawn' as worn by bishops and 'Lorne', *Punch* may have been making a veiled reference to the rumours about Louise and the Rev. Robin Duckworth. *Punch* also reported that 'a great Croquet Match was on the *tapis* at Balmoral in which PRINCESS LOUISE was to take a prominent part. This arose from there being a Lorne Party constantly at the Highland Royal Residence' – the same pun again, plus a reference to the arguments over Lorne's suitability.

After running to death the jokes on Lorne and lawn, the journal concluded with some lengthy word-play on *Lorne* and *forlorn*:

> The Princess is remarkable for her studious habits and neat wit. Knowing *David Copperfield* by heart, Her Royal Highness lately asked *Mr. P.*[*unch*] . . . 'why the Marquis was likely to propose for her hand?'
>
> *Mr. P.*[*unch*], of course, gave it up.
>
> 'Because', said her Gracious Goodness, 'he is like MRS. GUMMIDGE.'
>
> The Right Hon. MR. P.[unch] laughed but being evidently expected to pursue the subject further, submitted to H.R.H. The Princess that he (Mr. P.) did not exactly see why the Marquis resembles MRS. GUMMIDGE.
>
> 'Because', answered the dear PRINCESS, 'he is Lone and Lorne.' [Mrs Gummidge always described herself as a 'lone lorn' creature.]
>
> Whereupon, hearing her Mamma call, she left the right hon. gentleman to himself and his note-book.
>
> *Notice to Correspondents*
>
> Already the anticipated storm has begun. *Mr. Punch* has received forty-nine letters enclosing witticisms, the 'point' of which is that his respected and beloved Princess is
>
> All For-lorn
>
> He hereby gives notice that, as a loyal subject of the reigning House and as an indignant member of the Republic of Literature, he not only rejects all such rubbish, but designs a dire revenge on all persons who shall presume to send such impertinence.
>
> Respect this.

So much for sparkling wit in the 1870s.

At long last the wedding day, 21 March 1871, arrived. Louise dressed first in the Queen's room, after presenting her mother with a small locket in which to preserve a piece of her wreath. The Queen, in black satin trimmed with jet, at least wore a ruby tiara and parure. The *Amberley Papers* show that Lorne himself had expected the wedding to be in February. It was held in St George's Chapel, Windsor. There were plenty of Louise's rejected kilts around, but not on Lorne, to the Queen's regret. He wore the uniform of the Argyllshire Regiment of Volunteer Artillery, of which he was colonel. Though Louise's wedding dress and those of her eight bridesmaids were of conventional white satin and silk, Louise introduced new notes by drawing the design for the Honiton lace of her veil and choosing bouquets of brilliant red roses for the bridesmaids, whose crystal and jewelled lockets she also designed. Lorne gave her a diamond necklace and sapphire pendant. Two diamond daisies held her veil in place, presented to her by her three youngest siblings, Arthur, Leopold and Beatrice. Judging by other royal presents mentioned in the letters, the daisies must have provoked endless discussion between the three about size, price and a fair contribution from each. The bridal pair, according to Louise's biographer, were naturally nervous at entering a new world: Lorne into a life of semi-royalty, Louise into something more like ordinary existence than she had ever known before. To make it even more of a strain, neither of them really knew their companion on this pioneering journey.

Characteristically, the Queen noted that Louise did not look as lovely as usual, being pulled down by one of her bad colds and suffering from earache. Lorne was made aware of his half-and-half social position when he first entered the chapel. Though the trumpets heralded his arrival, the glittering congregation did not know whether to give this handsome commoner a standing or sitting welcome. They hesitated, until the Princess of Wales rose to her feet resplendent in blue satin. The whole congregation followed her lead. At least Louise and Lorne were allowed to exchange an official kiss at the Castle afterwards, as the Queen told her chief marriage broker, Lord Granville.

All accounts of the wedding agree on the shower of old shoes thrown after the bridal pair; one writer adds that a broom was also thrust into their carriage, though what it traditionally symbolized is not revealed. Perhaps a sweeping away of the past. If so, the broom was but a frail instrument for such a task.

On 15 April the Queen wrote to Vicky that Louise's happiness was 'strong' though undemonstrative. She would never say what she felt; to try to make her would have 'the worst effect'.

The next seven-and-a-half years in the Lornes' lives were to be like Louise's temperament and the English weather (which incidentally had sometimes been compared) – frequent changes from sunshine to cloud and back again. There were disappointments in the two key areas of Lorne's career and Louise's hope of children. But they had plenty of interests in common, one being foreign travel. So their honeymoon in Germany and Italy was in every sense a holiday in the sun. They visited Louise's sister Alice in Darmstadt, whose husband Louis was heir to the Grand Duke. Despite the Queen's fears that the sophisticated Alice would corrupt Louise's innocence, the honeymooners enjoyed themselves. In Florence they contentedly sketched together its terracotta roofs. Their hostess was the 'lithe and graceful' (according to Lord Ronald Gower)

Walpurga Lady Paget, wife of the British Ambassador Sir Augustus Paget. Wally had known Lorne as a 'pedantic and a little priggish' schoolboy, quite without his present 'sterling' qualities. In her memoirs this old friend of the royal family gives a picture of Louise as both enchanting and *difficile*. She was the life and soul of one party given in her honour – until suddenly, feeling she had had enough, she vanished into Wally's bedroom and never reappeared. The same thing was to happen many years later in even more bizarre fashion. Having dined alone after an exhausting day in Cannes with her friend Ethel Badcock, she presumably retired to bed early. But the Princess unexpectedly returned to her friend's room where Ethel was undressing, clad 'in her knickers and danced reels *beautifully* ... like the madcap she is, and finally flew out of the room with a military salute and a kick up behind'.*

During the honeymoon another interesting trait in Louise's character showed itself: her passion for anonymity. She and Lorne travelled part of the time as Lord and Lady Sundridge, one of the Argyll titles. She explained to Wally that she had not at first called on the King of Italy because 'we are by way of being incognito'. Of course Queen Victoria would also sometimes travel incognito, but when her true identity was spotted, as in the Highland expeditions, no one could have been more amused and delighted than she. Louise on the other hand seems to have had a growing obsession with anonymity, as if her identity might be actually changed by her assumed name. When recognized, she was not at all amused.

The first year ended with a distinct hiccup in the couple's relationship, that Queen Victoria's intervention did nothing to soothe. In late November the Prince of Wales's desperate attack of typhoid began. The family came hurrying across the snowy wastes of Norfolk like mourners to a death-bed, Louise and Affie from Windsor, Alice and Louis from Darmstadt. The house – Sandringham – was already overcrowded and not improved by the gas leak that was worst in Louise's bedroom and necessitated her sharing a room with Beatrice. Word had evidently gone out that there was no room in the house for Lorne. He took umbrage at not yet being treated as 'one of us'. The letters show the Queen suggesting that both Louise and Lorne were in the wrong, Louise for not letting him come and see the crush for himself, Lorne for expecting to barge in on such a family crisis.

The truth was that Queen Victoria rarely regretted the absence of a son-in-law until Beatrice married Henry of Battenberg. She had a curious theory that when one of her girls married, she lost a daughter; when a

* Badcock's diary quoted in Jehanne Wake's *Princess Louise*.

son married, she gained a daughter (in-law). Probably Louise's passion for Lorne was not strong enough, and her reverence for her mother too strong, for her to confront the Queen on this problem at an early stage. Thus all three of them – Victoria, Louise and Lorne – gave and received several minor stab wounds until the 1880s, when the Lornes' relations with each other radically changed – for the worse.

Meanwhile, it was Ponsonby who most vividly reported the stresses and strains of living as a grown-up under the same roof as the Queen. During the Prince of Wales's illness the family divided itself into 'improvementors' and 'depressors'; the latter (which did not include Louise), when Arthur and Affie went skating, accused them of 'bad taste'. A group of princes were exercising in the Sandringham gardens when they suddenly caught sight of Victoria's bent little figure – after her grave illness that August and September – advancing on them. 'The Queen! The Queen!', they shouted in panic as they stampeded for cover, the Duke of Cambridge in the lead, with Leopold bringing up the rear. Ponsonby turned to Douglas Haig, Prince Leopold's equerry, who was strolling into the garden with him. 'This is that "oneness" we hear of,' said Ponsonby sarcastically, referring to the public's devotion to the idea of united royalties. And yet the 'oneness' was there, as Ponsonby well knew, in this astonishing family; a 'oneness' both created and endangered by the small tyrant at its head.

These years of Louise's marriage were occupied in the main by three things: the charitable work already mentioned, domestic life and artistic activities.

Again with hindsight, it looks as if Louise's youthful instincts to assist women's liberation were gradually redirected by her family into more conventional channels, though her interest in women's education and artistic work never wavered. Regiments and hospitals gradually outnumbered other causes, hospitals predominating on her list of charities. This must have been partly Lorne's doing. Though at first a political Liberal, he was distinctly old-fashioned about a woman's place. His wife, for instance, was not allowed to play billiards or make speeches, even as chairman of a committee. Lorne made the speeches for her. One can assume that he did not say anything too radical on her behalf.

Lorne was also Louise's chivalrous champion during royal family 'rows'. The letters touch on one, for instance, in 1872 that raged around Francis Knollys's suitability to be the Prince of Wales's Private Secretary. As reported by Ponsonby to his wife:

> First it was said that Princess Louise said that Knollys took the Prince of Wales to places that he ought not to go. This on being enquired

> into was modified into that he was not a good companion for the Prince of Wales. Princess Louise however said it was Princess Alice who said it. Princess Alice denied this though she admitted she has said something to the effect that better companions than Knollys might be found. It was complicated by Lorne answering Knollys' remonstrances, that he should not mind the mutterings of a mischievous minx – which was meant to allude to Miss Knollys. Rather a strong observation to make about a man's sister.

Presumably Miss Charlotte Knollys had told her brother that Louise was criticizing him and Lorne was defending his wife.

By the beginning of 1872 the Lornes and Argylls were becoming anxious about Louise's failure to produce a child. Whenever Louise cancelled an engagement because of a cough or bad knee, the Duke would telegraph hopefully. Lorne had written a poem about marriage in which he conventionally extolled the fruitful 'vine' around the house. There were still no grapes on Louise's vine.

The marriage was not yet unhappy. Indeed, Ponsonby wrote to his wife in 1873: 'I believe they get on as well as possible: though her manner is sometimes complaining in style, I really doubt whether she always means it.' An American visitor to Inveraray in September 1875, when the Lornes were there, described them as a fond pair: Lorne handsome and 'manly', Louise 'a happy woman' with whom he himself was 'a bit in love'. All the same, the Lornes' relationship was no longer 'bright confident morning'.

Nor was Queen Victoria above sometimes encouraging Louise to criticize her husband. After they had been married three years: 'I pity you so much', she wrote, 'for being *made* to yacht and think Lorne should take a sister or brother and let you stay quietly at home. It is not right for it is bad for you....'

On the subject of possible children for Louise, Queen Victoria was ambivalent. The death of Louise's best friend, Sybil St Albans (formerly Grey), in childbirth in September 1871 did nothing to blunt the Queen's arguments, which appear in the letters. At the beginning of 1876 she was writing to Vicky that children were usually 'a bitter disappointment. No one should be pitied for having none.' Nevertheless, Louise's own love of children and desire to produce the Argyll heir was decisive. She made frequent visits to German spas in search of 'health' and tried out the scores of remedies for infertility suggested by well-wishers – none of which, she saw in retrospect, 'did any good'.

Did the recipes include one recommended to Queen Elizabeth of

Roumania? 'Eat a pregnant rabbit complete with the young inside to bring fertility.'*

On the whole Louise got on very well with her in-laws, though Ponsonby reported on the 'two-dinner' row between them as early as 1872. The Queen sided with her daughter, being shocked that Louise never got a separate dinner at Inveraray, but always dined with the family as Lady Lorne. When told by her staff that the Duke could not afford two dinners, the Queen retorted, 'He ought to have thought of that before.'

There was another skirmish in 1875, mainly due to Lorne's hot temper. According to Ponsonby's account to his absent wife, Louise was full of complaints about life at Inveraray: she found her rooms unsatisfactory and still could not dine alone when she felt like it (a taste she had learnt from her mother); she was bored by the Duke's favourite guests – professors and 'meenisters' – though she loved the Duke himself; she wanted a proper country house of her own, not the property called Macharioch, set in a wilderness and not used exclusively by them; worst of all, she was spoken to rudely by her sister-in-law in front of the servants.

This incident is mentioned in a letter from Louise to Queen Victoria in this collection. Contrary to Ponsonby's opinion, the Princess tried to smooth things down, but Lorne, who always took Louise's side (as Ponsonby indeed noted), flared up and made a row. One feels that Ponsonby's castigation of Louise was overdone:

> Louise plays old Harry with every household or person she touches. The once happy home of the Argylls seems to be a perfect pandemonium now and the departure of the Lornes for the rest of the winter in the sun has caused but little grief to the worthy parents. I presume that Lorne is overborne by her.

To do Ponsonby justice, he was Louise's fan as well as her critic, coming to believe that any royal party without her was bound to be dull.

The Campbell daughters regarded themselves as a vigorous 'sisterhood'. However, Louise was not excluded, at least according to the memoirs of Blanche Balfour, daughter of the fifth Campbell sister, Lady Frances. The other girls in order of age were Edith, Elizabeth (Libby), Victoria, Evelyn (Evey), Mary and Constance. Blanche in her memoirs, *Homespun* (1940), wrote:

> In the year 1871, when my mother [Lady Frances] was about thirteen years old, her eldest brother, the Marquis of Lorne, married Princess Louise. The daughter of Queen Victoria and the Prince Consort had been educated on rather more practical lines than her new sisters-in-

* Hannah Pakula, *Queen of Roumania* (1989), p. 184.

law. She delighted to relate [to her nieces by marriage] how she had taught one of them the way to sew on a button which had come off the [8th] Duke's coat. 'They hadn't an idea of it,' she would explain in her rich guttural voice. 'They put it on quite flat. Oh, your poor grandfather!' Peels of laughter accompanied such glimpses of the incredible past when Mamma and the aunts were in a position to be taught and criticised. Princess Louise gave my mother her first pair of spectacles and transformed her existence.

Lady Frances herself supported women's suffrage and was a skilful platform speaker – more than Louise was allowed to become. But Aunt Louise stood out in Blanche's memory for her untiring energy, quick temper, racy conversation and 'insatiable interest in everything, great or small'. At one point, while still hankering after the perfect retreat of her own, she burst into the Balfours' drawing room in Addison Road, without waiting for the shocked parlourmaid to announce her, as she had an exciting piece of news: one of the small houses opposite was for sale.

'I shall take it. It would just suit me. I could get away and be quiet.'

'Will Aunt Louise bring her sentry?' asked Blanche.

'I do not think Aunt Louise will come,' said Lady Frances, drawing on past experience.

Blanche liked the way Aunt Louise 'talked and laughed from the back of her throat'. Specially delightful was her habit of rolling her *rr*'s when shouting for Lorne: 'Lorrne, Lorrne, where arre you?' It reminded Blanche of the Prince of Wales's guttural voice. (Bertie was famous for his pronunciation of 'arrt' and 'ar-r-r-angement'; at the latter activity he considered himself adept.)

It seems probable, indeed, from this and other evidence that the voices of Queen Victoria's children were a good deal more Germanic than history has given them credit for.

In 1874 the Lornes came to live in Dornden, a middle-sized country house near Tunbridge Wells. Louise was happy there, only apprehensive lest Lorne should sell it to save expense. (He eventually did so.) Vicky called it a 'sweet little house', though it needed children to furnish it properly. The Queen thought it too far away from her – and the Kentish people, she remembered from her own childhood, had always been obtrusive. She thoroughly approved, however, of the Lornes making their London home, at her invitation, at Kensington Palace in February 1875. Up till then they had rented the far too expensive 1 Grosvenor Crescent from Lorne's uncle, the Duke of Westminster, or stayed with Lorne's family in Argyll Lodge on rural Campden Hill. Kensington Palace was a scene of 'dirt and desolation' when they arrived, not having been decorated to Louise's standards since George III's day. There was a bronze plaque over the bed in the room where Queen Victoria was born.

Queen Victoria never grasped the Duke of Argyll's shortage of money. Louise's first visit from her mother to Inveraray Castle took place in September 1875. It was not altogether a success. The Queen admired the magnificent trees, but felt that the estate was run down. Moreover, she kept up her old domestic habits as if she were at home. There was no reason why the Duke and Duchess should not surrender their own rooms to Her Majesty, as they did, but Ponsonby was shocked that the Queen often expected, and received, a royal dinner apart from the Argyll family. The Argylls were sometimes treated almost as guests in their own house.

Inveraray Castle delighted the painter in Louise, as it had so much impressed J. M. W. Turner in 1801. He admired the Castle and Loch Shira, picking out 'the fine lines of the mountains and the large masses'. The interior of the old Inveraray must have been much like Osbert Lancaster's 'Scottish Baronial' in his *Homes Sweet Homes*: ancestors, antlers and ancient weaponry on the walls, a stuffed eagle in a glass case, a suit of armour and a stuffed bear on either side of the huge fireplace which is still incapable of keeping warm the laird and his friend, who wear the thickest possible clothes indoors, against the penetrating cold.

Louise's best letter in this collection is a vivid account of the Castle's devastating fire on 12 October 1877. The Queen stuck the description into her own journal. It was Louise who had suggested the human chain of buckets that saved pictures and furniture. Perhaps she remembered her father, Prince Albert, telling the children the story of how he had once organized a human chain when Windsor Castle caught fire. Seven months after the Inverary fire, the shattered and semi-invalid Duchess of Argyll died, thereby touching off a permanent state of difficult relations between Lorne and his father. Lorne's filial feelings finally died too when the widowed Duke remarried, was re-widowed and remarried yet again to a lady who had actually *served* both Louise and the Queen in their households. The letters cover an episode at the Duke's death in 1900 from which Lorne emerges as a strangely perverse character.

Meanwhile, while Lorne was away at his mother's funeral in 1878, Louise showed signs of treating him as the son she never had. 'I have been thinking so much of you my poor little Boy,' she wrote, '... poor darling you must bear up you know.' The family moved to Rosneath after the fire, a Campbell castle on a peninsula between Loch Long and Gareloch.

The Campbell boys, after Lorne as the eldest, were Archibald (Archie), Walter, George and Colin. Louise was devoted to Walter, and defended his *mésalliance* with a cotton-spinner's daughter, Olive Mills; Walter was in

Coutts Bank, but preferred escorting Louise around the picture galleries. And through the amusing and artistic Archie, who married, unhappily, a turbulent, theatrical beauty named Janey Callender, Louise widened and deepened her understanding of the art world. Janey introduced her to the designer Edward Godwin, lover of Ellen Terry the actress and epitome of Bohemian values. Max Beerbohm described him as 'the first of the aesthetes', a customer of Liberty's shop for oriental goods, along with Ruskin and Whistler. He designed a studio for Louise when she and Lorne moved into Kensington Palace. The Godwin studio was to be the scene of lights, laughter and sky-larking, and was tucked away at the bottom of Louise's garden. It is ironical to think that King George VI's very proper Private Secretary, 'Tommy' Lascelles, was to live there in the next century. Society in 1875 heartily disapproved of Louise's choice of Godwin as her architect.

At the Grosvenor Gallery, with its 'greenery yallery' aestheticism, Pre-Raphaelite revival and Art for Art's Sake creed, the Lornes would meet the painters G. F. Watts (from whom Godwin had stolen his child-bride Ellen Terry), the increasingly fashionable Whistler and Burne-Jones, the diplomatic Mitfords and the two interesting sculptors, Edgar Boehm and Aimée-Jules Dalou, a Frenchman who had got mixed up with the Commune and fled to England. In 1876 Louise visited Whistler's famous 'Peacock Room' in Prince's Gate. The founder of the Grosvenor Gallery, Sir Coutts Lindsay, and his artist wife Blanche Fitzroy, became Louise's intimate friends. She first took the plunge of exhibiting there in 1877. Lady Lindsay painted Louise's portrait in her South Kensington studio (5 Cromwell Place), and the Lindsays would invite her to stay on afterwards for dinner and conversation with other scintillating guests. One was Violet Lindsay, the portraitist, who afterwards was to become Duchess of Rutland and mother of Lady Diana Cooper.

In the portrait by Blanche Lindsay, Louise is wearing a silver articulated necklace made by the 'Craft Revivalist' jeweller, Carlo Giuliano. Her rather fussy frill, bow and short curled hair are balanced by the smooth harmonious features – though there is sadness in the eyes. Did the painter Sir Edward Poynter use Louise as his model for Helen of Troy? The eyes look faintly sad, like those in Blanche Lindsay's portrait. When representing Mary Queen of Scots, Louise wore pastiche jewellery possibly made by Robert Phillips, whose customer she was. Phillips may have helped Louise to make jewellery herself, a craft that grew on her.

John Ruskin, according to his cousin Joan, loved all the royal family, but his favourites were Louise and Leopold. It was said that he would only accept correction from pretty girls, whom he called 'my girl friends':

like Rose La Touche or the May Queens of Whitelands College. He may have seen Louise as another of them.

In 1877 Louise was excited by the sight of George Eliot, now passing as Mrs Lewes, at a concert, so she asked George Goschen, the Liberal politician, to include the redoubtable novelist and her 'husband' in a party he was giving in Louise's honour. George Eliot had lived with George Lewes for many years, but had never married him – not a 'Victorian' thing to do. On arrival at Goschen's party, Louise ignored royal protocol by immediately asking to be introduced to 'Madonna', as George Lewes called his 'wife', instead of waiting for Mrs Lewes to be presented to her. Louise talked to the novelist again at great length after dinner, probably about women's education.

At an 'aesthetic' dinner given on 3 March 1878 by Percy and Madeline Wyndham in Belgravia, Louise again met Robert Browning, still as handsome as he had looked nine years before to the twenty-one-year-old girl in the Westminster deanery.

Louise was plunging even deeper into aestheticism when she introduced Lillie Langtry to her brother Leopold. The link between the Marchioness of Lorne and the 'Jersey Lily' was a significant one, and in no way connected with the 'Lily's' future lover, the Prince of Wales, as Jehanne Wake points out. Lorne's intimate friend and relative, Lord Ronald Gower, had also become a friend of his wife's. He would travel with them and visit them at Dornden, where he was impressed by Louise's bustling about like a thorough German *hausfrau*. Through Gower, Louise met Frank Miles, who shared a house with Oscar Wilde, and through Frank she met Lillie Langtry. There is an unsubstantiated story that Queen Victoria, finding the portrait of Lillie on the wall of Leopold's room, tore it down.

As early as 1872 Louise was getting even Bertie interested in modern art. 'Your account of Millais' and Leighton's studios', he wrote to her, 'seems a very good one, and I shall look forward to see their pictures at the Royal Academy.' Earlier still she had achieved a bust of the Queen, another of Prince Arthur (presented to Woolwich) and a portrait of the distinguished American ambassador and famous writer, J. L. Motley, which he considered 'very good'. Her bronze equestrian statue of the Black Prince had been presented to her parents-in-law and escaped the fire of 1877. She was now working on a relief of Geraint and Enid.

Into this exciting new world, where morals were 'peculiar' but aesthetic values which she could truly appreciate – beauty, imagination, liveliness of actual impressions – seemed to reign, burst in unforeseen and unwelcome bombshell. Benjamin Disraeli, the Tory Prime Minister, decided to honour Lorne by appointing him Governor-General of Canada.

For Lorne the prospect was bliss. He adored travel, felt romantic about the British Empire and was more than ready to serve in a sphere which would allow him to show his mettle. His career, so far, in the House of Commons had disappointed both him and Louise. He was not a skilful debater and he lacked party political ambition.

As for Louise, the *Punch* joke of eight years ago seemed at last to have come true. She was indeed 'all forlorn' at having to cross the stormy ocean, face a series of icy winters and leave the family and friends she loved, especially her younger brothers. Arthur was to be married to Princess Louise of Prussia (Louischen) in February 1879 and she would miss his wedding. Leopold was possibly the person she loved best in the world, now that she and Lorne had failed each other in the matter of children. Nevertheless, it was her duty to go and she did it 'all for Lorne'.

II

1878–1900

The voyage to Canada was appalling. Lord Beaconsfield (Disraeli) had expected Louise's departure from England to be a 'wrench'. Poor sea-sick Louise expected it to be a wreck. She moaned and prayed until battered RMS *Sarmatian*, two sails in shreds, was eventually towed into Halifax harbour. They reached Ottawa, the capital, on 2 December. Six days later Louise's sister Alice caught diphtheria and died on the 'fatal' 14th (the same date as their father), having already lost her baby May from the same disease. Vicky's Waldy, aged eleven, had also died of it in March, killing the life-spark in his mother. Louise arrived looking beautiful but deathly pale. The omens seemed sad.

For Lorne the omens were hard to read. Six months before his appointment his gift of second sight had granted him a vision of a brilliant future abroad. The only member of the royal party not to be sea-sick, he sketched a seagull that had been blown on deck. He was the youngest and fourth of Canada's Governors-General since Confederation. Some people, however, thought that the outstanding success of Lord Dufferin, his predecessor, would show up the inexperience of this young man. Others retorted that his marriage to a royal princess would be counterweight enough; still others saw the royal factor as a further disadvantage.

Lorne's Private Secretary, Major Francis de Winton, made a bad start with the Canadian press. (Ponsonby remembered that de Winton had previously been with old General 'Fuzboz' Williams in Montreal, and thought he knew everything about Canada.) What was known as 'the New Brunswick incident' concerned four journalists being turned off the royal train without the Lornes ordering it or, indeed, knowing anything about it. But it was assumed to be their wish and got them an unfair and early reputation for *hauteur*.

Sir John Macdonald, the Conservative Prime Minister, had not been able to meet the Lornes on arrival owing to one of his drinking bouts.

He was perfectly loyal, as was his strong-minded but touching wife, the mother of one mentally handicapped child. The Opposition naturally seized on Sir John's little weakness as an insult to the Princess, adding for good measure that Lady Macdonald was high-hatting her.

Louise's first state ball was a fiasco, for Ottawa was still 'a rough and boozy' little lumber town of some 15,000 inhabitants. The hospitable hosts provided too much champagne-punch and several ministers had to be assisted out. One drunken senator found that Louise's train was getting in his way and kicked it aside.

Major de Winton made an even worse start with the prickly question of etiquette. No doubt there were Canadian politicians on the alert for the imposition of royal ritual on their hitherto untainted democracy. Some of the Ottawa wives did not help by taking lessons in 'the backward walk'. 'A nation of flunkies', sneered one Canadian paper. Would their husbands have to wear knee-breeches? Louise, horrified by this speculation, was heard to say, 'I wouldn't care if they came in blanket coats!' (This famous remark has been wrongly attributed to Lorne, according to Sandra Gwyn in *The Private Capital*, 1984).

A Yankee journalist, using the pen name of 'Captain Mac', published in 1881 a survey of Canada including a lively skit on Mr and Mrs J. Muggins Jones being presented at the viceregal court. Married to a retired eating-house keeper, Mrs J. M. J. has at last won her heart's desire after months of 'supplication, solicitation and fees innumerable'. They arrive in their own carriage, with the 'newly-emblazoned family coat of arms – une saucisse, deux pommes de terre assiette, fourchette à la crosswise. . . .' They return home already beginning to despise the 'vulgah horde, who had never been presented at court. . . .'

A real-life senator was described by the Opposition leader as a 'vain-glorious fool', who put on a velvet coat and knee-breeches for the opening of Parliament; he got congestion of the lungs.

There were many acts of gaucherie on both sides. When Louise asked one Cabinet minister what he thought of the notorious Whistler–Ruskin lawsuit (Ruskin had accused Whistler of charging guineas for throwing a pot of paint in the public's face), the ignoramus replied that Whistler had for ever stained the army's good name – confusing James McNeill Whistler with an old soldier writing in Ottawa as 'Whistler at the Plow'. There was British gaucherie too in Canadian eyes. The navy, when they visited the Great Lakes, equipped their two gunboats with fresh-water tanks.

However, it was de Winton's starchy attitude that caused the real trouble. It was feared that he was establishing a regular 'court'. *Truth*, the anti-imperialist, anti-Canadian and anti-monarchist British weekly run by Lorne's cousin Henry Labouchere, reported a revolt against court dress:

> The extremely stout old ladies, in the name of decency protested. The lean Kine were furious. Those subject to bad colds and bronchitis said they acquired their ailments from having a Royal Governor-General, who had no sympathy with human weakness.

A contemporary writer on Lorne's administration (J. E. Collins, 1884) denounced de Winton as an 'unadjustable, frigid, and repelling person', a 'tactless and oafish blockhead'. His excesses were attributed to the Lornes' personal orders – until the 'icy ring' formed around them was thawed by Lorne's 'warm-hearted manliness'.

Despite all this Louise was happy. Everyone had told her she would like the Canadians and she did, especially the elegant ladies of Quebec, with whom she could discuss French novels in French. (This caused some jealousy in Ottawa.) Everyone had warned her against the frightful winters. But once she learnt to keep warm by skating, going for walks in much admired stout boots (though with a stick because of her knee) and wearing superb furs, she could enjoy the amenities of Government House.

Rideau Hall was a comfortable-looking villa surrounded by gnarled pines, which Louise liked even more than the gnarled politicians, for at least she could sketch the trees. And the artistic Lady Dufferin had constructed a studio. Louise added an outdoor sketching box that could be trundled around in the grounds. She redecorated her rooms, painting crab-apple branches on the white doors. One still remains, now in a corridor. Rideau could only be kept warm by enormous fires, but also at enormous expense, as Lorne was to discover. Canada could without doubt be liked and even loved – provided one was in good health. The *New York Times* had patronizingly credited Lorne with 'no blemish on his name', and they were manifestly a young couple for a young country.

After admiring Niagara Falls in January as Lord and Lady Sundridge (their expedition being spoilt none the less by an over-attentive press), they spent the summer visiting the people in their towns and villages, including the Wild West; fishing in the splendid Canadian waters; sketching and entertaining enthusiastic Campbell relations from home. Louise began to feel the pinch of home-sickness. She had been promised home leave by her mother in the autumn of 1879, and home she went. Lorne rightly felt it his duty to stay put. It was perhaps a pity that Louise took her leave so early – she left Ottawa on 18 October – and returned so late, not arriving back in Halifax until 3 February 1880, because new rumours were spreading that she did not like Canada, which was untrue. Someone said it was due to fear of a Fenian kidnapping. The *Church Record* said she was only returning to Canada because she had become 'a pervert to Rome'. Others kept alive the old rumours about the Macdonalds being insulting;

and the oldest rumour – dating back to 1867 – about her alleged illegitimate baby was resuscitated in a new form. She had returned to England so soon, it was said, in order to have her child – which was clearly not Lorne's – and bring it back to Canada. So that particular rumour also implied that she and Lorne had quarrelled. *Truth* supported the rumour of a quarrel with its usual inventive journalism. On the other hand, a scurrilous wit carved neatly on the wooden wall of a Nova Scotia public toilet verses to the effect that 'Louise loves Lorne'.

Meanwhile, Louise was planning to exhibit in the new Royal Canadian Academy: two flower pieces, a sketch of an old house in Kent, a pencil portrait of Lorne's sister Libby and another of J. L. Motley. Lorne was to open the Academy in 1880.

Only eleven days after her return, on St Valentine's Day of all days, a dreadful accident occurred that was later to give some truth to some of the rumours. Smashed up as she was, how could any place seem to her enjoyable? – which meant Canada; and how could any person seem lovable? – which meant Lorne.

On the evening of 14 February 1880, three covered, horse-drawn carriages on runners set out down the frozen drive of Rideau Hall for Louise's first Drawing Room of the season in the Senate Chamber. There is a sharp bend in the road to the left before the gates on to the Ottawa highway are reached. The English coachman, who was driving the third sleigh carrying Louise, Lorne and an attendant lady and gentleman, took the bend too fast, the sleigh suddenly slewed out to the right and, as the frightened horses bolted, turned over on its side and was dragged for 350 metres. At last the ADC Bagot in the second sleigh stopped the tiring horses and brought Louise's sleigh to a halt. The coachman and footman had been thrown clear; not so Louise.

She was hurled on top of Lorne opposite, who thus pinned down beneath her could do nothing to help. Hit on the head by the metal framework of the sleigh, she was momentarily concussed. When she came to, she was covered in blood, her own, the earring in her left ear having been wrenched out, tearing away half the lobe. Despite this she managed to hold Mrs Eva Langham's head off the ground, probably saving her from death. Weeks later Eva's arms and shoulders were still black and blue while their rescuer, Bagot, was to feel his leg injuries for the rest of his life. The other two, Lorne and Colonel McNeill, were less badly bruised. Did Louise, in her state of shock, feel deep down that Lorne, once her perfect 'Arthurian Knight', had resigned his chivalrous post to another (Bagot) in the hour of crisis? She could not have realized at first that it was not Lorne's fault that he lay there helpless beneath her.

The reception in Ottawa was cancelled, Louise and Eva were helped upstairs and put to bed. De Winton now took over and his handling of the situation was again disastrous. Over-anxious lest the Canadian and British public, above all the faraway Queen, should jump to exaggeratedly horrific conclusions, he deliberately played down Louise's injuries – the battering and the shock – letting the press and people believe that the accident was trifling and that the Princess was making a rapid and complete recovery. As the Leader of the Opposition, the Liberal Alexander Mackenzie, wrote to his wife on the 18th:

> I think there was no injury done worth mentioning. I am told she shewed good pluck. The cut [on her ear] was from the glass and the bruise simply from striking against the carriage side. The Sleigh slewed round turning the corner at full speed, in other words it was all bad driving by the English coachman. No Canadian would drive full speed on an icy road turning a corner.

Louise's royal training in the keeping of a stiif upper lip at all times encouraged the illusion. Added to this, the lingering shock was probably responsible for her bursts of animated conversation, noticed by all but wrongly interpreted as signs of restored health.

Lorne himself knew very well that she was far from recovered – quite apart from the fact that she woke him up at all hours to renew her cold poultices. For a long time she could not sleep without bromides, suffered from agonizing headaches and neuralgia in her face, and was in a permanent state known to Victorians as 'nerves'. Her biographer thinks there was later a recurrence of the youthful meningitic symptoms. Small wonder, then, that when Prince Leopold arrived on a long-planned visit in mid-May, she was eager to get away from it all by touring Quebec and Niagara, followed by ten days in Chicago (rebuilt after the great fire of 1878) and concluded by fishing on the Cascapedia river.

The *Chicago Tribune* happily named the royal pair, 'Vic's Chicks'. They went about incognito, Leopold twirling his cane like any 'young sprig' and Louise attracting no attention, though she wore a short black dress with a canary yellow straw hat, feathers and flowers. Their being incognito puzzled everybody. What had she to hide? Nothing – except that she was a human being.

The *Tribune* little realized that one of the 'chicks' was a game chicken indeed, but still very sorry for itself. Robert Collins, who had come out with Leopold, noticed the change in Louise – she was 'unstrung and restless'. So when Leopold had to go home in July, having injured both legs in one of his frequent falls, she went too. There was general agreement in her family, including her mother and husband, that another winter of public duties performed in freezing temperatures would be the worst thing for her. The public was still not allowed to understand her situation. They believed the chick was 'malingering'.

In spite of her continuing neuralgia, Louise was to find the old threads at home as silken as ever. There was Boehm, in due time to be knighted and already recognized as one of the most accomplished conversationalists at Grillion's famous club. Though conventional, he was sharp. Jules Dalou had returned to his native France, as the Commune, from which he had fled, was already a whole decade away. But there was Whistler with his jaunty walk and darting eyes, no doubt still sending invitations to Louise through her secretary and getting her to attend his most glittering events, as he had when she was home in 1880. The Canadians may have noticed that her neck hurt less in the Chelsea artists' Tite Street than in the politicians' Rideau Hall.

There had been changes among the dukes. Early in 1881 Lorne's father had resigned from the Liberal Cabinet over an Irish Land Bill that he opposed on the grounds that it might unsettle the Scottish crofters. Leopold called him 'our fiery little duke'. And Leopold himself had been created Duke of Albany on the Queen's birthday. With this position he felt equipped to seek a wife. Perhaps that 'very nice and pretty girl', Frances Maynard, thought Queen Victoria. But Frances settled (for the time being) on the heir to the Earl of Warwick. Later she was to entertain the heir to the throne.

There were two other weddings that boded no good for Lorne. In August 1881 Lorne's father remarried – a widow, Amelia (Mimi) Anson. It required all Louise's arts to reconcile Lorne to the fact. And in February 1882 Leopold married his Helen of Waldeck-Pyrmont, producing a daughter, Alice, a mere ten months later. It would require all Louise's charity to reconcile herself to these facts. Leopold's unexpected paternity did not make her think more kindly of Lorne.

Lorne had come home for eight weeks' leave in November 1881, greeting his wife at Liverpool with 'a regular downright emphatic hug' – a journalist's report that made Lorne sound more like a bear than an Arthurian knight. He had already opened the new Royal Canadian Academy (later the Canadian National Gallery) and written for Sir Arthur Sullivan's music a new Canadian national anthem, described by Louise as a 'rumtitum, glory and gunpowder affair', which did not catch on. It was to the arts that he returned in England, going, among other places, with Louise and Lord Ronnie Gower to hear William Morris speak. Lorne's sister Frances had married Eustace Balfour, the architect, and through them Louise met the Burne-Joneses.

Back at his post after two months, Lorne seemed more enthralled by the prospect of a Canadian Pacific Railway than of his wife – 'apparently happy without her', wrote Ponsonby; a note that had also been struck by the Canadian Opposition leader at the end of 1880: 'Lord Lorne seems to be tolerably happy in the absence of his flighty spouse.' That did not stop *Truth* from attacking her. Why did not 'Miss Carry Loo, daughter of the landlady of the Crown Inn, Windsor,' go back to Canada with her husband? Ponsonby called the article 'shameful'. Lorne's enthusiasm for the development of Canada made him popular, though there was the occasional cross voice saying it was all self-advertisement.

It was 5 June 1882 before the Governess-General arrived back in Canada. She was attended by a new temporary lady-in-waiting, her chief lady being always the devoted, childless Lady Sophie Macnamara, known as Smack. The newcomer, destined for a sweet-sour role in the Argyll family, was Miss Ina McNeill, a niece of Lady Emma McNeill. Lorne's Aunt Dot. Ina's former fiancé had died on their wedding day and Louise was hoping to revive the sad young woman.

Louise had spent the whole of 1881 and five months of 1882, besides the last two months of 1880, in England or on the continent seeking health. She had probably given up the quest for fertility though she was only thirty-four. As we shall see, her marriage was in the quicksands if not on the rocks, and it is by no means certain that it was due to her rather than Lorne that there were still no children. The reunion of 1882 was brightened by three glorious months in British Columbia, 'halfway between Heaven and Balmoral', as Louise said, not hesitating to damn Balmoral yet again.

The people loved her unaffected manner, though one small boy, according to Robert Stamp (*Royal Rebels*, 1984) was disappointed in the Princess Louise – 'She's only a woman. I thought she was a steamboat.' After a winter tour together in the United States, where a railway accident as usual left Louise the most damaged with cuts and bruises, the Lornes again separated, Louise spending three months resting in Bermuda. Their reunion next time, in April 1883, was little short of calamitous. The press got wind of a row. Some people thought it was due to Lorne's alarmist line on the Fenians; Louise seems to have ignored them ever since a Fenian sympathizer brandished a stick at her in Paris, when she was twenty-one, shouting, '*À bas les Anglais!*'

Others held that Lady Macdonald was again becoming uppity owing to Louise's absences, and Louisc had to write a letter to Sir John denying that there was any truth whatever in the allegation. Louise also had to stand up beside Lady Macdonald at the opera to show solidarity; this was interpreted by the 'Clear Grits' (Opposition) as yet more presumption on the Macdonalds' part, who were making 'puppets' of the Lornes. But Sir John was appeased. He thanked the princess for her 'gracious note', which more than compensated for the calumnies of the 'degraded press'.

The real truth was that Lorne had taken a decision, without consulting his wife, to resign from the Governorship-General of Canada at the end of his five years (in November 1883), instead of completing the sixth year now available to him.

Lorne told Sir John that after so long it was time for a change, for a new man; he none the less minded much, weeping tears on Ottawa's departure platform for the end of 'the five happiest years of his life'.

It was understandable. But why did Louise mind his leaving so much? Enough to quarrel with her husband over it?

Ponsonby had already noted that she did not like being bossed by her husband or having her views ignored. She was also genuinely fond of the Canadians and had particularly enjoyed her last session among them when she was visited by her fun-loving, devoted young naval nephew, George of Wales. Queen Victoria supported Louise in the quarrel, arguing that Lorne was jealous – not of Georgie, of course, but of Louise's success with the Canadians. They had always fallen for her royal look of 'unobtrusive but fearless self-possession'. It was 'the pride of the Campbells in Lorne', said the Queen.

There could also have been a deeper reason for Louise's unwillingness to return to normal life. While Lorne was occupied in Canada, she could live apart from him for long periods. Once home again, separate lives might be more difficult. That brings us to the key issue: why was her marriage now loveless?

It will not prove easy to answer this question. That much must be admitted at once. But the problems will not be diminished by delaying further the necessary discussion of Lorne's possible homosexuality; though here again it is difficult to decide on the best moment for tackling it. Jehanne Wake postpones it until a late page of her long, impressive and detailed biography of Princess Louise. She has found no evidence whatever for homosexuality either in Lorne's family archives or traditions. Rather, in Scotland he is remembered as having had an eye for the girls when young, to the extent of fathering 'the odd child'.

Sandra Gwyn, the prize-winning Canadian historian, on the contrary, attributes the marriage failure to Lorne's alleged homosexuality, which she believes Louise 'discovered' as early as the Canada period. She cites among other evidence the fact that when Oscar Wilde spent two days in Ottawa on his celebrated 1882 lecture tour, Lorne did *not* invite him to

Rideau, but played golf with de Winton instead, fearing, she supposes, lest his own proclivities should be indicated by intimacy with Wilde. (This point can be rebutted to some extent: Wilde was also a notorious republican, whom the Queen's representative at Rideau might have legitimately ignored.) Clearly, if Lorne were indeed homosexual, it would make all the difference to any interpretation of the Lornes' lives together after the early 1880s. From the reader's point of view it seems best to get the complex question into our sights as soon as possible, remembering that this method will involve some chronological leaps forward, as we collect the total evidence for and against.

Sandra Gwyn is specifically followed by Robert Stamp, Canadian author of *Royal Rebels: A Life of Lorne and Louise*, and apparently by several American biographers. The British writer Nina Epton (*Queen Victoria and Her Children*) is the only one to have interviewed Princess Alice of Athlone, niece of Louise, and to have learnt from her that the Princess ran after everything in trousers. (John van der Kiste remarks that Lorne appears to have done so too.) Homosexuality, however, never cropped up during the Epton interview, for as Nina Epton said to me, 'Princess Alice would never have mentioned the subject in any case.'

In answer to a letter from me, Robert Stamp kindly enumerated the four reasons why he thinks Lorne was homosexual: 1. The male friends he chose, such as Lulu Harcourt and Lord Esher (both homosexuals), but especially Lord Ronald Gower. 2. Lorne's observations on attractive males in his writings. 3. Louise's desire to separate herself from Lorne from 1880 onwards – a factor on which Stamp lays great stress. 4. The opinion of other writers, especially Sandra Gwyn (*The Private Capital*, 1984), A. L. Rowse (*Ambivalence in History*, 1977), and H. Montgomery Hyde (*The Other Love: Homosexuality in Britain*, 1970).

Writers on this same side of the fence are impressed by Lorne's friendships as a schoolboy at Eton, emphasizing his admiration for the homosexual master, William Johnson Cory, whose photograph he stuck into his album; but far more for his young uncle (more like a cousin), Lord Ronald Sutherland Leveson-Gower, a self-confessed homosexual.

The argument from Eton does not necessarily cut much ice. *Amitié amoureuse* among adolescents was neither rare nor taken too seriously; except perhaps by Cory, who, according to T. D'Arch Smith's *Love in Earnest*, celebrated the romance of two Etonians, Frederick Wood (later Lord Halifax) and Lord Lorne, in a poem called 'An Epoch in a Sweet Life'. (It was Lord Esher who later identified Lorne as having been the other half of the 'sweet' relationship.)

Lord Lorne's lifelong and close friendship with Lord Ronald Gower carries more weight. Gower's talents probably outnumbered Lorne's. A

Scottish MP before Lorne was elected, he took his nephew under his wing when he too won a Scottish seat and introduced him to London life. (This is taken to mean the young homosexual world of the 1860s.) Gower was a sculptor, who achieved the imposing Shakespeare monument by the bridge at Stratford-upon-Avon, besides representations of Lady Macbeth, Falstaff, Prince Hal and Hamlet; he was a trustee of the National Portrait Gallery; he published biographies and also his own *Old Diaries 1881–1901*, in which interesting entries such as the following (summarized) occurred:

> *August 1894, Naples*: Gower did not like 'lardy-dardy' young men, preferring 'manly' types.
> *1897*: Nor did he like 'morbid' or 'decadent' writers.
> *1898*: He was very fond of children and envied friends whose loneliness was cheered by having them. [In this year Gower adopted the young journalist Frank Hird.]

He moved among the continental homosexual set represented by John Addington Symonds in Venice. He also had the distinction of furnishing Oscar Wilde with the model for Lord Henry Wootton in his *The Picture of Dorian Gray*. What need for more proof of Lorne's proclivities, it might well be asked. The best friend of Lord Henry Wootton is hardly likely to be a stranger to the love that dare not speak its name.

Nevertheless, Gower's intimacy with Lorne introduces a puzzle. After the Lornes returned from Canada they would go abroad a good deal in company with Gower. Sometimes it would be all three together, sometimes Lorne and Gower alone, and at least once Gower and Louise alone. It seems strange that Louise should, according to this argument, turn violently against Lorne because he was a homosexual – and then choose to tour the European resorts in company with a far more active member of the same brotherhood! Of course there are always possible answers to that kind of logic. For instance, the artist in Louise was by this time acclimatized to aesthetes. She and Gower had much in common, including sculpture, loneliness, a yearning for children and an admiration for Prince Henry (Liko) of Battenberg, whose 'manly and unaffected' character Gower specifically praised. And anyway Louise did not have to sleep with Gower.

A little ingenuity can also explain an odd incident of hand-holding. While Lorne sat beside Lord Esher's hospital bed in 1911, he is said to have held his friend's hand. But holding hands by a sick-bed, even another man's hands, is surely in a category all its own. Most of Esher's visitors kissed him.

Harford Montgomery Hyde, an authority on the subject, but, alas, no longer here to be questioned, assumed that Lorne was a homosexual because of his connection with the unsolved 'Case of the Missing Dublin Crown Jewels' in June 1907. The jewels were in charge of Sir Arthur Vicars, the Ulster King of Arms, who moved in a bizarre set which was both homosexual and heraldic. He was made drunk and his keys were stolen and copied by Frank Shackleton, Ulster Herald, and a villainous colleague named Richard Gorges. After stealing the jewels from the safe in Dublin Castle, Shackleton pawned them in Amsterdam for £20,000, a quarter of their value. Vicars was dismissed, but Shackleton, though known to be the thief, was never arrested. Described as 'very handsome and very depraved', Shackleton was Vicars's liaison with the Gower set and therefore also with Lorne. Although the King ordered an enquiry (the Crown Jewels belonged to him), it was mysteriously allowed to drop after sitting for only one week. Shackleton is supposed to have admitted his guilt, but threatened to involve the King's brother-in-law if exposed.

In defending Lorne against the charge of homosexuality-by-association, Jehanne Wake points out that Lorne was no friend of Shackleton; indeed, Lorne warned Gower against him – but apparently in vain. For Gower allowed Shackleton to handle the Gower property and to bankrupt him by, in all probability, embezzling it.

But this was to come later. In July 1907, on the very Monday morning that the disappearance of the Dublin Crown Jewels was announced in *The Times*, Lorne was travelling by train with Shackleton back to London, both having stayed the previous weekend with Gower at Hammerfield, his house near Lorne's old home of Dornden. Lorne passed his newspaper to Shackleton to read the news. If Shackleton had been arrested later, the inevitable mention of this weekend in the law courts, let alone other meetings, would have made embarrassing reading, however unfairly, for the court at Windsor. Besides being the King's brother-in-law, Lorne had held the official court position of Governor of Windsor Castle and Constable of the Round Tower since 1892.

Without further evidence, the conclusion would seem to be that Lorne was indeed mildly ambivalent. But it is time to turn to Queen Victoria's own account of Louise's dislike of Lorne, which naturally did not include homosexuality. It means a return journey of thirty years, back to the chronological order.

The marriage touched bottom in the year 1884. The sudden death of Prince Leopold in this year did not help Louise to recover her equilibrium. Her love for him was probably balanced by some jealousy of his wife Helen, to whom he left two treasures beyond the reach of Louise: not only the daughter Alice, but now a posthumous son Charles. Also, Lorne's hope of the Indian Viceroyalty was defeated in 1884 by the older, more experienced and more suitable Dufferin.

But 1884 was the year when the Lornes were supposed to restart life together at home. That Louise had no intention of doing so is made clear in the Queen's emotional and sometimes frantic confidences to her eldest daughter, the Crown Princess of Prussia.

Vicky was the obvious confidante. She had common sense, daughters of her own, a responsible position, and she had opposed Louise's marriage in the first place. It says much for Vicky's wisdom that she never said, 'I told you so.'

Our first date is 24 July 1884, when the Queen sent a very private note about Louise and Lorne:

> *24 July*: She has taken a perfect aversion to poor Lorne (who still adores her!!??), and is bent on separating from him. This dare not be for we cannot have a Scandal in the family!

The Queen explains that Louise has never been the same since the accident in Canada, and Lorne's love and attention now irritate and aggravate her. 'The whole is full of danger.'

Two months later the Queen seems to have accepted the general situation. On 30 September she rejoices that poor Louise is going to stay with Vicky, who should try to cheer and soothe her. She will never live again as Lorne's wife, under the same roof. Lorne must understand that this is a necessity for her health, and 'at last it will become an established habit. That is all we can do.'

After a fortnight the Queen still cannot see the harm of 'living alone'. Why should ill-natured people, she asks, spread reports? 'The only chance for Lorne', she adds after another eleven days (26 October), is to be 'cold and distant'. On 5 November, from Balmoral, the Queen writes that Louise's aversion will be permanent. 'She will never look up to him for protection or lean upon him' – and though the Queen feels for him very much, she also quite understands how, with Louise's 'peculiar disposition' and state of 'nerves', she just cannot get on with him.

So far, the Queen has no criticism for Lorne, only sympathy for him in a situation that neither he nor Louise can change. (Note that in her eyes it is Louise's disposition that is 'peculiar', not Lorne's.) But between 9 and 26 November the atmosphere at Balmoral has deteriorated all round. Meetings have been 'cold', the Duke of Argyll treating her 'very coldly. It was a relief when all left – alas!' The Queen writes sadly for she always liked and admired the old Duke.

Over three years appear to have passed before we read of more confidences about Louise from the Queen to Vicky. Meanwhile, Beatrice married Prince Henry (Liko) of Battenberg in 1885 and Louise began falling under the Battenberg spell. She told her mother that his brother Sandro reminded her somehow of Papa. One of the letters in this collection shows Liko flirting, so to speak, with Louise by criticizing her clothes.

Lorne stood for Hampstead as a Liberal and was defeated in the general election of 1885 – another blow to both of them, for the more work Lorne had to take him away from Louise, the better pleased she was. His defeat indirectly caused a divergence in their political beliefs which had hitherto been similar. The next time Lorne became an MP in 1895 he was a Unionist. Lorne, like his father, left the Liberals on the issue of Irish Home Rule, to which they were both opposed, while Louise, drawing on her Canadian experience, was attracted to a solution known as Home-Rule-All-Round. She also supported the idea of life peers as a means of diluting the extremely reactionary House of Lords – three times to be the destroyer of Home Rule. The Liberal Prime Minister, Sir Henry Campbell-Bannerman, was to welcome Louise's presence at Balmoral – 'noisy and talkative' though she was. Louise herself defended the policy of a Liberal minister, Lord Ripon, in India, arguing that his more humane policy towards the 'natives' would stop them from plotting against the Raj.

At the same time in this year, 1885, and those that followed, we find Louise and Prince Arthur drawing closer together. Life seemed to be treating both badly. Arthur used his sister as a go-between with his Mama, whom he no longer refered to consistently as 'dear'.

At the beginning of 1888 the Queen, though still sorry for Lorne, no longer attributed Louise's aversion entirely to her own nervous condition. She asks Vicky on 20 January how she finds 'poor Louise, morally and bodily?' While unable to prevent it, the Queen is very sorry that Louise is going to Malta, after all that happened last year – perhaps a reference to Louise's flirtatious behaviour, as observed by Marie of Edinburgh (see below). And on the 26th the Queen writes again of Louise and Lorne: though she pities Lorne very much, 'he is totally unsuited to her, very *unsoigné*, not overfond of soap and water, all of which is very uncongenial to her. He bears her open dislike wonderfully well in public' – but in private the Queen fears the scenes are 'dreadful' and make Louise 'ill'.

From the Queen's letters, it is difficult to draw any firm conclusion in regard to the homosexual issue. One thing only is absolutely plain: that the Queen regarded Louise's aversion to Lorne as serious. She attributed it to his personal habits, for which the word '*unsoigné*' was a cover-all.

Finally, how does this picture of the '*unsoigné*' Lorne fit in with what we know of Louise's antagonistic feelings towards him? Jehanne Wake has stated that Lorne's untidiness and eccentricity in dress angered the clothes-conscious Bertie, who conveyed his criticisms to his sister. She in turn began to resent Lorne's personal habits, thinking that he might be behaving thus on purpose to annoy her. The Garter ribbon might appear across her husband's chest at breakfast, while for a really formal occasion he might turn up wearing a tweed jacket.

Though his nieces adored him, one of them tells a story about Uncle Lorne's behaviour that makes him out to be a very odd fish indeed. Having been given the prestigious post of Governor of Windsor Castle and Constable of the Round Tower, Lorne had to receive the German Emperor William II on a visit to his uncle King Edward VII. There was to be a banquet, so Lorne said to his brother 'in his funny voice', 'I think I shall have a nice lil bath – a nice lil bath, before dinner.' Just then a message arrived to say that the German Emperor was on his way up to confer the Order of the Black Eagle on the Duke of Argyll (Lorne) so that he could wear it at the state banquet. Lorne's brother therefore knocked on the bathroom door with the message about the Emperor and a request to dress at once. 'Oh, no, no, dear,' replied the Duke, 'I'm having a very nice bath, I'm not going to get out of the bath.'

'But the page says the Emperor is on his way to decorate you. . . .'

'Oh, no, no, dear, I'll see him at the banquet, it's a very nice bath.'

Eventually Lorne's brother got him out in time for the Kaiser to decorate him in his dressing-gown, to the great amusement of Lorne but not of the Kaiser.

At least Lorne seems to have taken to soap and water in a big way. This might be represented as a success for Louise. However, she could not stop him growing stout, despite her passionate interest in diet, nor from doing eccentric things nicely calculated to displease the touchy Kaiser. And what of that 'dear'? Surely a curious way to address one's brother in middle age? His family probably accepted it as part of a good story, and of Uncle Lorne's genial charm. As we shall see, Louise herself was to become fonder of Lorne again in the 1890s, when the 'separate' regime, as described by Queen Victoria, was working rather better.

One last incident of a very strange kind must be mentioned before we return to the chronological story.

A rumour began to circulate during the last quarter of the twentieth century regarding certain nocturnal adventures of Lorne. It was said that he used to let himself out through the French window of their Kensington Palace apartment at midnight for assignations in Hyde Park. In desperation Louise – so ran the story – eventually resorted to having the French window bricked up. There was no hard evidence, however, that the window ever *was* bricked up, or, if it was, as to who Lorne's outside friends were.

In 1990, thanks to the most effective researches of HRH Princess Margaret, Countess of Snowdon, the first point was cleared up. When

Princess Margaret came to live in Kensington Palace, occupying half of what had been the Lornes' apartments, she found that the way into her garden was blocked by a bricked-up French window. The Princess had it unblocked; at the same time she asked the housekeeper why it had been bricked up in the first place and was told that it had been done on the orders of Princess Louise to keep her husband inside. But there was no further information on whom Lorne was visiting in the Park.

There is a third possibility: that Lorne was dating no one. In his last years, though still only in his sixties, he became senile. Today he would probably be said to have had incipient 'Alzheimer's', a term loosely used for loss of memory and concentration at any time between fifty and eighty. One characteristic of this affliction is wandering about aimlessly at night, sometimes even going outdoors. This may well have been Lorne's trouble. Unfortunately, there is no record to show in what year the window was blocked up, despite Princess Margaret's renewed researches; but if it ever was discovered to be 1911 or later, this theory would be strengthened. In any case, all three possibilities – man, woman or senility – would have made things wretched for Louise. One of her much younger German relatives, who could never have known her personally, can none the less remember her always being referred to in the family as 'poor Louise'. One way or another, there is an impression that she had 'a fairly poor time'.

In returning to where we left off in the 1880s, we come across the first picture of Louise drawn by a pen that was, if not poisoned, dipped in acid. Marie Alexandrovna, only daughter of Tsar Nicholas II of Russia and married to Prince Alfred Duke of Edinburgh, did not get on with her sister-in-law Louise. The Edinburghs had married in 1874 against the better judgment of the Empress and Queen Victoria – the two mothers. Marie and her mother were terrified of Queen Victoria when they visited England. All the same, Marie loved the prospect of the prestigious English court and Affie loved the prospect of Marie's wealth. So they loved one another, at least for the first years of marriage. As the Queen wrote hopefully to Vicky, Marie was very sweet and had married Affie 'entirely for his sake (!!) – I wonder – but never mind that'.

Marie was plain, badly dressed and exceptionally well educated. She was married to a husband for whom she successfully produced beautiful daughters and one son. Apart from the 'failing' of nursing them herself, which shocked the prim English court, she could not produce the magic to stop Affie from drinking and bring out his best qualities. By 1887 the marriage was no longer happy. Ponsonby noticed that after Marie had been married for eight years, she would go about at Balmoral 'speaking to no one, with an expression of disgust on her face'. The year before,

Affie had been ill with what Ponsonby heard was incipient *delirium tremens*. He was 'chastened' by the experience. This year seems to have been the last when Marie made an effort to 'cheer' the royal family, writing to Lorne on New Year's Day 1882 that the very 'dullness' of the royal residences raised her spirits, inspiring her to make Louise and the rest of the family laugh.

On 31 January 1887 Marie wrote an interesting letter intended to tell her correspondent about Louise's visit to Malta, where Alfred was in command of the fleet. Addressed to 'Dearest Mama' (Queen Victoria), it expressed Marie's pleasure at having Louise to stay. They had met her and Lorne in Naples and brought Louise from Syracuse to Malta, while Lorne went back to England. 'I think it almost better that Louise should be here without him first,' wrote Marie, 'so this arrangement seemed a very good one.'

Marie would have preferred to send Louise back to England and keep Lorne. She was to thank him profusely for once coming especially to see her off at the end of a London visit, and after his death she was to remind Louise of her many pleasant conversations with Lorne through the window at Kensington Palace. Perhaps it was the famous French window.

On board *Surprise* in 1887 Marie had been annoyed to find Louise criticizing her sister-in-law's relations with the ship's officers, which were no more than comradely. The Duchess of Edinburgh, in fact, accused Louise of the same foibles as Louise attributed to Marie, adding for good measure Louise's unpunctuality and tendency to complain. Marie's daughter Missy was to sum up her mother very justly: 'Poor dear stormy old Mama!'

As the 1880s drew to an end, fate continued to bludgeon the royal family. Vicky's invalid husband Fritz, after reigning for 100 days as Emperor of Germany, met his agonizing Waterloo from cancer of the throat. It was now 'poor Vicky' as much as 'poor Louise'. In 1889 Vicky's daughter Moretta reported from Windsor to her mother: 'Auntie Lou is not right at all – she complains of every sort of thing, but is charming as usual to look at.' Nor did Louise neglect her public duties. Winston Churchill, a fourteen-year-old Harrow schoolboy, used the Princess's visit to the Harrow Technical School on 14 May 1889 as an excuse for not writing his letter home: 'My dear Papa ... I would also have written yesterday but I was part of a Guard of Honour *all* the afternoon for the Princess Louise....'

Towards the end of 1890 a more personal blow struck Louise. For the first time it enabled the gossips to put a name to one of her suspected romances.

On a December evening she met her former instructor and present helper and friend, Sir Edgar Boehm, at his studio by appointment to advise him about a sculptural design. Boehm had five rooms in Avenue Studios, a large block of studios at 76 Fulham Road. They had been originally occupied by Carlo Marochetti, the sculptor of the recumbent statues of Queen Victoria and Prince Albert in the mausoleum at Frogmore. Among Boehm's neighbours were Alfred Gilbert, his friend and pupil; Edward Poynter, president of the Royal Academy; and John Singer Sargent, known as 'Wriggle-and-Chiffon' from his portraits of Edwardian ladies.

What happened next must be told in Louise's own words. Her biographer discovered a letter from Louise describing the tragedy in detail to the Duchess of Atholl:

> It was a terrible shock, doubly so as he was quite well when he met me in the long passage: as you see I did not go (unattended and unannounced) as all the papers please to say. Lady Sophie Macnamara and I were talking to him some twenty minutes and then Sophie said 'As your carriage will be here in a minute I think I will walk home' and in much less than five I heard that awful cry, Sir Edgar had carried a bust [of Lord Dufferin] to show me which I entreated him not to, also pushed some heavy things and must have over-exerted himself. It was found to be aneurism of the heart.

The Queen wrote in her journal of 13 December that Louise had given her 'the ghastly details of his last shriek, fall and gurgle'.

Boehm was a workaholic. 'I work like an engine,' he once said, and in the words of Mark Stocker, his biographer (*Life and Work of Sir Joseph Edgar Boehm*, 1988), 'The engine stopped in the early evening of Friday 12 December 1890.' The Princess may have got the detail about the aneurism from the doctor who was fetched by Alfred Gilbert after Louise had alerted him.

According to 'Skittles' (Catherine Walters), described as 'the last *poule de luxe*', Boehm's doctor gave her a different and far more melodramatic account of the death, which she passed on to Wilfrid Scawen Blunt, the diarist. (Blunt was particularly interested since he knew Boehm, the great expert on horses having visited Blunt's Arabian stud in 1879. He had also met Princess Louise.) Blunt duly entered in his diary Skittles' account of Boehm's collapsing in Louise's arms while making love, Louise 'covered with blood' dashing in a cab for a doctor, and the two returning to find Boehm dead. Blunt commented: 'There is a great deal of truth mixed up with the invention.' His own invention was the theory that Boehm had made up the Queen Victoria/John Brown liaison in order to cover up his own love affair with Princess Louise.

Great interest was shown in the affair by the press, some of it scandalous. *Truth* pointed out gleefully that Louise could not have got into the studio without being 'admitted' (presumably by the dead man), so that *The Times*'s account of the death was 'quite incomprehensible'. (The Princess was said to have found Boehm dead on arrival.) The gossips believed that Boehm was passionately in love with the Countess of Cardigan as well as Princess Louise, described by Boehm's biographer as 'both beautiful, talented and uninhibited women'. Boehm in fact produced very similar statuettes of each of them on horseback.

Blunt understood from Skittles that she knew of Boehm's liaison with Louise from Boehm himself and of the death-scene from Sir Francis Laking, the Queen's physician, whom Louise allegedly fetched. In fact it was Gilbert who fetched Boehm's own doctor. Skittles could at least claim with justice that she herself had sat to Boehm for the semi-nude statuette of a nymph commissioned by Bertie when Prince of Wales. Skittles also explained Louise's alleged affair with Boehm: Lorne was 'unsatisfactory as a husband'.

There are plenty of 'inventions' to dismiss without having to deny an *amitié amoureuse* – that perhaps overworked phrase of the historian – between Louise and Boehm. Thanks no doubt partly to her intervention, he was buried in the crypt of St Paul's next to Sir Edwin Landseer. Louise was friendly with the Boehm family as a whole, a fact that these letters bring out. Incidentally, the Boehms' daughter Effie married the brother of Marion Sambourne. The famous Linley Sambournes of Stafford Terrace, Kensington, were great friends of the Boehms, which helps to put Boehm into a respectable rather than a Bohemian niche, despite his wild curls and bright blue eyes.

It looked as if the 1890s were going to be another sad decade for Louise. Her nephew Eddy (Prince Albert Victor of Wales) died of pneumonia in 1892, to the great distress of his family who loved him despite his glaring defects as heir to the throne. Georgie, her much closer nephew (the future George V), had caught typhoid the year before, but fortunately recovered. At last, in 1893, came the start of some good years again. The letters show Louise much involved with the art world; better still, she completed her most famous piece of statuary, to be unveiled on 28 June 1893.

The marble sculpture represented Queen Victoria at the time of her coronation as a girl of nineteen. It was to stand on the south side of Kensington Palace where she had been born. So good was it that Ponsonby heard people say it was really the work of Boehm. That could not be, at least in regard to the last two or three years, since Boehm was dead. Boehm's son had given Louise the pick of his tools as a souvenir, so they may have inspired her. And there was in fact Alfred Gilbert to help when necessary. This seems to have been fairly often, for Gilbert's wife was heard to say: 'I shall be very glad when that tiresome princess has finished her work.'*

Why did Louise take so long over it? It had been commissioned by Kensington in the Queen's Golden Jubilee year, 1887. Some biographers say that Louise was ever idle. Others point out that her studio hours were continually interrupted by her royal duties. Besides, even if it had been ready by 1892, it could not have been unveiled, with due rejoicings, in the year of Eddy's death.

The unveiling ceremony was planned by Louise's brother-in-law, the Rev. Teddy Glyn, who was married to Lorne's sister Mary. The Queen herself was to perform the ceremony. Twelve little girls and twelve small boys, who were to present Her Majesty with flowers or wreaths, were rehearsed by Louise. Two of them let her down. The terrified Esther Canzioni, when she approached the old lady in the carriage, thought that she, Esther, was going to be carried away and burst into tears. (There seemed to be an echo here of Victoria's own youth, when her anguished mother suspected that her wicked uncle King George IV was going to make off with her in his carriage; the difference being that the young Victoria longed to be carried away.)

Another child, Meg Campbell, was seized by blind panic as she approached the Queen. Shutting her eyes and lowering her head, she charged on and on – until suddenly brought up short by something large and soft; the ample stomach, not of the Prince of Wales but of the Archbishop of Canterbury.

As the years passed, Louise's relations with Lorne seem to have settled down into a fairly stable companionship. He would write verses to the Queen which Louise forwarded, calling then indulgently his 'little weakness'. Or she herself would get a tender line from him: 'It is a great comfort to hear from you' – if only on a telegram or postcard. One can hardly imagine him sending her little jokes by post or addressing her as 'Dearest Alba' (his pet name for her) – as he did – or missing her company when abroad, if she was still liable to fly at him, as in the 1880s. Incidentally, their rows also were often conducted by note, just as Victoria and Albert, when quarrelling, had exchanged terse recriminations in writing.

The reactions of her friends and relatives, however, were still liable to vary from one extreme to the other. Her two new great friends, Constance

* Jane Roberts, *Royal Artists*, 1987.

and Cyril Battersea, found her an enthusiastic supporter for their work for adult education; she was none the less 'restless', 'queer' and 'capricious', though 'attractive'.

It was the attractive side that got her made honorary Colonel-in-Chief of the Argyll and Sutherland Highlanders in 1892. Her designs for bits and pieces of their uniforms were more successful than her father's attempts to model headgear for the Crimean War: his efforts were said to look like close-stools.

Ponsonby (who was to die in 1895) could hardly bear Balmoral, with its cold and its 'balmorality', when Louise was not there; her presence made all the difference between flatness and fun. Louise herself was beginning to enjoy Balmoral on her own terms. She liked getting up early and driving out alone in her little pony-cart, no one knew whither. But a bright young maid-of-honour like Marie Mallet saw the very worst in Louise: though 'amiable enough' and even 'fascinating' to all men, she was 'dangerous', a 'mistress of intrigue' and told 'more lies in ten minutes than most people do in ten years!' Lady Wolseley, wife of the war hero, observed that Louise sat with the household instead of with the family at an Osborne concert in order that she might enjoy a flirtation with one of them. She was not prohibited, however, from flirting with the family also when occasion arose, as we shall see in due course.

For Louise the 1890s were not exactly 'naughty' – rather, full of temptations, to some of which she would succumb. Two of those who have seen private papers agree that in her forties she was at her most 'alluring'. The Batterseas made much of her, entertaining so lavishly in her honour that even the experienced Lady (Wally) Paget commented on the interesting people one met there. It might be the Russian ambassador, or Millais the painter, Gilbert the sculptor, Henry James the novelist or John Morley the Liberal historian-statesman.

Louise's Liberalism still seemed as strong as ever and she had recovered all the sparkle that Ponsonby had missed during the second year of her marriage – 'not so bright and lively'. Indeed, most of Louise's anecdotes date from the late 1880s and 1890s. In Aix she related how the Governor of Malta's little son told them a story: 'There was once a naughty king who blew his nose on the curtains [loud laughter].' The king turned out to be Peter the Great when visiting England. If Louise's talk became too free, Ponsonby noticed that the Queen would begin admiring the fireworks.

There was the famous dialogue that same year (1891) in Balmoral. After Sunday service at Crathie church Dr McGregor asked Louise if the Queen had liked his sermon on the Devil. Louise said she had not heard but thought *not*, as Her Majesty 'did not altogether believe in the Devil'.

McGregor looked pityingly towards the Queen but only said, 'Puir body.'

Or there was the incident in Grasse when Louise went out for a walk with the household. Suddenly she spotted the Queen coming down the road. She tried to dive for cover into a shop-entry, but was prevented by twelve young priests coming out of the shop at the same moment. Louise roared with laughter at the look on the Queen's face as she recognized her daughter in the centre of a priestly throng. 'She makes it lively for us here,' said Ponsonby. (The Grasse incident seems to echo the similar Sandringham incident of taking cover from the Queen, exactly twenty years earlier.)

But however 'lively' Louise would make it for the household, there was always frustration gnawing at her. This alone can really explain her pathological need to criticize or tease her siblings. It was Ponsonby who was again to note these paradoxical moments, when Louise made evening parties pleasant 'with such a sweet smile and soft language – and saying such bitter things'. For instance, there was the failure of the Gordon Hospital. 'Poor dear Bertie,' said Louise, '– so nice of him to stick to a wrong idea even when he sees its folly.' Who could resist laughing?

Her jealousy of two out of her three surviving sisters, Helena and Beatrice, was to plague Louise during the last years of their mother's life. They both had sons (though Lenchen had lost two in infancy and two of Beatrice's were haemophiliacs) and also spent more time with the Queen than Louise was able to do.

Her teasing of Beatrice was not funny and Beatrice was terrified of Louise's tongue. Once at Balmoral Beatrice wanted to tell Ponsonby something about new blinds for the house, but she spoke so low, in order to stop Louise hearing, that Ponsonby had no idea whether she was talking about 'trigonometry or women's suffrage'. Next year, 1892, at Osborne, Beatrice was trying out a new horse when a carriage came tearing up 'like a fire-engine'. Beatrice, thoroughly scared, entreated Arthur Bigge, the Queen's Assistant Secretary, to make the driver slow down. But the driver was Princess Louise with Lady Ely seated beside her, both convulsed with merriment.

Louise's special mixture of emotional warmth and mischief reached its peak between the deaths of Ponsonby in 1895 and the old Duke of Argyll in 1900. Her kindness and support were fervently praised by the Queen's last and most admired doctor, Sir James Reid, who had nothing evil to put against her acts of generosity. It was she who persuaded the Queen to give him and his young wife an apartment in the Castle when Susan Reid was expecting her first baby. When the doctor wanted Louise to open a new hospital wing in Aberdeen, she replied: 'If they want an "Eclat" ... I fear I am not the right person. At the same time I would much like to do anything to help you in assisting a work you yourself are interested in.' The Reids called their second son 'John Lorne' and Louise was his godmother. There was never a hint of flirtation with Sir James, but only genuine helpfulness. 'Princess Louise – always a great support in times of difficulty', he wrote. Marie Mallet said the same thing: 'At her best when people are in trouble,' but added, '– oh, so ill-natured I positively dread talking to her, and not a soul escapes'.

After Ponsonby died Louise would have 'long talks' with Reid on the subjects that interested or worried them both. She sided with him against the Munshi, her mother's greatly indulged Indian secretary. She discussed with Reid the Queen's possible abdication: yes, she should go. 'The people are learning to do without her . . .' said the Princess, 'and she is reducing the future role of the Prince of Wales to a nonentity.' Most anxiously of all, she reviewed the available successors to Ponsonby as the Queen's chief Private Secretary, arguing strongly for Sir Arthur Bigge, while her sister Helena backed Sir Fleetwood Edwards. Louise's candidate won. And the situation gave rise to fresh jealousies in Louise's life.

It was in November 1895 that Beatrice sent for Reid and painted a highly coloured picture of a 'scandal' between Louise and Sir Arthur Bigge. 'Something must be done.' Beatrice emphasized that both Lenchen and Alix had been in touch with her about the scandal and Lady Bigge was 'in despair'. Louise 'had ruined the happiness of others' and would surely ruin that of the Bigges.

Was Beatrice thinking of her own happiness and herself as one of the 'others'? It has always seemed strange that none other than the Princess herself should have persuaded the Queen, against her better judgment, to let Prince Henry, Beatrice's husband, join the Ashanti expedition in 1895. The explanation may lie somewhere in the situation revealed by Reid.

Michaela Reid, married to Sir James's grandson and editor of his diaries (*Ask Sir James*, 1987), believes that Beatrice may have exaggerated the Bigge–Louise relationship. Be that as it may, the big guns were brought up: the Queen and Beatrice arranged for Randall Davidson, Bishop of Winchester, to tackle Bigge while Reid spoke to Louise. She in turn complained bitterly to him of her mother's and sister's unkindness: 'They had laid their heads together to ruin her position here [at court] and succeeded.' This time it was Louise who exaggerated; indeed, she was on the verge of a nervous breakdown. But the 'scandal', if such it ever was, collapsed.

One month later came a real tragedy.

The attractive Prince Liko of Battenberg, whose brother reminded Louise so much of beloved Papa, and through whom she again enjoyed family charades and acting, had begun to find domestic life lacking in adventure, even when spiced by the frequent presence of his sister-in-law. The Queen had insisted on his living under her roof in England or Scotland with his wife, Princess Beatrice, and their four children. It was not a man's life. Some people said that Louise's attentions only made things worse; that he fled from her, as well as from his family, when he left England for Africa in December 1895.

At the beginning of January 1896 the family heard that Liko had a 'slight fever'; on the 22nd – five years to the day before Queen Victoria's own death – came the news that he had died on the 20th. The devastated widow had to listen to her sister Louise 'calmly announcing, that *she* (Louise) was Liko's *confidante* & Beatrice nothing to him. . . .' This story comes from the Duchess of Teck and its truth has never been doubted. Louise also called Liko, perhaps with more truth, 'almost the greatest friend I had'.

It was always said of Louise, as we have seen, that she was at her best when people were in deep trouble, and even though she was partly responsible for her sister's misery, Louise did genuinely attempt to make reparation. Having joined the prostrated widow in the South of France and stayed on with her, Louise offered to design a memorial to Liko in Whippingham church on the Isle of Wight near Osborne. The result was the second of her three most famous *œuvres*: a bronze reredos of the Crucifixion with Christ supported by the Angel of the Resurrection. Alfred Gilbert was responsible for the bronze screen and marble sarcophagus in the memorial chapel.

Lorne praised its 'medieval German' idea of the Cross's dead wood springing into the tree of life. In technical skill it was a successful example of art nouveau and showed originality of feeling. Memorial sculpture, during this period, was sometimes under attack. Lady Ponsonby, the 'advanced' wife of Sir Henry, demanded an end to all sculptured memorials, which should be replaced by 'scholarships, fellowships and parish pumps'. Even Louise's mentor, Boehm, had been sarcastically described as a master merely of the 'coats-and-trousers' school of sculpture. At least Louise had brought poetic imagination even into a military monument.

During the year after Liko's death, Louise's interest was thought to have been awakened by the charming and witty Sir Edwin Lutyens, her architect friend. The Argyll family objected to Lutyens being given the coveted job of restoring Bishop Teddy Glyn's palace – Louise said Eustace Balfour, also an architect and Lorne's brother-in-law, was jealous – but Louise prevailed. Lutyens introduced her into a new high-powered set – Barbara Bodichon, the founder of Girton College; Gertrude Jekyll, the magical gardener; Hubert Parry, the musician; and Hercules Brabazon, the painter, who thought Louise herself painted 'rather well', and with whom she enjoyed holidays incognito. At times Lutyens found her exhausting, and when his wife Lady Emily complained of his attentions to the Princess, he replied, 'I squirm at the thought of the Princess fascinating me!' However, 'Hoheit' (Highness), as he called Louise, got him work, joked and flattered. It was all very friendly, but not friendship.

Jehanne Wake sums up Louise's flirtations with Bigge and Lutyens in an epigram: 'It was sons she sought, rather than lovers.' Certainly none of her siblings was without at least one son and there were plenty of sons among the Campbells.

The last two scenarios in the uneasy drama of conflict within and outside Louise's family both came to light through Sir James Reid: the first in his diary, the second among his correspondence.

Over two years after Liko's death, Louise came to Sir James in June 1898 with an extraordinary revelation, that nevertheless has the ring of truth. She confessed during one of her customary 'long talks' with Sir James, about 'Prince Henry's attempted relations with her, which she had declined', in consequence of which he had made efforts to expose her and Bigge out of revenge. This was the reason, she said, for Beatrice's continued 'unkindness'. Finally Louise could stand it no longer. She decided to write a letter to her mother 'complaining of her treatment'. She took the precaution of sending it to Reid so that it could be vetted. The letter duly passed the test and after the Queen had read it the family situation improved. There were no more long, complaining talks with Reid after 12 August 1898. At least, as far as we know, until twenty-four years later, in 1922. And then it was a letter rather than a 'long talk'. Louise wrote:

> I am feeling very much that some of my family would be glad if I were out of the way. It's always been so but I am not as strong as I was and I cannot throw it off so easily though it will never disturb me. One can rise above minding, and I try to. I remember when you were in trouble years ago, you used to write to me; so now in my loneliness I cannot help having a talk on paper with you. Pray excuse, and *please burn* this when *read.*

Sir James died not long afterwards and the letter was not burnt, fortunately for Louise. Though it shows how sadly indestructible were these family jealousies – Louise had grown up with them and they were still alive when she was in her seventies – at least her lifelong moods become more understandable. One could almost say that her failed marriage caused her less pain than her loving sisters.

For Lorne in the 1890s was relatively successful, therefore less of a problem in the home. Though he had missed the viceroyalties (India and Ireland) and Louise had turned down Australia, his name was discussed as King of Roumania after 'Foxy Ferdy'! Then, in 1895, he found a niche in the Liberal Unionist party (a move towards the Conservatives), as MP for Manchester South and in the Government. His looks improved with middle age, the gossip writer Augustus Hare calling Lorne 'a good Rubens', while Ronnie Gower was 'a bad Bronzino'.

True, a tiff developed between Lorne and Louise over the purchase of Rosneath Castle from the Duke of Argyll *with her money*. She thought this infra dig. Nevertheless Rosneath, with its exquisite views and kindly people, was to bring her intense joy in the future. Again, in March 1896 we find them celebrating their silver wedding separately, Lorne with Alix at Sandringham, Louise with Bertie on *Britannia*. Later that year Louise enjoyed an independent incognito 'biking' holiday with the late Sir Henry Ponsonby's daughter Maggie.

In 1897 Lorne wrote the script for an opera, *Diarmid*, which was produced successfully two or three times and then never again. The Queen at first thought that Lorne must have written the music as well. 'Oh, only the words,' she remarked. Lorne in fact was tone-deaf, facetiously referring to musical items like oratorios as ''orrid borios'.

The old Duke, having lost his second wife in 1894, married Ina McNeill in 1895. She was probably the person who kept him alive, though fading into senility, until 1900. When the Duke died on 24 April, Lorne was found tactlessly to have already ordered a selection of various sized coffins.

Louise was in for a new, short sharp struggle with her husband. But at least it was the 9th Duke of Argyll with whom she would be sparring. At last she herself was a chatelaine – the Princess Louise Duchess of Argyll.

III

1900–39

The burial of Lorne's father was even more traumatic than the old Duke's death-bed – unattended by his son and heir. A regular family row broke out between the Dowager Duchess Ina and the rest of the family over the burial place, with Louise at one extreme as conciliator and Lorne at the other as sea-green irreconcilable. Not that Ina was by nature implacable. Ronnie Gower had met her in 1899 at Argyll Lodge and found her 'very pleasant; she certainly has charm and that peculiar and rare one, a sympathetic voice'. Unlike Lorne. But she could not cope with the family's hostility and broke all the rules by having the old Duke's heart cut out before his eventual burial at Kilmun. She had wanted him to be buried at Iona with herself eventually beside him, but finally agreed to Kilmun as long as no family were present. When Louise, having hidden with some Campbells in the Kilmun church, suddenly emerged and ordered the service to begin, Ina promptly left the church and the country.

Lorne had called Amelia Anson, his first stepmother, 'a tiresome woman'; but Ina was 'Bitchina' and 'Hell-Cat'. No wonder the Queen was shocked by the long-delayed funeral (till 11 May), which Lorne did not attend anyway; while Bertie was scandalized by Lorne's threat to change his title from Argyll to something unpolluted by Ina. Louise settled the title question by saying that if Lorne changed it, she would leave him.

The early years of the young century seemed focused on death rather than life. The Boer War was raging and enteric fever swept Pretoria, killing the Queen's grandson Prince Christian Victor (Christle). The only two males of the Edinburgh family were also dead. Young Alfred had been dismissed from the army and sent to his sister Missy to be cured of drink and women, but in 1899 he died from untreated venereal disease at Meran, in the Austrian Tyrol, deserted by his mother and alone except for two servants. The year before, his father, who was parted from Marie, had come through an attack that drew from Lorne the comment, 'This illness ought to frighten him away from Beer.' Instead he was frightened away from life: he died of cancer of the throat on 5 August 1900.

But at least Affie had founded something – the Royal Philatelic Society. He eventually sold his stamp collection to Bertie, Prince of Wales, through whom it passed to George v, with spectacular results. King Carol II of Roumania, Affie's grandson, also became a collector. While he was trying to arrange his collection, Carol's newly wed wife would crawl into his lap – a problem King George can never have faced with Queen Mary.

By contrast with the two Alfreds' sad ends, the death of two valued art teachers, Ruskin in 1900 and Corbould in 1905, seemed triumphant: Ruskin 'winging his way into glory' at sunset, in the words of his adoring niece, and Corbould living beyond ninety. At the head of each coffin was a wreath from Princess Louise.

It was a gloomy Christmas 1900, as the letters show. The Queen's and Louise's lifelong friend, Jane Churchill, died in her sleep at Osborne in the early hours of Christmas morning. Queen Victoria, herself failing fast, had to receive the news in stages, through the tactful handling of her doctor, Sir James Reid, and her three daughters, Louise, Lenchen and Beatrice. Louise was determined that her mother should not be made more miserable by hearing of Jane's death too suddenly; not to mention having Vicky's despairing letters read aloud to her by Beatrice or Lenchen. (Vicky was to die soon after the Queen from cancer of the spine.) Louise was probably in the right, but caused havoc in the house by her sharp criticisms of her sisters, who refused to believe the Queen was dying. Reid wrote: 'Louise is as usual much down on her sisters. Hope she won't stay long, or she will do mischief' – again that word.

On the other hand, Louise had at least recognized the seriousness of the situation and telegraphed Reid: 'Could I be of any help to you, ready for anything?'

Louise liked dramatic action, including self-sacrifice. At Rideau Hall, Ottawa, for instance, she had nursed people with scarlet fever when the servants refused to come near. But deadly dull co-operation with others, particularly sisters? No!

She had done her best to support Reid when Jane Churchill's death struck. 'I am so truly sorry for you', she told him on New Year's day, 'in all this extra worry and fuss. The dear Lady [Churchill] how she would *hate* causing any disturbance. The Prince [of Wales] has just come into the room and bids me say again what a comfort your letters and telegrams are to him, and he has such confidence in your judgment.'

On 22 January 1901, Queen Victoria died, aged eighty-one, having reigned sixty-three years, three years longer than her grandfather King

George III. She died in a 'simple, narrow' bed with a 'small canopy', her family around her, Sir James on her right, the Kaiser on her left and a nurse sitting on the bed behind her – which would have been impossible if she had really died in 'the great canopied bed' that more than one writer has liked to imagine. At the very end Louise was kneeling on Reid's right. She told Lord Esher afterwards that she had held her dying mother's hand for five hours and that the Kaiser's 'tenderness and firmness were extraordinary, so unlike what was expected of him'.

The tensions between herself and her mother had steadily relaxed as the years passed and the trials mounted. It was her mother who decided that the icy Canadian winters were not for Louise after the accident. It was her mother who understood that she could not live as a wife with Lorne. And if the other side of the coin was jealousy of her sisters, that too seems to have diminished except when the situation was unusually stressful. Towards the end of her mother's life Louise wrote to Niall Campbell, her nephew and the future Duke of Argyll, 'Poor Mama, so deluded by Beatrice, my dear, and by Helena.' They were looking after the Queen; Louise was tied to Lorne.

Her last brush with Lenchen seems to have been in 1916, when Arthur described Lenchen's coming to live opposite Louise as 'a bore', and 'Pretty thoughtless' not to tell Louise first; though when Lenchen collapsed at a party seven years later, it was Louise who succoured her and was fervently thanked by Lenchen's daughter Thora.

Louise could not look to Lorne for protection, as she had to her mother, but he had his uses. He was an intellectual stimulus, he discussed books and artists, and he was able more and more to be treated as a child. Florita Thesiger, who became the Princess's extra lady-in-waiting in 1904, told her daughter Patience of an extraordinary little scene when she remembered the Princess springing up at lunch one day, running round the table with a tit-bit on her fork and offering it to her darling boy: 'Lorne, do eat this. It's so good.' Lorne's second childhood was just around the corner.

Indeed, Louise was to derive pleasure from many of Lorne's child-like moments. After his death she bequeathed his beloved scrapbook ('the dear little old Book') to his sister, Lady Mary Glyn, lest something so precious should fall into 'the wrong hands'. She would always remember his breathing hard as he gummed things in, like an absorbed child.

For the moment, however, he was every inch a Duke (though there were not all that number of inches: strangers would describe him as 'a nice little gentleman'). As Governor of Windsor Castle since 1892 he was deeply moved to be receiving the body of his Queen – 'my second mother' – at the end of its long journey from Osborne for burial. He had been present at her death-bed and it was he who, with impeccable literary style, summed up Queen Victoria's last hours: she went down like a great three-masted ship. (Sir Frederick Ponsonby heard the simile from Lorne and used it in his own memoirs.)

Lorne's manifest reverence for his late sovereign did not please the royal family so much when he promptly sat down and wrote a life of Queen Victoria – far too soon. But he needed the £1,300 advance.

There were still strains over money that the dukedom did nothing to relieve. Lovely Rosneath, for example, belonged to Lorne, but was paid for by Louise. There were rows over its restoration. Like Inveraray it had to be let for part of each year, when Louise and Lorne would stay at Dalkenna (wet and cold) or the Ferry Inn, for which Louise painted an inn sign. Argyll Lodge was sold, and is now remembered only through the name of a Kensington street. Kent House, on the edge of the Osborne estate, had been given to Louise by her mother by deed of gift in 1897. After Lorne's death she gave it to the Battenbergs, her favourite Louis and Victoria, since the unfortunate Admiral's resignation in 1914, on account of his German birth, had left them homeless.

Louise resented the thought of Lorne and one of his sisters staying at her beloved Rosneath without her, and altering things when she was abroad – but, of course, she would not stay there with them. She is still remembered at Rosneath by Flora Stewart, one of the gamekeepers' daughters: her trim, agile figure arriving at Rosneath pier, her constant visits to Flora's family at Green Isle Cottage, her deep voice, her presents of jackets and boots. She would attend the Presbyterian church every Sunday – 'always in the front pew, always late!'

She and Lorne were both becoming subject to gusts of furious temper. Louise's flare-ups could be controlled by Lorne's soothing enquiry: 'Now, now, Louise: what's the matter?' Lorne's outbursts were less amenable to reason, but were more transient, if also more frequent – described by Louise as 'hourly'.

His eccentricities were remembered by his nieces with indulgent affection. The protocol of chaperonage, for instance, seemed to him absurd and he took no notice of it. When 'a very tiresome young man' was about to go with their party to the Oban Gathering, Lorne thought it would be nice for the young man to drive over one of the Campbell nieces whom he fancied. Unfortunately, the fancied niece refused to go – 'I simply couldn't bear it, you must go,' she protested to her sister. The young man was not pleased at the substitution and the substitute sister was scolded by her aunt, Lady George Campbell, for a jaunt she had not enjoyed. 'How *dare* you go in a motor alone with a young man? It's *absolutely monstrous*!' But neither sister blamed their beloved Uncle Lorne.

It was said that at home in Kensington Palace Lorne's behaviour was also endearingly odd. He liked using the servants' entrance and helping with the cooking, especially baked potatoes – then considered strange uncouth fare for a gentleman.

Meanwhile, Lorne's public career had one more chance of taking off again, in its new ducal guise. Three months before he inherited his dukedom, the Colonial Secretary, Joseph Chamberlain, approached the Prince of Wales with the proposal that Lorne should be Governor-General of Australia. But if the idea had been a non-starter in 1884, it was even less likely to appeal to Louise sixteen years later. Instead, Lorne entered the House of Lords, where his late mother-in-law had always wanted to see him. His Liberalism was a thing of the past; he nicknamed Lloyd George's followers 'Preda Tories', a typical little Lorne joke.

Louise was working up to a spurt in her career as a memorial sculptor. She experienced keen frustration, however, over the colossal monument to Queen Victoria, to be erected outside Buckingham Palace at the top of the Mall. Fearing lest this key site should be used by the mob as an alternative rallying ground to Trafalgar Square, Louise argued for a monument in Green Park. It would have the added advantage of surrounding Mama with leaves and flowers, which she loved, instead of with tarmac, which she hated. Her views were ignored, Lord Esher asserting that she had not been consulted in the first place (why not?) and her later objections were therefore 'pure pique'. Certainly the committee's chosen site was the right one.

The end of the Boer War came in 1902, and for the next two years Louise was working on another poetic memorial, such as she had devised for Liko. This time it was in memory of the 'Colonial Soldiers' (including many Canadians) who fell in the war. Again a central figure was an angel, supporting the head of Christ on the cross, suggesting that those who had died had shared in Christ's sacrifice. Erected high up on the south transept wall of St Paul's Cathedral, the bronze group was unveiled in 1905. The model for the angel had been a Mrs Lloyd, suggested by her dashing friend Sir William Blake Richmond. With her 'splendid head' and 'beautiful arms', it did not matter that Mrs Lloyd had no aitches.

In the same year Louise produced a new nude study of a woman with long hair that was *not* used to cover up her body. The model was a married lady, again with no aitches, who had been recommended by none other than the magisterial Sir Edward Poynter, president of the Royal Academy. What combination could be safer?

Louise was no longer stylish, Florita Thesiger noticed, particularly when, at one charity sale, the Princess's hat and coat found their way into the second-hand clothes' box. Indeed, her new public position was edging her more and more into the serious world of charities, leading politicians and the establishment generally. Mrs Thesiger was fond of Louise and would cheer her with pleasant anecdotes from the workaday world. When King Edward VII died in 1910, for example, Mrs Thesiger saw from the top of a London bus a tramp in the road pushing a trolley. He was wearing a respectful black tie. Louise was deeply touched. 'I must tell Alexandra,' she said.

Louise and Bertie had always got on particularly well, for they had much in common (though not racing): jokes, cigarettes that he brought her back from Constantinople, a jolly way with the crowd. 'Good old Teddy!' they would shout at race-meetings; and at a charity do in Battersea Park, 'Good old Loo!' One cannot imagine similar cries for the equally 'good' and conscientious Helena and Beatrice. Louise was probably somewhat in awe of Bertie. She would never let him stay at Inveraray after she had become duchess and they were economizing; when Mama had visited there were seventy servants, now four; seventy-four dogs, now two.

Louise loved giving presents of jewellery she had made to her friends; Florita Thesiger received a necklace of fine opals and enamels. Unfortunately, the rather grand marble clock, another present, would not go. Only once was Florita sharply reminded that she had a royal employer. Inadvertently she stood on the royal hearthrug and was 'frozen off it'.

Another extra lady attendant was the Austrian Mme Klepac, who revealed something of her royal employment to the *Saturday Evening Post* in January 1930. Klepac's chief impression was of Louise's obsession with physical fitness, to be brought about by exercise (like hunting, even in her sixties) and a diet supported by a capacious medicine chest from which she was never parted, especially on her travels. The letters are full of 'thank-yous' from grateful patients, including Prince Arthur Duke of Connaught, who was cured of his dyspepsia by taking powders and resting before meals, and his son 'Young Arthur', who, short of exercise in Pretoria, received a punch-ball. She sent remedies round the family and round the globe, the Swedish palace receiving in 1913 'stuff for Gustaf's throat'.

All this health care seems to have had an excellent effect on Louise's own complexion, which Klepac found lovely and fresh, while her eyes were sapphire blue and her 'sandy' hair almost free of grey. To those who laughed at her exercises she would retort, 'Never mind I'll outlive you all. . . .' And she did. Nor would she ever 'get fat like my mother', which she never did.

The year before Klepac left Louise's service (1912) was not a happy one. Indeed, Louise may have had to make these and other domestic changes because of the drastic deterioration in Lorne's health. He had begun 'babbling', repeating himself and showing every sign of incipient senility. Christmas 1911 was a particularly sad one. It had been Lorne's favourite festival and he enjoyed it 'like a little child'. Now Louise felt again her need for real children, not this mockery of childhood. She longed for 'a house full of young voices and cheery faces.... I just love children at Christmastime.' Her interest in the Victoria Hospital for Children and the Chailey Craft Schools for Crippled Children may all have benefited from Louise's own childlessness.

The letters begin to show increasing instances of Lorne's being 'ill' or 'better' or again 'not looking well'. He suffered from bronchial trouble. In spring 1914, while Louise was at Kensington Palace and Lorne at Kent House, she went down with flu, he with bronchitis. She was sent for on 28 April. He had double pneumonia and died at Kent House about an hour before midnight on 2 May 1914.

The number and tone of the letters of condolence in this collection alone make one thing clear. Louise wanted to remember the ten years of her marriage when she had been in love with Lorne as if they had never vanished; and in understanding this feeling, her relatives thought to please her. True, a belief in Lorne's utter devotion to *her* comes through even more strongly in the letters, and may have been sincerely held by Louise's relatives. Whether or not the belief was true remains a mystery of Lorne's character. Lorne depended on Louise, who was not always there when he wanted her. Edward VII once met Lorne at the Royal Academy, where a new portrait of the 9th Duke was being exhibited, writing a foreign telegram. 'Lorne is asking where Louise is,' joked the King. She was as usual abroad.

No other name beside Louise's emerges as forming an important part of Lorne's latter-day story. If there was someone, male or female, they were most effectively concealed. One of his nieces did occasionally speak of a man with whom he would stay at Inveraray, but the two were only ever spoken of as companions, never anything more. Of course people were not always able to recognize homosexual relationships. Princess Louise's biographer states that when in 1893 Lord Ronald Gower was miserably wondering how to hide his own emotional propensities, neither Lorne nor Louise had the faintest idea what he was worried about. Gower was subtle and shrewd enough to keep the forces of the law in the dark. According to this account, he seems to have done the same for his best friend: Lorne thought it was drink; Louise saw him as restless and 'effeminate'.

Did Lorne's sister Frances mean anything special when she said he was too 'chivalrous' with women – perhaps suggesting detachment – instead of passionate? We may never know. In Canada, as we saw, he came out of the crucial Victorian 'manliness' test with credit. He was often praised for being 'manly'. Ironically, it was Oscar Wilde, on the look-out in artists for regrettable 'unmanliness', who found it in Burne-Jones, while the mother of J. E. C. Bodley, the writer, described Wilde himself as 'a mass of unmanly absurdity!'

As soon as Lorne was dead, Louise had a breakdown. Her nervous temperament burst out in anger with those she most loved, like Lorne's young nephew Ralph Glyn, the nearest she had to a son and destined to be her new 'darling boy'. There were no quarrels over the burial, though, this time; Lorne quietly joined his father in the solitude and beauty of ancient Kilmun.

Did the phantom 'Galley of Lorne' – a Gaelic vision comparable to King Arthur's galleon, but sailing through the skies – come for Lorne as it had for his brother Archie? And was the wonderful music of the harper heard? Perhaps the Isle of Wight was too far from Scotland for Gaelic mysticism and psychic phenomena to flourish. The 'watch lights' that appear whenever a Highlander is dying were clearly seen rising in their arc of red, green and yellow globes over the Scottish hillside by those kneeling beside a later Mac Cailein Mor, despite the lights of cars mingling their beams where the 'watch lights' met the Inveraray road.

Judging by Lorne's Gaelic interests and poetry he was not likely to have been a rationalist like his father, who was quoted by Lady Frances as calling the 'Cherry lights' mere will-o'-the-wisps and the shepherds' sightings 'rubbish'.

Louise at any rate would have believed. She amused the sceptical Ponsonby by telling him one day that she had got a real case of second sight for the Psychological Society. Her own poetic tribute to Lorne, however, dwelt on his contribution to the natural world:

> ... lofty the goal he sought
> Beside the chosen comrade of his love
> Labouring to make the Empire nations one
> His best was given to serve his country's cause.

Louise was clearly thinking of Canada, whose attachment to the Empire, with independence in trade and defence, Lorne had fervently upheld. Canada was going through a zestful period in its history, and Lorne's successes in the spheres of art and culture were in keeping. To have been responsible for the foundation of a national art gallery in a place like Ottawa, where 'all the artists in the town could have ridden together in one street-car' (Sandra Gwyn), was no mean achievement. At the same time, Canadian party political jealousies, playing on Louise's largely unexplained absences, left Lorne's career without the steady shine either of his predecessor, Lord Dufferin, or his successor, Lord Minto. There were those who said that Lord Beaconsfield's 'great experiment' with a young royal couple for a young country had been a failure. Others praised Lorne's awareness of Canadian sensitivities, which led him to be a Governor-General who did not use the throne but adopted what one Canadian woman called 'almost a republican simplicity'. This picture, however, was modified at times by the Princess's occasional fits of regality. 'Is your mother well?' she was asked at a children's party. The corrective reply came: '*Her Majesty* is very well, thank you.'

Louise was sixty-six when she became a widow. People said that she was getting more like Queen Victoria. They probably meant in her intense loneliness. 'My loneliness without the Duke is quite terrible . . .', she told her friend and informal lady-in-waiting, Ethel Badcock. 'I wonder what he does now.'

Many things kept her going. The Great War broke out three months after Lorne died and there was her public war-work for soldiers' and sailors' families, for an American women's hospital ship, and for the wounded in suitable homes like the Savoy Hotel and private houses, including her own. She had sick officers in Scotland and at Kensington Palace. Arthur hoped they were not 'terribly in the way'.

From Ottawa, where Arthur had been Governor-General since 1911, he thanked Louise for her message 'to "our boys", as they are called here', and for attending the service for Canadians at St Paul's. Louise, indeed, had always kept up with Canada after her departure. She received Canadian visitors in London and had sent Lord Minto one of her unusual presents – a musk ox robe. Lord Grey (like Minto, a Governor-General in succession to Lorne) had told her in 1905 that the door she had once painted with crab-apple blossom was still the chief object of interest in Government House. Arthur described to her in 1912 the glorious spectacle he had seen at the foot of Mount Victoria – Lake Louise!

Alix sent Louise a card sold in aid of troops' comforts. It well expressed in rhythm and words the dogged spirit of Christmas 1914:

Just keep on fighting, conquer all your fears,
Just keep on waiting till the darkness clears,
Just keep on smiling, though you smile through tears,
Just keep on trusting, for 'tis faith that cheers,
Keep on, on, on! each day the Victory nears,
Press on! Keep on!

Louise's private life was henceforth divided between a number of interesting friends and her family. She sent advice to Balfour on spies, and to Haig and Kitchener on various subjects. Kitchener replied coolly that he would 'see what can be done'. Baldwin thanked her for her sympathy over the Abdication drama and Neville Chamberlain for her encouragement over Munich. (At that date, the royal family, like the Cabinet, were appeasers.)

She kept up with the artists she had known for years, such as the theatrical Sir William Blake Richmond, with his swings between asceticism and panache, his handsome bearded face and shining hair parted down the centre. Anna Maria Stirling (*The Richmond Papers*) tells a story of Louise visiting her friend Richmond one day when he was absorbed in painting. The maid opened the studio door and announced:

'Please, sir, Princess Louise is here!'

'Tell her to go to the Devil!' shouted the exasperated Richmond.

'Not till I have seen you, Mr Richmond!' said the Princess demurely, as she slipped into the studio behind the maid. (Some say that what Richmond really shouted was 'Bugger off'.)

On the other hand, many years later Richmond was to address Louise effusively, if incoherently, when she was nearly seventy: 'My dear Madam, When I have made a friend, if I may call you that? I believe!! and nothing would move me from perfect faith.... You could never bore me.' Her lack of 'nerve power' would be restored by sleep, he said, and he would pay his respects on Sunday morning – his only free time.

There was also a clever set of friends headed by her architect Baynes Badcock, husband of Ethel, with whom she would go travelling. They found her incredibly volatile, sometimes the life and soul of the party, sometimes impossibly 'trying', treating a hotel as if it were her private house. Travel indeed linked her to both friends and family.

She saw a good deal of her brother Arthur in the South of France as well as in Surrey. He was by now a white-moustached old gentleman in a trilby hat, with a woollen scarf, gloves, stick and spats. Widowed in 1917, he tried to look after his sister, insisting in 1922 that she overdid the royal patronage of charities: 'that may be very well for the younger members of the family,' he wrote, 'but not for *you* or *I* [*sic*]'. In return for his love and advice she would send him a more amusing variety of presents than anyone else: waistcoasts to go under his uniforms; pills, pastilles and pickmeups galore; 'Pilenta', an English soap not irritating to the skin; fruit to eat between meals; articles to read; ideas for his 'blue garden', seeds of red cabbage; a 'delightful' Christmas cake with a 'female head and shoulders peeping out from it'. George v, however, ran Arthur close in her generosity. In 1925 he received a 'bunny' tray, for which he thanked her with the advice that she needed a rest cure for 'nerves'.

When Louise bought her Surrey house, Ribsden, near Arthur's Bagshot Park, his comment was, 'How Lorne would have enjoyed being so near the golf course.' Louise was no golfer, even if Lorne had encouraged her to play – which is doubtful, considering his veto on a typical Edwardian ladies' game, billiards. Her injured knee, dating from 1870, was getting worse, and she had frequent severe headaches and neuralgia. One of her great-nieces thinks that the sleigh accident must have caused more damage than anyone suspected; perhaps a slipped disc.

Prince Arthur's forcefully expressed letters to his sister resulted in a barrage of reactionary views gradually competing with and taking over the Princess's earlier Liberal instincts. The Beaverbrook and Rothermere press were presented by Arthur as '*poisonous* and *ultra socialist*', Lloyd George and trade unionism as 'dangerous', and Anthony Eden as 'very dangerous'. She must have begun to wonder how she and the Greys and at least one of Lorne's sisters had ever come to support votes for women.

As early as 1913, Charles Ashbee of the Arts and Crafts movement had found her 'Guelphic and a bit conventional'. When the Great War broke out the Connaughts had no trouble with their German connections: Arthur considered the Germans 'savage' and his wife Louischen called the war 'the deed of the D[evil]!!!' It was Victoria Mountbatten who, twenty years after the war, asked Louise to contact Kaiser William, who had become 'kinder and gentler' since his long exile. Arthur was also deplorably anti-Semitic. However, when it came to actions rather than opinions, the constitutional training of both brother and sister saved them from the worst errors. Ex-Queen Ena of Spain, for instance, hoped to elicit charitable help for the families who supported General Franco in the Spanish Civil War; Louise and Arthur kept firmly out of that dangerous zone.

King George v (little 'Georgie' of Malta days who loved dancing and Aunt Louise's jokes) was another influential friend and not all that much more advanced than his Uncle Arthur. One can see from the letters that Louise agreed with, and sometimes seems to have propounded, their characteristic political ideas, such as 'a firm hand and firm government in India' (1930); any Indian troubles were due to Moscow – quite a change in Louise's views since the days when she was a Liberal.

Nevertheless, she did not lose her individual spirit. Johanne Wake has a new story of Louise standing between Queen Mary and one of the Kensington Palace clocks that her niece coveted. 'The clock is here, and *here* it will stay.'

One of the later letters heralds a visit from Louise to Elizabeth, the future Queen and then Duchess of York, for tea with her great-great-nieces, Princess Elizabeth and Princess Margaret Rose. This may have been among the occasions which convinced Queen Elizabeth II that there had never been such 'great talkers' as 'the Aunties'. (Princess Beatrice also no doubt found her tongue when not in danger of being overheard by her sister.) The young Princesses learnt to call Kensington the 'Auntie Palace'; alternatively, the 'Aunt heap'. Princess Alice, long-lived daughter of Prince Leopold, smiled at the recollection of Louise's loud 'whooping' laugh all over Kensington Palace yard.

Louise continued to cultivate the household and get on well with them. A letter of condolence to Lord Wigram, the late George V's Private Secretary, evoked touching thanks for her sympathy in his 'loneliness and sadness', together with the unexpected remark that 'His Majesty left us on the crest of the wave with his pennant flying full length.' Wigram evidently did not know that the pennant had been hauled down by the King's doctor in an act of euthanasia.

Princess Louise was the first of the royal family to be photographed by an essentially modern artist, Cecil Beaton. A shrewd and witty account of Beaton's initial attempt to photograph her was given by Edith Olivier, the writer, who was present. Louise had been invited to lunch at Cap Ferrat by Lord and Lady Grey on 8 March 1927. Unfortunately Louise, who was usually the most unpunctual of people, arrived with her lady attendant before her host and hostess. Edith wrote:

> ... we observed that two retiring, rather embarrassed ladies had entered and were standing near the door. It slowly dawned on us that one of them was Queen Victoria's daughter. I hastened to greet her with a curtsy and we all presented ourselves and walked with her in the garden till the host and hostess came. Very bad of them. We all loved the Princess.... She stayed for hours and it was so agreeable. A Miss Slingsby in attendance was hated by all. Cecil wanted to photograph HRH. She refused but made him take Miss S. and he only made a sham click and took no photograph!

About six years later Beaton at last succeeded in photographing Louise – his first of so many royal portraits. She was taken in his drawing room at Sussex Gardens in what he called 'a variety of conventional period poses' wearing a grey tea-gown and the equally conventional ropes of pearls. Beaton found her charming with 'pale hair and features'; though the aftermath was less charming when Louise set about having the chosen photograph correctly touched up. It involved a lengthy correspondence with the lady-in-waiting, of which this was part of the final letter:

> Dear Mr Beaton ... Owing to the delicacy of the whole picture, the cheek should not be so light against the deep shadows, left side, as

> also the eye, the bone above the eye requires slightly toning down; the right eye should be a tiny bit higher towards the nose, upper lid.*

There were also alterations to be made to the left nostril, left eye, left side, and hair; and lastly, in an addendum, not so much light on the nose as it had been made 'too prominent'. What it was to photograph a sculptress! Louise evidently thought it as simple to change a photograph as to add or take away a pinch of clay from a bust.

Though Louise now looked rather more like Queen Mary than any less conventional figure, she still had a determined toe in the unconventional camp. Her favourite great-nephew and great-niece were Prince George and Princess Marina, Duke and Duchess of Kent. It was the beautiful Marina who was given the train Louise had designed for herself and had had made by her Ladies' Work Society to wear at Edward VII's coronation. Princess Marina wore it at King George VI's. Louise responded quite naturally to this second 'little Georgie's' interest in art, bequeathing many of her treasures to him and his family. His younger son, Prince Michael of Kent, inherited among other things two portraits in oils of Princess Louise, one by Queen Victoria, the other by László, some of Louise's watercolours, and emeralds.

Her relations with her great-nephew David (Edward VIII) were warm but see-through. Wake has another new story, this time of David doing what the young frequently think is a good ploy, despite it usually being found out. He sent Aunt Louise one of his own snuff boxes as a late birthday present. She returned it, writing back, 'Dear David, Do look inside this box.' Inside was a note, 'To David from Aunt Louise'. The old Princess saw the joke of getting her own box back. But she agreed entirely with Prince Arthur about Mrs Simpson and made a 'strong' joke against her. Whoever let Wallis Simpson out of Pandora's box had gone beyond the joke.

On the Campbell side of the family, Louise hit it off particularly well with Janet Aitken, who married Ian Campbell, a future Duke of Argyll and nephew of Louise's Lorne. Louise was nearly eighty when Janet got engaged in November 1927. In her autobiography (Janet Aitken Kidd, *The Beaverbrook Girl* [1987]), Janet described her as 'one of the nicest people I have ever known'. She telephoned Janet to come to lunch at Kensington Palace, saying, 'I have a wedding present for you.' Janet found an 'utterly charming' old lady dressed in Victorian clothes with a high lace collar. She hated Janet's curtsying and advised her not to pluck her eyebrows. 'After a rather heavy meal served by a butler and two footmen in royal livery, Aunt Louise presented me with a large jewel box

* Cecil Beaton, *Photobiography* (1951).

and told me to open it.' Janet saw in the subdued light a diamond and emerald tiara. Ian secretly popped it on their honeymoon to help pay his gambling debts.

Janet's marriage was to be even less happy than Louise's, though the Princess became 'a warm and understanding friend', perhaps seeing in Janet the daughter she never had. Janet's own daughter, Jeanne Louise, was called after the Jersey Lily's daughter and Princess Louise.

For several years Louise had needed to take to her bed in a darkened room after every public appearance. As early as 1907 she had spoken of her 'treadmill' – shades of Albert – yet she was to live into her tenth decade. A touch of Florence Nightingale here?

Her last public appearance was in December 1937 at the Home Arts and Industries Exhibition. After that she became too ill to move around. She had developed a carbuncle in 1936 and from 1937 neuritis in the arm, inflammation of the nerves between the ribs, fainting fits, and what Queen Mary called 'that dreadful sciatica'. Her sister Beatrice was not in much better shape as the letters show. Despite her disabilities, Louise took great interest in encouraging the statesmen who had to cope with the run-up to the Second World War. She loved drafting prayers, one of which had gone to the Archbishop of Canterbury on the General Strike, while another gave great satisfaction to the Neville Chamberlains in July 1939. It was not all that different from the Book of Common Prayer ('Guide our Ministers of State and all in authority over us . . .'), but it was remarkable that a ninety-year-old princess should write it at all. The interesting thing is that her brother Affie's daughter Missy also wrote prayers. A family trait?

Princess Louise died at 6.50 on the morning of Sunday, 3 December 1939. She had learnt from her old friend Lord Ronnie Gower – who died in the Great War, 1916 – that the best thing was to be cremated. She was duly cremated so that her obsequies were in three parts, an arrangement well suited to an unconventional princess. As there was a war on, Louise had sensibly decided to be buried where she fell, so to speak: at Kilmun if she died in Scotland, Frogmore if in England. It turned out to be Kensington Palace, where in the past Louise had often heard the ghostly voice of George IV. If her own voice is ever heard, like his, somewhere above stairs, it will surely be calling for a 'darling boy'.

After the cremation at Golders Green, the casket of ashes was placed in a plain oak coffin and laid in the Prince Albert Chapel at Windsor. The burial in the vault of St George's Chapel took place on 12 December 1939, as recorded in the Chapel Registers:

The Body of H.R.H. Princess Louise Caroline Alberta daughter of Her Majesty Queen Victoria & Widow of John Douglas Sutherland Duke of Argyll was buried in the vault under St. George's Chapel Windsor by me. Cosmo Cantuar.

The Military Knights of Windsor brought a glow of scarlet and gold into the Chapel as they filed slowly in; otherwise all was black, khaki or the blue of naval and air-force uniforms. A bearer party of the Argyll and Sutherland Highlanders carried the coffin, which was covered by a Union Jack. Two members of the Campbell clan held her insignia on velvet cushions. Among the wreaths lying just outside the main doors was one from the pearly kings and queens of London, remembering her work for their charities.

Three months later, on 13 March 1940, her final resting place was ready. 'The ashes of HRH Princess Louise Caroline Alberta were removed from the Vault and buried in the Burial Ground at Frogmore. Albert Baillie. Dean.'

The *Ottawa Journal* of 4 December 1939 had chosen to emphasize her courage and unconventionality. She refused to leave London on the outbreak of war or 'fortify' Kensington Palace with sandbags and gummed paper on the windows. She had no special air-raid shelter, but decided to make do with a tunnel near the kitchens, no doubt built in the old days, according to custom, to keep the kitchen smells out of the house. Her only concession was to have the main gas turned off when the sirens sounded. (Of course, she died before the Blitz.)

On her unconventionality, the Ottawa paper quoted a snatch of dialogue after some event the Princess had attended in London.

'May I summon your car, Ma'am?'

'No thanks, I'll take a taxi. You see, on Saturdays the car goes to Frogmore to fetch the weekend vegetables, so I just manage without.'

The Times said that she was 'the least bound by convention and etiquette of any of the Royal Family'.

Louise did not work long or hard enough to become a memorable artist. But as the royal art historian, Jane Roberts, has written of her sculptural *œuvre*: 'A truly extraordinary output for a woman of gentle birth in the nineteenth century, let alone a Princess of the blood royal.'

In between being a sculptor, she was carrying out her public duties with the thoroughness shown by all Queen Victoria's daughters. Octavia Hill became friendly with her through their major work for the National Trust, venturing to invite the Princess for a cup of tea at her cottage at Crockham Hill, after visiting her 'beloved Mariners Hill' near Chartwell.

Invited to visit the Royal Academy after the Great War, she spent two-

and-a-half hours there examining every single exhibit and incidentally wearing out the young niece, Blanche Balfour, whom she was showing around.

Jean Hamilton was another, much younger relative whom Louise would choose as a companion. 'I've got to open a hospital today. You must come with me. We'll put that vulgar crown on the car and go off!' Louise had wanted to adopt one of Jean's uncles. She left an impression on the young girl of brightness, liveliness and animation. Her visits were a thrill.

Owen Morshead, the Royal Librarian, compiled a list of institutions in which the Princess was involved, 'before her correspondence was broken up'. These included twenty-five hospitals of which she was president, President of the National Trust, Patron of Queen's College, London, Colonel-in-Chief of Princess Louise's Own Kensington Regiment and of five Canadian regiments.

Of late years Louise had begun to accept the daunting fact that the public might actually recognize her in the street. Anonymity at its most extreme, powered by a pathological need for it, had been reached many years before, when she opted for the infinitely neutral title of 'The Lady'. She would refer to herself in the third person by this name that was no name at all.

This 'complex' lady, as Marie Mallet had called her, who could be equally amiable and mischievous, was never to come down completely on the sunny side of the equation. (The Kaiser summed up her temperament with typical ineptitude as 'joyous and sunny'.)

In the end it did not matter. She finished as a remarkable and fascinating woman, who was no longer frustrated by her joint royal and artistic roles, and so could face her 'complex' identity.

LETTERS

I

Youth

1856–71

PRINCE ALFRED TO PRINCESS LOUISE GENEVA, 22 DECEMBER 1856

A Christmas letter, with its original spelling:

Dearest Louise, I wish you a very very happy Christmas and I hope you will like all your prents and also my little pesant. I shall have a Christmas tree also and I will send every one of you a little thing from it I am going to have it some thing like a lottery; there will be numbers put on every little thing and then the same numbers are written on pieces of paper and then put in a bag then everyboddy pulls out one paper and see what his number is then he cuts off the little thing which has a lable corresponding with his paper. I remain your affect. brother Alfred.

(5)

Prince Alfred, or 'Affie', was twelve and his sister Louise eight. He was given his own tutor in April 1856 and spent the winter at Geneva with a full complement of teachers. It was probably to get him away from his elder brother Bertie (they were thought to be a bad influence on each other), to improve his French and to prepare him for long stays away from home, as he was to join the navy the following year.

PRINCESS LOUISE TO PRINCE ARTHUR BALMORAL, 13 OCTOBER 1861

My dearest Arthur, I miss you so much; I am so glad that you arrived safely in London.

I have bought you a beautiful squirting ball I hope you will like it. We took our general Sunday walk by the Dee, and we were nearly blown into it. Leopold [her youngest brother] and I are going to play with your fair. Mr. Leitch [their drawing master] said that he misses you very much. I am going to paint you some pictures for your book and I will give you them at Windsor. Baby [Princess Beatrice] speaks nearly all the day of you.... I will soon write to you again and a longer letter too.

(Add. A15/106)

Louise was thirteen, her brother Arthur eleven, Leopold eight; Beatrice, the baby of the family, was five.

PRINCE LEOPOLD TO PRINCESS LOUISE
CANNES, 20 DECEMBER 1861

The Prince Consort had died of typhoid on 14 December at Windsor while his son was abroad.

Dearest Louise I was so very very much grieved when I heard of the death of poor dear Papa, who I loved so very very much, I got a letter from you this morning in which you said a great deal of the death of poor dear Papa, it is such a fearful loss I am so very very much grieved. Dear Louise please do not forget to send me the studs ... for Dr. Günther as a Christmas present.... I hope Mama is quite well.

(48)

Queen Victoria's state was about as far from 'quite well' as possible. Her children were to suffer from her protracted grieving.

PRINCESS LOUISE TO PRINCE ARTHUR
WINDSOR CASTLE, 30 MARCH 1862

Dearest Arthur, I write to you today because I am afraid I will not be able to write to you again before we come, I have so many letters to do in the weekdays. Mr. Ogg twice a week, the Dean twice a week, and Mrs. Anderson three times a week, besides my lessons with Tilla, Lina, Bauerlein; so you see, dear Arthur, how little time I have to write, and I dare say you have very little time also.

Dear cousin Mary [of Teck] came yesterday to have dinner with us, and after dinner Lenchen [Louise's sister Helena] and I walked down with her to Frogmore and we showed her dear Grandmama's Mausoleum, which she thought was very beautiful: dear Papa's is getting on so fast Mama goes down every day to see it.

We are going to St. George's and I think I am going to put a wreath from you, Leopold and me together; you asked me to do so. Dear Vicky [her eldest sister Victoria] is going away tomorrow at 12 o'clock, I am so unhappy she is going.

We were photographed together we five sisters it is not very good so we are going to be done again tomorrow before Vicky goes.

Pray *do not show* these hurried lines *to any body.*

Your most affectionate sister
Louise

(Add. A15/157)

Louise's third sister, Princess Helena, was seventeen. Her sister Vicky, the Crown Princess of Prussia, was twenty-one.

THE PRINCE OF WALES TO PRINCESS LOUISE
NAPLES, 10 NOVEMBER 1862

He thanks Louise for her kind congratulations on his twenty-first birthday.
I was very sorry to have been prevented from spending it with you all at home as usual – But as this year is one of mourning and sadness, it is perhaps better that I should have been away.

(59)

PRINCESS LOUISE TO PRINCE ARTHUR
12 JANUARY 1863

Dearest Arthur, Mama told me that you have been to the Crystal Palace and seen a Christmas tree of sixty feet and been in a merry-go-round, that you amused yourself I am so pleased....

I have lessons every day from Mr. Leitch which I like very much, he told me that you do such beautiful straight lines that he had never seen a boy of your age do them so well, and he calls you a most charming youth full of talent, so I hope you will always appreciate being called so....

(Add. A15/228)

SAME TO SAME
3 FEBRUARY 1863

... Mama gave a council this morning and the Archbishop of York did homage, Lenchen was present, she said that Mama held his hands up whilst he was taking [the] oath and then afterwards he kissed the Bible. Lenchen said she felt such an inclination to laugh.

(Add. A15/249)

SAME TO SAME
9 JULY 1863

Dearest Arthur, I am sure you will be very much grieved to hear of the sad news of Baron Stockmar's death; Mama knew one or two days ago that he was very ill she feared then he would never recover, poor Mama it is so very sad for her, he was one of her greatest Friends now she has dear Papa no longer.

Dear Mama wishes me to tell you that she will write to you soon, and she hopes you are working very hard for your examination. She is very anxious that you should pass it well, for if you did not it would make her very unhappy, she fears you are rather lazy. Believe me ever dear Arthur your most loving sister Louise.

(Add. A15/316)

Baron Christian Friedrich Stockmar of Coburg was Prince Albert's closest adviser until he left England in 1857 for health reasons.

THE QUEEN TO PRINCESS LOUISE ROSENAU, 15 AUGUST 1863

She was visiting Albert's birthplace.

Dearest Louise Tho' still suffering much from the *fearful* heat which we endured in the railroad yesterday from Brussels till the night – I will try and write you a few lines. Your letter gave me much satisfaction *all* but the dreadful Musk Smell which I must ask you not to use again for it is *really very nasty* dear; let them get you some more sweet violet powder which is *so* very nice.... Oh! this sweet spot is lovely and peaceful – but it is *all* the same – *lonely* and pleasureless – and *dreadful* without my own darling Angel! *Nothing* interests or attracts me *any more*.

(74)

The Queen was forty-four.

THE PRINCE OF WALES TO PRINCESS LOUISE SANDRINGHAM, 10 NOVEMBER 1863

Bertie's twenty-second birthday: he thanks Louise first for the pretty carpet she has worked, which does the greatest credit to her workmanship. Also:

The little statuette is really admirably modelled, and I strongly advise you to continue taking lessons with Mrs. Thornycroft as you certainly have great talent in modelling, and may perhaps become some day an eminent sculptress.

(88)

If underrated by her mother, the fifteen-year-old Louise was certainly encouraged by her eldest brother. The Queen would frequently refer to her as 'poor Louise'. Mary Thornycroft was the daughter and wife of a sculptor and a sculptor in her own right *(see page 14)*.

PRINCESS LOUISE TO PRINCE ARTHUR WINDSOR CASTLE, 15 NOVEMBER 1863

Prince Arthur was not yet in the army, but living at Rangers' Lodge, Blackheath, with his governor and attending lectures at the Royal Military Academy, Woolwich. He entered the Academy in 1867.

... you will be sorry to hear that poor Leopold has had the rheumatism in his leg, and it was very much swollen yesterday, but it is better today, but he must be carried up and down stairs, the doctors say it comes from wearing the kilt in such cold weather, but dear Mama does not think so, poor little boy he says it hurts him very much.

The Queen would not hear a word against Scotland from the climate to the kilt.

I hope Major's [Elphinstone] foot is better and that he can walk a little....

William [the future Kaiser] rides with us nearly every day in the School, he rides so nicely, and is so happy on this little pony.

I suppose by this time you know that Lady Augusta is going to be married to whom do you think – to Dr. Stanley; it seems so very odd that she should marry after being with us for such a long time.

(Add. A15/388)

Lady Augusta Bruce was to marry the Dean of Westminster, Arthur Stanley. At this stage Louise was still echoing her mother's feelings.

SAME TO SAME
11 MAY 1864

I write to you the few spare minutes I have here in London. Mama wishes me to thank you very much for your letter and to say that you do not gum the covers enough, they always arrive open.

I am sorry I did not meet you here today, the soldiers came by just now playing, and I thought of you very [*sic*].

(Add. A15/470)

SAME TO SAME
10 MARCH 1865

Lenchen and I are going to a ball this evening at Bertie's, being their wedding day [anniversary] it will be very nice, it is my first ball.... I envy you having been to Naples, such a beautiful place, I should give anything to see it. We have such dreadful cold weather here again we had a snowstorm two days ago but none lay on the ground, it must be charming weather with you now.

(Add. A15/654)

Louise's frustration and envy of her brothers – one married and the other in Italy – comes out very clearly in this letter. She was about to be seventeen.

SAME TO SAME
OSBORNE, 11 MAY 1865

... You will get my letter when you are at Venice. Oh! what a lovely place to see, I will ask you to tell me a great deal about it, I have always longed so to see it.

(Add. A15/686)

SAME TO SAME
VICTORIA & ALBERT, 9 AUGUST 1865

Dearest Arthur, I write you a line or two whilst we are still on board. I was so sad at leaving you yesterday, the last I saw of you was when you were surrounded by all those ladies and Colonel Du Plat behind you. What a quantity of people there were, but I was pleased to see that Mama did not mind it very much....

I have had nothing to do this morning so I have been drawing the sailors, and Leopold was delighted with them. My head aches very badly and this letter is very stupid so I give you a reason why it is so. I shall soon write again and tell you *how* we feel after having slept *two nights* in the train.

(Add. A15/740)

Louise hardly slept on a train. She was on a family visit to Rosenau.

SAME TO SAME
ROSENAU, 11 AUGUST 1865

... I forgot to say when we landed at Antwerp it was quite dark, and there was nothing but lanterns everywhere, and there was such a crowd of people, some men held torches: as we were getting into the carriage, a man put his head in, blew a quantity of smoke from his cigar in my face, and screamed 'God bless Victoria' I think he was rather mad, he screamed the same thing out several times already when we were walking up the pier, it was rather alarming seeing poor Leo carried down the ladder from the ship but Archy [a ghillie] managed it very well.

I am *so* tired, I hardly slept at all in the train, the first night not a bit, last night a little, I travelled with Lady Churchill she likewise hardly slept a bit.

Forgive this scribble I have only got one old pen, and the ink is so blotty.

I am looking forward with great impatience for the time when you will come here. We must have some nice walks and drives together and rides.

... Leopold's leg is much better. Believe me darling Arthur your most loving sister Louise. I am quite ashamed to send such a letter.

(Add. A15/742)

THE PRINCE OF WALES TO PRINCESS LOUISE SANDRINGHAM, 2 JANUARY 1866

Trouble over the Christmas presents, which he sent labelled, late, for Louise to distribute.

The desk is for Arthur and not for Princess Arthur – unless he likes to keep it for his future wife. ... I am very glad that your Xmas went off well – tho' *very* lively it cannot have been – I wish that you could once spend it with us – how nice that would be and what fun we would have. I think you did quite right to buy pipes and cigar cases for the servants, although Sir Thomas [Biddulph – Privy Purse] was very much shocked.

(131)

Bertie was making a joke about the mistake over the labelling of Arthur's present: there was no 'Princess Arthur' in view, since the Prince was only fifteen.

THE QUEEN TO PRINCESS LOUISE OSBORNE, 1 MAY 1866

Louise had whooping cough.

Dearest child ... I can't say how grieved I am not to be able to be more with you and to *hold* you, darling, when those nasty coughs come on, – but it is a *trial* I *can't*, which is as *great* for me as for you – and we must be so thankful that you are as well as you are – and *once* over you have done with *all* illness which is a *great* blessing! God bless you darling. *Your* print after Winterhalter's picture is *quite lovely*. Ever your loving Mama.

(147)

PRINCESS LOUISE AND PRINCE LEOPOLD TO LIEUTENANT WALTER GEORGE STIRLING, 6 AUGUST 1866

Today is Monday, Affie's birthday bye the bye, *wretched* day too for a birthday, in consequence of it, to our *great* delight, breakfast was laid in the council room, it was not much warmer, though, the draughts being quite *dreadful*. Bertie for a *wonder* appeared at 9.30 a.m., but Alix could not be up so soon, her usual time for breakfast being about 11 a.m., a big birthday cake was put in the centre of our feeding table, next to this one another table stood on its legs, with *the* birthday's presents, few in number, but yet rather pretty, ours of *course* were the *best*, being Cupids (little ones) meeting and holding shells for salt, the cupids (bless their little hearts!) we hoped would prevent every chance of a salt quarrel in Clarence House. We wondered what the new extra groom in waiting in the R.H.A. [Royal Horse Artillery] would be doing today; not having organs to grind or dogs to whip or cats to run after or pushing painters to sky daddle, *we* thought our best employment would be to write a joint comic epistle to our well beloved W.G.!!! a very kind friend of ours, in Scotch political troubles, but (thank God!) is out of it now though got out of it in an unpleasant way.

Louise and Leopold
(poor girl) (little man)

(Add. A30/317)

All the lines of the letter are written alternately, beginning with Leopold. Stirling was Leopold's ex-governor, who was appointed in March 1866 but left in July to rejoin the RHA – sacked after a quarrel with the ghillie Archie Brown, brother of John Brown. It is clear whose side the children were on.

THE PRINCE OF WALES TO PRINCESS LOUISE ABERGELDIE, 28 AUGUST 1866

We give on Thursday evening what is called here a 'Quality' Ball at 10 o'clock – and we shall be only too happy if you or anybody else at Balmoral like to come. You know best if Mama will allow you to come or not – at any rate I hope you will come. We have the Fifes, Farquharsons, Forbes etc. – as we thought it better to get the 'smart' dance over first – before the ghillies' Balls later....

(153)

According to the Queen's Journal, 'all' went to the ball, 'good Leopold remaining with me'.

PRINCE LEOPOLD TO PRINCESS LOUISE BALMORAL, 4 OCTOBER 1866

Leopold has an adventure at last.

... On Monday a most curious thing happened to us, in the afternoon I drove out in the little waggonet with Mr Sahl [German librarian], and Mr Duckworth [Leopold's tutor] rode behind us, we drove to Aberarder to have tea there and to bring some toys to some children who lived in a house near Colonel Farquharson's sawmill, when we drove home (it was on the day of the fair and cattlemarket at Braemar) we were driving quite quietly and Mr Duckworth was riding on the side of the carriage, a drunken man came riding at a furious rate after us, it was just dusk and the man was riding on a snowwhite horse, he dashed between Mr Duckworth and the carriage but he being frightfully drunken could no more hold himself on his horse and he reeled off his horse under our horses' feet he caught hold of Mr Duckworth's leg and tried to pull him off his horse but at that minute Mr Duckworth's horse shied and ran to the other side of the road so that saved him, but the drunken man was in an awful rage and sprung up swearing on his horse and galloped off again at a dreadful rate.

(157)

THE CROWN PRINCESS OF PRUSSIA TO PRINCESS LOUISE
BERLIN, 8 MARCH 1867

... I am so pleased and thankful dear Mama has made up her mind to stay there [in London] a little while, perhaps she will take to it again by degrees which would be a *great great blessing.*

(193)

THE PRINCE OF WALES TO PRINCESS LOUISE
MARLBOROUGH HOUSE, 6 MAY 1867

... I cannot tell you how sorry I am that you were not allowed to come and stay here with Alix while I am at Paris, but I was afraid that there would be difficulties in the way. I saw Lenchen on Friday and she seemed very well. Both Alix and I are very anxious that you should be Godmother to our little girl, especially as she is to bear your name. The christening is to take place here (quite privately) in Alix's sitting room on Friday next. When you see 'King Charming' remember me to him. I hope Mama will ask him to dine with her some day.

(193)

'King Charming' may have been the superlatively attractive Rev. Robinson (Robin) Duckworth, Leopold's instructor in 1866, to whom he and Louise were devoted. He was Louise's first love. Promoted to be Leopold's governor in 1867, he had to leave in 1870, much to the regret of Louise and her brother (see page 18).

SAME TO SAME
MARLBOROUGH HOUSE, 23 JUNE 1867

Bertie has written to Louise on the day before asking her to approach Mama to have the date of the state ball changed either to the 5th or the 8th, as he is going to Paris for the Exhibition and will not have enough time there if the ball is on the 3rd. He gets his answer and writes again the next day.
My dear Louise, I must own I was very much surprised to receive the answer from Mama about the Ball in your letter and I think it is very hard that I should be obliged to be back on the 3rd which will give me no time at all at Paris, only affront the people there by my short stay and I think it will probably be hardly worth while to go at all.

I have never shirked any public duty yet, and have been *always* ready to do anything State or Public for Mama, and I think it is very hard that the first favor I ask should be declined. I feel certain that the people – that is London Society – would not think it odd that I should be absent from one ball, and it is not likely that I shall be in Paris again in a hurry – and as this is an exceptional year, on account of the Exhibition (which is not likely to occur again) it would be *perfectly* understood. If it is *so* absolutely necessary that I should be there I cannot see why the 5th (the Review day) or the 8th should be inconvenient to Mama. Lord Bradford at first proposed the 5th. It is only to please dear Mama that I go to meet the Queen of Prussia. I am sure it is no pleasure to me, however I know it is a duty, and I do it, so I really think I might be allowed to absent myself once. If I don't go to Paris the Emperor will think it very odd my not coming after Lord Coventry has announced me. I leave it now, to you, dearest Louise, to do what you think best and you can send me a line tomorrow here.

(197)

Louise had become the Queen's secretary on family affairs, replacing Lenchen after her marriage in 1866.

PRINCE ARTHUR TO PRINCESS LOUISE
RANGERS HOUSE, WOOLWICH, 11 AUGUST 1867

Arthur, aged seventeen, is homesick.
Dearest Louise You have no idea how sad I was at leaving Osborne yesterday: I have enjoyed my stay there so very much. This place feels very dull and triste without you. But my spirits will be better after I have regularly got to work again at Woolwich. I have a proposal to make: I intend writing to you regularly twice a week (namely Tuesday's and Saturday's) to let you know all that I am doing, do you think you could

manage to do the same, even two or three lines will do; pray let me have an answer to this. Let me also know your movements for next week.

(200)

On the next Tuesday, as he has heard nothing to the contrary, he assumes that the arrangement stands.

SAME TO SAME
GREENWICH, 10 AUGUST 1867

Balmoral under fire.

... You must summon your courage and energy now for the *amusements* of your approaching Highland life, which I must say I think will be very tiresome for you. I hope you will have nice weather for your visit to Floors [Castle], for if it is wet (a thing which *occasionally* happens in Scotland) it will be rather a bore.

(202)

SAME TO SAME
WOOLWICH, 24 AUGUST 1867

Dearest Louise I hope you will forgive me if I do not write to you quite as regularly as I had intended, for my time is so much taken up that I can find very few moments to write to you. Besides that I write to Mama regularly 3 times a week, and I am obliged to write it in the middle of the day (when I have only ½hrs time to spare, namely between dinner and afternoon study) so as to save the post which leaves at 3 P.M.

Towards the end of the letter he writes:

I saw Capt: Rideout yesterday and he told me all about the fun you had on board the yacht together.... Good bye old girl....

(203)

SAME TO SAME
WOOLWICH, 31 AUGUST 1867

Dearest Louise I thank you very much for your letter and for kindly asking me not to write when I was busy. To write to you is I assure you one of my greatest pleasures, and I shall always try and write to you twice a week.

(205)

SAME TO SAME
WOOLWICH, 3 SEPTEMBER 1867

Dearest Louise, Many thanks for your kind letter received yesterday, it gave me so much pleasure. As to the great secret, I did not know that I could not mention it to you, of course I would not speak of it to anybody else.

(207)

SAME TO SAME
WOOLWICH, 7 SEPTEMBER 1867

Home is not best.

Dearest Louise I do not think I thanked you in my letter for the photograph of yourself which you sent me. I like it very much and I thank you extremely for sending me it. The time when I am going to Balmoral is now fast approaching, but I do not know that I thoroughly appreciate the pleasure, for as you well know one is under a good many restrictions at home. There are also constant squalls and squabbles which give rise to a great deal of bad feeling and jealousy. Here I can do very much as I like, as long as I do not do anything contrary to the statutes and regulations of Her Majesty's service, there are also lots of nice fellows here who I am very intimate with and whom I am very fond of. The only reason why I do not dislike the idea of going to Balmoral is that we two shall be able to see a little more of each other and that I shall be able to keep your company on long expeditions. I am going in two days time to a Croquet party at General Ormsby's which I rather dread as I always feel shy and awkward before ladies. Now goodbye dearest girl ever your most affectionate brother Arthur.

(208)

THE CROWN PRINCESS OF PRUSSIA TO PRINCESS LOUISE
POTSDAM, 7 SEPTEMBER 1867

At Vicky's request, Louise has commissioned for her a miniature of her son Sigismund, who had died of meningitis.

Dearest Louise a 1000 thanks for your 2 dear letters, and for all the trouble you have given yourself about the miniature which has safely arrived. It is beautifully painted as all that Mr. Taylor does, but I cannot see any likeness to my dear little Sigie except the *outline* of the head which is quite right. The eyes look in different directions, the mouth is quite different and the colouring about cheeks and chin quite wrong. I think I had better bring it with me and see whether it can be altered. I am so grateful to dear Mama for giving it to me and I am very glad to have it, even though the 1st impression was almost a painful one.

(209)

THE PRINCESS OF WALES TO PRINCESS LOUISE
10 SEPTEMBER 1867

Alix begins by saying how distressed she is by the death of her Papa, of whom she was 'dreadfully' fond, and goes on, wrily, to wish Louise a happy time at Balmoral.
I wonder how my little pet is getting on at Balmoral!!! Write soon to me ... I am longing to hear from you and all your doing there '*en famille*' I hope you are not teased too much!!

(211)

SAME TO SAME
MARLBOROUGH HOUSE, 1 NOVEMBER 1867

Alix was battling with the after-effects of rheumatic fever. She remained lame for the rest of her life.
My beloved Louise, a 1000 thanks for your dear letter and I am delighted to think we shall meet so soon, and that I know my little Louise is looking forward a little to see her *tiresome old* sister-in-law appearing again....

I have to go about on two sticks which makes me rather *shy* before people, and I don't know quite ... how I am to manage about *driving* in an ordinary carriage like *other people*....

Louise has written on behalf of the Queen to ask what Bertie wants for a birthday present and Alix replies:

I am very sorry to say I cannot think of *a thing*, as he has so many *things* and I am always in despair *myself* not knowing what to give him –

She goes on to say however that

anything pleases him – your suggestion of the 'egg boiler' is I am sure very pretty and that is a thing we don't possess in *our household*, at present.

(219)

SAME TO SAME
SANDRINGHAM, 21 NOVEMBER 1867

My own dearest Louise I must send you a little line to hear how you are, and hope that you miss me a little bit.... I am quite alone here now as my Bertie went the day before yesterday ... and won't come back till Saturday, so I feel rather lonely just now, and wished I could have you, my little pet, here just now for a little while.... The Chicks are very flourishing and send their love.... What do the Rangers do? do they dance perpetual *jigs*? every day?!! Or are they seldom performing....

(227)

'The Rangers' were Princess Christian (Lenchen) and Prince Christian of Schleswig-Holstein-Sonderburg-Augustenburg, who was Ranger of the Great Park at Windsor. The Queen wished to have her daughter living close by, but Christian was terrified of his mother-in-law and once, when asked to get permission for a big replanting of trees, he 'shook in his boots'. The marriage had divided the royal family into two camps: the Queen and Vicky in favour and the rest, led by an indignant Alix, against. Prince Christian's family had backed the German side in the German–Danish War.

SAME TO SAME
SANDRINGHAM, 1 DECEMBER 1867

Alix begins by thanking Louise for two presents and a letter: the 'happy pug family' – she knows her weakness for pugs – and a lovely locket.

I shall wear it *very* often in remembrance of its dear giver.

My poor little pet I am afraid you have not been enjoying yourself so *very well* lately and as you say the *Rangers* seem to have been doing nothing but that lately and left you to *dance* the *Perpetual* jig all by yourself, which I think a *horrid shame* as they *ought to entertain their guests* THEMSELVES!!

(230)

The Rangers' guests – or rather guest – was Christian's younger sister, Princess Henriette of Schleswig-Holstein, who was staying with them at Frogmore; but on 26 November they went off to stay at Blenheim for two days, leaving Henriette behind. She dined with the Queen (at Windsor Castle) on the 26th and doubtless during the two days Louise was expected to look after her. She was much older – thirty-four.

SAME TO SAME
SANDRINGHAM, 8 JANUARY 1868

I see that you have got rid of the Ranger family & Company for a time, it must be a *blessing* for a while!!! They seem to be very fond of paying *visits.*

(236)

THE QUEEN TO PRINCESS LOUISE
OSBORNE, 29 JANUARY 1868

One of the haemophiliac Leopold's attacks:
Dearest Loosy, Dr. Jenner has *just* been and given an excellent *account* of our darling Leopold – *no* sickness to speak of, for 12 hours – *no* bleeding since 2 – a *steady* good pulse, and *every hope* that he will get on well. We must still hope with trembling but we may feel *very very differently* than last night and far more *hopefully* than this morning. God is *very* merciful to us in the midst of *all* our troubles and we must be *very, very grateful.* Send this down to Lenchen. Ever your devoted Mama.

(238)

THE PRINCESS OF WALES TO PRINCESS LOUISE
3 FEBRUARY 1868

A characteristic example of Alix's light touch, combining family affection with poking fun at certain members, probably Henriette again.
My own dearest Louise, Thousand thanks for your dear letter, which gave me so much pleasure. Thank God that darling Leo now is getting on and now is out of danger. How easily can I understand your feelings and your anxiousness about that darling boy! What your poor little heart must have suffered in seeing your darling brother in such danger and in so critical a state. How anxiously you must have been watching his bedside and how dreadful to think how soon and easily everything might have been over!! Oh! Sometimes one may wonder how human beings can bear so much! and it makes one shudder to look back upon! I was so glad when I heard *dear Mr. Paget* [the Queen's doctor] had gone to Osborne, as I have the *greatest* faith and confidence in him, and besides he is always so kind and good natured to one which is a great comfort.

My *darling* husband left today for Kimbolton. I hate when he is away, the house seems empty and desolate and lonely. Next week we go to London, I cannot say that I am looking forward to it much! But I hope you will soon come to Windsor and *often* come to see me!! *Somebody else* has already given me the *happy prospect* of *very often* coming to see me at Marlborough House. I suppose you *know* '*the* one' – ? – ? –

Goodbye and God bless you my sweet Louise think sometimes of your loving sister Alix.

(239)

THE PRINCE OF WALES TO PRINCESS LOUISE SANDRINGHAM, 10 FEBRUARY 1868

The Queen did not wish Louise to be drawn into the Wales's 'fast set'.

. . . I wish you could be allowed to come and see us in London for a few days. How nice that would be. . . . How does 'Henriette' get on? Is she still so much in favour. I hear from everybody who has met her at Country Houses, how awfully tiresome she is. I am so glad that dear Vicky has another son, how delighted she will be.

(243)

PRINCE ALFRED TO PRINCESS LOUISE SYDNEY, NEW SOUTH WALES, HMS *GALATEA*, 21 FEBRUARY 1868

How much Lenchen seems to have been visiting about I have no doubt she enjoyed it amazingly; I only wish you could have some amusement of that sort. Is not it too bad sending me out orders to remain away so much longer I shall not be home till January next year, goodness only knows what may not have happened before then; I don't expect I shall know anybody after being away two years. I am going off this afternoon to Queensland which is only removed by a very short distance from the infernal regions I believe; they say the heat is fearful and that one is eaten up by mosquitoes. I send you one of the last photographs done of me out here so that you may know what I look like in case you were to see me in about a year's time.

(246)

In fact Prince Alfred was to be ordered home early, owing to the Fenian assassination attempt made on him in Australia. He was wounded during a picnic held in aid of charity on 12 March. See Letter 271, in which Arthur is not exactly enthusiastic at Affie's return, to absorb Louise's attention.

PRINCE ARTHUR TO PRINCESS LOUISE
WOOLWICH, 29 FEBRUARY 1868

Arthur's complaint:
Dearest Louise, How unkind and cruel of you not to have written to me for so long; I have deferred writing to you expecting that every day must bring me a letter from you – but in vain. Do write to me as soon as possible or I shall begin to think that you intend to desert me. From a letter which Mama wrote to me four or five days ago I heard that you are making a bust of her, so I suppose your time is very much taken up with it.

(247)

PRINCE LEOPOLD TO PRINCESS LOUISE
18 MARCH 1868

His own composition on Louise's birthday:

I think of thee, my sister,
In my sad and lonely hours;
And the thought of thee comes o'er me
Like the breath of morning flow'rs.
Like music that enchants the ear,
Like sights that bless the eye,
Like the verdure of the meadow,
The azure of the sky;
Like rainbow in the evening,
Like blossom on the tree,
Is the thought of thee, dear Sister, –
Is the tender thought of thee.

The Queen also arranged a birthday surprise for Louise in the form of a serenade at 7 in the morning under her window by some boys of St George's Chapel choir. Dr Elvey, the organist, conducted many favourite songs including, 'Merrily wake music's measure', 'Hail, smiling morn' and 'I saw lovely Phyllis'.

PRINCE ARTHUR TO PRINCESS LOUISE
CHATHAM, 9 JULY 1868

I suppose you know that nobody wrote or telegraphed about the birth of Alix's little girl and that all I have heard has been entirely from the newspapers. You might I think have written a couple of lines to me to say how Alix was getting on and what the baby was like, but I know that since Affie has come home you do not care any more for me. Mama did telegraph yesterday but it was only to say how very hot the journey to Osborne had been, which I can quite imagine for it was really overpoweringly hot here.

(271)

Arthur was to complain after the Queen's death that no one ever told him anything now.

SAME TO SAME
8 SEPTEMBER 1868

I hope you will have been able to see a little more of Paris on your way back [from Switzerland]; I think I shall spend a day there if I can. I have been trying to make a few watercolour sketches but the result has been very disappointing as you can easily imagine, however I intend to persevere. I am afraid you do not look forward to going back to Scotland, you must however make the best of it.

(279)

PRINCE ALFRED TO PRINCESS LOUISE
DEVONPORT, 1 NOVEMBER 1868

On the question of Louise's marriage:
In wishing you goodbye I would only say I wish you all happiness which I am sure you do not completely get at home and recommend you to take my advice and not forget Albert of Prussia. He is good and excellent, clever and rich, wishes it himself and I think would make you happy. If I don't find you at home when I return it will be my loss, but I sincerely hope you will seek your new home where I am sure you will find a happy one. This may be what I ought not to say, but believe me, my affection for you would not allow me to leave without putting it before you again, let alone the regard I have for him.

Goodbye; all happiness be with you; don't forget your old brother at sea and write to him some times, Alfred.

(284)

The family was divided between those who wanted Louise to marry a German such as the wealthy Albert of Prussia – Affie, Vicky and Alice – and those who did not – the Waleses, the Christians, the Queen and Louise herself. The Queen did not want to lose yet another daughter abroad nor to have even more foreigners coming to stay. Louise was not in love.

THE PRINCESS OF WALES TO PRINCESS LOUISE 14 DECEMBER 1868

Louise's marriage:
My thoughts have been a *great* deal with you my sweet Louise, and I have been wondering how things have gone on since I left, and hope they have not again been teasing you dear, like the last day I saw you when you looked quite *worn* and sad!! Pray don't *let* yourself be *guided* by so many!!! but better go straight about *that* kind *of thing* to your Mama. I am sure she would not then misunderstand you, and she surely would give you the *best* advice – and don't ever believe that she would think *first* of herself in *such a case as this*!!! Those who tell you that, give you the very worst of advice, and don't either do *any good* by it but *harm you*! So pray Darling, follow my advice, and listen to a sister who, God knows, means well and loves you very much.

(288)

THE PRINCE OF WALES TO PRINCESS LOUISE COPENHAGEN, 2 JANUARY 1869

Louise's marriage:
. . . I can quite understand your wish that we should not be absent from England too long, but you must not take too gloomy a view of matters at home. If dear Mama will only open Parliament and say just a few words, that will be a great point gained.

It would be far better if Arthur did not hold the Levées, (that is) Mama instead of him, but if she positively does not wish it, I would not if I were you press the point, as there are other more important things for her to do. Nobody can object to Arthur holding Levées. He is popular, and will do it very well. With regard to the other part of your letter concerning P. A. of P. [Prince Albert of Prussia] I have promised Mama to speak to no one on the subject but herself, so I cannot break my word, but my advice to you is not to do anything in the matter behind Mama's back, or she will lose confidence in you, and your position towards her will be gone. When at Berlin, I shall keep my eyes open – that at least I can promise you – and I have no doubt all will end well, and that you will find a good husband, as P. A. is not absolutely the *only* one in existence.

I am glad to hear better accounts of Lenchen and she writes to me very often. I suppose you will remain at Osborne till February. I must say I pity you, as it must be very dull there but I trust that some nice people may occasionally make their appearance, and it will amuse you to see the new ministers.... Now goodbye, dearest Louise, write to me whenever you have a moment to spare, and with Alix's best love, ever your affectionate brother Bertie.

(291)

Accounts of seasickness took up a considerable part of letters after visits from dear ones on the continent; in fact General Grey, the Queen's Private Secretary, wrote a whole ballad on the subject with a final verse:

Until at last, on Calais jetty, –
Where men for 'yes' still answer 'oui' – ee – ee
They all agree it is a pity
That England lies beyond the sea – ee – ee.

(292)

Arthur wrote that these verses amused him very much and ought to be set to music 'and then you might sing them'.

THE CROWN PRINCESS OF PRUSSIA TO PRINCESS LOUISE BERLIN, 9 JANUARY 1869

Louise's marriage:

Darling Louise ... As regards your own affairs dearest which are never out of my head – and which keep me awake at night, I will write a little word to the General [Grey]. Bertie and Alix have been evidently and most successfully worked on by the Hessian relations. I would advise you not to begin the subject again to them unless they do to you, and then just tell them what you think. I do not think there will be any row at all. But should Mary T. [Teck] speak to you I would advise your telling her that you would rather she did not meddle in your affairs. You will have the dear kind Countess [Countess Blücher, at Vicky's court] to help you and later dear Aunt Feodore [Princess Hohenlohe, the Queen's half-sister], so set your mind at ease and be as quiet as you can; I really do not see what on earth there is to ferret out. You spoke to dear Mama yourself – if she asks you again you have but to tell her what you wish and what you think. I do not believe she can fancy anything so unjust or absurd as that *we* should wish to try and *make* you marry anyone you do not like for *wishes* of *our own*.

We only wish *your* happiness and dear Mama's too. Only see for yourself – compare and reflect on all the different circumstances brought to your knowledge and decide for yourself. I would not for the world take the responsibility on myself of pushing you into anything. But you can have no kinder wiser better counsel than the dear Countess who will be only too glad to help you as she loves you so much.

I am sure dear Mama knows enough of me (and I am *near* 30) to know that I am not an 'intriguante'. I have certainly never painted inviting Pictures of Berlin to lure you over.... Indeed I have often underrated things, so I cannot be accused of trying to influence you.

I shall never deny to dear Mama that I think it only *right* and *fair* and due to BOTH parties that you should have a FAIR opportunity of judging for *yourself*. You are no longer a baby. I would not press anything on dear Mama that is distasteful to her – she is easily excited, it would only annoy and irritate her and then you would most likely have a difficult time of it. I trust to all coming right in time as it mainly rests with your own dear self.

Vicky passionately wanted her sister to marry a German. In this letter she hoped to succeed by a show of impartiality.

How nice all that you tell me of Mr. Bright [John Bright, the Liberal] is, I wish I could have seen him too. We give a dance tonight. I wish you could be here so as to show people that English Princesses are not all as ugly as I am.... I am looking forward to dear Bertie's visit with so much pleasure. I am afraid dear Alix will be much annoyed at having to come here – it will be a very good thing that she does. How people will admire her, dear lovely thing.

(295)

The 'dear lovely thing' was treated offensively by the Queen of Prussia, though the King found her charming. She remained anti-Prussian all her life, and in 1867 had at first refused to meet the King.

SAME TO SAME
BERLIN, 23 JANUARY 1869

What a wonderful thing that Mama will hold a levée.

How *glad* and how grateful I am! I am sure you have done your best to bring it about. The opening of Parliament is of *paramount* necessity, it *must* be brought about, I shall quite give Mr. Gladstone up as a statesman if he does not bring it about. If Ireland could be done [visited] *this* year instead of next it would be far better. Can you not consult General Grey and Uncle George [Cambridge] whether in the spring Mama could not go to *Aldershot*, have some reviews, give a Lunch at the pavilion and have a *whole lot* of officers presented to her either out of doors – before or after Lunch – it would be *such a good thing*! Cannot *3* Breakfasts [garden parties] be given instead of 2, in London? Cannot dear Mama be persuaded not to go away before the Drawing Room is over – or at least *not* to *show* herself out driving while the drawing room is going on? Could she not give *2* largish dinners at Buckingham Palace with her Ministers?

Can you not get her to pay visits in the country in *England* on her way *to* or *from* Scotland – to show herself either in Birmingham, Liverpool or Manchester, it would be such an *excellent* thing. It *ought* to be *tried* at any rate. . . .

Dear Bertie's and Alix's visit went off *very well.* They made the best of impressions and charmed everybody – they were *so* nice and *so* kind. . . .

I am going to write a little word to General Grey. – You were *quite right* in what you said to dear Mama about *servants.* The mischief it is doing her dear self, England and us *all* is *not to be told* – I sit and cry over it!

(296)

The comment about 'servants' and 'mischief' is probably a reference to John Brown.

PRINCE ARTHUR TO PRINCESS LOUISE GREENWICH, 24 JANUARY 1869

I want to know whether you can tell me if on account of poor little Leopold's death [Lenchen's baby] you think I should not go to a dance at the mess next Wednesday. Please send me an *immediate answer* as I shall abide by whatever you say. I see that's your handiwork that Mama intends holding a levee on the 5th of March. I am delighted to hear it. Please answer me this question 'is Mama going to open Parliament or not,' I do hope she will. . . .

(297)

LOUISE IS SERENADED.

Astroea Regia to Princess Louise:

As you fair Star that neighboured by the Moon
  Burns meekly pale beside the greater light, –
So, set within the blaze of England's throne,
  Thy soft effulgence half evades our sight.

And yet unerring Science may divine
  That Star, – a *Sun* to tributary spheres; –
As I, with prescient vision, see thee shine
  A sovereign Presence, in the onward years.

(Signed: Dufferin. March 1869)

(1963)

He evidently expected her to marry a prince.

THE PRINCE OF WALES TO PRINCESS LOUISE
SANDRINGHAM, 22 MAY 1869

I am so sorry we saw so little of you on our return, and how tiresome that you must be away for *so long in Scotland*.... Arthur treated us in rather an offhand manner as we asked him to dine with us on Monday evening, but he preferred a *boat race* to our society....

(304)

PRINCE ARTHUR TO PRINCESS LOUISE
ORONSAY, SKYE, 7 JUNE 1869

... On our way here we visited both Iona and Staffa, two most interesting places and well worth visiting. There are two of the oldest crosses in Great Britain at Iona and there are likewise some very curious old tombs, the whole of this island belongs to your *great friend* the Duke of Argyle [*sic*].

(306)

Louise's 'great friend' was to become her father-in-law fifteen months later.

THE CROWN PRINCESS OF PRUSSIA TO PRINCESS LOUISE
9 AUGUST 1869

Not one word have I heard from you for 2 blessed months! – Have you quite forgotten your old Vicky?

... I sometimes fancy you wished I were with you, and that we could walk and *sit and paint together*, is it so?

(307)

Vicky was a talented painter, who went to art school and encouraged Louise to do so.

PRINCE ARTHUR TO PRINCESS LOUISE
12 AUGUST 1869

The enclosed cover contains some of my hair for Mama, you can tell her that I could not cut off very much as she forbid my hair being cut too short. With a kiss and a hurried adieu.

(308)

SAME TO SAME
14 AUGUST 1869

Arthur is going to Canada with his regiment, the Rifle Brigade, into which he was commissioned as lieutenant in 1869.

I feel so sad at leaving old England but I suppose it is all for the best so I must feel parting as little as possible. Leo wrote me a most kind letter which gave me a great deal of pleasure.

(309)

SAME TO SAME, ON BOARD THE *CITY OF PARIS*, 'APPROACHING HALIFAX AUGUST 22ND 1869'

It has been 'a capital' passage apart from the Atlantic swell.

We have a very motley set of passengers on board, most of them Americans, some of whom are most amusing. I cannot say very much for the ladies on board. There are really only one or two that can be called *ladies*.

(310)

SAME TO SAME
CANADA, 17 SEPTEMBER 1869

Arthur has had to make many extempore little speeches in French, which is not easy. The Governor's ball in the theatre was meant to hold 600, but 900 came.

I must say the ladies made a very good show, there were two or three American ladies who were very pretty. Is it not odd that they do not allow the Canadians who are Roman Catholics to dance valses under pain of excommunication. I like Canada much better than either Nova Scotia or New Brunswick, the country is better cultivated and the people are nicer....

Smoking:

I hope you liked your stay at Invertrossachs, and that you smoked in your bedroom to any amount. I am very glad I was not there, I should certainly have got into another scrape like at the Glassalt.

(314)

PRINCE ALFRED TO PRINCESS LOUISE
HMS *SALAMIS*, GULF OF CHILE, 1 OCTOBER 1869

I am glad to hear that you have a proper studio now in which I hope to see a whole collection of your works of art when I return. I must then give you a sitting for a bust for the last was far from successful.

He looks forward to tiger-shooting: 'splendid fun', and must now stop his 'stupid letter'.

P.S. No signs of a husband yet???

(316)

THE QUEEN TO THE PRINCE OF WALES
24 NOVEMBER 1869

Louise's future:
Dearest Bertie . . . I wish just to say that Louise is most *decided* in her wish to *settle* in her *own* country (as she has told you both) and indeed I am equally of this opinion, – having ascertained that there are no difficulties which will not be easily overcome; and I have written to Vicky *without mentioning this* that neither Louise or I would ever hear of the Prussian marriage, which must be considered *at an end.* Louise would *never* hear of Adolphus or the young Prince of Württemberg. I wished you should know this, dear Child, but would beg you *not* to mention it to a *soul* but to dear Alix; you might however, if you liked, speak to Lord Granville and the Dean [Wellesley] who are the only ones I have talked fully to about it and who are strongly in favour of the plan I have mentioned and decided on; – Ever your devoted Mama V.R.

(322)

SAME TO SAME
WINDSOR, 26 NOVEMBER 1869

Louise's future:
Dearest Bertie, I received dear Alix's letter this morning for which pray thank her, with the extraordinary proposal of Prince Albert of Solms. My two letters of the day before yesterday and yesterday . . . which I hope you will receive tomorrow will be the best answer to any of these proposals: viz: that Louise wishes to settle here in her own Country and that I think she is quite right. A poor, small German Mediatized Prince, *one* of 6 brothers with no Home or fortune would never do, unless I wished to do again what I did for Lenchen [financially] and that *I* could not. I can't

conceive *how* he [Albert] could *dream* of such a thing. He is so [German for 'commonplace'] *besides*. I will not here repeat *what* I said in my two letters, but Prince Albert of Solms may be told there is no chance for him. (323)

THE PRINCE OF WALES TO PRINCESS LOUISE CLARIDGE'S HOTEL, BROOK STREET 28 NOVEMBER 1869

Marriage to Lorne?

... I understand your feelings with regard to the other business but I still maintain my opinion – that it is still a highly *unadvisable* proceeding. (326)

THE QUEEN TO THE PRINCE OF WALES CLAREMONT, 29 NOVEMBER 1869

Louise's future:

I thank you for your letter received on Saturday. There is nothing about which I am more anxious than that you and I should hold together about so important a subject as this concerning Louise's future. What I am *irreconcilably against* is the Prussian alliance and I have every reason to think that you agree with me.

That which you object to *I feel* certain will be *for* Louise's happiness and for the peace and quiet of the family. Times have much changed; great foreign alliances are looked on as causes of trouble and anxiety and are of no good. What could be more painful than the position in which our family were placed during the wars with Denmark and between Prussia and Austria. Every family feeling was rent asunder and we were powerless. The Prussian marriage supposing even Louise wished it and liked the Prince (whereas she has not even seen him since she was a child) would be one which would cause nothing but trouble and annoyances and unhappiness, and which *I never* would *consent* to. Nothing is more unpopular here or more uncomfortable for *me* and every one, than the long residence of our married daughters from abroad, in my house with the quantities of foreigners they bring with them, the foreign view they entertain on all subjects; and in beloved Papa's lifetime this was totally different and besides Prussia had not swallowed everything up. You may not be aware as I am with what *dislike* the marriages of Princesses of the Royal family with small German Princes (German beggars as they most insultingly were called) were looked [on] and how in former days many of our Statesmen like Mr. Fox, Lord Melbourne and Lord Holland abused these marriages and said how wrong it was that alliances with noble-men of high rank and fortune which had always existed formerly and which are perfectly legal, were no longer allowed by the Sovereign. Now that the Royal family is so large (you have already five, and *what* will there be when your brothers marry?) in these days, when you ask Parliament to give money to all the Princesses to be *spent abroad,* when they could perfectly marry here and the children succeed just as much as if they were the children of a Prince or Princess, we could not maintain this exclusive principle.

As to position I see *no* difficulty whatever. Louise remains what she is, and her husband keeps his rank (like the Mensdorffs and Victor [Leiningen, the Queen's German relations]) only being treated in the family as a relation when we are together.

I wish you would talk to the Dean and Lord Granville about it; you would see how well every side has been weighed, and how strong the reasons are for such an alliance [with a commoner]. It will strengthen the *hold* of the Royal family besides infusing new and healthy blood into it, whereas all the Princes abroad are related to one another; and while I could continue these Foreign Alliances with several members of the family, I feel *sure* that *new* blood will strengthen the Throne *morally* as well as physically. In Mary's [Teck] case it would have been more difficult as she would hardly have been able for many reasons to maintain her rank as my daughter could.

(327)

A copy of this important letter was included in the published Letters of Queen Victoria, *Second Series, vol. I, pp. 632–3.*

THE CROWN PRINCESS OF PRUSSIA TO THE QUEEN GRAND HOTEL, CANNES, 29 NOVEMBER 1869

Retort from Vicky to Mama about Louise's future:

My beloved Mama, ... In reply to your few words about Louise, I can only say that *I* must most positively decline to transmit your intentions to the King [William of Prussia]. You will I am sure, understand that any message conveying so unmitigated an affront to the Head of my family from you, cannot go through *me*.

As you have never permitted me to write or speak to you on a subject you must know I had deeply at heart – *not* for *my* own sake – I have never had an opportunity of explaining much to you which might have been of value to you to know. To Bertie as our eldest Brother, I shall say what I think is my duty as your eldest child, and a member of the family to which I think it an honour to belong. I am well aware that my opinion has since long had no weight with you, and therefore refrain from discussing the subject again. Ever your most dutiful and affectionate daughter Victoria.

(328)

THE QUEEN TO THE CROWN PRINCESS OF PRUSSIA WINDSOR, 2 DECEMBER 1869

On Louise's marriage: the Queen begins by saying that she has been caused much pain by the lines which Vicky must have written in a hurry, under the influence of irritation, which has produced this tone.

Yet what just ground was there for irritation? In the *commonest* family the *one* surviving parent would have the right of determining that her daughter had better not make an acquaintance which might lead to her affections being engaged to any person, a marriage with whom was against that mother's own feelings and views.

The Queen emphasizes that though she had made her views plain, the idea was

still pressed on me (through *you yourself*, you must remember) by the King's wish.

The King of Prussia wanted Prince Albert of Prussia to be allowed to come over to England.

But meanwhile I had – independently of my repugnance to that Match – come to the conclusion that it would be for my own happiness and Louise's (who quite agrees with me) that a decided end should be put to the whole matter!

If the King and Albert still have hopes, they should be 'undeceived'.

... Among *all* families, marriages are every day *declined* for various reasons and without any *insult* taken or given, and why is this one to be otherwise?

I can see no ground for your regarding my request that you should tell the King the true state of the case, in the light of an insult to him!

The King and Prince would have far more reason to complain that they had been insulted if they were allowed to continue under an illusion.

At all events as my intention was to insult *no* one or ever to be *ungracious* to any one, I cannot but think that both your own excellent reason and your affection for and sense of duty towards me will prevail after reflection and that you will do all in your power graciously and kindly to bring this matter to a *decided* conclusion between the King and myself *without* any offence to him.

But as to your carrying this matter further by referring it to Bertie, so as to create out of it a *cause* of *dispute* between me and him, I cannot venture to express my feelings – only – I still trust to his good heart and to my own reason with him, to prevent this mischief – and I must leave you to regret from a distance – as I am sure you will – that you the eldest Daughter and Sister, wife to the 'heir' of a throne, might be the means of causing disunion on such a question as another sister's marriage, between mother and son in such positions as we are here at your early home.

(329)

THE PRINCE OF WALES TO THE QUEEN
MARLBOROUGH HOUSE, 4 DECEMBER 1869

I candidly confess that I can easily understand how much vexed and annoyed you are at Vicky's letter. I feel sure as you yourself say in answer to her letter that she must have written under irritation – or on a few hours reflection she would never have sent you the letter – I know how great her love and devotion is to you and that her last wish would be to give you a moment's pain.

I think, if I may be allowed to say so, that your letter to her is most kind and just, and I cannot myself see how the King of Prussia and his Family could consider themselves affronted or insulted by your not accepting Prince Albert as Louise's future husband.

You and, I am sure, all of us must feel flattered by his desire to be allied to our Family and preferring Louise to any other Princess but you must indeed be the best judge whether he is accepted or not. I never had any idea how strongly you had written to Fritz in 1868 on the subject – and I must say that I think it wrong and to say the least highly injudicious to encourage Prince Albert in hopes which there was but little chance of being realised – as Vicky and indeed I fear also Alice [of Hesse-Darmstadt, Louise's second sister] have done.

It is an unfortunate business, and I can well understand how worried you, dear Mama, must be about it, as you are naturally anxious to keep on good terms with the King and his Family. Vicky must now bear the blame herself, as she is alone responsible for what has happened.

Might I suggest however perhaps a few kind lines to the King from you expressing your regret etc. but that you had other plans for Louise, and that Fritz knew a year and a half ago that you did not wish the match.

With the exception of Louise, might I ask you to consider this letter as *private*.

(331)

Bertie was the peacemaker, both within the royal family and between the British and Prussian families, at this date.

THE PRINCE OF WALES TO PRINCESS LOUISE
MARLBOROUGH HOUSE, 5 DECEMBER 1869

He thanks her very much for her letter – he has written to Vicky and thinks he has said everything to Louise's satisfaction. He has written kindly, as a breach in the family 'will never do', and ends with a plea on his own behalf:

... I trust I shall be informed *before* it is *actually* settled what future Mama intends for you – and not like Lenchen's marriage when *everything* was settled before I had even a suspicion. That is all I ask, and I think you will agree with me that it is not asking *too* much.

(332)

THE CROWN PRINCESS OF PRUSSIA TO THE QUEEN
GRAND HOTEL, CANNES, 6 DECEMBER 1869

Louise, the Queen and the Prussians: Vicky begins by apologizing humbly for having written a letter wanting in respect if this were so, but adds at once that it is not unreasonable for her to feel it an offence that a marriage between Louise and any member of her family should be cut off.

That other Princes should be admitted to make her acquaintance and win her favour whilst he who in all fairness has a prior claim, is refused and shut out without a reason which either the King, Fritz or he can understand, *is* and *must* appear to us *hard* and *unjust*.

She has never led him on to feel there was a chance of his success,

as I know the violence of your feelings against him, but I have not refrained from again repeating in the interest of *both* our families what a *1000* pities it is that you will not consider the matter.

Louise has always I believe put her duty to you before her own interest and her own happiness, your command would I am sure make her refuse even the best chances, but whether some day in later years when she sees what she has lost this will contribute to her comfort, one is surely at liberty to doubt. You know that I am the last person to wish to make mischief between you and Bertie, but being forbidden to speak to you, what other course have I than to turn to our eldest Brother. Fritz feels so much more strongly on the subject than I do and *has resented* the treatment of his cousin so much more, that *I cannot say or do* anything to anyone without his express desire.

(333)

PRINCE ARTHUR TO PRINCESS LOUISE
ROSEMOUNT, MONTREAL, 18 DECEMBER 1869

I miss you very much, and at Xmas time I shall feel your absence very much. It is my first time away from home at that season of the year, and I shall feel quite lonely without you all. It is too bad of you not writing to me any more, I have not heard from you for three weeks or more....

How I wish you were here. I should drive you out with my four in hand every day, teach you to skate, snowshoe, toboggan, and even to flirt, the latter you would learn here to perfection.

(335)

THE PRINCESS OF WALES TO PRINCESS LOUISE
MARLBOROUGH HOUSE, 23 DECEMBER 1869

She begins with the usual discussion of Christmas presents and hopes that they will be liked. Then,

I hope my poor pet has not been worried and bothered lately about that tiresome old affair of yours! and that your sisters have given you a *little rest* now.

(336)

THE DUKE OF ARGYLL TO THE QUEEN
OSBORNE, 25 JANUARY 1870

Lorne and Louise: a possible match, Lorne is using his father as a go-between.

What Lorne wished the Duke to convey to your Majesty was that provided other views were not already entertained, he would avail himself of whatever opportunities might be offered of making farther acquaintance: – and this on the footing which would be least embarrassing to the Princess – that neither should be considered *in the least degree compromised* by such acquaintance.

The Duke thinks that in seeking this farther acquaintance he does not wish to put himself forward as a suitor, *unless* and *until* the acquaintance should lead to *real* mutual liking – without which the Duke thinks it much better that the matter should never go further; and he must repeat to your Majesty that he hopes your Majesty will not feel the *smallest* reluctance or difficulty in telling the Duke that this last is your Majesty's conclusion.

The Duke was very sorry not to have the opportunity tonight of saying *one word* to the Princess Louise to thank her for her kind sympathy. The Duke hopes the Princess does not mean to be shy of *him* – in any event.

(343)

SAME TO SAME
OSBORNE, 26 JANUARY 1870

The Duke of Argyll presents his humble duty to your Majesty and has the honor to acknowledge your Majesty's most gracious letter.

He rejoices to hear that your Majesty was somewhat better yesterday.

He encloses the excellent telegraphic account he has received from Inverary [*sic*].

The interest which the Duke could not but feel in the Princess Louise began long before late suggestions had been even thought of, and is entirely independent of them, and the Princess need not therefore be the least embarrassed in any friendship she may be disposed to entertain for him.

He has had, like your Majesty, experience of the happiness which arises from a marriage of perfection, and he has no wish that H.R.H. should make any other – neither can the Duke wish for any other for his son.

(344)

The tone of the last paragraph is typical of the dignity and pride of a great noble in the nineteenth century.

PRINCE ARTHUR TO PRINCESS LOUISE
NEW YORK, 31 JANUARY 1870

Impressions of America:

Most of the young ladies are very pretty and extremely well dressed, they are great fun and come out with no end of queer Yankee expressions; at the end of a dance the correct thing is for the lady to say to the gentleman, 'Well sar I guess we've had quite a gorgeous time of it'. Mind I am spelling it as they pronounce it; I have quite a selection of Yankee phrases to fire off when I get back to England.

(345)

THE CROWN PRINCESS OF PRUSSIA TO PRINCESS LOUISE
BERLIN, 5 FEBRUARY 1870

The Queen's public duties:

... *What* a 1000 pities it is that dear Mama does not open Parliament and that it was put into the newspapers about her being unwell! You must try and get her to do something more in London instead, or else we shall

Princess Louise by Queen Victoria, aged four. On the back of the portrait is written: 'Louise after Winterhalter, my first effort in oils'.

Princess Louise and the Prince of Wales as 'Winter' in the Tableau of the Seasons, Windsor Castle, 1854

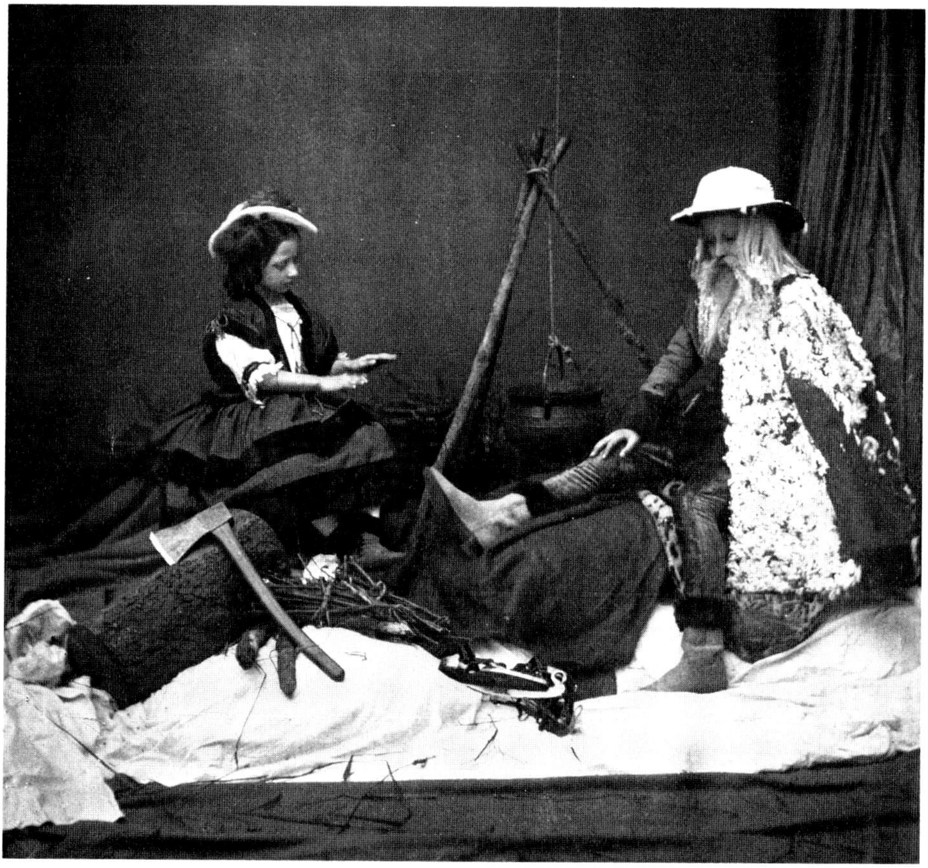

Above: Prince Alfred, Geneva, 1857

Left: Princess Louise as a Vivandière, Windsor Castle, 1856

Group at Osborne, 1857: left to right, Prince Alfred; Prince Albert; Princess Helena; Princess Alice; Prince Arthur; Queen Victoria with Princess Beatrice; Victoria, Princess Royal; Princess Louise; Prince Leopold; Albert Edward, Prince of Wales

Princess Louise, Princess Alice and Princess Helena in the dresses they wore at the Princess Royal's wedding, 1858

Princess Louise (right) and Louise Van de Weyer, her friend, c. late 1860s

Princess Louise as a girl

The inconsolable widow: Princess Louise, Queen Victoria and Princess Alice, Balmoral, 1863

Right: Princess Helena and Princess Louise (right), 1864

Below: Princess Louise and Queen Victoria attended by John Brown, Osborne, 1865

The Prince and Princess of Wales with Prince George, 1865. Bertie is the only member of the royal family in this collection to be photographed smiling.

Above left: Princess Louise aged twenty

Above: Thought to be Princess Louise with her painting; she had probably posed for the photograph

Left: Prince Leopold sculpted by Princess Louise

Opposite: Princess Louise and Prince Arthur, 1870

Top left: Princess Louise in her wedding dress

Top right: John (Ian) Marquess of Lorne, c. 1870

Above: Marriage of Princess Louise and the Marquess of Lorne, St George's Chapel, Windsor Castle, 21 March 1871

have no end of unpleasant things written and said which will irritate and pain her.

(346)

PRINCE ARTHUR TO PRINCESS LOUISE
MONTREAL, 13 FEBRUARY 1870

I enjoyed my visit to the States very much but am glad to get back to Canada again for I dislike the Yankees awfully as a *nation* although I like some of the *individuals* very much. I earnestly pray that this Dominion may never be given over to the States as it will be the ruination of it; for I feel certain that British rule is the only really free one; for in the States the mob tyranny is something fearful, and bribery and corruption are practised to any amount.

(348)

Lorne, who was to be Governor-General in eight years' time, was a strong exponent of Canada as a British Dominion.

LORD GRANVILLE TO THE QUEEN
16 BRUTON STREET, 12 MARCH 1870

Princess Louise has decided she does not love Lorne after all.

Lord Granville presents his humble duty to Your Majesty. He ventures to think Your Majesty has taken the honorable and kind course with regard to Lord Lorne. Lord Granville will lose no time in obeying Your Majesty's command, and he has no doubt that although the young man may feel a little present mortification, both he and his family will perfectly appreciate the considerate manner in which Your Majesty and Princess Louise have acted and that there will be no diminution of the deep and affectionate loyalty which they feel towards Your Majesty.

(350)

THE QUEEN TO LORD GRANVILLE
WINDSOR CASTLE, 13 MARCH 1870

The Queen has had some conversation with Princess Louise on the subject she yesterday wrote about to Lord Granville and she has been confirmed thereby in the opinion she expressed, viz: that while the Princess thinks Lord Lorne very clever and agreeable, she does *not* think she could have that feeling for him which would enable her to wish for any nearer acquaintance with a view to a further result. He is too young for her and it would not be right or honourable to encourage hopes where the Queen sees there are none.

Under the circumstances the Queen thinks that the kindest and least formal way would be for Lord Granville to see Lord Lorne and to mention this to him in the kindest way.

Princess Louise is so fond of the Duke that she is most distressed to think he might be hurt by this and it would be a distress to her and to the Queen were it to make any difference in the feeling which exists between us and the Argylls, the connection with whom the Queen had much wished.

The Queen will herself write to the Duke of Argyll after she has heard from Lord Granville. If the Queen could have seen Lord Granville she could have explained more to him than she can in writing.

(351, copy)

Perhaps it was a pity this decision was not adhered to, as the marriage was not happy.

LORD GRANVILLE TO THE QUEEN
16 BRUTON STREET, 13 MARCH 1870

.... It was impossible for Lord Lorne not to show a little regret, but he spoke in the highest terms of Your Majesty's considerate kindness to him, and added that Princess Louise's conduct had been faultless as regarded him.

He admitted that knowing his fate was a relief to him, that the uncertainty of the prospect together with the almost impossibility in the circumstances of making himself known to Her Royal Highness had weighed much upon him, and that he could not help feeling if Your Majesty had allowed the matter to drag on, that his feelings would have been irretrievably engaged, with probably no final success.

Lord Granville is convinced that the Duke of Argyll will think the same.

Now it was off with the old love and on with the possible new:

Lord Granville thinks that Lord Cowper is so much a man of the world, that it does not much signify with whom your Majesty invites him. If Your Majesty thinks of having Lord Hartington at Windsor they would do well together.

The weakness of Lord Cowper's character is indecision, which may be a difficulty in the outset as well as a drawback for the future.

(352)

DEAN WELLESLEY TO THE QUEEN
THE DEANERY, WINDSOR, MARCH 1870

New candidates for the post:
All about Lord Lorne is most satisfactorily over. But the Dean from experience judges that everything must depend, not upon what might be actually best, but upon what suits the Princess. It will therefore be no use in urging Lord Dunglass upon her in preference to Lord Cowper, but let her see both, and make her own preference. The Dean will, and so will Mrs. W[ellesley] enquire further about Lord Cowper. But Your Majesty must recollect that the Manchester admiration [for the Duchess of Manchester], and it was nothing more, is a thing past years and years ago and that Lord Cowper is now universally thought a steady man. As Your Majesty wants the letters back, the Dean has no time for more, Lord Hartington is not necessary – Your Majesty might have another or two [to Windsor] who were going afterwards to Frogmore, which would save appearances.

(353)

BIRTHDAY LETTER FROM PRINCE ALFRED
HMS *GALATEA*, 18 MARCH 1870

My dear Louise, Many many happy returns of today and you know all what besides I wish you, a wish which has so long remained unrealised and . . . so I must besides wish you patience.

(355)

The wish was for marriage.

DEAN WELLESLEY TO THE QUEEN
22 MARCH 1870

Everything seems to have gone well (he hears) so far, as to Lord C[owper]. But his manner is awkward, and if the Princess should observe this at first, it is not to be wondered at. Time should be given and further acquaintance to get over these things. He is certainly very agreeable. Mrs. W[ellesley] has known him long, and assures the Dean (as he himself has always heard) that he is kind hearted and very amiable. He seems to have been well pleased with the Princess, and it does not seem unlikely that on his side, he would not object were he to come to know what was contemplated.

It appears to the Dean, however, that none of these men who have yet been seen are calculated to make a strong impression. Lord C. is the best, but allowances should be made for the Princess, if she cannot make up her mind to any of them.

(357)

SAME TO SAME
31 MARCH 1870

Marriage with a subject?
The Dean thinks that although there has been fresh disappointment, no attachment can have been really formed for anyone, so as to occasion any real unhappiness. Meanwhile, so far, ground has been gained, that without any positive authority, there has arisen a general idea that the marriage with a subject may be permitted – indeed it is impossible to suppose that many young noblemen should have been lately admitted into the company of the Princess without some such surmise, and the matter does not appear to have been received anywhere with opposition. Time then may be taken, and men of promise looked out for without any unusual efforts being made. But the Dean would be most sorry if the Princess were not ultimately to marry someone, as, although she might for a while be of great comfort to Your Majesty at home ... yet in after years her position might become wearisome and insignificant from want of duties and interests. She ought with her talents and attractions to marry, while still young, and it should be a question only of time.

(359)

THE DUKE OF ARGYLL TO PRINCESS LOUISE
26 APRIL 1870

A present from Iona:
Madam, May I ask Your Royal Highness to accept the Cross which I now send, made of the Iona Stone.

This cross is out of a piece which I picked up in Iona last September and which was the only specimen which I have ever seen of sufficient size for such a purpose.

Professor Maskelyne of the British Museum does not seem to be sure what the mineral is – whether a soft jade, or a soft serpentine. It is half transparent when held up to a strong light. I have the Honour to be Madam your sincere friend, Argyll.

(1967)

The Duke was highly cultured, and interested in science and natural history.

LORD GRANVILLE TO THE QUEEN
16 MAY 1870

More candidates?
He hopes your Majesty will not think he neglects your Majesty's commands, but having made no confidant and everybody being on the qui vive, it is very difficult to get information which would be of value.

Lord Bessborough has told Lord Granville that Lord Gosford is well off, but he would not say the amount.

Lord Granville is told that Lord Camperdown is poor, but that he will be rich at his mother's death. She is the daughter of Sir George Phillips of Manchester, and sister of Lady Caithness. Some of the Household might know what Lord Caithness' circumstances and expectations are which would be a guide. Lord Granville will not relax his efforts. Lord Granville is not surprised at the part of the Family having made themselves disagreeable on the subject, there is much gossip on the subject and must come from some such source.

(362)

M. VAN DE WEYER TO THE QUEEN
16 MAY 1870

Van de Weyer was the Belgian Ambassador. Marriage with a subject is 'the idea'. The letter is written in French.
After a conversation with His Royal Highness the Prince of Wales I am not at all surprised at the contents of the note from Your Majesty. The Prince with his usual frankness spontaneously brought up the question and explained to me his regrets when I expressed a favourable opinion at *the idea* which your Majesty had deigned to convey to me. I replied to His Royal Highness that the question, as posed to me by your Majesty could never have received any other than this solution and that in the absence of a Prince 'convenable' in all respects, the combination proposed seemed the only one which could assure the happiness of the person principally interested, a combination which would be in my opinion more popular in the country than the candidates whose names I have heard mentioned.

'I don't believe it', retorted the Prince; 'and the *idea* which has been entertained could create great embarrassment for us. But there is a prince who has not been thought of, a prince of Mecklembourg, who seems to unite all the desired conditions. The other *idea* is subject to very grave objections and I would wish you to have an occasion to speak of it again to the Queen.'

I replied to His Royal Highness that what had made me seize and understand the *idea* is that it was above all important that a person so accomplished should find, in making such a choice, a worthy appreciator of all her qualities, and that one in no way believed, as had been claimed, that your Majesty did not wish for any marriage at all.

He continues that knowledge of 'the idea' has begun to spread in the world.

I myself have heard it talked about without surprise and without disapprobation. I have equally heard speak of the Duke of Aumale and I said this to the Prince of Wales who did not think that the quality of Catholic was acceptable for any candidate whoever he was.

I ask pardon of your Majesty for going into all these details which I place very confidentially at your feet. But I think it important that the Queen should know without restriction and without reserve all that is said. The realisation of the *idea* presents without doubt difficulties, like everything in this world. But a solution is only possible by perfect knowledge of the ground and of the dispositions both hostile and favourable.

(363)

THE PRINCE OF WALES TO PRINCESS LOUISE 22 MAY 1870

More criticism of Mama:
I can't tell you how horrified I am at the idea that Mamma is going to have her 'breakfast' [garden party] at Windsor instead of here (London). It is a thousand pities and when I first heard the report I would not believe it till Lord Sydney told me that Mamma had settled upon it. Can nothing be done to change it? How will everybody get down there and return? It will be most unpopular, and the whole object gone, as it was to give something in London that the breakfasts were first started.

(365)

PRINCE LEOPOLD TO PRINCESS LOUISE 28 MAY 1870

Please ask Mamma to show you the letter I have written to her for I have written about 'not being left behind at Balmoral'; I have said that I can't come at all. I see she wants to drag me up there 'par toute force'; but I *won't* come; *nothing on earth* shall make me come, as it would be too fearful to be left behind.

I send you some verses by Tom Taylor, out of Punch, but they are not very good; but I thought they might amuse you. The Saturday Review in its criticism of the Academy sits on Mr. Boehm frightfully.

(367)

SAME TO SAME
30 MAY 1870

P.S. It is all settled that I am not to come to Scotland. Sir W. J. [William Jenner, the Queen's principal doctor] has behaved very well about it.

(368)

Leopold is still laid up with a knee like a pumpkin and a dreadful headache.

SAME TO SAME
6 JUNE 1870

I am mad with pain, so I must stop. I am in such agonies at this moment – Mr. Collins [Leopold's tutor] is going on all right. I don't think it ever was typhoid.

(370)

Four days later:

I go on as usual suffering frightfully, at this moment I am in agonies of pain; my knee gets worse daily and I get more desperate daily. If this continues long I shall soon be driven to Bedlam or to Hanwell, where I shall be fortunately able to terminate a wretched existence by knocking out my brains (if I have any) on the walls; that is the brightest vision that I can picture to myself as a future.

But I must stop on account of the *awful* pain, which is torturing me. Your wretched brother Leopold.

(371)

Robert Hawthorn Collins was to become Leopold's comptroller in 1874 and his wife's comptroller in 1884, dying in 1908. His brother was to go out to Canada on Princess Louise's staff when her husband was Governor-General.

PRINCE ARTHUR TO PRINCESS LOUISE
MONTREAL, 12 JUNE 1870

Arthur will soon be home.

I feel sure you will think that I have grown very ugly since I left, my face is nearly as black as my coat from the heat of the sun, and I have grown fat as a prize pig and my face is likewise adorned with whiskers of a pea green colour; you will likewise find that I have grown rather of a woman hater, I believe chiefly due to my having followed strictly that advice you gave me before leaving.

(372)

We do not know what Louise's advice was that resulted in Arthur becoming 'rather of a woman hater'.

SIR THOMAS BIDDULPH (PRIVY PURSE) TO THE QUEEN 17 JUNE 1870

Candidates again; the letter is written in the third person

He has only today received any answer to his enquiry respecting Lord Gosford, and that not so full an answer as he could have wished in consequence of the absence from London of a person who could have furnished more precise details. This person will however probably be in London again in a fortnight. The impression Sir Thomas Biddulph has from the information he has received is that Lord Gosford is a man of high character, and careful habit of life, as regards his expenditure. He thinks it pretty clear that his fortune is not what is called a large one, though he is not at all ill off.

But on a matter of such importance Sir Thomas is very diffident in giving an opinion without further information. As to income a great deal depends on what your Majesty would consider sufficient.

(374)

To sum up, his information on Lord Gosford's fortune was so vague that he hardly liked to say anything.

SAME TO SAME 21 JUNE 1870

Many a landed proprietor has a nominal income of £20,000 a year, when in fact he has not more than half that sum to spend, on account of mortgages and jointures and expenses of keeping up an Estate and place. These drawbacks are most difficult to ascertain.

All Sir Thomas's informant could tell him was that he thought Lord Gosford was not ill off, but whether he has more or less than £10,000 a year to spend he could not say.

(375)

LORD GRANVILLE TO THE QUEEN
LONDON, 6.30, 9 JULY 1870

Suitors still sought:
Princess Louise was charming last night, and won the hearts of everybody. H.R.H. had Lord Ilchester on her side and Lord Rosebery opposite, the table being very narrow there was some general conversation. The latter seems anxious to put himself 'sur les rangs'. Lord Dunglass is pleasing, not good looking, and engaged but not to Lady M. Scott, but to Miss Grey, Lord Grey's niece. Lord Dalrymple (pleasing but young) never took his eyes off the Princess, but was too shy to speak. So was Mr. Compton and Mr. Robartes. Mr. Wellesley talked to H.R.H. for some time. Lord Cowper who dropped in in the evening, with Clanwilliam, Harcourt, Calcraft, and many middle-aged men, was marked in his attention to Miss Compton. [He became engaged to her.] Lord Granville does not think much progress was made last night, but it will not be without use for the future, in encouraging young men to approach the Princess. Lady Clifden's tenue [behaviour] in attendance is perfect.

The Prince of Wales had heard of the dinner and sent to propose himself for the evening, but afterwards sent an excuse.

(376)

MR GLADSTONE TO THE QUEEN
11 CARLTON HOUSE TERRACE, 11 JULY 1870

Mr. Gladstone presents his humble duty to your Majesty and humbly thanks your Majesty for having permitted the Princess Louise to honour his wife and himself by her visit to their house today. The Princess's gracious demeanour is the delight of all who see her.

(377)

The Queen was breaking her rule against Louise dining out (except with Bertie and Alix) in the interests of her possible marriage. Louise renewed her contact with Lorne at this dinner and was impressed by his cleverness and charm – at least compared with other candidates. The Queen must have known Lorne was to be present.

LORD GRANVILLE TO THE QUEEN
16 BRUTON STREET, 11 AUGUST 1870

Lord Granville thinks Lord Lorne still much in love. He talks of going to India.

(379)

THE QUEEN TO LORD LORNE
BALMORAL, 3 OCTOBER 1870

The engagement: Queen Victoria consents to the marriage of her daughter to a commoner.

... I cannot go to bed tonight without telling you that I give my ready consent to what Louise has informed me of – and earnestly pray for God's blessing on you both. I know that my dear Child will be safe in your hands and I trust that you will protect and guide her and be that support which every Husband ought to be.

Your very high character gives me every confidence and I doubt not that you will, with your kind heart, good sense and devotion to her overcome the difficulties which will naturally be unavoidable in a marriage with one of my daughters.

I trust that you will receive the sanction of your dear, kind Parents to this important step, which however must for the present be kept a secret, at any rate till we hear from them, and till (after we do so) I have informed my own family of this event. Dear Lady Ely having been here and acting the part of chaperone to Louise, besides being a dear friend of ours, has been informed of today's Event in strict confidence. She can bring any message from you which it might under present circumstances be difficult for you to convey to me personally.

(380)

It is interesting that the references the Queen makes in this letter to the nature of the 'Event' are carefully controlled. Lorne would be well aware of the 'difficulties' of marrying a royal princess, if only through the somewhat strained atmosphere of this first letter.

PRINCESS LOUISE TO THE DUCHESS OF ARGYLL
BALMORAL, 7 OCTOBER 1870

Louise's engagement to Lorne had taken place on 3 October. On the back of the double sheet is written 'For The dear Duchess'. Front page:

Dearest Duchess, How very kind of you to write to me yourself, and to wish me joy of this most happy event. How lovingly you speak of my becoming a daughter of yours; believe me how truly I shall love you and the dear Duke and strive to be a comfort and happiness to you.

You can guess how proud I already feel of Lorne, and how I shall love and respect him.

I hope this sudden news has not been too much for you.

I hope it will not be very long before I see you, and can by word of mouth assure you *how anxious* I am to do all that will be expected of me. YOUR VERY AFFECTIONATE Louise.

(1701)

THE PRINCE OF WALES TO PRINCESS LOUISE
DUNROBIN CASTLE, SUTHERLAND, 10 OCTOBER 1870

Lorne's 'position' as a commoner:

Dearest Louise, Your kind letter which I received this evening has touched me deeply, as by all you express you only convince me that the ties of brotherly and sisterly affection between us are strengthened. My greatest wish, as I wrote to you yesterday, is your happiness – and if you think that your marriage to Lorne will give you what you have a right to desire – as it is for your whole life – I am satisfied.

But I cannot change my opinion which I expressed so strongly in my letter to you yesterday. Don't think me unkind, dearest Louise, for adhering to my opinion, which resolves itself into firm conviction, and I can only trust that these numerous difficulties of position etc. which now come before me, may never give you cause to regret the step you have taken. I always liked Lorne – but his position will require tact and discretion which cleverer men than him would find difficult to maintain.

I think on the whole, if he has not already done so, he had better not write to me at present, as it would be a very awkward letter for me to answer. You may rely on my always showing him all the kindness and friendship which lies in my power. Alix who sends you her best love, agrees with everything I have written, and that God may bless and protect you, dearest Louise, and make you happy as you deserve is the wish of your most affectionate brother, Bertie.

(381)

One of the 'difficulties of position' concerned Lorne's precedence on formal occasions, when he would have to enter a room near the end of a procession of royalties and ambassadors and separated from his royal wife.

PRINCE ARTHUR TO PRINCESS LOUISE
RANGERS HOUSE, GREENWICH, 12 OCTOBER 1870

Dearest Louise, I feel most anxious to know what kind of answer you got to Bertie's letter – I heard from him today and he said that regarding your engagement he would make no comment, but that you would be very happy.

Pickard asks me to send you his best congratulations on your engagement, when I first saw him I told him that one of the ladies at Balmoral was engaged to be married and made him guess who it could be; he guessed all the ladies one after the other except you.

(383)

Lieutenant Arthur Pickard, RA, VC, was attached to Prince Arthur from 1867 to 1870, and his equerry from 1871 to 1877. He died in 1880, having been the Queen's Assistant Private Secretary.

THE PRINCESS OF WALES TO PRINCESS LOUISE
STAFFORD HOUSE, 14 OCTOBER 1870

Alix writes to congratulate her.

I must confess it took me rather by surprise as neither of us had thought you had made up your mind. Let me now wish you all possible happiness for your future, and may you never have cause to regret the step you have taken! God grant that the husband you have chosen may prove worthy of you my dearest Louise in every respect!

Alix goes on to say that she has heard so much good of Lorne, but as Bertie says they will have difficulties to go through though true love will bring them through.

... I hope you feel VERY VERY HAPPY!!!

Have you heard from your sisters? What do they say to it? Vicky particularly! Please write soon to me and very ausführlich [fully] as I am longing to hear from you myself. You know my pet in me you will always find a *true* friend whatever may happen!

Alix continues with three more pages of mostly family news – including the fact that 'My naughty little Man won't be back till Wednesday which seems such a long way off' – to end with the message:

I must wish you good-bye now my darling Louise with God's best blessing for your future

Ever your own affectionate sister Alix.

(384)

COUNT GLEICHEN TO PRINCESS LOUISE
ST JAMES'S PALACE, 14 OCTOBER 1870

A German cousin congratulates her. He was a sculptor.

... I can't tell you how glad I am for your sake to know that you will soon have a home of your own – but at the same time I fear you will be very much missed not only by the Queen but every one at Court – I always used to look forward to a little chat with you but I hope this will not be quite at an end when you become a stately married party, but that we may see even more of each other's lovely countenances than hitherto.

Lolo [his wife] joins with me in the warmest possible good wishes – I don't know Lord Lorne yet, but hope soon to be able to make his acquaintance and to claim cousinship and criticise him from head to foot. I hear his head is a good one (both steady and for sculpture).

(385)

LORD LORNE TO QUEEN VICTORIA CAMPBELTOWN, 19 OCTOBER 1870

Lorne's engagement:

Dearest Mama – the dinner was certainly a success. I did feel very nervous – much more so than I expected when the dear health was given – but do not think I said anything indiscreet. The people behaved very well, and there was no allusion made in a disagreeable way. I had sent round to warn them beforehand. They cheered her name very heartily – and were evidently much pleased when I spoke of her living sometimes among them.

You were frantically cheered.

I send a note from the Duchess of Roxburghe which is very kind – considering what she must have wished.

The Volunteers do not parade till tomorrow – and I go to Carradale to see the site of a new Battery there, early in the morning. It is a drive of sixteen miles so that I shall only get back in time for Parade at 5.

We had quite a gale yesterday.... The yacht behaved very well in the morning – and Louise was a charm to me against evil by sea as well as on land.... Your affectionate Lorne.

(1787)

THE PRINCE OF WALES TO THE QUEEN MARLBOROUGH HOUSE, 23 OCTOBER 1870

Objections:

My dear Mama, I have to thank you for your last letter. It was not my intention to make allusion to Louise's intended marriage in another letter, but as you mention the subject in your letter, I cannot help doing so also. I have not the slightest remembrance of advocating such a marriage when you spoke to me on the subject on December 14th last year and I think you must have misunderstood me, as from the first to the last I have always been against it, and spoke most strongly to Lord Granville, the Dean of Windsor and M. van de Weyer in that strain. I have seen by the papers that the Press (which does not always express Public Opinion) are strongly in favour of the marriage. I can only repeat again that I trust my views on the subject are wrong, but I cannot at present alter the very strong opinion that I entertain on the subject. . . .

I decidedly maintain that a marriage with a subject is lowering the position of the Royal Family and in the instance of Lorne, he is excessively poor, and Louise's position will naturally be less good than if she had married a rich man. When I spoke to her about Lorne before we left Abergeldie she certainly did not seem to care much about him, and when she wrote that she was so 'much touched by his devotion', that she accepted him, it did not give either Alix or myself the impression that she was in love with [him].

I suppose you know that Lorne was half engaged to one of Lord Shaftesbury's daughters and that the Family are naturally furious that he has thrown the girl over.

(390)

Louise, while in Mentone with Lorne in 1872, had to call on the family and noticed one of the girls staring at her. The same thing happened on the training ship Cumberland *in 1871. Shaftesbury was a great friend of Lorne's family, the Duke of Argyll being godfather to his youngest son.*

THE DUKE OF ARGYLL TO THE QUEEN INVERARAY, 29 OCTOBER 1870

Louise's knee:

. . . In the last letter I had the honor of receiving, your Majesty mentioned that the affection of the Princess's knee seemed rather obstinate; and as each day's account was rather less good than better, Lorne became rather anxious this morning on hearing from the Princess that she had suffered a good deal – especially as she evidently thinks very little of it, herself, and bears pain so well. Our own doctor here made him more so by telling him that *any* affection of the knee joint is very apt to be very tedious and troublesome.

. . . Your Majesty will no doubt readily understand Lorne being rather fussy on the subject, and he was SO anxious about it this morning that I PROMISED to write to your Majesty today.

I hope your Majesty has not been annoyed by any disagreeable letters. There can be no doubt of the hearty approval of the country, an approval indeed which seems far more enthusiastic than could have been anticipated.

(393)

The Duke felt that a good surgeon's opinion would be valuable. The Princess had sprained her knee while riding with Lorne on 15 October. It was to give her trouble for the rest of her long life.

QUEEN VICTORIA TO LORD LORNE BALMORAL, 4 NOVEMBER 1870

Louise's knee and Lorne's visits:
I think you may like to have a few lines from me to say how the *young lady* is. The leg is no worse – indeed we hope better – but the progress is very *slow*, and she is obliged to keep quite still which in this fine weather and at the end of nearly 3 weeks (for I am afraid that *all* think the *ride* to Birkhall [with Lorne] that Saturday did the mischief) is very trying and annoying. But she is quite well and very cheerful: much occupied with many necessary arrangements. I think another fortnight must elapse before we can come south. If it were not for so distressing a cause I should be only *too* happy to be remaining here in the dear Highlands ... all so quiet and the dear people so kind. All of them in and out of the House take the same interest in her as if Louise was their own child – but of course are greatly distressed at her being shut up during the last time that she is here still as my child, and I think you both *owe them and me*, a visit here on the first occasion to make up for this. I trust that by the end of the month (for I understand you were not going to remain in the south but in Scotland particularly this constituency) Louise will be in a fit state to see you, because as she is now it would be almost impossible.

You will not I hope object to staying *occasionally* for a night or 2 at Windsor, gloomy and formal tho it is – as well as coming over from Cliveden, and I hope to show you Osborne too, which *we* all like best *after* this. We shall naturally be going there before Christmas.

The Crown Prince has written very kindly and so have the Duke and Duchess of Coburg....

There is nothing whatever of a *serious* nature in Louise's knee and you and your parents need not fidget yourselves about it, but trust to me who am *still* the *only* one responsible for her *well-being*. There is more fear of *over care* than the contrary.

(397)

SAME TO SAME GLASSALT SHIEL, LOCH MUICH, 15 NOVEMBER 1870

... I write to tell you that Professor Lister ... has found the knee of Louise is considerably better and has *no* objection whatever to the journey south of the 23rd, by which time she will have made further progress as to movement (I mean rolling and lifting) and therefore will, I hope, be able to see you a day or two after our return, of which I shall instantly inform you.

The Queen goes on to say that he should not hesitate to write or telegraph whenever he is anxious to come and see Louise,

for I shall then always be able to arrange the time, which will generally be best between five and seven. But I hope you will also come for luncheon and sometimes also for a day or two at a time. All can be arranged if you will only let Me know.

(404)

On the same date (15 November) the Aberdeen Free Press *reported on the huge bonfire that was lit by Prince Leopold at Balmoral to celebrate the engagement. It was 100 feet round the base and 30 feet high and could be seen for miles around despite the bright moonlight. The toast of the affianced pair was cheered 'until the distant hills gave back the sound'.*

PRINCE ARTHUR TO PRINCESS LOUISE
MARINE BARRACKS, WOOLWICH, 17 NOVEMBER 1870

... Tuesday I hear is now the date of your departure [from Balmoral to the south] and I hope you will be well enough to start on that day. I hear that Mr Gladstone is most anxious for Mama's return and now that this Russian business has occurred it is most essential that Mama should be in constant communication with her Ministers.... I was very much pleased to see Lorne and very glad to hear from you that he enjoyed himself; his hair I remarked immediately and I think it is a great improvement....

(405)

THE QUEEN TO LORD LORNE
BALMORAL, 21 NOVEMBER 1870

The 'difficulties' of being married into the royal family:

Dear Lorne; I have this moment received your kind and affectionate letter and would wish to explain that I *must* ask you *not* to ask to see Louise *till* Saturday – as the doctors and I wish *absolute* rest for those 2 days. And if *she* knows that you are in *Windsor* she will fret and agitate herself and do herself harm. She can, I know, unfortunately not have the complete rest she has had *here*, and not having been out of the house or gone down stairs for a *whole* month, this long journey will try her *very much*. It is for *her* sake as well as for mine ... that I *beg* you *not* to let *her know* that you will be *there* till *Saturday* which she *knows* herself from me, is the day on which she is to see you *first*....

If, when you come, you send in your name to me, I shall see that Louise is ready to see you, which she will always be able to do in a room near mine (her dear Father's room) where her 3 sisters *before* have always had their *Interviews* with their *Bridegrooms*. . . .

I am so pleased to see that you write openly to me and I *long* for the opportunity of *knowing* you, which I do so little as yet.

(407)

SAME TO SAME
WINDSOR CASTLE, 25 NOVEMBER 1870

Many thanks for your kind note. I am glad to say that Louise has had a very good night, that though she suffered on the Journey from pain and discomfort she has not suffered from it [since] and Mr Paget wishes much more moving about except, of course, *walking*, or as yet putting the foot down.

(409)

SIR THOMAS BIDDULPH TO THE QUEEN
2 DECEMBER 1870

Re the Marriage Settlement:
I know the Duke of Argyll is very particular and sensitive about having his money matters talked about. . . .

(410)

SAME TO SAME

It appears that the Duke of Argyll has a strong objection to entailing his estate on the eldest son of the intended marriage. It is usual to do so in cases of landed estates particularly where there is a title, so as to ensure the title and the estate going together. The Duke's objection may be partly of a private, and partly of a public nature. It seems that the Lord Advocate brought in a Bill last year (which did not pass) to alter the system of entails. The Duke appears to have no intention of leaving his estate away from his son, but dislikes entails. Should he persevere in his objection, it will be for Your Majesty to consider whether the settlement, without it, will be satisfactory.

(411)

THE QUEEN TO LORD LORNE
4 DECEMBER 1870

Wedding arrangements:
As at *all Royal marriages*, 'the Bridegroom' is always 'supported' by *two* and not as at *Private* marriages, only by his 'best man', I am anxious to know if there is anyone (of course of high rank) who you would like to have beside your uncle Ronald [Gower]. He need *not* be *unmarried*.... The Prince of Wales was supported by his uncle the Duke of Coburg and by the Crown Prince [of Prussia].

Louise's leg is improving, and she can stand and even walk a few paces (of course with *quite* a stiff *knee*) I have no doubt it will yet be for some time. She has written to you about your sisters and brothers coming here on Thursday – and we both wish *Libbie* [Lorne's sister, Lady Elizabeth Campbell] would stay to dine and sleep here on Thursday ... – your parents would *not* object.

The Queen then discusses the difficulties of the bridal couple's planning to travel abroad in these uncertain times. She adds:

There are many more difficulties in the way of a journey abroad, considering my daughter's position which cannot be overlooked, than would appear on the surface – and everything would have to be well considered and weighed before starting any project of the kind.

I shall hope to see you at Osborne soon after New Year for a week's visit.

(413)

Lord Ronald Gower was Lorne's closest friend (*see pages* 52–3).

SAME TO SAME
WINDSOR CASTLE, 7 DECEMBER 1870

Scottish enthusiasm:
... Respecting the Journey, I must still urge you not to think of it as a thing settled, but to wait till we see what happens and how Louise is herself. Climate is not the only important thing. You should have a good talk with Sir William Jenner about it. And to make too sure of one's plans is not a good thing.

The gift from the dear Balmoral people is *entirely* new and comes entirely from their *delight* at Louise's marrying a *Scotchman*: and their generosity and feeling of loyalty, and pride that it should be *worthy* to be *worn* with anything else, is really touching. My good Brown who has as noble and true a heart as ever breathed with an independence of character and straightforwardness which are invaluable to me, was one of the chief promoters of this present and says: 'We consider her as our *Scotch* Princess, and we wish her to have something from the Balmoral servants to remind her of them.'

You must, dear Lorne, not let your marrying my daughter, make you *less thoroughly Scotch*, than you *ought* to be.... How proud you must, and she ought to feel to belong to 'the country of worth'. The Scotch are behaving so kindly and nobly to you both that I am sure you will feel more and more proud of your dear country. My dear Prince, who had such a very high opinion of the Scotch and of their immense superiority both as to heart and head said a very short while before his fatal illness, 'England does not know what she owes to Scotland.' ...

(414)

SIR THOMAS BIDDULPH TO THE QUEEN
7 DECEMBER 1870

The Marriage Settlement; Biddulph writes in the third person.
He has seen Mr White to-day and Mr Morton Your Majesty's Lawyer in Edinburgh. They both consider the entail of the Inveraray and Kintyre estates as proposed satisfactory and it will accordingly be done. They both agreed that the Duke's proposal to have power to give a jointure of £5,000 a year to a possible future wife of the Duke's was rather a large demand, but it is understood that the Duke is tenacious on this point, so it is not worth while to dispute what very probably will never come into operation.

(416)

In fact this may have come into operation, as the Duke was to marry again after the first Duchess's death in 1878; and again after the second Duchess's death.

THE QUEEN TO LORD LORNE
WINDSOR CASTLE, 8 DECEMBER 1870

My dear Lorne, I send you here a little pin made out of a piece of granite I picked up on the path to the Dhu Loch, when I went to the Glassalt Shiel on the 26th October, with the *3d* October engraved on it at the back, and with a wreath of *bog myrtle* round it, which I hope you will sometimes wear. Louise has a brooch just like it made out of the same stone.

(417)

PRINCE ALFRED TO PRINCESS LOUISE
AUCKLAND, NEW ZEALAND, 11 DECEMBER 1870

My dearest Louise, Your letter of the 6th October made me rejoice very much for you, and I wish you every possible joy and happiness but selfishly I am very sorry to hear of your good fortune as I shall miss you terribly at home. Lorne was an old playmate of mine when we were very little boys, but I have met him but once or twice since. The last time I saw him was at Chiswick two years and a half ago. Neither you nor Mama say when this important event is to come off, but the papers say that it is to be in February, if so I shall not be in time for the wedding as my orders won't allow of my being home before the end of March or beginning of April at the very earliest....

Give my kindest remembrances to Lorne and tell him I shall be very happy to have him as a brother-in-law.... What does Aunt Cambridge say to it????!!!! The photos are very good but you ought to have been leaning on a stile with Lorne instead of Arthur, who was very sorry to have missed the last mail but did not write by the following one.

(419)

SIR THOMAS BIDDULPH TO THE QUEEN
12 DECEMBER 1870

The Settlement:
The remark your Majesty has made about the sale of Roseneath [*sic*] has been already suggested but there is a difficulty in introducing a clause in a legal document to the effect desired as the Duke must have the matter in his own power as to value. Sir Thomas is a little afraid that the Duke expects more for the property than he will get. If he *should* effect a good sale, however, it was agreed that he should increase the allowance.

(420)

It was not sold.

THE QUEEN TO LORD LORNE
OSBORNE, 23 DECEMBER 1870

Dear Lorne, I write today to wish you a very happy Christmas and every possible happiness and blessing and to say that I send you Louise's statuette on horseback. If the bronze one cannot be ready in time you shall have a cast in the meantime.

This will be a very quiet and in some ways a very sad one, from the thought of the dreadful sufferings and miseries of so many many thousands and millions [through the Franco-Prussian War] – and also from the feeling that it is dear Louise's *last* in her own *Home as* my OWN Child! You must not be angry at this, but I dare *not* think of the changes which another 2 months and a ½ will bring.

Kind love to your dear parents.

(421)

SAME TO SAME
OSBORNE, 24 DECEMBER 1870

Dearest Lorne, Though I wrote to you yesterday I cannot leave so very kind and affectionate a letter as I have received this afternoon unanswered.

Many many loving thanks for the dear words it contains which have done me good.

Mine is a nature which *requires* being loved, and I have lost almost all those who loved me most on earth.

She had lost her parents, her Uncle Leopold and Prince Albert.

I hope Louise will not be spoilt by too much adoration and by the touching amount of devotion and kindness of the beloved *Scotch*!

That she will be safe and happy with you I *don't* doubt – and trust she may prove worthy of such a blessing.

Of course married life brings trials and anxieties unknown before, but with mutual affection and confidence and trust in God's goodness and guidance – all then may be overcome, at least all that lies within human power.

(422)

SAME TO SAME
OSBORNE, NO DATE BUT PROBABLY A NEW YEAR WISH

The Queen's dread:

To *me,* I must repeat it, *for it is* inevitable, as Louise will tell you *herself* – it brings a *very great* trial, which *she* must to a certain extent feel herself. I know how much you will wish to lighten this to me and I have no doubt that in *many* ways it will be *far* less trying to me than the marriages of my other daughters. Still, the separation and the change are *inevitably* there, and I look with sorrow and dread to this, because one's daughter has other interests, and *those must* be *her* first – and her Mother and old Home can, if she is happy, only be her *secondary* one.

In wishing your happiness I feel I am also wishing *hers,* which for the future can *never* be but *inseparable* from yours.

(424)

LORD GRANVILLE TO THE QUEEN
9 JANUARY 1871

The Franco-Prussian War. Confidential: should the marriage be postponed until peacetime?

Lord Granville presents his humble duty to Your Majesty. He will ask Mr [Odo] Russell to do what Your Majesty wishes, but he doubts its being expedient. Any leading question from him will produce an affirmative reply, as there is no doubt that the marriage is unpopular among the princes. But it will not be less so after the Peace, when they have more time to think of it. It appears unreasonable that they should object to a marriage in England on account of a war of some duration, when it is reported from Versailles that marriages are taking place among the Prussian officers.

Here the marriage is exceedingly popular among the middle and the poorer classes, and the postponement of it for the reason Your Majesty mentions, would cause great disappointment. Some of the Republicans who are trying to make a little capital out of it, would hit it both ways, and they would then have time to do some harm. Lord Granville will not tell the Duke or his family what has passed, unless Your Majesty permits it.

(425)

Odo Russell (later Lord) was at this date an Assistant Under-Secretary at the Foreign Office, on a special mission to the German Army HQ at Versailles.

THE QUEEN TO LORD LORNE
OSBORNE, 10 JANUARY 1871

Dear Lorne, These lines are to welcome you here and to send 2 photographs of the picture of myself in the dear Prince's room at Windsor.

I wished also to say I hoped you would come up at 6, to the Prince's room here, to see Louise. But I have given her permission to meet you at tea in Helena's room, as she is anxious to see you and Ronald [Gower] at tea this evening.

(426)

SAME TO SAME
OSBORNE, 12 JANUARY 1871

On the 11th, the Queen had sent Lorne a letter from the Prussian Crown Prince about the marriage for him to translate into English for Lord Granville.
Dearest Lorne, Many many thanks for the masterly translation of a very difficult letter. You have left out the *right* things.... I send you a little bust of myself, hoping you will place it on your table.

(428)

The Queen had said that it might be wise to send a copy of the letter to Granville. The Crown Prince was dead against the marriage.

SAME TO SAME
OSBORNE, 25 JANUARY 1871

My dear Lorne, I was just going to write to tell you that I have definitely settled to have the marriage on the 21 of March, by which time I hope Louise will be far more strong and recovered than she is yet.

(429)

SAME TO SAME
OSBORNE, 28 JANUARY 1871

Parting from Louise:
My dear Lorne, I could not write before and now do, to thank you for your 2 kind letters. Both *rather* surprised me. The 1st from the expression about '*unnecessary* delay' – and the 2nd from the extreme delight expressed at the day being *settled*! They seemed to imply want of confidence in me. Most painful as it is to me to look to the day which takes my *own* Child for *ever* from me, you know that I would settle it as soon as I *could* do so without fear for Louise's knee or political affairs abroad obliging me to put it off again. I do not see any cause for either at present, though I fear the knee will long be painful – and I own I am in fear and doubt about the journey [abroad on honeymoon] though very much may happen between this and the end of March.

... I *do* hope you will soon get a *Highland* Servant ... as it quite shocks *my* feelings, that *you* my future Highland Son-in-law should not have a Highlander attending on him, when Alfred *always* has one and Ld. Huntly ... and the Duke of Sutherland *always* brings them as well as your father. *Does* this look well for *you* to have *none*?...

And now dear Lorne before I conclude I *must* say one word on your observation that it was 'intolerable' for you to be without Louise! If you feel that – who are only parted for a few days, or at the outside 3 weeks – what must the feeling be to those who to a great extent lose her altogether? Is this not a selfish thought and feeling? You must accustom yourself to occasional partings, for it would be very cruel and not just, could you not spare her sometimes to her *own* Mother, who parts with her for you, for a few days. My own sad experience has taught me that it is a misfortune to be quite unable to be ever apart, as it makes your life so dependent on one other that you are quite lost when separated even for a very short time. *My* dear Husband felt that *much* himself and often spoke of it.

(431)

DISRAELI TO THE QUEEN
31 JANUARY 1871

Assurance of devotion in reference to her confidential appeal respecting Princess Louise's dowry:

Mr. Disraeli with his humble duty to your Majesty, has the honour to acknowledge the receipt of your Majesty's confidential communication. Mr. Disraeli has no tie to public life but the desire to serve, however humbly, a gracious Sovereign, whose kindness to him, under trying circumstances, he never can forget, and which he can only feebly repay by devotion.

(432)

The Times *castigates electors of Birmingham for objecting to the dowry. After explaining that the Crown receives its Civil List and grants in return for its surrender of Crown Lands to Parliament,* The Times *goes on to analyse the specific objections in this case.*

Already, during the present reign there have been half-a-dozen such grants, and what, then, be the justification for suspending or renouncing the custom in the present instance? Is it meant to express a popular objection to the match itself? On the contrary, the match, exceptional as it certainly is in character, is of a kind to commend itself especially to popular sentiment. The daughter of the Queen, with her mother's full consent, descends from the charmed heights of Royalty and marries a subject. What can the most advanced Liberal object to in that? For once the money will not even be spent out of the country, but will be kept at home and spent among the people. We can understand objections, perhaps of no small weight, to the step thus taken; but they are not such as would be sustained by popular constituencies. In their eyes, the marriage ought to appear peculiarly promising and satisfactory, and why, then, should the opportunity be selected for an invidious and irrational demonstration?

... Time was when Ministers came down to Parliament with demands for half a million or so in liquidation of Royal debts, but nothing like such profligacy in high places has ever been known in our own days.

(434)

GLADSTONE TO THE QUEEN
1 FEBRUARY 1871

The dowry:

Mr. Gladstone presents his humble duty to your Majesty and entirely shares your Majesty's sentiments of regret and disapproval with reference to the objections taken in some quarters to the moderate proposal about to be made to Parliament for a Dowry to Princess Louise.

These objections, Mr. Gladstone thinks, may really be referable in a greater or less degree to causes quite independent of that proposal and its merits.... These objections, as far as he knows, have been taken in few places, and for the most part by persons possessed neither of influence nor of information. He has heard of two members of Parliament as joining in them; one of them, though well meaning, is weak; and the other is perhaps the most fractious spirit in the House of Commons.... In any case, when the time arrives, your Majesty will have no cause to complain of any want of explicitness or decision in the language which will be held by the Government in putting aside, and endeavouring to discredit, what your Majesty most justly describes as a vulgar error; an error venial in ignorant persons, but discreditable enough in those who mislead them.

On the whole Mr. Gladstone hopes and thinks there is no reason for the least uneasiness on the part of your Majesty with reference to this subject.

(433)

The vote on the Princess's dowry of £30,000 went through with only one 'No'.

THE QUEEN TO LORD LORNE
OSBORNE, 3 FEBRUARY 1871

After discussing politics and saying that she is glad to see 'the right and good Scotch feeling coming out in the little extract you have sent me', she goes on to the weather and then the real point of her long letter:

I *cannot* deny that the tone of your answer to my observations has *surprised* and *pained* me. I think you forget in speaking to *me* of people not knowing *what* married happiness was *if* they *could* wish to be a *single* day apart, – that for 22 years there were *no* two people more united and happier than my dear Husband and I were, and that to us separation was always a trial. But *my position*, he always said was *very exceptional*, and he always maintained that the man *ought not* to be so *tied* to his wife as to be *unable* to be at all away from her, for that if a man could *not stand* alone – he could be *no support* to his wife and that he *ought* to do so.

And I also know well *how* deeply I regretted *my* selfishness in having kept him from going oftener for a few days to his own dear country, which he said he felt sure would have done him good and that I myself expressed, just before his fatal illness, my readiness to facilitate this in every way for the future. I am the *first* to disapprove the style of the present day when wives go out to amusements alone, the Husbands going to their clubs etc. and think that their life should be *as much in common as possible*.

But that the Husband should not *readily* and *gladly* bring his wife to *her Mother* from whom he has taken her, and leave *her occasionally* for a *few days alone* with her, as is *constantly* done, or let her come *often* to see her for the day when near by, *especially* when *that* Mother is the *Queen, bereft* of her beloved Husband and who *cannot* like *any other* [incomplete]

(435)

II

Marriage

1871–1900

THE QUEEN TO PRINCESS LOUISE
28 APRIL 1871

The Lornes are travelling abroad after their wedding at Windsor on 21 March, their honeymoon tour of over a month being followed as closely as possible by the Queen at home.

You did quite right to visit the Gd.Dss.M. [Grand Duchess of Mecklenburg-Strelitz] but I am glad Lorne was there, for she can *say dreadful things* – and this makes me now answer you rather tardily about Alice. I would rather you had *not* met her *so* soon, for I know her *curiosity* and what is *worse* and what I hardly like to say of my own daughter, – I know her *indelicacy* and coarseness – and therefore if you go wish *you* and *Lorne* (painful as it is to me to say it – as she *was* as nice and *refined* as any of you and has learnt all this from the *family there* [Hesse-Darmstadt]) to be on your guard. When she came over in '69 and saw Lenchen again she asked her *such things*, that Christian was shocked – and Mary Teck, who *is* very *nice* in her feelings unlike *her Mother,* told me *she never* was *so shocked* as she had been at the things Alice *said to her*! . . .

(475)

The Queen probably feared lest Louise should be questioned about the prospects of her having a baby. Princess Alice was genuinely interested in gynaecological matters, as affecting women in general, and in hospitals.

PRINCE LEOPOLD TO PRINCESS LOUISE
WINDSOR CASTLE, 15 MAY 1871

After an account of his doings, all in good humour, he goes on:

The day after tomorrow we go to that *most* VILE and *most* ABOMINABLE of places Balmoral; I have never been there without you and I shall hate it more than ever, and meanwhile you will come back to England, and *everybody* will see you before *I* will, it angers me to a degree. Poor Lenchen looks anything but well, it is most sad. Uncle [Ernest of Saxe-Coburg-Gotha], I believe, is going on much better now. . . . Nothing has yet been heard of Affie. . . . With love to the Marquis.

(481)

'Uncle Ernest', Prince Albert's brother, lived until 1893, despite his extremely dissolute lifestyle.

MAJOR ELPHINSTONE TO PRINCESS LOUISE
BUCKINGHAM PALACE, 21 MAY 1871

Prince Arthur's accident:
Madam, The accounts of Prince Arthur's fall will have already been conveyed to Your Royal Highness, and I feel sure that you will sympathise with him and share in the general regrets at this unfortunate accident. I cannot tell you how sorry I am; especially just at present when he had made all his arrangements for the London season, etc. etc. We must however be thankful that the result was no worse. With an older, or a heavier person it would certainly have proved fatal.

We had been dining quietly here, before the State ball, with Prince Christian, Colonel G. Gordon, Mr. Pickard, Mr. Fitzgerald and myself and went afterwards to the billiard room, next to the Equerry's room and the grand entrance hall. The windows of the billiard room descend to the floor, the lower part being protected from outside view by a slight wire gauze screen lightly fixed. The windows were wide open, and Prince Arthur, without thinking, lent with his back against this wire screen. It gave way at once, and he was thrown backwards and head foremost out of the window, 7 feet high, on to the granite slab pavement. He lighted apparently on the top of his head, and was stunned for the moment. Two policemen outside picked him up at once, and carried him indoors. By that time he had recovered consciousness, but trembled violently. I saw that there was nothing broken, nevertheless sent at once to Sir William Jenner and Dr. Paget. About an hour after the fall a large swelling appeared on the top of his head, which caused some pain. He was still too stunned to feel acutely. His toe was bruised severely; how, I cannot imagine.

For the following day, the Prince was very poorly, and feverish, and complained of pains in his head. He was utterly unable to retain any food or medicine.... This evening however there is a decided improvement, and the swelling on his head has greatly diminished.

22 May

Prince Arthur has made rapid progress since yesterday. He has commenced to take food and even appears to enjoy it. The swelling on his head has entirely disappeared, and the toe is mending rapidly. He has not however recovered from the effects of the shaking, and the weakness caused by the absence of daily food has brought on his old complaint of neuralgia. Last night, these pains prevented his sleeping, and today they have been very acute; almost to make him cry. Both of his eyes became much inflamed likewise. There is no doubt however that he is much better, and that there is not the slightest cause of apprehension.

(483)

THE DUKE OF ARGYLL TO PRINCESS LOUISE
INVERARAY, 31 MAY 1871

After discussing the new stables and projects for the artillery, he comes on to the date of the Lornes' visit after returning from their honeymoon.

We have fixed, – as nearly as anything can be fixed so long before – the 23 August as *the Day*. I am to preside on the 9th at Glasgow at the Scott Dinner. Then comes the *grouse week* of the 12th and the next again seems the earliest that we can well fix it for. The Queen can't make up her mind whether she can come or not.

I am very vexed to hear that you still feel that disagreeable knee. We must try to get it right, else it may bother you all your life. Ever my dear Louise your affectionate father, Argyll.

(1968)

The knee did bother her all her life.

THE QUEEN TO LORD LORNE
BALMORAL, 1 JUNE 1871

She defends Balmoral.

The country is in its greatest beauty. It is such a contrast this peace and quiet and lovely pure air and glorious scenery here, to the *awful horror* – really *quite unparalleled* in that sink of iniquity – Paris!! ... Your parents are enjoying Inveraray and your dear Mother is none the worse for the journey.

(484)

She reports that dear Arthur is getting on well, but must not join in any gaieties for another fortnight.

THE QUEEN TO PRINCESS LOUISE
BALMORAL, 2 JUNE 1871

Prince Alfred's love affair:

... I hear such great praise of the Grand Duchess Marie from Vicky and also from others, that I own I begin to *think*, if Affie *really* likes her, she would be the *best after all*. Affie is quite reasonable and sensible about her and Thyra will see both.

Thyra of Denmark was Princess Alix's sister, later married to Ernest Augustus, Duke of Cumberland (former Crown Prince of Hanover). The Queen then discusses her proposed visit to Inveraray and whether to arrive with, or after, Louise. In a postscript she writes:

Don't let Alice pump you. Be *very* silent and cautious about your 'Interior' and about Lenchen and Christian.

(486)

PRINCE LEOPOLD TO PRINCESS LOUISE
BALMORAL, 4 JUNE 1871

My dearest Loo, I have been a long time answering your letter and thanking you for the charming photographs you sent me of yourself and Lorne. I am so glad to hear that you have been able at last to see dear Aunt [Feodore, Princess of Hohenlohe-Langenburg], who seems to have been pleased with your worthy husband, and I am so pleased to hear that you have been in the dear Countess's house and have seen her rooms. Mamma tells me you have seen a good deal of my august but intolerably tiresome godmother, the Empress Queen [Empress Augusta of Prussia], is she very grand since her assumption of the imperial dignity? I send this to Darmstadt, whither you are going I understand either tomorrow or the day after. Poor Arthur might have had a very dangerous accident the other day and he has had a most wonderful escape, he is nearly all right again now, and is stopping with Lenchen who has been and looks anything but well since you left, I don't attribute her indisposition to that though. I am so very happy at the thought of seeing you in at most a fortnight, as we will leave this on Friday the 16th inst. But you will be changed and not the same to me as you were before your departure, I fear. Give my very best love to dear Alice and Louis and their kids....

I am very well, yet I am pining for England.

(487)

THE QUEEN TO PRINCESS LOUISE
BALMORAL, 6 JUNE 1871

Many thanks for your dear letter of the 31st from Waldleiningen where I rejoice to think that you have found a little of what *you* call: 'sharp air' but which is wholesome, invigorating air, far more beneficial for *you really*, than the soft, tepid air and broiling sun of '*beautiful Italy*'. Waldleiningen must be very pretty. I am glad Ernest was so amiable. It is sad to think of the little creditable life he leads in England.

(488)

Ernest, Prince of Leiningen, Queen Victoria's nephew, was in the British navy and was in command of the Royal Yacht at the time. He was said to have had an illegitimate child.

SAME TO SAME, BALMORAL, 12 JUNE 1871

Darling Loosy, I am all impatience to hear how you *get on* in your new home, for it will be stranger to you than *anything else yet*. Pray *don't rush* about in London, as you always used to do! visiting and going to exhibitions, shops and studios, without ever getting fresh air and exercise which you know always ended in making you *quite* ill. Pray be prudent and reasonable. And don't ever go out (when Lorne is *not* there) without *sòme* lady *or other*.

(490)

The Lornes' first country home was Macharioch House on the Inveraray estate (very run down) and their first London home was 1 Grosvenor Crescent (rented).

THE QUEEN TO LORD LORNE OSBORNE, 4 AUGUST 1871

Dearest Lorne, These few lines are to wish you all possible joy and happiness on your birthday. May God bless and protect you and may you see many happy years with my dear child, in the enjoyment of mutual affection, regard and confidence! Louise will give you my offering.

I am very glad the visit [to Ireland] has gone off so well – but I think the Irish are far too much *buttered.* It makes it almost an advantage for them to be so troublesome, unreliable and unmanageable.

(491)

LORD LORNE TO THE QUEEN INVERARAY, 4 SEPTEMBER 1871

Madam and dear Mama, I cannot say how grieved all here have been that you are still feeling so unwell, and are therefore unable to think of making the journey to see us at this time. Sir William's [Jenner] letter received this morning makes us fear that the arm has caused you great discomfort, and it is indeed most hard that you should have had this additional suffering. Everyone we meet enquires about you, and is so anxious to hear how you are, and I do hope that we shall soon be able to give more reassuring accounts.

Since people are gone and we have been quiet here, we have had fine weather and Louise has I think taken a liking to the place. Our rooms look towards the Loch, and get plenty of sun as their exposure is to the South and East. We have been putting up in them some pictures and prints that we brought with us, and I have the dear miniature you gave me of yourself in front of me on my table as I write.

Before long Louise will I hope send you some sketches of the views from the windows. Till now all her disposable time has been occupied in driving and sometimes riding about to see the neighbourhood, and in paying visits to the people. I send two photographs with this letter. One is of the Pavilion in which the balls were given and which is now to remain up as it will be useful for dances, dinners etc. Only half of it is shown in the photo. It is built much in the same style as the ballroom at Abergeldie, but is 150 feet long by 50 broad. The other photo is one taken of the pony carriage given by the towns-people. It is a most useful carriage, but is adorned with lamps and embroidery that are much too wonderful.

The visit to the 'Cumberland' training ship in the Clyde went off well on Saturday....

(1788)

The Queen had been suffering from acute blood-poisoning since 4 August.

THE QUEEN TO PRINCESS LOUISE
BALMORAL, 11 SEPTEMBER 1871

A Victorian death in childbirth:

Dearest Loosy, I saw by your letter what distress you were in about dear Sibyl [Duchess of St Albans]! It is an awful tragedy. How thankful I am that you *did dine* with the poor dear that day – for else how you would reproach yourself. She had a presentiment she would never get over it, and told Mrs Smart the nurse so. She ought not to have been *left* all that *hot* time in London; it is *very bad* for people and London was and is very unwholesome.... At present I am still very weak and cannot walk up and down stairs without support.

(493)

Sybil Grey, later Duchess of St Albans, had been one of Louise's very closest friends. Both she and her baby died. Queen Victoria was still suffering from the dangerous blood-poisoning that had attacked her – at Osborne! Nevertheless, she stuck to the 'unwholesomeness' of London as one reason for avoiding her public duties in the capital.

SAME TO SAME
BALMORAL, 12 SEPTEMBER 1871

The Queen's illness:
I am going on well, the appetite quite returning – only I can eat but little at a time. I had taken a great dislike to *all* that I liked most. Tea I could not touch. The arm is healing very fast.

(494)

This letter, written only a day after the above, illustrates the volatility of Queen Victoria's moods. How were her children to cope?

THE PRINCE OF WALES TO PRINCESS LOUISE
BRAMSHILL CAMP, 13 SEPTEMBER 1871

I quite agree with you, and so does Alice that on no account must Vicky's celebrated letter be sent to Mama for some time to come, as there is no doubt that her illness – and she has really been very ill – has been produced by worry, from what the Ministers have said to her and from what she has read in the newspapers [criticizing her seclusion]. All alas! was only too necessary for her to know, but I think if the letter is to be sent at all it should be at the end of January or beginning of February.

I am so glad that all your festivities, the account of which I read in the papers, at Inverary [*sic*] went off so well, but you seem to have been very unlucky in your weather, which was a great pity.

(496)

A long letter with news of his travels follows, with a postscript in German, which says: 'Is it true that the Duchess of A. is expecting a child, as I hear?!!!!!!'

Vicky had drafted a splendid appeal from the whole family recalling Mama to her duties.

THE QUEEN TO PRINCESS LOUISE
BALMORAL, 1 OCTOBER 1871

A tribute to John Brown:
I am decidedly *better*, unberufen [touch wood] – able to walk – and though very *ailing*, still beginning to be *less dependent*. Still it is a very slow progress – and one which keeps one rather nervous from the way in which it *lingers*. I wear a bandage on both feet – though only *one* was bad – but the thighs were so stiff that it threw the whole of my weight on my ankles and I find the bandages a great support. I was twice out yesterday in the pony chair and today which was misty and wet – I went out in the closed carriage.... Yesterday was the 1st night I was able to get into bed without

being lifted. For 12 nights good, kind Brown lifted me and the *amount* of pain he has *saved* me then, and in helping me on the sofa and lifting me up when I slipped and could not move myself is *not* to be *over-estimated*, and my *gratitude* for all his kindness and continual thoughtfulness is *true* and *deep*. My poor maids have also been indefatigable in doing all they could.

(499)

SAME TO SAME
BALMORAL, 14 OCTOBER 1871

A relapse:
I am sorry to say my right foot has been quite as bad as my left was, though I was less ill than with the first attack, but I suffered again last night and got only about three hours sleep. The foot is however much better today. I am however obliged to be carried up and down stairs and lifted in and out of bed again.... Nine weeks since I began being ill. Is it not *dreadful*.

(501)

The Queen goes on to discuss Louise's future home, which she says the Duke had promised to build her somehow or other and somewhere. The question of 'a home of their own' was a subject of continual discussion between their families.

SAME TO SAME
BALMORAL, 2 NOVEMBER 1871

Three of the Queen's obsessions – doctors, visitors and childbirth:
Darling Child, Many thanks for your last dear little letter. I am glad that you are going to try about the wing [of a house]. Use my name as much as you like and I will support you for I have a perfect right to do so, the *Duke promised it me*. The reason that I am so anxious that you should see Dr. Fox and Sir J. Paget is because (*in* confidence I tell you this) the Duke and Duchess and all the Howards are very fond of trying new and half quack doctors which is very bad and very dangerous and don't see Mr. Hewitt without his being agreed with Sir J. Paget who knows all your constitutions so well. You will see Dr. Marshall at Windsor and Osborne.

Alice and Louis left yesterday. I warn you that (besides *begging* for much money again which [you] must never let her think you know or tell anyone else) [she] is moving heaven and earth to stay, taking the children's coughs as a pretext, the *whole* winter in *England* living at my expense and letting Louis remain alone at Darmstadt after having been so long separated from him!! But I declared I would *not* allow it on any account and Sir J. is *very stout* about it and Sir William Jenner too. I have had enough of large families this year and I shall not ask Alice again soon, if she *always* tries to remain longer than she is asked. Alix quite shares my opinion. I want indeed a quiet winter.

In many ways nothing can be more sensible, reasonable and right-minded than Alice is – and you can only profit by her *experience* and listen to her. But as regards questions like the *very indiscreet* one to poor Janie Campbell [Lady Archie Campbell, Lorne's sister-in-law], she is most *indelicate*, and tells anyone *how* sick she is, and that there is a new and most unnecessary Event impending; when really one would never SO early think of mentioning it except to one's mother!!

(505)

SAME TO SAME
BALMORAL, 11 NOVEMBER 1871

Strained relations over travel:
Darling Loosy, I have received both Lorne's letters of yesterday with *much surprise* and, I must add, *pain* and think it better to write the answer to you, for else I should have to write a sharper letter than I would wish (if I could) to do. In the first place you *both* know well that I have always only wished you to do what was for your good *physically* and *morally*. But I *certainly* expect that *confidence* and *consideration* which are due to me both as a mother and as the Sovereign. You should have told Lorne that *none* of the Royal family *can* go abroad without the Sovereign's leave and I have even as a *Mother* a *right* to be consulted as to what you think of doing. What shocks me *still* more is, that *others know* of your *wish* to go abroad, and that *therefore* THIS cannot be *only* the doctor's advice. Aveline Campbell told it Alice who told it me – and thought it not wise, very properly (I must say).

Why make a mystery of your plans to your loving Mama, and then let Lorne announce to me that *you are* going as a *necessity abroad* without asking my opinion which you so often blamed Lenchen for *not* doing, and without asking for my consent, which I shall not give till I feel *certain* that you *can* undertake this journey in a *pecuniary* point of view.

If you *can* go away anywhere else, and not to so hot a climate why rush abroad (whence you returned only in June) and again incur that great expense of apartments (*not* very fitting for a Princess of England) and waste your money which you want so much for that expensive house in London and for your future home in Scotland?

Reflect well on all this and let me be quite assured that you cannot do *quite as well* in England in some *dry* and *not* hot place, for you know that

that never does you *real good* and you have had *only that, this* year. *Beware* of incurring debt (as Alice has to a *very* serious extent) for I shall *not* be able to help you – I *cannot* with the help I have been *asked* and maybe *obliged* to give your other sisters. As I give you £2,000 a year I *have* a right to see that the money is not improperly or at least improvidently and unnecessarily spent.

All these observations would have been avoided if you had openly consulted me and it is indeed most *painful* for me to have been treated with so little confidence. *How you* blamed Lenchen for want of the same, and yet she and Christian would never have dreamt of going abroad without asking my opinion and consent. There might be many reasons rendering it undesirable, and I think it will have a very bad effect as it is. People will think you are very ill, and I must say that nothing but serious illness would justify your going abroad again so soon.

In the summer some German baths would be far more efficacious.

(506)

PRINCE LEOPOLD TO PRINCESS LOUISE BALMORAL, 15 NOVEMBER 1871

My dearest Loo, Many thanks for the charming bézique box which I received from you this morning, it is very pretty indeed and will be of great use to me, as my old one is worn out.

Is it true that you are going abroad this winter? I hope not as then I shall see nothing of you this winter at all, however that does not matter if it is necessary for your health that you should go.

Mama won't go away from this dreadful place till the 23rd or 24th, isn't it tiresome?

I am getting on all right, and walk a little with two sticks.

(507)

THE QUEEN TO PRINCESS LOUISE BALMORAL, 15 NOVEMBER 1871

Another argument about going abroad:

Your dear long letter of yesterday reached me this morning and I have been much relieved by it and pleased by the very *proper tone* of it, as alas! from Bertie, Vicky and Lenchen (*not* from Alice) I am accustomed as you know too well, to the very reverse.

I *cannot* deny that I *regret* in *every way* the physician's decision and cannot help fearing that Mr. Hewitt (who is no doubt very clever but knows *nothing* whatever of the constitution of yourself and your family) has suggested this, for the Duke tells me he told him so in a letter received today. *If* it is to *cure* your knee – *right* and *well*, I shall *not* object – but my fear is that it will weaken you (who require bracing as much as all of us) and make you only *more* sensitive for the future, which as your home is in the North, would be a terrible misfortune.

You misunderstood what I said about your sisters. I meant that for this journey or repeated journeys I could give you no help as I am obliged to help the others – and I wished to warn you well before you incurred *more* expenses – as Alice has got herself *sadly* in to debt. This you must keep to yourself. You are quite wrong if you think Alice set me against you – and altogether you know perfectly well, as I have so often told you (when your sisters thought the same) I am *not set* against people or ever *made* to believe things which I have not *good reason* to believe. No, she only casually mentioned what Aveline had said and I replied I was *quite* sure it could not be true. We both thought a German bath next summer would be so much better.

As for Alice's being very sly and scheming as to obtaining her own objects – I am alas! too well aware of that and have therefore resisted her most vehement attempts to remain here all winter which she has been moving heaven and earth to effect but which has been stopped....

Of course I am most anxious to see you again – but not on any account will I have a *large* family party together. It would tire me far too much. I am still *very* easily tired ... and even 6 people at dinner *quite* upsets me.

Your simple fare and economical arrangements are in every way good, wholesome and wisest. I am very glad that the Scotch cook and housekeeper answer so well....

(508)

PRINCE LEOPOLD TO PRINCESS LOUISE BALMORAL, 22 NOVEMBER 1871

The Prince of Wales's illness, typhoid, struck on 21 November.

Dearest Louise, I write on Mamma's behalf, she desires me to ask you to come down to Windsor next Monday or Tuesday as you are, of course, not going to Sandringham now. Mamma wishes me to thank you for your last letter and to say she does not write herself as she is writing to Sandringham. I am so very sorry for Bertie, it is most unlucky, I think *one* of us is doomed always to be laid up.

A thousand thanks for the book of Acrostics, it is capital. I hear Mamma has asked you to stay Xmas with us, I do *so* hope it will be practicable, for otherwise it will be horribly dull.

(509)

THE PRINCESS OF WALES TO PRINCESS LOUISE
SANDRINGHAM, 23 NOVEMBER 1871

My darling Louise, Many thanks for your dear kind little letter in the midst of my grief – You will easily understand my grief and anxiety about my own darling Bertie!! But thank God he is going on as well as can be expected and although the night was not at all very good, as the poor darling suffered a great deal from his head, he seems certainly easier today and has been changed to another bed which he seems to like better.

We have *nice* Dr. Gull here whom he likes and in whom we have the *greatest confidence.* My dear little Lou you know that I should have liked to have you here with me now, also for my darling Bertie's sake, but at present at least dear Alice *remains* whom he seems to like to see about him too, and therefore it would not be wise if he was to see anyone else *now*, as the doctors are very strict about it – but I hope a little later when he is getting better and when Alice is gone that you will come for a little, which I am sure he would like very much!

I am sitting near his bedside while writing as he seems to like to see me about him – to me it seems like a bad dream having my own darling laid up – I wished it was me instead – I can't *bear* to see him suffering so, how willingly I would change with him! God grant that he may SOON *get over it*!!

(510)

THE QUEEN TO PRINCESS LOUISE
SANDRINGHAM, 29 NOVEMBER 1871

Dear Bertie is very ill still; Dr. Gull says he is rather more anxious tonight, as the breathing is more rapid and the pulse and temperature higher – but he hardly speaks; he dozes and the fearful delirium seems past. Poor dear Alix and Alice both came down to meet me. She [Alix] was upset and looks thin and wretched but calm. She is *very* deaf just now.... I am well but tired and *shaky*.

(511)

THE PRINCESS OF WALES TO PRINCESS LOUISE
SANDRINGHAM, 29 NOVEMBER 1871

I knew that your dear loving heart would be with us at this dreadful time of anxiety and misery – A thousand thanks for your kind little letter just received. How gladly would I have welcomed you here darling Lou, but I am sure you will understand Alice being here now and as NO ONE is allowed to go near my darling it was better to wait till later when he is sure to wish to have you near him to cheer him!! Pray don't think me *very* unkind and unfeeling in this, but his welfare must be our first thought, and it was the doctor's wish to keep everybody from him at present. I have explained everything to dear Leo who I hope has told you all, so will not repeat it all, but I only hope and trust darling Lou you don't misunderstand me, nor think that I, wretch, am trying to keep you away from your beloved brother whose life indeed has been in such great danger!

Oh! darling Louise no words of mine can EVER fully express to you how fearful and MISERABLE these days of AGONY have been to me, indeed the three *last* days were a fearful time of *torture* to me, as he was so VERY VERY bad, my darling husband. The fever was so high and he was perfectly delirious, at times he did not even know me, and the day before yesterday, I was hardly allowed to nurse him or go to him at all, which was TOO AWFUL!! He called me 'his good boy' and when once I told him that I was his little wife he said 'that *was* once but is *no more* you have broken your vows!' as he thinks occasionally I have left him altogether. It is *dreadful* to listen to all he says, but God be thanked today he is much more himself and only occasionally delirious.

It is such a blessing that he continues to take his food so well as that alone can save my own darling now!

(512)

THE QUEEN TO PRINCESS LOUISE
WINDSOR CASTLE, 5 DECEMBER 1871

Jenner's report:
You will have received Sir William's last telegram. I have also had a second letter from Sir William dated today, in which he speaks of this having been the best night, but the respirations are still 32, the temperature 102 2/5ths and the breathing retains its peculiarity. The weakness Sir William writes is not very great for the period of the disease, as he can still turn and hold the feeding glass with both hands.

(513)

TELEGRAM FROM PRINCESS ALICE TO PRINCESS LOUISE
SANDRINGHAM, 8 DECEMBER 1871

I find Bertie worse, his state as grave as possible.

(514)

THE QUEEN TO LORD LORNE
SANDRINGHAM, 14 DECEMBER 1871

The tide turns on the 'fatal' 14 December, the date of Prince Albert's death.
Dearest Lorne, I must write you a line to say I have left much for you in this your first separation and that dear Louise is well, and behaving as I would indeed wish her to do – very calm, most unselfish and discreet. Everyone sees and feels this and it is a great comfort to me to have her here.

Though the dreadful alarm of yesterday and of Sunday already is *less*, the state is STILL MOST precarious and anxious. We all dreaded today but *till now* this saddest of anniversaries has been one of the least trying of the many days of cruel anxiety, watching and uncertainty!

He still wanders and the breathing is still bad. . . . The dear Princess of Wales bears up admirably and is most touchingly devoted.

(515)

THE QUEEN TO PRINCESS LOUISE
WINDSOR CASTLE, 19 DECEMBER 1871

A tiff between Louise and Lorne over staying at Sandringham:
I was grieved to see your meeting as I fear there must have been rather painful explanations.

I think darling Child that you were both wrong. You *ought* to have let him come to the Cottage or to Sir William Knollys' for a *night* when dear Bertie was so ill, as he would then have *seen* how impossible it was to remain as there was not room for a mouse and he should have come on Monday. And I think you should perhaps have gone back on Saturday with your brothers. However if you repeat to him that it was a great comfort for me to have you, and that there was *no* room for any one more *in* the house I think he will understand it and not feel annoyed.

I can't pretend to say that *I don't* like *sometimes* to have my daughters *alone* with me for one cannot feel as much at ease with *2* (and especially when one's daughter is only lately married) as with one's own child *alone*. I have often said this to the other sisters. Still there are reasons which make it essential *you* should respect Lorne's wishes and feelings as much as possible – his own position being different to my other sons-in-law.

(516)

SAME TO SAME
WINDSOR CASTLE, 21 DECEMBER 1871

Bertie's slow convalescence:
I am feeling very tired and *very much* shaken and my nights since I returned have become bad – I start and see all before me – and long to know all that is going on at Sandringham. The account today is so far satisfactory. But there seems *no* REAL improvement *yet.* The respirations are still very rapid whenever he speaks or exerts himself. The mind wanders, 'the double consciousness continues'.

(517)

PRINCE LEOPOLD TO PRINCESS LOUISE
21 DECEMBER 1871

My dearest sister, Though always delighted to receive the shortest note from you, I was very sorry about the contents of the dear letter I received from you yesterday. I am very anxious about your poor knee, I fear an injured knee is nearly always incurable, look at mine, and at darling Alix's, but I *do so* hope that it will soon give you no more pain; since the seven months experience I had last year, I firmly believe that no pain can exceed that of neuralgia in the knee.

I am very sorry also about other matters, but I *sincerely trust* that what you say will not be the case, and that you are taking a gloomier view of affairs than necessary.

Thank you so much for the excellent jam and jelly you sent me, Mamma liked hers very much; she does not yet come to any meal, though she has decidedly improved during the last 4 or 5 days. Alice's children have got the whooping-cough, imagine what a nuisance, they caught it from Bertie's chicks. There is a report going that your mother-in-law is about to present the Duke with a 13th – is it true? Presumably not. If it's a joke, I wonder who started it.

(518)

What were the 'other matters' of which Louise took such a gloomy view to Leopold? Possibly the doubtful prospect of a home of their own? Or of a family? Or both?

After a number of satisfactory accounts of the Prince of Wales, an unsatisfactory telegram arrived on Boxing Day 1871: his temperature had reached 101, probably due to trouble in his hip.

THE CROWN PRINCESS OF PRUSSIA TO PRINCESS LOUISE
BERLIN, 26 DECEMBER 1871

After describing the present of a picture done by the same lady artist who 'painted' Louise's table, Vicky continues:
I never 'fancied' you were going to write to me, as you say, only Mama had told me you were going to do so – so I was on the look out for a letter which I should certainly not have been otherwise, as we are not in correspondence, and you dislike writing so much.

... I feel rather low-spirited shut up indoors [she has neuralgia] while everyone else are enjoying themselves. My thoughts are all at Sandringham with dear Bertie, Alix and Alice, also with you all at dear Windsor. The 10 grandchildren (the hopes of 'Esse' [Hesse] and Wales) scampering about the corridor would be a delight to me: – I wonder when there will be a host of small Campbells to keep them company, I hear of none as yet.

(522)

Vicky was never the soul of tact.

THE QUEEN TO PRINCESS LOUISE
SANDRINGHAM, 28 DECEMBER 1871

She refers to another most alarming spasm yesterday.
How much has happened since we parted! I hope you got all my telegrams?

That spasm poor Bertie had at 5 yesterday morning was most alarming, and they feared at the time he *was gone*. Mr. Thomas told me so. And this naturally made both doctors anxious I should come.... His poor hip hurts him dreadfully, but it is rather better this morning and the night has been passed without any severe spasm. But there is mischief in the hip ... and one *cannot* tell *what it might lead to*. But dear Alix does not know this, and they think for dear Bertie's sake it is better she should not be unnecessarily alarmed – so don't talk about this.

(523)

SAME TO SAME
SANDRINGHAM, 29 DECEMBER 1871

I regret much your going abroad altogether but think if you are to go that it is better you should not delay it longer. *Pray* let me know your route and also just send me a telegram announcing your arrival at Calais, Paris, Cannes and Menton. I feel very much your going so far away – after all the trouble we have gone through.

Dear Bertie is quite himself except *occasionally*. I was with him twice yesterday and he spoke about everything *quite rationally*. I helped to arrange his pillows. He was very feverish yesterday evening – this morning *less*, and in less pain but I *think* him *hardly* as clear or at least as acute as yesterday, and I observe a sort of pant or gasp (*very slight*) while he speaks which he had *not* last time we were here – which shows still oppression of the chest and something wrong there. The leg or rather more hip, has been carefully examined and nothing can be found – which *I* like less than if there *was* a cause for all this peculiar state. There were two spasms in the night but not very severe ones. The nurses looked tired and worn....

God bless you. Let me now wish you and dear Lorne a very happy year and *all* possible happiness to you! This has been a very eventful year to you....

(524)

SAME TO SAME
WINDSOR CASTLE, 6 JANUARY 1872

The Queen expresses a wish that Louise would let her have a word about the New Year to our good faithful friend Brown. He is more like one of the family in fact from being so constantly with me....

She feels that a friendly word from afar about his care of the Queen would gratify

the kind soul who has truly anxiously watched over and nursed me and shared our sorrow and anxiety about dear Bertie. It is when children leave the Home that those who have known them from their Childhood and who serve their Parents (alas only one Parent) devotedly feel *so* much marks of kindness and recognition and the absence of the same.

(526)

SAME TO SAME
OSBORNE, 26 JANUARY 1872

Louise and children: she had now been married nearly one year.
I am so sorry you have headaches. Be careful in your diet and in *not* omitting aperient medicines....

The Queen goes on to criticize Lenchen and Louise for being too active:

You younger sisters arc always *moving* and sightseeing, and *I* think that this is why you are so far less strong than the elder ones, who besides have always kept such early hours. Alice is not a bit ill.

The Queen then answers points in Louise's letter:

In the 1st place, you misunderstand me if you think I wish you *never* to have any children; I fully believe that in a case like yours – and I dare say in *most* – to have *none* would be melancholy in one's old age – and if one has a son as devoted to his father (and a father so kind almost too indulgent to his children) then it is a great blessing. But *think* of the reverse. ANY, ANY thing is preferable to have all destroyed by wicked children – and *how* far more (in the higher classes) *this* latter position is *far* the most common. And you will both admit that any thing is better than that.

In the case of daughters, their interests are inevitably different from their home interests and the Queen feels this fearfully with 'my own enormous family'. She thinks that

in a *royal* family especially *it is a very great misfortune*.... In the *lower* classes the position is in fact *reversed* and makes the position far more *natural*. The *children* have to work for their bread and how constantly and beautifully do they support their aged Parents, who had supported them by the sweat of their brow?... I am sure if you *reflect* you will be struck by this observation.

Why did you not tell me of the little Duchess's [of Argyll] indiscreet questions? I feel so pained at the want of confidence this shows; though I dare say it was merely as you forgot it. This is another thing I never could do to a daughter even but to a daughter-in-law – it is really most indelicate. This again is a practice peculiar to the *refined* higher classes.

(527)

THE PRINCESS OF WALES TO PRINCESS LOUISE SANDRINGHAM, 7 FEBRUARY 1872

After Bertie's illness:

Darling Louise ... You can hardly think *HOW* happy I am now every thing seems bright and beautiful around me, which only so short time ago threatened to become dark for ever!! – Oh! dearest Louise you know WHAT I suffered, and saw my utter despair and misery – you would hardly *know* me now in my happiness. We are *never* apart, and are now enjoying our *second* '*Honey Moon*'.

She thanks Louise for her lovely Christmas presents:

that sweet cross, I wear so often, and the dear prayer book with the very appropriate verses written on the title page gave me also the *greatest* pleasure!

(528)

THE QUEEN TO PRINCESS LOUISE
OSBORNE, 16 FEBRUARY 1872

The death of Feodore, the Queen's niece, and Alice's views:
What a blessing true resignation and faith are! God only knows what I should have done had it not been for that. It is the want of that which has spoilt the characters of Vicky and Alice but especially the latter.

Painful and dreadful as it is to me, it will be my *duty* to warn you *all* (especially Affie and Vicky who are her devoted admirers) against *her,* for she has behaved so badly and has written so ungratefully and shamefully to me that I feel she is *really very* dangerous. You, Lenchen and Baby (for she saw and heard enough) are *quite* safe, but the two younger brothers *must* be kept out of her *web.* Bertie has had his eyes opened and is greatly shocked. Alix sees all. Can you wonder if I speak of the terrible troubles, trials and annoyances of a large Royal family?...

(531)

Alice's views were considered dangerously 'modern', ranging from an interest in anatomy to a study of books like Renan's Life of Jesus. *She criticized her mother for being a reluctant hostess.*

PRINCE LEOPOLD TO PRINCESS LOUISE
OSBORNE, 21 FEBRUARY 1872

Birth of an Argyll heir to Louise's sister-in-law:
My dearest Lou, ... In the first place let me congratulate you on Janey Campbell's safe confinement, and on the birth of the possible future (*I hope not*) Duke; I suppose *you* and *Lorne* would have been better pleased had it been a *girl.*

Mamma holds a drawing-room on the 12th of March, and a levée on the 14th, and she hopes you will be back by that time to help her, as otherwise Beatrice would have to finish the drawing-room, which would be somewhat ludicrous. We go to Baden on Monday the 25th of March so we shall be abroad during Easter; but Mamma considers this a mighty secret, so don't mention it to her when you write. Bertie will go, as soon after the St. Paul's business [the Thanksgiving Service on 27 February for his recovery] as possible to Rome, by way of Paris, Marseilles, Nice etc., so you will see him but he says he will *never* forgive you if you *breathe a syllable* of it to any mortal soul save of course your worthy spouse.

Your excellent father-in-law made the other night a most choleric, and I think injudicious speech in the House about that hateful Collier business, everybody on every side is abusing him for it, it is most unfortunate; to call the Lord Chief Justice of England's letter 'claptrap rubbish' *in* the House of Lords, is most indecorous in my humble opinion.

Leopold ends with news about the horrible hunting accident that befell little Lady Charles Ker, who was thrown from her horse, kicked on the ear and had her skull cracked from side to side:

It is said that one ear was torn off, and that Prescott Hewett sewed it on again. Bertie's leg is yet far from well, and I think he looks *much aged*, the top of his head is quite bald – Alix is looking very well, and more *lovely*, I might say *angelic*, than ever; she is so dear and kind; I have played lots of duets with her on the piano.

(532)

SAME TO SAME
BALMORAL, 21 MAY 1872

The trials of Balmoral:
I have received the charming photos which you and Lorne sent me, and I am very much obliged both to you and to him for sending me so many, I like them all, the ones of Lorne the least, though; they do not do him justice in my opinion.

My knee is much better and today for the first time I am sitting in my wheeling chair writing. Ever since our arrival here it has rained, hailed and snowed *unceasingly*; on Sunday I went out for the first time, and today already Mamma has insisted upon my going out twice-a-day, consequently I obeyed orders, and both times got caught in the rain. Mamma has been as unkind and disagreeable as she *possibly can be* since she has been here; has been and is in and out of my room all day, without giving me ever warning.

(535)

THE QUEEN TO PRINCESS LOUISE
WINDSOR CASTLE, 19 JUNE 1872

A family row over Francis Knollys:
My darling Loosy, For three dear letters have I to thank you.... How grieved I am at dear Lorne's illness and weakness. He will never be fit for the House of Commons. He *must* not try, unless he feels quite strong.

The Queen goes on to denounce the abominable mischief and malice of Alice. Francis Knollys was Bertie's Private Secretary, raised to the peerage in 1902.

May not Affie also have made mischief? You may be sure *I* will stand by poor good Loosy, but *Alice* must be shown up to *all* the family. Long before this I meant to write to Vicky even to warn her, and I think you should let me speak to Leopold about it, for *he* dislikes F. Knollys, for his being a nonentity which was my objection to him, and I shall always maintain this; and he (Leo) ought to be warned against Alice. Does Lenchen know anything about it?

(537)

It would appear that Princess Alice had spread a story that Princess Louise had criticized Francis Knollys as an unsuitable companion for the Prince of Wales, while Princess Louise maintained that it was Princess Alice herself who had criticized Knollys.

PRINCESS LOUISE TO THE QUEEN
CALVERLEY HOTEL, TUNBRIDGE WELLS, 20 JUNE 1872

Death of Dr McLeod, the family's favourite 'Meenister':

My dearest Mama, The letters you were so good as to let us read about our dear friend Dr. McLeod have affected us both much; his own letter to Lady Ely is very very touching and quite a bit of his dear noble minded self. It is too sad to think that he is taken from amongst us. The last time I saw him was when he christened Archie's [Campbell] and Janey's child, his words were very few but so beautifully said, no one else could do it like him. He was like a loving Father, with a large heart ready to help everyone however old, young, rich or poor. Lorne loved him much and looked up to him. Your dutiful child, Louise.

(D43/21)

THE QUEEN TO PRINCESS LOUISE
FROGMORE, 26 JUNE 1872

The continuing row about Francis Knollys:

Darling Child ... Both (Bertie and Alix) spoke to me about what has passed about you. *I stood by you*, and Bertie was very kind and affectionate and I think Alix will be so too. But *she IS* to blame, though not intentionally so, by repeating the story – and Alice is a real *Devil* in the family. It is terrible and makes it *very trying*. Ask Jane C[hurchill] – to tell you what passed.

(538)

Three days later Robert Collins, Leopold's tutor, was telling Henry Ponsonby that 'he believed the row about Francis Knollys had been allowed to drop'.

PRINCE LEOPOLD TO PRINCESS LOUISE
BALMORAL, 22 AUGUST 1872

I suppose you have heard that we are going to Dunrobin on the 5th or 6th, I wish it were to Inverary [*sic*] instead. So Lenchen has at last done her duty, and I am so sorry that she is suffering so much from neuralgia. Christian regretted that it wasn't a *boy*, what an old fool!

I fear I must end now, do write to me, and send a good long letter too. When are Lorne and his officers going to offer me the honorary Colonelcy he spoke of?

Now goodbye, dearest, with love to Lorne, your devoted brother Leopold. Bertie has got some divine photos of Janie Campbell, taken in the Isle of Man, I think, I wish you could get me one.

(539)

Lord Archie Campbell's marriage to the striking and artistic Janey Callender was a stormy one. She staged amateur theatricals with the help of the famous actress Ellen Terry and Ellen's lover Edward Godwin, who painted the scenery. Through Janey, Louise plunged into Bohemian circles. Janey also attracted the Prince of Wales, although she never became another 'Lillie Langtry' to him.

THE QUEEN TO PRINCESS LOUISE
BALMORAL, 28 SEPTEMBER 1872

A lament for the death of Princess Feodore, the Queen's half-sister and Louise's aunt, the last person that Victoria could confide in freely and openly; 'she lived so much out of the world that nobody was jealous or suspicious of her'.

How willingly would I have *kept* you *always near* me but you would not and *therefore* I felt *you too* could no longer be what you had been.

The Queen feels that none of the children showed the right feeling, although Bertie wrote kindly.

But *still, HE* wanted to go out *hunting the very next* day! . . . He can't live without amusement and excitement! Now there is my poor good Brown, who knew Aunt very little tho' he felt her kind friendliness. . . . But he WOULD not hear of going out shooting. . . . If only dear Lorne by and by would let you come and stay alone with me a little and Christian do the same with Lenchen, it would be a great comfort. . . .

(546)

PRINCE LEOPOLD TO PRINCESS LOUISE
BALMORAL, 6 NOVEMBER 1872

I would have written to you sooner, but I really have had nothing to say. I continue to improve in health, I walk always up and down stairs, and I walk a good deal also out of doors. I believe we are going away from this charming place on the 21st, and I expect to go to Oxford on the 25th, and I trust by that time to be *all right* on my pins.

What do you say to Eliot Yorke's [a member of the court] marriage with Sir Anthony de Rothschild's daughter? Bertie wrote to me the other day to tell me about it, and I am very pleased at it, I suppose you have heard of it already? Mamma is in a great rage with Lorne just now on account of the letter he wrote to her, but I don't suppose it will last, you yourself are in great favour....

Lady Erroll, the future Lady-in-Waiting, is here. She is about the ugliest woman I have ever seen, of course Mamma is tremendously taken up with her. The weather is most awful daily wind and rain, I think if it continues, we shall be able to float over the hills to Inverary [*sic*] and pay you a visit there.

(548)

THE PRINCE OF WALES TO PRINCESS LOUISE
SANDRINGHAM, 12 NOVEMBER 1872

... I am sorry to hear that that brute J. B. [John Brown] made himself disagreeable during your stay at Balmoral. I wish you would let me know what he did.

(549)

Perhaps Louise had declined to write a letter praising Brown's virtues, as the Queen had earlier requested.

PRINCE LEOPOLD TO PRINCESS LOUISE
WYKEHAM HOUSE, OXFORD, 2 DECEMBER 1872

Prince Leopold had just gone up to Oxford University.

Darling Loo, It is a long time since I last wrote to you, and I have got a great deal to tell you. First of all I must thank you very much for your two dear letters, and for the engravings, which I shall have re-mounted at a charming print seller's shop here, Ryman by name, who sells the most beautiful engravings.

Leopold goes on to rejoice in the beauties and freedom of his new house, situated half a mile from Christ Church. It would be

almost in the country were it not for the immense number of villas which have sprung up all round it, where most of the professors and 'coaches' live.... My housekeeper and cook, Mrs. Scott, is a very nice, good-looking, rather fat woman of about thirty-two or thereabouts, with a faultless pronunciation, and cooks (in my humble opinion) quite as well as Franceatelli or Jungbluth, she is also a very good-tempered woman, and makes no difficulties, which in my eyes makes up for a multitude of defects (if she had any). Now haven't I described a model?...

On Wednesday morning I went to the Deanery, Christchurch [*sic*], and there went through the ceremony of 'matriculation'. In the evening the Vice-Chancellor, Dean of Christchurch [Dean Liddell], and Dr. Acland dined with me. On Thursday I went to my first lecture, which was one delivered by Professor Ruskin on the art of engraving, it was *most* interesting.

Leopold then describes the professors he has met and the lectures he has been to, including Professor Rolleston on physics, Professor Montague Burrows on history and Professor Clifton on the human eye and another by Ruskin on art.

In the afternoon I went to the Deanery and heard the charming Miss Liddells play and sing, they are very pretty indeed, and very nice.

On Sunday he went to the University sermon at St Mary's.

Dr Pusey preached for AN HOUR AND TWENTY MINUTES, I assure you, not a minute less, I never was so tired in my life; it was all about the Athanasian Creed. In the afternoon I took Sahl [German tutor] a walk all round Christchurch Meadows which are quite under water....

He has had many professors to dine and one morning worked at chemistry in the Christ Church laboratory. On the afternoon of that day,

I went to a most interesting lecture delivered by Mr. Chandler on 'the transmission of genius etc., from father to son', which consisted mainly in proving that most great men had stupid parents and stupid children....

Tonight Ruskin comes to dine alone with Mr. Collins and myself, as he does not like going out to dinner parties....

Show this letter to Lorne, it may interest him.

(550)

It might well have interested Lorne, since Ruskin was a famous man by then and Slade Professor of Art. One of the very pretty and nice Miss Liddells was the 'Alice' of the Rev. Charles Dodgson's ('Lewis Carroll') classic.

SAME TO SAME
WINDSOR CASTLE, 16 DECEMBER 1872

I was very sorry to leave Oxford of course, though most people had gone down, but I shall look back on the short time which I spent there, as having been the first time when I was really happy, and knew what it was to be happy; I shall be very much annoyed if I can't get back there by the beginning of next term (January 24th), but I foresee that I shall have a hard fight about it.

As to the Volunteer business, I think Lorne had better send me a letter setting forth that he and the other officers of the Corps desire me to become their Honorary Colonel, and explaining that it is purely a honorary affair, and he must write it so that I can show it to Mamma, it will be best if he sends it to me *just after New Year*; and perhaps you might at the same time write to Mamma, and mention it to her, and say that it would give great pleasure to you and Lorne, and explain that it is *purely honorary*.

My Xmas present for you is (as you desired) one of Carlyle's works, his 'French Revolution'; and if you will let me I will gradually give you *all* his works....

(552)

THE QUEEN TO PRINCESS LOUISE
OSBORNE, 25 DECEMBER 1872

Alice's two little boys have been very ill with sort of diphtheria attacks. ... I *hope* you will write oftener than once in 10 days in future.

(557)

PRINCE LEOPOLD TO PRINCESS LOUISE
OSBORNE, 27 DECEMBER 1872

Darling Loo, Many many thanks for your and Lorne's good wishes and for your present. I assure you I am most *delighted* with the slippers, they are the most comfortable ones I have *ever worn*; and as you know, red and grey is my favourite combination of colours; I was also told that you made every bit of them yourself, which makes me value them doubly, and you can't know what pleasure you have given me; for I felt so unhappy missing you, this was the *first* Christmas since 1861 which we have not spent together, and I can't tell you how I missed you and *do* still miss you.... I send you and Lorne my best wishes for the New Year, you *know* what I wish for you!

(558)

The wish for a child?

PRINCESS LOUISE TO THE QUEEN INVERARAY, 9 JANUARY 1873

Death of the Emperor Napoleon III and a Tennyson poem:
Dearest Mamma, How dreadfully sad about the poor Emperor. What agonies he must have suffered. I must confess that I did hope he would live to return to France if only for a short time. What a distressing end. And the Times wrote such heartless articles on him, all these days. The poor Boy [his son, the Prince Imperial] what will become of him? Poor Empress she seems so young to have gone through so much, how very wretched she must be now, I do feel so for her, what a blessing she has that boy now. Where do you think the Emperor will be laid?

Many thanks for your letter received yesterday and for Tennyson's poem. As you said you did not wish it spoken about or shown, I thought it was prudent *not* to send it to the Duke and Duchess [of Argyll] as they *never can* keep anything to themselves, if even they have promised not to say anything they always do to everybody they meet. You will be so taken up with the poor Emperor's death that I will not write more now. *Please* do *not forget* to mention my name in any letter or telegram you may be sending to the unhappy Empress. Ever your dutiful affectionate child Louise. I hope you are well.

(J84/15)

At one time there was an idea that Louise might marry 'the Boy'. The unfortunate Empress Eugénie was to 'have' her son for only another six years. He was speared to death in the Zulu War, 1879.

LORD LORNE TO THE QUEEN INVERARAY, 11 FEBRUARY 1873

The Tory victory; Lorne is writing as a – Liberal!
Madam and dear Mama, It is very good of you to so kindly say you are glad my election has gone by quietly. A contest would have been a trouble, as I should have had to make speeches everywhere over a county 150 miles long by 30 or 40 broad, and to have visited the Islands – not an easy task in winter – besides the incurring of a very great expense.

I must say I am very glad that the Tory Party will have a good majority. What I much feared was, that the two great parties would be very evenly balanced and that the 'Home Rulers' would occupy a commanding position, by being able to turn the scale either way, and thus to make each bid for their support. This danger is now I trust greatly lessened. I should not have said so much, had you not asked Louise what I thought of the election?

I think it is a good thing too that the country should have plenty of time to consider before it makes up its mind to wish for any further changes, as such things are always best done if well considered beforehand, and there is no denying we have done much during the last five years. What is most encouraging is the good class of representative the people are electing under the free action of secret voting....

I am looking forward very much to kissing your dear hand again. I am, Ever with the greatest love, Your dutiful and loving son, Lorne.

(1789)

As members of a family of great landlords, Lorne and his father, the Duke of Argyll, were against Home Rule for Ireland, on which issue they eventually left the Liberal Party.

PRINCE LEOPOLD TO PRINCESS LOUISE
OXFORD, 27 FEBRUARY 1873

I have had a *screaming* row with Mamma, last week, but it is now patched up again, only Mamma will now see that I am not going to submit to all her little bullyings.

... Tomorrow afternoon I go up to town to go to the play in the evening with Baby (unless the Duchess of Inverness dies before, which God forfend!) We are going to Covent Garden Theatre to see a play called 'Babil and Bijou', which is very pretty, but somewhat indecent (so saith report at least), I believe the dresses of some of the fair females are not very extensive and somewhat transparent; I can't understand how they let Baby go to such a thing, however it is not *my* business, and old Car knows best.

Lady Caroline Barrington ('Car') had been the royal children's much loved governess.

I dare say you have seen in the papers that Captain Buller, who married Mrs. Kingscote, (you know) has got 'a son and heir *prematurely*'. It is indeed *very premature* but why put it in the papers, he must have lost all sense of shame or self-respect.

I heard from Arthur today, he seems to be as happy as the day is long; but I don't envy him as I am very happy here; but the hateful prospect of going in May to Scotland, and then losing the whole of the Summer Term at Oxford, makes me rather unhappy.... Now, dear, I shall shut up, with love to Lorne, ever your devoted brother Leopold.

(564)

PRINCESS LOUISE TO THE QUEEN 10 MAY 1873

A blue leatherbound, fat volume, tooled in gold, entitled 'Memoranda Balmoral No. 3. Stalking, shooting etc. Confidential family papers'. Part of the 'etc.' includes a letter from Princess Louise, recommending a housekeeper to her mother.

Dearest Mama, I have heard of a housekeeper that I think will suit you for Balmoral. Her name is Mrs. MacHardy she is born in Aberdeenshire, is not fine or grand, her age is 50, she is very quick, and active, she has been *9 years* in her last place with Mr. and Mrs. Aston 1 Princes Gate she is I am told a highly respectable and trustworthy person. She is quick at her needle. I am to see her on Monday morning, and shall tell you what I think of her looks when I see you.

If you thought it best Sir Thomas [Biddulph] could write to Mrs. Aston to ask himself for this woman's character. I have heard of her from a lady who is very particular and would not have recommended her unless she thought very highly of her.

(Add. Q2/114)

Finding servants was another of Louise's jobs.

THE QUEEN TO PRINCESS LOUISE BALMORAL, 19 MAY 1873

A note on Prince Alfred:

Affie is a *strange* person and I fear will always remain so. He was not quite satisfied with some passages in my letter to the Empress and so I have had to write it all over again!!

(567)

The Empress of Russia was mother of Affie's future wife, Marie.

PRINCESS LOUISE TO THE QUEEN 26 JUNE 1873

A royal visit:

Dearest Mama, Many thanks for your letter. All went off well yesterday. The Shah seemed much pleased at the Ball. The reel he was *delighted* with, the waltzes he said made his head turn to look at. Count Buist's thin pink stilk stockings amused him much. He said 'presque nue' and laughed a great deal. He was in fact most amusing, and we could not help laughing all of us princesses. The poor Grand Duke [the Tsarevitch, future Tsar Alexander III] *hates* Balls and was very unhappy at being dragged to so many, and point blank refuses to go to any more: I am so sorry for him. Minny his wife [the Grand Duchess, sister of Princess Alexandra], seems to like going out as much as Alix does.

The Bazaar went off very well. I will send the things I got for you tomorrow. There were not many pretty things....

(Q18/41)

THE QUEEN TO PRINCESS LOUISE
OSBORNE, 12 JULY 1873

Affie's engagement to the Grand Duchess Marie, daughter of the Russian Emperor: You know so well what I think that I need not say that I can rejoice as if it was a match I much wished for, and I see many difficulties. Still as *she* and *he* were both determined we parents have done I believe right in giving way. Anyhow, as she is said to be so amiable and good and there is *no* legal difficulty I could not refuse my sanction. In Affie's telegram he says 'Am very happy', more I don't know, though I may hear tomorrow. I had a letter from Alice saying it would be, but I did *not* expect this very rapid dénouement! God grant it may have a good effect on *his* character which would be a blessing! If *that* has not – nothing will.

(568)

SAME TO SAME
OSBORNE, 31 JULY 1873

The Queen grieves when Louise is away
... without a Home of your own. What makes *me* even sadder, is to feel Loosy belongs to another and *not to me*, and that when I go to your room even, I never find you alone! I did not go to the door and see you go as I thought it would be sadder still for us both.

(569)

The Duke of Argyll's offer of Macharioch was unsuitable, and their house in Grosvenor Square, rented from Lorne's uncle the Duke of Westminster, was much too expensive for them.

PRINCE ARTHUR TO PRINCE LEOPOLD
TROUVILLE, 19 AUGUST 1873

This is the enclosure to the following letter:
For fear that any absurd rumours may reach Mamma of what might nearly have been an unpleasant accident to Lane and myself I write you the particulars and will ask you kindly to tell Mamma about it.

We were all four of us out bathing this morning on the sands where there were lots of people bathing. We swam about for some time enjoying ourselves so much that we did not observe that there was a strong tide running, which was carrying us away from the shore. Of course when we began to swim back to the shore, which Lane and I did not do till the others had nearly reached it, we found it no easy work, and very soon got pretty well blown. A lot of Frenchmen, who as you know get very easily excited on the least provocation, made a great 'hullabuloo' said we were going to be drowned, and rushed out to us with ropes and lifebelts. I don't deny that we were more pleased than otherwise to be towed in, instead of having to swim the whole way. 'Signed' Arthur.

(572)

Lieutenant Ronald Bertram Lane (later Major-General Sir) was a friend of the Prince in the Rifle Brigade and accompanied him on other journeys. He died in 1937.

THE QUEEN TO PRINCESS LOUISE
BALMORAL, 23 AUGUST 1873

She sends her daughter an extract from a letter from Arthur to Leopold.

He has been *most* foolish as indeed he is.... But I was *not much startled*, as General Ponsonby fortunately gave the telegram [about Arthur's accident] ... to Brown (who is always the happy person to have the agreeable task of breaking startling or painful news to me) and he gave it me saying 'General P. thinks it is *not* true.' So seeing he [Arthur] was quite safe, I at first thought but little of it, and only by degrees began to think there must be some foundation for it. But I thought of *you* my good Child and *you* thought of *me*.

(571)

PRINCE LEOPOLD TO PRINCESS LOUISE
BALMORAL, 5 OCTOBER 1873

A Campbell engagement:

I was much astonished at the news you gave me, however, if it is an event which will give pleasure to the family, and particularly to the Duke and Duchess, I am very pleased to hear of it. I presume there is no want of tin? You did not mention the lady's names, pray congratulate Walter [Campbell] from me when it is made public....

The lady's names were Olive Mills, a local cotton-spinner's daughter, so there was plenty of tin, but no other advantages. Louise liked her amusing brother-in-law

Walter and managed to 'sell' the marriage to the doubtful Duke and Duchess; but it proved stormy and eventually broke up.

I would be very much obliged if you would ask him for me *where* he gets his *cheroots*, as I took a fancy to them, please don't forget this.... I am very pleased that dear old Car enjoyed her visit to Inverary [*sic*], but I'm *not astonished*, as everybody *must* be charmed with Inverary [*sic*], *and* with its inhabitants. Pray don't forget to get me the photos of W. and Mary Stewart.

(581)

THE QUEEN TO PRINCESS LOUISE
GLASSALT SHIEL, LOCH MUICH, 6 NOVEMBER 1873

I answered yesterday a kind letter of the Duke's in which he tells me of poor Evie's [his daughter] not being very well and of Walter's marriage which had appeared 3 days ago in the Scotch papers. He does not seem much pleased and said they did not know the young Lady – nor, said I, did I know Affie's bride! I also told him of my having taken the Sacrament (and he told me you had taken it) last Sunday at Crathie – which you know I had for some time intended to do – as I wished much to do it – besides that I think *all Protestant churches* SHOULD have *inter-communion*; and all DO have excepting the *very exclusive* and alas! *not really Protestant* English church.

(585)

SAME TO SAME
WINDSOR CASTLE, 14 DECEMBER 1873

The anniversary of Prince Albert's death twelve years earlier:
This *dear* and *hallowed* though dreadful day has been as *quietly* passed as it could be with the whole family. But *all* is *very harmonious.*

(591)

PRINCE LEOPOLD TO PRINCESS LOUISE
WINDSOR CASTLE, 18 DECEMBER 1873

Presents:
I returned here on Saturday after having enjoyed my short stay at Oxford very much indeed. I must now ask you about a confirmation present for Beatrice; we have all agreed to give one present together, so as to give a handsome one. We have selected a most lovely bracelet, pendant, and

ear-rings from Phillips', costing £150 – Bertie and Alix meant to give £49, – Affie and Arthur £25 each, I £15 and Alice and Lenchen each £12, and we want you to give also £12, and I was asked to write to you about it. I suppose you are sure to agree to this arrangement but all the same I should like an answer....

I send you for Christmas as usual some more Carlyles, 5 volumes of his 'History of Frederick the Great'; but I fear they will not be quite ready by Christmas, they shall be sent, however, soon after to Inveraray.

How do you like Miss Olive Mills? Is she worthy of Walter? It must be [*rest of letter missing*]

(592)

LORD LORNE TO THE QUEEN
INVERARAY, 19 DECEMBER 1873

Louise's illness:

Madam and dear Mama – The account tonight is favourable. The pain in the throat which is always felt, and is severe when anything is swallowed cannot be expected to diminish much for some time, but there is less inflammation and the strength has been well kept up.

All that is necessary to ensure a pretty quick recovery seems now to be due precaution against any fresh cold being caught. We are keeping the temperature of the room as even as possible, and the weather is not against this, being uniformly mild and open. The doctor lays great stress on constant feeding – day and night.

The nights have not been good, as the discomfort has robbed her of a great deal of sleep. She is now on the sofa, and sends you her very best love, and hopes you will excuse her for not writing, and thanks for your kind enquiries. I am ever your dutiful and loving son Lorne.

(1791)

THE QUEEN TO LORD LORNE
OSBORNE, 21 DECEMBER 1873

How very annoying and provoking that poor Louise should have this horrid throat.... I hope she will not be kept long in bed, for she has never been accustomed to it and would get so weakened by it.... Alfred's marriage is on the 23rd January but they will not be in England before the 5th of March D.V. I wish you both to be at Windsor for the arrival which I mean to make as much of a *State one, as possible*, as I shall [not] be at the marriage [which was to take place in Russia].

(594)

PRINCE LEOPOLD TO PRINCESS LOUISE
OSBORNE, 23 DECEMBER 1873

A sad Christmas for everybody, including the schoolchildren:
I am going over to Southampton in a little while to meet Arthur, Affie comes tomorrow, and goes away again on Friday; Arthur only stays till Monday, the 28th, so that on New Year's Day, we shall be *quite alone*, the smallest family party there has ever been, it is very sad, and I feel that this is not like our ordinary Christmases and New Years. There will be no Christmas Tree for the school children tomorrow, on account of the bad behaviour of all the people here last spring.

(595)

THE QUEEN TO PRINCESS LOUISE
OSBORNE, 25 DECEMBER 1873

It was a very harmonious but not a very *merry* Christmas. Richmond's picture of Alix is *too dreadful*! It is just as it was – so flat and so green and deathlike. I *cannot* hang it up anywhere. It is too dreadful.... Do send me a photo of Walter's young Lady. The Duke writes pleased about her. When is the marriage to be, and where?

(597)

William Blake Richmond was to be one of Louise's artist friends.

SAME TO SAME
OSBORNE, 8 FEBRUARY 1874

The Queen is delighted with the election results: Gladstone defeated and Disraeli victorious.
Darling Loosy, I received your dear little note this morning for which many thanks. I am very glad Lorne has had so satisfactory a reelection! But *what* a *wonderful* and *unexpected* (to a great extent) result these Elections have brought! Did Lorne *expect* this? I thought they would lose, but never that the Conservatives would have a majority which they have not had since '45!!...

(609)

Lorne, of course, was a Liberal and therefore on the losing side!

PRINCE LEOPOLD TO PRINCESS LOUISE UNIVERSITY MUSICAL CLUB, OXFORD 13 FEBRUARY 1874

Artistic taste in dispute:
Dearest Loo, I write to you from this delightful club; at this moment there is a delightful trio being played by some friends of mine ... we are of course *all* amateurs, and *nearly* all of us are undergraduates. We only allow strict and good music.... I am *really* working *hard* this term.

I daresay you heard that Mamma again objected to Richmond's lovely picture of Alix, so she lent it to me to bring here for a while, and two days ago young Richmond came up to Oxford and dined with me, and then I pointed out to him *some* of the things which Mamma would like to have altered, and he was very nice about it, and said he would do what he could; I *could not* say *all* that Mamma wished changed, as if I had done so I would have made a fool of myself, as she wanted to ruin it altogether, and *I* won't lend myself to *that*, she must get *others* to say it if she wants further changes made, but I trust and hope that she will be satisfied with what Richmond *is* going to change. Everybody is leaving the room so I must end in a hurry.

(610)

SAME TO SAME WYKEHAM HOUSE, OXFORD, 15 FEBRUARY 1874

Mrs Josephine Butler, the women's champion:
... Mrs. Butler is staying here and I shall probably meet her to-morrow, you must remember her, by name at least very well; she is by many people considered the most beautiful woman in the world, and she is very clever and a great speaker; but she has done herself a great deal of harm by violently taking up a subject which had better be left alone, by ladies at any rate.

Josephine Butler eventually succeeded in getting the infamous Contagious Diseases Acts of the 1860s regarding prostitutes repealed. She and her family had once lived in Oxford; Louise had supported her in the past.

... I had a letter from Christian [Princess Helena's husband] to-day crowing over me tremendously on account of the elections, what a dreadful majority the Conservatives have got!
The royal family were certainly not monolithic in their political feelings.

(613)

THE QUEEN TO PRINCESS LOUISE
OSBORNE, 16 FEBRUARY 1874

On the election again:

I write this from here, *very sad* to go, for at least I am quiet here and I shall have so much to do; for – though from the overwhelming majority, in all places, and *all* classes of the Conservatives – my course is very clear and simple, it entails trouble and work which I am not feeling very fit for, for I am not feeling strong and am weary. I am *most* anxious that the Government should resign at once, as it is inevitable and as *I could* not receive Affie and Marie [about to return to England after their wedding] with no real Household or Government or in the midst of a Ministerial Crisis.

For the Country to have a good strong Conservative Party is most important for it keeps a *check* on the extreme Liberals. *No* one is more *truly* liberal at heart and in spirit than *I* am, but there must be *limits* to this; the *principles* of the Constitution *must* be maintained, and I must say (as Lord Russell and Lord Halifax said, but please don't mention the latter's name) Mr Gladstone didn't care for these and tried to remove the *Land Marks* of the Constitution, and was a *danger*. Now the Country has declared (for in all *parts* and in all *classes* it was the same) that they WON'T have any more change. For that *perpetual changing* and altering and pulling down is a *very bad* thing. Your father-in-law himself said to me, two or three years ago – 'I think we are going too far!' There must be a limit.

(616)

Gladstone had passed the 'limit' by introducing reforms to 'pacify' Ireland, according to Queen Victoria. She was anxious that his Liberal government should resign after losing the election instead of waiting to meet the House of Commons and being defeated there.

SAME TO SAME
WINDSOR CASTLE, 21 FEBRUARY 1874

Gladstone on his defeat:

I am so tired that I can hardly write, but I wish just to write a few hasty lines to thank you for your dear long letter of the 18th as well as for the one of the 15th. I took leave of Mr Gladstone yesterday; he resigned on Tuesday. He is very sore, but says it is idle to say it is *all* the Publicans; – of course they all went against him – but it is the divisions *in* the [Liberal] *Party*, and the dislike taken to the Government. ... Mr Gladstone talks of retiring and making the Party *feel* what they have done. He says they have no *Cohesion*.

(620)

SAME TO SAME
WINDSOR CASTLE, 6 MARCH 1874

Lorne's rank:
There is a thing which I – and *most* of my *people* [courtiers] think ought to be done – but which I wish not to do *without* your speaking to Lorne. It is that in *my Home* and on State occasions he, *as my son-in-law* (just as well as I let Victor [Leiningen, her nephew] and the Mensdorffs have rank) or just as well as the Lord President and Privy Seal have official rank *whoever they are*, should *go before* anyone but Princes and Ambassadors. It *ought* to be – and I think Lorne should let me do it – just as much as Christian and Louis were made Royal Highness. Now that the other Party [Conservatives] is in, it would be much easier to do. If I *approved* of Lorne *marrying* MY *Daughter* he *ought* to have rank as her Husband. Hoping to hear from you either verbally or by letter about this,

Ever Your devoted Mama VR.

(621)

This was to be a long-standing point of argument. If Lorne were to accept 'rank', he would no longer be able to sit – as a Liberal – in the House of Commons, nor be required to be in London so much. He would also be higher up in processions.

SAME TO SAME
WINDSOR CASTLE, 21 MARCH 1874

My best loving congratulations to you *both* on your wedding day. May God continue to bless you as he has hitherto done! It is a pleasure to see you contented, so sensible and *satisfactory* in every way. It is a comfort to *me* though alas I see so little of you. . . .

To-day's horrid steeple chases which I purposely did *not* go to, had a *dreadful* ending in poor young Lord Rossmore's horse *falling* on him and crushing him so dreadfully (I *fear bursting* of the bladder!!) that he is not likely to recover! How awful – and oh, how shocking and wicked to throw away one's life for nothing but stupid and cruel amusement. The poor Duchess of Roxburghe is very much upset by it. Lord Charles [her son] *rode* and *won*!

(622)

The 4th Baron Rossmore died on 28 March after the accident at the Windsor military steeplechase.

Right: Princess Louise, Marchioness of Lorne, 1871

Below: 'The entry into Ottawa': arrival of the Governor-General's party, 1878, Princess Louise is in the centre

Princess Louise with a group in front of the toboggan slide at Rideau Hall, Ottawa, c. 1880

The Marquess of Lorne and Princess Louise in a group on the verandah at Rideau Hall, Ottawa. Prince George is dressed in white.

Princess Louise, wife of the Governor-General of Canada, photographed in Ottawa

Above: Princess Louise by William Blake Richmond, 1881. Richmond was Slade Professor at Oxford.

Right: Joseph Edgar Boehm. A *Punch* cartoon of February 1882 entitled 'THE HORSE AND HIS MASTER', satirizing Boehm's becoming a member of the Royal Academy. He rides his 'NEW R.A.-BIAN STEED'.

Princess Louise photographed by Vianelli in Venice

As Mary Queen of Scots: Princess Louise in fancy dress, c. 1890

The font in St Mildred's Church, Whippingham, designed by Princess Louise, c. 1860s. The carpet was also designed by her and worked by her, Princess Beatrice and their ladies.

Above left: The bronze figure over the communion table at St Mildred's was designed by Princess Louise in memory of her brother-in-law, Prince Henry of Battenberg. He died of malaria in the Ashanti War, January 1896, aged thirty-eight.

Above: Memorial to the 'Colonial Soldiers' of the Boer War in St Paul's Cathedral by Princess Louise

Left: Statue of Queen Victoria at her Accession, designed by Princess Louise for her mother's Golden Jubilee. It was unveiled by the Queen in 1894.

Princess Louise, Duchess of Argyll (holding the bouquet), opening a hospital in Clapton, accompanied by the Duke, 1913

Princess Louise as a widow, painted by László, after 1914

Above: Members of the royal family at the Cenotaph, 11 November 1925: left to right, Princess Helena Victoria; Duchess of York; Princess Beatrice; Princess Louise, Duchess of Argyll; Queen Mary; Queen Victoria Eugenia of Spain

Left: Princess Louise in old age, c. 1920s–1930s

SAME TO SAME
OSBORNE, 6 APRIL 1874

Louise's new home, Dornden, in Kent and Leopold's coming-of-age:
Many thanks for your little note from your new House which I am so grieved to think is so far from me! I fear that you may be molested by the neighbourhood of Tunbridge Wells, for the papers speak of people going to Rusthall Common to try to see Dornden and to see you at Church!

The Queen goes on to consider another gloomy matter:

To-morrow is poor Leopold's 21st. birthday. Little did we *dare hope* that he would *ever* attain that age and for that we *must* be very thankful! But in other respects you will, I am sure, understand that I *cannot* rejoice at it; for, though of course *fortunately* in *his* case, he will be, by reason of his health, far more restrained from *follies* than other young men who think that when they are 21 they may set *all* good and useful advice at defiance; still it will make my task far more difficult – for *many* will try to make him foolish and unmanageable. As yet he has no allowance from Parliament, and I don't know if that will be proposed soon. We must see. I have appointed Mr Collins his Private Secretary ... and he will not go out into Society of an evening except on rare occasions. You will I know feel as anxious as I do – and so will Lenchen. Others may *not*, and in the family may not *wish* even to help me! The Parents are always the *last* thought of....

(624)

The unhelpful 'others' were mainly the Waleses.

PRINCE LEOPOLD TO PRINCESS LOUISE
BALMORAL, 11 APRIL 1874

Leopold did not approve of the family habit of being late with birthday presents.
I would have answered you sooner to thank you for your kind letter and for the lovely mezzotint (so tastefully mounted and framed), which you sent me for my birthday [7 April]; but as your letter and present only arrived here the day before yesterday (the 9th), and I had such a number (35) of letters to answer which had reached me *on* my birthday I put off writing to you till to-day....The number of letters and presents I received showed me I was not wanting in friends, and it was very pleasant to find that *not one* of my friends had forgotten me on that day.

(625)

THE QUEEN TO PRINCESS LOUISE
OSBORNE, 12 APRIL 1874

Childlessness – the advantages:
I can think of nothing else but the dreadful news of the death of the poor Bagots' daughter in her confinement – and the poor baby too! It is so terribly sad. *No* death is *sadder* than *that*. I hope your dear Mama-in-law will feel that it is *not always* such happiness to have such prospects. *Lorne* I *know will*.

(626)

THE CROWN PRINCESS OF PRUSSIA TO PRINCESS LOUISE
SANDOWN, 7 JULY 1874

An Imperial grievance:
Dearest Louise, Many thanks for your dear letter which I was doubly glad to receive as neither a line nor a telegram nor *any* sign of life from you or Lenchen has reached me since our arrival in England. However I trust we are soon to meet and what a happiness that will be, – it seems so strange to be in England and to have seen *none* of you – and *nobody* I know....

(1712)

THE QUEEN TO PRINCESS LOUISE
BALMORAL, 19 SEPTEMBER 1874

This is one of Victoria's most enthusiastic passages about Louise's sister-in-law Marie, Affie's wife. It also makes plain why Victorian mamas did not reveal the facts of life to their young: they were too grim.
... Affie and dear, good Marie leave us on Thursday (21st.) I shall be relieved when she is safe home, for her enormous size makes one nervous. But I never saw anyone make less fuss about it, or bear it better or be so well – though she is very prudent. She is a most pleasant companion – cheery, always good humoured and yet not noisy and always occupied, and *very quiet* in her tastes. May God carry her *safely* through the *great* trial which awaits her, and which luckily for her she knows nothing of!

(640)

THE CROWN PRINCESS OF PRUSSIA TO PRINCESS LOUISE
POTSDAM, 25 SEPTEMBER 1874

Children:
Darling Louise, It was a great treat, at last to receive a long letter from you! You do not often favour me with one – and I am always so glad to hear from you, as it seems so very sad to be so completely cut off from you when I leave England. You cannot think with *what* pleasure I remember the lovely balmy summer evening when I saw your sweet little country House [Dornden] in its nest of ivy, how picturesque, how inviting it seemed! To me it wanted nothing but a few little fair heads looking out of the windows above, – perhaps I may see that glad sight some day please God, – and if I *don't* I trust I shall see one which is still better, that of my dear sister and her Husband as happy together as they are now ... and each as contented with their lot!

(641)

PRINCE ARTHUR TO PRINCESS LOUISE
BALMORAL, 1 OCTOBER 1874

Prince Leopold:
Poor Leo is going on very slowly and I am afraid making but little progress, his leg is rather better – but it is perfectly powerless and he is obliged to keep it as still as ever. He has put it to the ground several times, but as there was more swelling about four days ago he has had to lay up entirely again. His health is good and he suffers no *pain* but it is a terribly tedious business and I don't know when he will be able to walk again. Leo hopes still to be able to go to Oxford this month but I think it is rather doubtful; however the sooner he gets some change and occupation the better for him.

(642)

PRINCE LEOPOLD TO PRINCESS LOUISE
BALMORAL, 22 OCTOBER 1874

The Oxford beacon:
Darling Loo ... You seem to be having a great number of visitors at Inveraray; with what pleasure do I look back to my delightful stay there last year, when I enjoyed myself so very much! Tomorrow morning I start for Oxford, where I expect to arrive about 4.30 the next morning. I fear the journey will be bitterly cold, I only hope my leg will not be the worse for it; but it is most important that I should go South, *important for my*

health, as the weather here now is something too *fearful* ... nearly *6* months now that I have been ill!! and now I can't keep warm on account of want of exercise.

(645)

THE QUEEN TO PRINCESS LOUISE
GLASSALT SHIEL, LOCH MUICH, 16 NOVEMBER 1874

The Queen on Mr Gladstone and religion:
... Mr Gladstone is a most inexplicable Man! After coming into Office to upset the Protestant Church in Ireland and cajoling and flattering the Catholics, he turns round and abuses them violently and will kindle a fire he will not easily put out. And yet he has *no true* Protestant feeling, for he admires and advocates Ritualism and Sacerdotalism which is the true spirit of Catholicism, and which pervades more or less *all* Episcopalianism ... and it is the *absence* of that in the Scotch which makes me love the Scotch Church so much and find that sympathy and satisfaction in it, which I *never could find* in the *English one*, brought up in it, *dosed* with it, as I was. Pray read what I have said here about Mr Gladstone and the 2 Churches to Lorne and the Duke of Argyll.

(647)

THE CROWN PRINCESS OF PRUSSIA TO PRINCESS LOUISE
NEW PALACE, 21 NOVEMBER 1874

Vicky as always encourages her young sister, but suggests the need for more professionalism in her art.
Darling Louise ... How dear and kind of you to remember the bangles which *delighted* me, and which I have now got on! I think them so pretty and peculiar.

How can you think I could be bored with having more photographs of your sweet little House – which is like a thing in a romance to me, so charming and small and picturesque, so snug and comfortable.

I am so glad you are enjoying your time at Inverary [*sic*], and that you have been drawing. Why do you not attend a class in the Kensington School of Art when you are in London, I do so at Berlin at our little *Gewerbemuseum* [technical museum]: and I think one gets on best by following a *very systematical course*, because it is the technical part in which all amateurs are so defficient.

Don't say my drawings are *good,* indeed dear they are nothing of the kind which often depresses me! But I have learnt a great deal as to how things *ought* to be done, of which I was once quite ignorant. Being able to use one's compass and ruler is also an advantage.

(648)

THE QUEEN TO PRINCESS LOUISE
WINDSOR CASTLE, 27 NOVEMBER 1874

A typically tart account of a family christening – that of the Edinburghs' son: Many thanks for your 2 dear letters of the 19th and the 26th. We have nasty raw, dreary sunless weather, which makes me feel the change from Balmoral and hate the place even more than usual!

The Christening I thought a flat, dull affair (I do like our service so much); the room was so *badly* arranged and *might* have been prettily so – and tho' very large – people did not see as well as they might have done.

The Archbishop made a great mistake (and *when* are there *not* mistakes at Royal Christenings?) and *christened* the Child without waiting *for me* to name it! I was so provoked.

The 'Babe' was in the *old* family Christening dress – worn by you 9 and Bertie's 5 – and was very good and quiet. He is a large, fine child – very fair – and *I* think . . . that he will take after his enormous Russian uncles. Mrs Johnstone [nurse] was in great force and looked very large carrying the Child in all its mantles, in white herself – with white gloves!

Dear Marie looked very pale and dragged; I think the Baby is a greedy boy and too much for her. He is *fed* too, but must be more so. Tell the Duchess of Argyll about 'Johnny' and the Baby.

The heat in *all* the *rooms* downstairs and even in the Green [drawing] room upstairs – on account of the poor Empress [of Russia] – was fearful and I was quite done up – having been *on* the go ever since 9 in the morning till 6.30 when I got back here. The Empress is much more pleasing and better looking than her photographs. She is *very* tall, *very* ladylike and amiable and *très grande-Dame,* with a sad expression and very delicate in appearance.

I went to see her on my arrival and was at once at my ease with her. Then I was with her after the Christening and she sat near me at the luncheon which followed the Christening very shortly – and I went to see her again for about half an hour before I left. I feel so much for her poor thing. The sons are very rough with her, tho' I think they are very fond of her. Marie has had a bad cold herself.

I am sorry your future Piper can't speak Gaelic, though I rather like his being an Aberdeenshire man.

(649)

PRINCE ARTHUR TO PRINCESS LOUISE
29 NOVEMBER 1874

The christening went off very well the other day but I thought the service very dreary; it always is when in a room.

(650)

THE QUEEN TO PRINCESS LOUISE
OSBORNE, 20 DECEMBER 1874

The Prince of Wales:
... Dear Bertie is *not* I think in a satisfactory state – so stout and puffy. *Often* oppressed and his poor leg swells so that he can't walk up hill at all! I think he is anxious about himself.

(653)

SAME TO SAME
OSBORNE, 28 DECEMBER 1874

Prince Leopold:
I am sorry to say that our poor Leopold has a feverish attack – though of a *very mild* kind, sleeping *very well* indeed, taking his food well, being quite himself – cheerful and taking interest in things – unberufen, unberufen, he is *without any anxious* symptoms. But he has had it now since Sunday 20th, and been in bed since the *21st*. It was however only on Saturday that Sir William Jenner ... pronounced it to be *the* FEVER [typhoid]. He is however, unberufen, unberufen, so well that Sir William went up to town today, to return tonight. You shall hear *daily*, after you get this letter as I know how anxious you will be and *how* much you will *feel* for ME. I have told *you* this as I know you would fidget so if you did not [hear]. And I have done so to *no one* else yet but Bertie, asking him not to talk about it. Arthur knows. He left this morning, as they wish Leopold and the house in general to be *as quiet* and *dull as possible*. He has every care and attention and we wish it to be as little talked about as possible. He himself does not know (we think) what it is.

Queen Victoria believed that Leopold's father, Prince Albert, lacked the spirit to fight back when he knew he had 'the FEVER'.

Alas! he contracted it at that unlucky Oxford – where on account of its *lowness* and *unhealthiness* I had such a horror of his going at this time of year!! If he had been with me this *never would have happened*. There was a smell in the house. He was able to have all his presents given him on Christmas Eve. Don't worry or fidget. You shall hear all.

(658)

The Queen recognized the closeness between Leo and Louise.

SAME TO SAME
OSBORNE, 30 DECEMBER 1874

Louise has had face ache.

... I am thankful to see that you are so much better.... Before I say anything else let me wish you *both* a very happy New Year in health and happiness for *many* years to come. May you continue in the path you have so worthily walked in ever since you married to be an *example* to *many many*!... I am sure Lorne made a good nurse and was very glad I *fear* that I could not be there to divide your affection.

(661)

Queen Victoria was the mistress of the sting in the tail.

THE CROWN PRINCESS OF PRUSSIA TO PRINCESS LOUISE
BERLIN, 3 JANUARY 1875

Many thousand thanks for your dear and welcome letter which I received yesterday! Let me wish you every blessing and all possible happiness for yourself and dear Lorne, for this year, may it bring you health and prosperity, and [may] you be an increasing comfort and blessing to each other, for there is nothing better I can wish you.

Vicky seems to have given up hope of Louise having a child.

Our boys are going back to school today so I am rather sad, and I said with tears in my eyes to Willy, the time will seem so long, darling, till I see you again; he comforted me with the answer, 'Oh, it will only seem long to you, you know, not to me!' It was very kindly meant and taken as it was meant.

(665)

THE QUEEN TO PRINCESS LOUISE
OSBORNE, 7 JANUARY 1875

After a series of telegrams about Leopold's progress in January, ending with 'All danger is now passed', the Queen congratulated her system, at least by implication, on its success as applied to Leopold.

... We have every reason to be very grateful to God for his mercy. But his very delicacy, and the regular, careful life he has led has been the cause of his getting through it as he has. Sir William told him today what it was [almost certainly typhoid], which he had not suspected excepting at the very beginning. He does not look so ill as in the summer except as to thinness which is very great and makes him look *old* and haggard. It is *not* becoming.

(673)

But all danger was not passed.

TELEGRAM FROM THE QUEEN TO PRINCESS LOUISE OSBORNE, 18 JANUARY 1875

Though he is no worse and there is no immediate cause alarm think you should come at once as you proposed.

(675)

PRINCESS BEATRICE TO PRINCESS LOUISE OSBORNE, 19 JANUARY 1875

Dearest Louise, You will have got my telegram tonight at Edinburgh saying that Lorne may come. Mama says though that it must only be for one night, as if he were staying here the brothers would naturally wish to come, and Mama says the only way to keep up under this terrible anxiety is to be alone with you and me.

She hopes you will not mind for that one night separate rooms, as she has had everything arranged for you on her side of the house to be all together. Mama will with great pleasure see Lorne on your arrival, but thanks him for his kind thought of dining with the Household. Mama has gently told dear Leopold that you might perhaps come, without saying of course that she had sent for you, and you ought to have seen his look of delight. Dear Louise, I cannot say what a comfort it will be to have you, but what a dreadful journey yours must have been. We are terribly anxious.

Mama hopes poor Lorne will be able to find some place to go to, as she says, you proposed in a letter to her not long ago to stay here *alone* with her. Perhaps Argyle [*sic*] Lodge [in London!] Your loving Beatrice.

(677)

THE QUEEN TO PRINCESS LOUISE
OSBORNE, 6 FEBRUARY 1875

I felt much grieved to see you go, as it seems always as though you were *taken away* afresh from your old Home, where, though you have a kind, good Husband, *your* heart is, as much as in your new one, I often think and perhaps even LIKE to think....

Would you ask Lorne to let me have a copy of his Lines on Kingsley?

... This sad and strange winter here with its terrible anxieties ... as well as God's mercy in restoring him to us, unberufen – for I own I always look to *some* mishap *yet*.... This last attack came so terribly unexpectedly

I like to think of you in MY old home and birthplace and only wish *you* had my rooms [at Kensington Palace].

(679)

The Lornes moved into Apartment I, Kensington Palace, that February. The rooms were shabby, but the Lornes now had a town and country home of their own.

SAME TO SAME
OSBORNE, 10 FEBRUARY 1875

Filial improvement ...

Many loving affectionate thanks for your *3* dear letters, which were a great pleasure to receive and I hope *show* a disposition to be more communicative in the future. Very many thanks for the pretty little frame.

(680)

SAME TO SAME
OSBORNE, 13 FEBRUARY 1875

... not kept up.

Lorne is right. You write almost in one day 3 letters and then none for a week *nearly*. I am longing to hear how you are getting on at Dornden....

(681)

SAME TO SAME
OSBORNE, 23 FEBRUARY 1875

An epileptic fit:

Leopold is going on well and was out again today.... But I must tell you that he had *a fit* on Sunday though not a very bad one – but he had a pair of sharp pointed scissors in his hand and cut his fingers rather badly – so that his right hand is disabled for the present! The bleeding was stopped without any difficulty, but only shows that he never must be left one minute alone. It is awful to think of what he might not do! I *hope* and think this will be a lesson to him. Mr Yorke [equerry to Prince Leopold] was with him and had some difficulty in wrenching the open scissors from him. Don't speak of it. Only really what a *life* is it! Is it even to go on? That is in the hands of a higher power.

I must end for tonight. On Friday we go to Windsor as Leopold is quite able to travel. He lunches with us since yesterday. Ever your devoted Mama V.R. Love to Lorne.

How did the concert go off? And how do you feel at my poor old home [Kensington Palace]?

(682)

SAME TO SAME
BUCKINGHAM PALACE, 10 MARCH 1875

Darling Loosy, I spoke fully to Dr. McDonald as he will tell you both, and I will not oppose it further. But I *fear* we *cannot* entirely rely on secrecy – and that it will ooze out from the *surgeon*. Dr. McDonald reminds me of our nice Dr. Profeit at Balmoral and certainly these sort of doctors are so much nicer than the great people.

(685)

LORD LORNE TO THE QUEEN
KENSINGTON PALACE, 10 MARCH 1875

Madam and dear Mama, Louise has just shown me your note saying that you have kindly arranged to make me a Privy Councillor, and that I am to be sworn in on Wednesday next. I prize this honour very much, because it is one that comes directly from you. It is a curious coincidence that my Father was admitted at the same age. I wish I could have thanked you this evening, and that the discussion in the House had not kept me so late. We only divided a few minutes before 6 o'clock, so that it was not possible for me to be back in time to see you here, which I am very sorry for.

(1792)

PRINCE LEOPOLD TO PRINCESS LOUISE WYKEHAM HOUSE, OXFORD, 15 MAY 1875

A visit to Oxford?

Dearest Loo, I am *most anxious* that you should come and stay here for Commemoration Week, I have also asked Arthur. This is my last year here, and the last chance you'll have of seeing me here; it would give me *such* pleasure if you would manage it.... I don't suppose you and Lorne would care to go to Ascot particularly; still if you wanted to be there, it would not prevent you being there on the *Cup Day*, which is after all *the* day.

I am sure that it would give the Dean and Mrs. Liddell great pleasure to put you and Lorne up during Commemoration, as they did Bertie and Alix; even if they couldn't there is a charming hotel close by my house, where I would get you very nice rooms. Pray send me an answer, if possible, by return of post; as I have just now so many arrangements to make.

With love to Lorne, your most devoted Leo.

(689)

PRINCE ARTHUR TO PRINCESS LOUISE ALDERSHOT, 17 MAY 1875

An artist at Dornden:

Dearest Louise You may like to know that I got up to town all right last night and not more than half an hour late. We were in plenty of time at the station having to wait even five minutes at the station. I enjoyed my stay at Dornden so much and was so sorry to leave in such a hurry. What a nice girl that Miss Montalbert (I don't know if that is the right way to spell it) is, she is so clever and so pleasant in every way; you must take me to the South Kensington school one day. I should like to see what she is doing....

Have you received any more meteorological reports from Mama. I have not. Hoping you have written to Leo and with my love to Lorne ever your most affectionate brother Arthur.

(690)

Henrietta Montalba, a student friend of Louise's, was to become a well-known artist. They studied together at Kensington.

THE QUEEN TO PRINCESS LOUISE
BALMORAL, 29 MAY 1875

... I was very glad you went to the Derby with all the family as it pleases them and Bertie and it is a thing to have seen *once*. I saw it twice – as a child with dear grand-mama and again with dear Papa.... I disliked it the 2nd time very much.... Pray tell me how you are this time dear child. *I* am (wonderful to say) become *quite* regular again!!! It is very uncommon to go on so long [the Queen was fifty-six]. But they say very good. My eyes are weak, which I think has also something to do with this.

(693)

This letter is important for a fair judgment both of Queen Victoria and Princess Louise. Those biographers who have attributed the Queen's seclusion after the Prince Consort's death to the change of life are clearly mistaken. The letter also refutes the suggestion made by some writers that Princess Louise had no children because she never reached full maturity.

SAME TO SAME
BALMORAL, 11 JUNE 1875

The Leopold problem:

... Many thanks for your very short letter from Leopold's *adored* Oxford, which contained very little information, and I wished to know *all* about what you were doing. I thought as Angeli [the artist, Heinrich von Angeli] had so much to do, that the Duke [of Argyll] was to be painted next year? But I suppose he could manage it....

I am *so* astonished at Leopold's coolly *writing* to me he is going 'to town' – but that is to *you* when I had told him before I left I expected him to remain at Oxford till I came back. He is so wanting in all *dutiful* and respectful forms and seems to delight in showing a childish defiance of my wishes. He ought to have said that he found there would be no use in staying on at Oxford while I was away, every one having left, and had asked you to take him in. But I rely on your keeping him quiet, not taking him out to *any* party *at night* which he knows is bad for him and only to such theatres where, as Sir William [Jenner] says, he can get away at a moment's notice in case of a fit. I have let *everyone* know that he does *not* go out to parties or large dinners and that *no one* is to ask him. But I am nevertheless *greatly annoyed* at his remaining *near* town or *almost in town* for a week, which he has never *done before*. I know that *you* will watch over him and *stop* any follies. But he is so very defiant and shows such utter want of proper égard in not telling me the reasons for things. He shall find, I shall no longer *care* for him as I *did*, for I find it is *sadly wasted* on an ungrateful, inordinately selfish nature.

One thing I am afraid of – viz: that Lorne, may have imbibed that very (I must say) unfortunate idea which all *British* young men, especially in these days, have of being *independent* of their parents and doing just what they like. With the Royal family and Leopold's health, this *cannot* be.

I hope to have a few reassuring lines from you, and that you will scold this stupid brother of yours for *not* telling me of his changed wishes. He is so very sly. But he shall find me *very different* and no confidence shall be shown him if he goes on in this way....

(695)

This letter shows the Queen's painful jealousy of her children's independent lives and suggests that her attempts to control Leopold were not entirely due to his illness and the physical risks involved in his leading a freer life.

PRINCESS LOUISE TO THE QUEEN
KENSINGTON PALACE, 13 JUNE 1875, PRIVATE

The great Leopold row:

Dearest Mama, I am very sorry to see by your letter of 11th how very angry you are. I have *nothing* to do with Leopold's arrangements. He asked me when I left Oxford if I could take him as if *not* he would go elsewhere in London. I of course said yes, as he is *better here* than elsewhere, and at his age he cannot unfortunately be told *to do*, and *not to do*. If he is careful I do not think that being here will do him more harm than being at Oxford would. I will try *what I can* to keep him quiet, entre nous I am always nervous about him, you know.

He has only told me now, that he has your answer, that he asked to go to the State Ball, I told him at once it was very foolish of him to ask for that, and when he did. The State Concert, he might do more safely, as that is over *early*, and it is not hot, and very easy to get away from. But of course all this is none of my affair.

Dear Mama I am really distressed and astonished at the tone of your letter, and fondly hope it was written under irritation, and so I have burnt it. Lorne and I are quite at a loss to know what you mean by saying 'that you fear Lorne may have imbibed that very unfortunate idea which all British young men have of being independent of their Parents'. Lorne never has done this, and never could; as all *reserve* between *parents*, and *children*, is quite foreign to him. His parents tell *him* everything, he is the first that they go to, and he consults his Father about everything that has any importance, and always tells him all he knows.

All Lorne has ever told Leo is to mind *not* overtire himself, he himself gets ill in a minute if he is overtired!

He says what we all say, that Leo is old enough to use his own discretion, and he must bear the consequences himself. Sir William, Dr. Acland I am sure and Mr. Collins and we all think the same, he has bought his own experience if he will only keep his spirits in bounds.

I am sorry you gave that order about the carriages, but he can of course use ours, when he wants them, and we must shift for ourselves. I was just able to go to the Ball, as my time came on two days sooner than I expected and as it was on my 6th day I was just able to go, I suffered much as usual. Dr. Macdonald says it will take some months before I am really better. Your dutiful affectionate Louise.

(Z264/46)

THE QUEEN TO PRINCESS LOUISE BALMORAL, 15 JUNE 1875

'A small Republic' ... Louise bore the brunt of her mother's exasperation with Prince Leopold.

Darling Child, Though my head and eyes are tired, and I am thoroughly *disgusted* with this luckless business, I must *write* once more to answer a few points in your dear letter of the 13th. It seems to me that you don't *quite* see *what* I and any Parent, but above *all* the Sovereign (who *can* forbid *any* of her children from going anywhere and have always done so in former days, but I have been *far* too *lenient*), object to. It is, that when I had *allowed* him not to go with me to Balmoral, on account of his wish to redeem lost time [at Oxford], I *told* him that it was on the condition of his remaining there till I returned, which Mr Collins and Sir William Jenner know, he never answered and above *all* he never said – as of course he ought and as Lorne (who you say always consults his Parents about all he does) would have done to his father – that he wished not to remain on at his 'dear little Home' [his digs at Oxford] when everyone else left.

He should at once have said this and that he hoped I would not be annoyed if he went to you for a few days to go to the opera and see his relations. This, any of the Brothers at his age, if a *prearranged plan* was altered, would have done, and still more when Mr Collins told him of it and he said, he would explain it, and did nothing but announce to me in what I must call a most impudent way, his going to *Town* – a thing which he could not do without my sanction.

Then it would really be well if you and Lorne were to tell him and show him how very wrong and disrespectful this was, and how this is the 4th or 5th instance of his having been so totally wanting in respect towards me. The Palace is the only place he could go *in Town*. But I have perfect confidence in his being with you and Lorne. It is a misfortune in one sense that he feels so strong. About the carriages, I am sorry you should be put to inconvenience. But *how* can it be allowed, when Leopold goes to Kensington without my sanction and does not ask my permission to have them – which has only been given when it was understood beforehand.

I am sorry to have said anything which hurt Lorne; but you know (and the Duke I know understands this) young people in England think at 21 they are quite their own master, which is really only in a legal point of view – and those who have not been brought up in Royal families can't exactly know what a difference there is and what Princes owe to their Sovereign.

I have my Position as Sovereign and head of a large and somewhat difficult family to maintain and if such want of respect is allowed – *where* is it to end? It would be a small Republic.

But you can both help me very much if you will point this out to Leopold.

I can't see anything in the tone of my letter (of which I have a copy) to be astonished at. If you were in my position you would be as indignant. And I shall never watch in the same way over one who, as soon as he recovers, tries to set me at defiance and make me *feel* he wishes to do *all* HE likes, and what he knows I disapprove of for his good.

Pray let Lorne see this letter. If Leopold is open, and does not do such things in future, all will do well, but I shall never take as much trouble again....

Let me say once more, it is not *the thing itself* I objected to – but the *concealment* and the *whole way* in which *it was done*.

I just hear of his being laid up! I am so sorry for you, as you, I know, watch so anxiously over him. But each time that he has behaved in that sort of way (without exception) he has fallen ill!

I must end, and rely on *Lorne's* doing what he can to make Leopold *feel* WHERE he always fails and thereby brings upon himself all this annoyance and vexation which could be avoided. It has made me quite ill....

(696)

It apparently made Leopold ill also. But the Queen won the battle of letters, having kept a copy of the one Louise burnt!

SAME TO SAME
WINDSOR CASTLE, 19 JUNE 1875

... Sir William told me all about Leopold. I can't say how annoyed and shocked we have all been! I hope you *will* read my long letter very carefully for it contains the full explanation of *the trouble*.

I miss my dear Balmoral much. I am *so sorry* Lorne is unwell again....

(697)

SAME TO SAME
WINDSOR CASTLE, 27 JUNE 1875

Still Leopold:
Darling Loosy, Your letter arrived just as my telegram left. But you really are a naughty child! Not one word have I heard of you since last Monday! Leopold goes up to town tomorrow for the Trinity House affair. He is not as *careful* about his knee as he *ought* to be, for he stands about too long and won't use a stick – but he is quite amiable though his manner is not more pleasant than usual. I fear it never will be. Mr. Collins leaves tomorrow for some time unfortunately. He is greatly annoyed at Leopold.

Poor Angeli does indeed take the greatest pains and I am quite afraid he has overworked himself. I hear your picture is lovely. He really is a great artist.... I enclose the direction for the drawing paper. It is made of different thicknesses. I must end to get dressed. I hope Lorne is better....

(698)

SAME TO SAME
WINDSOR CASTLE, 4 JULY 1875

Heinrich von Angeli's portraits:
I wrote in such a hurry that I said I would write again and I wanted to tell you all about the fine pictures. I imagine the senseless *Anmassung* [presumption] of my 2 good and not overwise ladies – the Duchess of Roxburghe who, I think, understands *nothing at all* about Art (as she said the Academy was particularly good this year when every one says it is very bad) and the 'White Elephant', alias Caledonia [Jane, Countess of Caledon]!...

The 1st said of my picture it was very like but hard and unpleasing; and the other that he seemed to have more talent than power!! But pray keep this to *yourself* and *don't* repeat it to anyone, for it would be dreadful if either he or they heard it again. They are the *only* people who have made such too absurd remarks (and they said something silly about each of the other pictures!!) *I* think yours very fine and a picture which requires long looking at. It gives your expression so truly. Is it not a pity that Lorne's of you is to have a hat and high up dress? For the *shape* of your head, neck and shoulders are so particularly to be admired and are so characteristic. You know how honest and *un*flattering-like Angeli is – therefore you may believe he thinks it, when he says your head and shoulders are quite like the *antique*.

Affie's and Marie's pictures will be quite excellent; the Duke's [of Argyll] marvellous, and also Sir John McNeill's. I must ask for a photograph of that. For whom is it? Lorne's will be excellent also. And Lenchen's is a splendid picture. In short they are all *real* works of Art – and the stupid remarks made by those ladies show how vitiated the taste in England is, by Watts' and Richmond's and [Sir Francis] Grant's colouring and [Henry] Graves' want of drawing! It would be such a thing if one could send 1 or 2 young men of promise to Vienna to study under Angeli. I would willingly help to pay for such a thing. Could you not help me?...

(699)

Angeli seems to have painted, between March and July 1875, portraits of the Queen, Princess Beatrice, Princess Louise and Princess Helena, and still had to complete portraits of Louise (again, for Lorne), Lorne himself, the Duke and Duchess of Edinburgh and a group of the Prince and Princess of Wales and their children. Not quite all the family! The Queen decided against having Prince Leopold painted, as she had a fairly recent portrait of him (though not by Angeli) and he did not look well after his recent illness.

The 'other pictures' on which Lady Caledon and the Duchess of Roxburghe had commented were presumably those of Beatrice, Louise and Helena.

SAME TO SAME
BALMORAL, 1 OCTOBER 1875

Problems at Inveraray:

... I must now tell you that I *hope* you and the Duke and Duchess will not make a fuss with Leopold, as *though he has been left to do exactly what he likes* (only not to drive a *dangerous* strange horse in a dog-cart, having his own pony and carriage and his own wagonette) he has been *perfectly* odious and so rude, and disrespectful to me, in his manner so cross – rude, impertinent to his sisters and indeed everyone.... No one is so, I must say, horrified as Alix! Indeed everyone, and I wrote him a few lines last night ... to say how pained I had been at his manner and I hoped it was caused by indisposition! *How* disappointed and pained I am at this child's behaviour to *me* ... – *words* cannot tell.... We are greatly relieved that he is gone! Poor little Mr Yorke, who is greatly distressed, is quite useless. He wants some severe handling....

(700)

SAME TO SAME
BALMORAL

Just before leaving Balmoral for Inveraray, the Queen wrote a note to Louise saying:
Leopold is most *amiable* and seems to have been quite unaware of the unfortunate manner which distressed and annoyed us all.

(702)

SAME TO SAME
4 OCTOBER 1875

The Queen added:
Leopold is in a very much better mood and seems to *begin* to *see* that he *is* really making himself disliked.

Of Inveraray the Queen wrote:

I think the scenery and trees *beautiful* – the house not good though I liked my rooms very much – and the place needing being better kept up.

(703)

SAME TO SAME
BALMORAL, 6 OCTOBER 1875

Trouble with the Argylls:
Darling Loosy, I have today received a letter from the Duke [of Argyll] with a memorandum in answer to mine, which I will send you in a day or two (or copies of them) but my letter has come *most* unfortunately after Lorne's decision or *meditated* decision, for he says: 'Elizabeth [the Duchess] and I are quite vexed that Lorne does not seem to wish to bring Louise back here this winter. I don't know whether he said anything to Your Majesty on the subject, or whether Your Majesty said anything which can account for apparently a sudden change of mind.' And at the end he says: 'I hope Your Majesty will understand that I do not at all wish to *interfere* with Lorne's plans or that they should reside more here than they like themselves.'

You will see in what a very awkward position this places me and it would be said by the *world at large* that *I had been displeased and told* you to *go away*!! There is not a doubt of this and I must most *earnestly* ask you to go back for *some part* of the winter – shortening it which ever way you like. But *don't keep away* all the winter....

(704)

PRINCESS LOUISE TO THE QUEEN
KENSINGTON PALACE, 11 OCTOBER 1875, PRIVATE

Staying in the south – an inter-family row:

Dearest Mama, I have just received your letter. I am very sorry you should be vexed with Lorne's intention of not settling again at Inveraray this year. I mentioned in one of my former letters that one of the elder girls was I think *un*intentionally rather rude to me, and that I casually told Lorne of it, which was perhaps stupid of me, but after this he said it would be as well we should not return this winter there being other good reasons for it. We would never never mention the fact to the Duke or Duchess [her parents] or else the poor girl would have no peace for months to come.

Having to come up to see the last of Bertie [before leaving for India] makes it so natural for remaining in the south now.

We have told the brothers and many other people, that as we have come up we might as well stay, instead of going through that long tiring (not to say expensive) journey again. Besides which we have a great deal to look after. The Tenants' farm at Dornden is undergoing repairs, and must be constantly superintended by us. Also the new gardener must be looked after. Then again we want to see if the bracing air of Dornden will do my headaches good which I have been suffering from all the time I was in Scotland, this year. No one can possibly think for a minute that you have influenced our movements as to our remaining or not. I hear everybody saying that you were so pleased with your visit. It would cause more surprise than otherwise if we did return, people think that since I am married I am not on such good terms with my family as I was I fear, as I have been staying so long away. I was perfectly happy at Inveraray each year, and I hope to be happy at Dornden. For two years we were 7 months in Scotland, life becomes monotonous if one does the same thing every year.

The old problem of a home:

As to the Duke's Memorandum! If you can find any written statement that he said he would build a wing, I should send it to him, but say at the same time that you see it would involve too much expense. It was unfortunate that Lorne decided on not returning at the same time as you were writing your letter.

Then about Macharioch, we went there for a few weeks for the *two* first years of our marriage to please the Duke and not to say it did not suit us before we had tried it. We never were consulted as to the building and we always regretted very much that the Duke should spend so much on a house in Kintyre which would be very little used. Lorne did approve of Roseneath [*sic*] being put in the market, but now he seems to have a longing that it should remain in the family and that he could live there occasionally. Your dutiful affectionate Louise. Private.

Don't you think the whole thing had better be dropped just now. I could not have refused to come to Lilah's marriage, as she asked me personally to do so, or it would have pained her, and I am too fond of her to do that. But I shall not remain to the breakfast, Leo will go with me, and I hope come away with me too. We are just going to say goodbye to Bertie.

(Z207/4)

Known as Lilah in the family, Eliza Lady Clifden was Lorne's cousin. She married Walter George Stirling, Leopold's former governor, on 12 October 1875.

THE DUCHESS OF ARGYLL TO PRINCESS LOUISE INVERARAY, 13 OCTOBER 1875

Dearest Louise – I feel for you the parting with your brother. I am almost afraid of telling you how much I miss you for fear I should be supposed to be complaining, and yet you must be glad to have made us so happy. I miss you constantly – I see you were at Lilah's Marriage. Is she still Lady Clifden? How I hope he will do well by the son....

I cannot get out of my tiresome way of waking too early.

We are thinking of going to Henry's marriage on November 9th and to Castle Howard and Alnwick after. Besides wishing to be at little Harry's marriage, a little country house visiting is the only thing I can do with the girls, and I suppose I ought to do what I can. London I can never do much of.... Most affectionately E. A.

(705)

PRINCESS LOUISE TO THE QUEEN 15 OCTOBER 1875, PRIVATE

Dearest Mama, I have just received your letter, and I cannot help saying that I am pained with the words you use in it, saying that 'I have shown you want of confidence.' As I mentioned in my former letters, two days after you left we were rearranging the rooms and things, and one of the elder girls spoke rudely to me, before three of the servants. I told Lorne of this, never thinking that he would be so angry, as he was, and he at once said 'order all your things to be packed up, and we shall not return this winter.' I *remonstrated* but with *no* effect, he ordered the boxes up, and packed his things and what could I do but obey? How can this be called 'want of confidence'?

I quite saw at once that your letter might be differently understood from what it was intended, but the Duke and Duchess know *perfectly* that *you* had *nothing* whatever to do with Lorne's sudden resolve not to return. We cannot tell them *why* and so I suppose, they think I am at the bottom of it, and then you are displeased. All because Lorne is impulsive, rather headstrong; and his sister was rude; and I was foolish enough to tell him of it. I do think it hard, and do not see how this can put you in an awkward position dear Mama.

I always try to make the best of things, and so I wrote to you, all my good reasons for not regretting that we are once here in my last letter. Please let this be the last time we discuss the stupid subject. As it is the poor little Duchess is fretting very much at not having what she calls an enough reason for Lorne's wish not to return, but if we told her, it would make her quite ill – so please never let the Duke and Duchess know I told you.

Bertie's departure for India:

The last day the 11th was a most painful one for Bertie, and I know he was thankful when it was over. He was dreadfully overcome when he parted with the children; and he said goodbye to all his servants and Alix's people. They drove in an open carriage to the station, and there were crowds of people all along the streets, and in the station. Dear Alix kept up wonderfully, she was fighting with herself all the time. On her return from Calais she was looking calmer, and better than I could have expected, but she was very tired; she was looking forward to a quiet time with the children at Sandringham.

A 'stupid marriage':

There is nothing much to say about what you call 'the stupid marriage'. It was *very* quiet, and there were *very* few people there, and it only lasted a $\frac{1}{4}$ of an hour. Lilah's three brothers, Lord and Lady Spencer and the Dowager Lady Spencer, Di Cook, Lolo [Gleichen] and the two children and her mother . . . his father, mother, two sisters, and Alice Enfield, Lord Enfield being a cousin.

I had never seen Lilah's mother, she is a very pretty old lady. Lilah looked very pretty dressed in grey with a white bonnet.

I said goodbye to dear Arthur on Tuesday evening, it is very sad to think we shall not see him for such a time dear boy. I do trust he will not have had a very bad journey.

Arthur went to Gibraltar as Assistant Adjutant-General for six months.

I never thought dear Bertie would have felt it so deeply as he did leaving, it was dreadful to see him but at the same time it brought out all his warm kind nature, which was very touching to see.

Alix said all these last months she has never known him so gentle and patient, that she felt she was the impatient one; only this is private of course.

Lady Walter C[ampbell] has a girl, it was born last Sunday, she is going on very well, she was ill a long time, 33 hours.

I am very sorry to hear about Brown's old Father, but I fear he has been but a poor creature these last years, the good old Mother will do all she can I know, I hope she will not make herself ill.

We have made no plans to visit about. Affie said something about seeing us later, and Lord Granville has given us a sort of general invitation, but this is all, and these are in the county, we go to Dornden the end of the month. We shall be very glad to come to you for a week or 10 days at Christmas time. I hope you see that I have had *nothing* to do with Lorne's wish not to return to Inveraray this winter, I only told him how his sister spoke to me; and he has now written to her to tell her he knows of it.

(Z207/5)

SAME TO SAME
OCTOBER 1875?

The question of the Lornes' home in Scotland:

Dearest Mama, Many thanks for your letter received this morning just when I was going to write. I think do you know dear mama after the Macharioch letter to the Duke, the subject had altogether [better] not be mentioned for a little time.

About Rosneath, we did write to the Duke about it, and say how much we wished he would not sell it, but lend it to us. He said 'he had to sell it, and if we were disposed to pay him £600 a year for it until he could sell it, well we might live there though he would not advise it.' I said at once I should never degrade myself by paying my husband's father for letting us live in his house, it looks too mean and bad....

I hope next year when we are at Inveraray, if I try and do my very best not to mind what the girls do or say, that Lorne will naturally stay on a month or two longer. Lorne is *so* fond of the place, and you know how fond I am of it. Of course he has nothing to do with the place except as member [of Parliament], and that is why I am so anxious he should keep on there. Lorne is no one, it is the Duke who the people look to, and the Duke does live there a good deal. And it does not do to tell Lorne I am very fond of the place, as he always says if I am it is high time I did not stay there too much, as if anything happened to him, and my having no children, I should have no right there, in fact his talk is rather wild on the subject, and I always try not to discuss it, as I see he only gets more strange ideas, so to let the subject die away is the best thing....

(Z207/6)

LORD LORNE TO THE QUEEN
DORNDEN, 9 NOVEMBER 1875

Louise at Dornden:
I have only just received some copies of my Riviera Story, and ask your acceptance of one that I send by this post to London to go by the messenger.

Louise wrote to you the day before yesterday that she had been suffering a little from sore throat. It is now better, but she is still kept to the house, as the weather has suddenly become very cold and raw after having been for two or three days most unusually warm.

The woods about here are still in great beauty, for the leaves are only just beginning to fall off in any quantities. Mr. Ward Hunt is staying with Lord Abergavenny and seemed the other day to loom larger than ever through the foggy atmosphere when we saw him at Charing Cross Railway Station. Lord Torrington was also one of Lord Abergavenny's party, and Lady A. was one of the ladies who met Louise at the opening of the Ladies' Work Society in Sloane Street.

(1793)

Ward Hunt MP was known as 'the Elephant'.

THE QUEEN TO PRINCESS LOUISE
OSBORNE, 11 JANUARY 1876

Louise's health:
Darling Loosy, I received your dear little note of the 8th ... I am greatly grieved to hear so poor an account of you and you ought seriously to do something. Inverary [*sic*] agreed much better with you in the winter and I hope Lorne will see and feel that you should try to go somewhere else for February and March; why not to Bournemouth, if you can't go abroad? and this next summer you *must absolutely* go to some baths in France or Germany.... then you catch continuously cold – and you will go on doing

that; and keeping in your room or in the house is the very worst of all, for it makes you more and more sensitive. Paying visits and going to an exhibition was *the* very worst thing you could do for a cold as well as staying in a cold house.

(708)

PRINCESS LOUISE TO THE QUEEN
KENSINGTON PALACE, 14 MARCH 1876

The new title of Queen Empress:
Dearest Mama, ... There is a great deal of bother and talk about your title of Empress. The people will not understand it. They think you wish always to be so called in future, instead of Queen, it is too stupid; of course there is no title so fine as that of our British Queen: and calling us the Imperial Family instead of Royal gives a very *unEnglish* sound and which the people are so against but I always say you never *thought* of such a thing. The opposite party think the bringing forward of the Title is a fancy of Mr. Disraeli's, are they not stupid.

(F16/36)

Critics professed to fear that Queen Victoria would drop the traditional title of 'Queen' in favour of the foreign and supposedly grander title of 'Empress'. In fact, she aimed, with Disraeli's encouragement, at getting the best of both worlds, by adding, in April 1876, Empress of India to her royal title. After a rough passage through Parliament, the bill became law. The new Imperial title was to vanish again in 1947 with the independence of India.

THE CROWN PRINCESS OF PRUSSIA TO LORD LORNE
BERLIN, 20 DECEMBER 1876

Engagement of Vicky's eldest daughter, Charlotte, to Prince Bernhard of Saxe-Meiningen:
My dear Lorne, A 1000 most heartfelt thanks for your dear letter of congratulations! It does indeed make one feel old, – at least *I* feel venerable! *Very grateful* and hopeful, and pleased but much shaken and upset by it all, as you can imagine! One never knows *what* such feelings are, until one experiences them, and it is *painful* to give up a daughter. I try *not* to feel jealous of course, but sometimes it give one a *little* pinch! However I am going to *try* to be the most amiable, '*facile*', easy going Mother-in-Law that ever was. Bernhard is dear and good and intelligent, worthy of your affection and esteem, and I trust you will become good and intimate friends some day, and I do not conceal from him how great an advantage I shall think that for him!

They are *exceedingly happy* and everyone in the House contributes to making them as comfortable as possible. Your kind words did my heart good! Now let me wish you a very merry Xmas and happy New Year for yourselves, your parents and all your family. Fritz sends his best love, Charlotte also. Ever your most affectionate sister Victoria.

(1714)

Lorne had already experienced a mother-in-law's 'little pinch' of jealousy. Queen Victoria made it clear that she competed with him for Louise's love.

PRINCESS LOUISE TO THE QUEEN 16 APRIL 1877

Dearest Mama, Many thanks for the enclosed and for letting me read them. The girl is very foolish but has acted well in her letter poor thing. I am so sorry for dear Arthur. No one will speak of it any more I think and so it will die out....

(Add. A15/2655)

This refers to Prince Arthur's search for a bride, in this case Princess Mary of Hanover, daughter of blind King George. He had met her in 1875 and was evidently much attracted to her. They met again a few times and he was still hoping to marry her in 1877. But she seems to have hesitated endlessly, and finally in March 1877 plucked up the courage to turn him down, in a letter to her father, which is the letter Princess Louise is referring to here, and which the Queen had sent to Princess Louise together with letters from the King and Queen of Hanover about it. Queen Victoria was very annoyed, and thought Princess Mary and her parents had behaved badly in not letting her know earlier that there was no hope. Princess Mary never did marry.

SAME TO SAME 16 JUNE 1877, PRIVATE

Dearest Mama, I have not written for some days pray excuse. Leopold has asked to come here on Monday. I wrote to him that we should be very glad to have him here provided he wrote it to you, and that I would write it to you, as I could not bear any underhand goings on. I went further to say that if he came I hoped he would be prudent and reasonable, and not overdo things as it would not be for his own happiness.

I fear it may make you fussy that he comes to town, but as he is anxious to come he is better here than elsewhere, and as he is over 24 it is so difficult to check his motions. I told Bertie that Leopold wished to come, and that I had written back that he must write his wish at once to you.

I shall be as anxious as anyone you know dear Mama and *shall try* and keep him with me as much as I can if he is not too sly for me.

(Z265/64)

PRINCESS LOUISE TO THE QUEEN
ARGYLL ARMS, INVERARAY, 12 OCTOBER 1877

Disaster at Inveraray Castle:
Dearest Mama, I telegraphed to you, as soon as it was daylight, about the dreadful fire; at that time we thought nothing could be saved!

All was perfectly quiet and peaceful till about 5 o'clock a.m. when I was woke by our big dog barking and making a great fuss. A few minutes after, Mrs Campbell of Isla's Scotch maid came to the door, and one of the men shouted 'the castle is on fire' – then Lorne woke, and jumped up and said we must be off that moment (not knowing wherabouts the fire was) – and so with only our dressing gowns, not even slippers, we went downstairs, and found all the inner part of the Hall was illuminated, and large sparks falling as we went; when we passed through the big hall, where the billiard-table is, large bits of the flaming roof fell on the furniture and set it in a blaze; most of the roof fell in about three minutes after Lorne and I had passed. All the others passed outside.

We joined the Duke and Duchess who were in a dreadful state. It was a bitter cold night; as the morning broke, we found all the hills white with snow. There was great difficulty in getting the [invalid] Duchess away, – she could not walk and would not be carried, though many kind people were ready to help her; – we helped her along at last, somehow, and got her safely to the stables, in the coachman's room. It was a curious sight to see us all huddled together, walking away from the burning house. Lady Caroline Charteris, who is very tall, having only a white blanket to cover herself, walked like a spectre in front of us; – poor blind Mrs Campbell being led by her devoted Scotch maid (who is more of a Companion to her than a maid); Archie's children [Douglas and Lilah] being carried along by the terrified nurse, the dear little things not uttering a sound.

When we were all out, the flames had got to their full height, and we saw them coming through the top of the house. The people from the little town were most efficient, though at first they lost their heads rather, and began tearing things down and shouting; but after a little while they formed a string (which Lorne organised) with buckets, to the river, and shut all the doors to prevent currents of air. At about 10 o'clock the fire was got under, though it still keeps smouldering and has to be watched and pumped upon. There is to be a body of men to watch tonight.

All the large Hall is burnt and the Culloden arms we were so fond of: the 91st old Colours, four or five valuable pictures, and arms of all sorts – *gone*! The room Sir W. Jenner lived in when you were here is quite destroyed, and the cupboard just out of your room was half burnt, also the Organ. The 2 passages on each side have fallen, and all the roof; otherwise all is saved. The very door of the large drawing room was burnt down, and part of the floor, and there it stopped.

A great many things were broken and spoiled in the moving of them, and the tapestry torn, and the curtains in getting them down, which was done not knowing how far the fire might spread.

Not a being knew (I mean those in the Castle) that it was on fire, till alarmed by some people outside. A fisherman was the first to see it. He had got up to look after his boat, as it was a stormy night, and he saw the fire from the loch. He at once roused the Clerk of the Works, and then, on his way to the Castle, called others. Had he been a quarter of an hour later we should none of us been able to get away!

In haste for the post – I am ever your dutiful and affectionate child Louise.

(Copy of letter stuck in Victoria's Journal, 1877, p. 317)

LORD BEACONSFIELD TO PRINCESS LOUISE
10 DOWNING STREET, 13 JANUARY 1878

The Prime Minister describes a present to Louise of roast cygnet in imaginative language. Louise would have liked nothing better than life on 'some moonlit isle'.

Madam and dear Princess, A cygnet for your Royal Highness's gracious acceptance. It is good for princesses, but should be tasted in the banqueting chamber of some moonlit Isle, surrounded by swans in melodious chorus!

Through Beaconsfield's interest, Lorne was to be appointed Governor-General of Canada – a great 'experiment'. Lorne accepted the post on 28 July 1878.

The Prime Minister concluded his letter to Louise:

Alas! I cannot offer your Royal Highness the Isle which you deserve, but deign to accept the humble tribute of your faithful servant, Beaconsfield.

(714)

PRINCESS LOUISE TO THE QUEEN
18 JANUARY 1878

On the writing paper there is a blue coronet beneath which the names Louise and Lorne are linked together.

Dearest Mama, Many thanks for your letter received this morning. I went to hear the speeches in the House of Lords yesterday. Lord Beaconsfield's voice was wonderfully strong and clear. Lord Granville made rather a mess of it I think although of course it was difficult to make a speech without anything to go upon, as is more or less always the case with the Opposition. The Duke [her father-in-law] was too violent, though he promised me two hours before he would try to be calm, which Lorne thought took the form of scolding. Lord Salisbury spoke very well, I had never heard him before.

(B55/24)

Louise was no longer inclined to the Liberals.

PRINCESS LOUISE MARGARET TO PRINCESS LOUISE 3 MAY 1878

'Louischen' of Prussia was engaged to Prince Arthur.

Dearest Louise, You will I hope let me send you a few lines to tell you with what interest I have heard that Lorne is appointed Governor-General of Canada. I hear from Arthur that you are in low spirits about it which you naturally would be having to leave behind you your dear country and all your friends and relations. But no doubt when you are more settled down there, you will like it very much as it must be a beautiful country and the people are very nice.

Arthur and I will miss you *terribly* and it is so sad that his favourite sister should not be there for our marriage but there is always a bright, sunny side in everything and so we are determined to go out and visit you there some day.

I hear that you have left for Kissingen. I hope the cure will do you good and strengthen you for all that is to come.... I remain dearest Louise your very affectionate sister Louise Margaret.

(718)

Louischen's marriage to Arthur was the 'bright sunny side' of her life, which had hitherto been miserable owing to the unpleasantness of her father, Prince Frederick Charles of Prussia. At the wedding in March 1879, he complained that Prince Arthur's house at Bagshot, where he stayed, had not enough rooms. The Queen wrote in her journal, 'I assured him I had just the same at Osborne!'

ANNE, DUCHESS OF SUTHERLAND, TO THE QUEEN STAFFORD HOUSE, 25 MAY 1878

Death of the Duchess of Argyll, Lorne's mother:

Madam, We thank Your Majesty from our hearts for the most gracious message we have just received. It is too terribly sad about poor Elizabeth;

last night we were dining at Marlborough House, when just after dinner a note came from Princess Louise to the Prince of Wales saying they could not come, as poor Elizabeth had been taken *very* ill while dining with Lord and Lady Frederick Cavendish in Carlton Terrace. We went there, and found the most distressing scene; Elizabeth (*I* thought then in the last agony) struggling for breath, though quite unconscious, laid on a mattress on the floor in the room next the dining room; Argyll and all her children and many friends round her, so that we felt we ought not to stay, there was so little air and room. In the general confusion and dismay Princess Louise looked such an angel of goodness and calmness, kneeling by her head. Stafford [Duke of Sutherland] stayed for a time, but I came away, and waited up here – it was all over at 4, still without consciousness, and I trust without much suffering.

Princess Louise writes this morning to me very kindly to tell me of poor Argyll, about whom we were very anxious, as he has always been in such a terrible state at her illnesses; but now he is better than we dared to hope, having dreaded this for so long that it has not been such a *shock* to him as it might have been. The Crown Prince and Princess of Germany had just graciously consented to honour us by dining here on the 3rd; of course this is now at an end.

I must also thank Your Majesty for the very kind answer through Lady Ely to my best wishes for yesterday [Queen Victoria's birthday], which I had wanted to *write*, not telegraph; but I stupidly missed the messenger.... A. Sutherland.

(1769)

LORD LORNE TO THE QUEEN
KENSINGTON PALACE, 27 MAY 1878

Death of Lorne's mother:
We have been much comforted in our sorrow, and much touched by your dear letter. Our loss has indeed at last come suddenly, but for some time past I have had a sort of conviction that I should make the most of the time which remained to me to see as much of her as possible, for the days would be few – and there is nothing I am more thankful for, than this: that I was able of late to visit her almost every day. There never was a Mother who more deserved all the devotion a child could give her, for she loved us with her whole soul.

We have laid her today in a chapel of the great abbey [Westminster] to which she so loved to go, and the dear Dean read the 121st Psalm, some prayers, and then we repeated after him the Lord's Prayer.

Caroline Leinster and Constance Westminster were the two sisters there, all her sons, Charles Howard, Leinster and Westminster.

The place where she rests for the few days before she is taken to Scotland is quite shut off from the rest of the Church, so that no one can enter it without having the key of the door that leads into it. It is very high, and there is an old fresco above a recessed altar. Kind as Freddy Cavendish and Lucy were, I feel it a relief that we have taken her from the floor of the little room in their house, where she died, and where the body lay in a bed made on the floor until today.

I took a photographer there on Sunday, and he has succeeded in doing something tolerably good of her. I hope Louise may be able to do something in clay from the likeness. Mrs. Gladstone and Lady Cavendish had covered her most beautifully with flowers.

The bracelet you gave to her was on her arm when she died, and my Father asked Louise to whom it had best be given, and she agreed that Mary [Glyn, her daughter] who had been most constant in her attendance on her should be the one to have it.

My Father has terrible fits of grief, but is usually wonderfully calm, and thinks much of details of the ceremony to be gone through in Scotland, and which he dreads so much.

If I may I should like to write to you from Rosneath after all is over at Kilmun [the burial place]. I am, dear Mama, ever your loving and dutiful, Lorne.

(1794)

SAME TO SAME
ROSNEATH, 6 JUNE 1878

Sure enough Lorne sends HM a long account of the funeral, which must have gladdened her heart. Here is an extract:

The beauty of the situation of the ruin of the old Church of Kilmun was much admired, and the modern church is not ugly. There is an avenue of fine old sycamores leading from the shore up to the gate of the churchyard, and high hills look down upon it on three sides. The name is supposed to be the 'cell of teaching' or 'instruction' as a collegiate church was founded there by an ancestor in 1453 – the vault is a larger place than I imagined. There are great stone platforms on both sides of a wide passage – the coffins lie on those platforms, and at the end of the broad passage is a recessed tomb with a fine monument of an old Earl and his Countess. His is in curious armour minutely carved in stone. The vault was draped with black cloth, and the old crimson velvet covered coffins looked ghastly in the half light. . . .

(1795)

Lorne included a sketch of Holy Loch to the left, then the vault on the side of the church, then the modern church, then the ruins of the old church, with trees on the right and hills behind.

THE QUEEN TO PRINCESS LOUISE BALMORAL, 18 SEPTEMBER 1878

Royal parting: Louise is off to Canada.

Most precious Loosy, This is a dreadful hard parting and I felt and feel more than I can say. God bless you my darling child is what I say and what in fact can I wish more truly?

Everyone felt it deeply but still let us think it will not be for so long – and you must try and come and see me *next Autumn.* If you say beforehand you *promised* to come and see *me*, then every one will expect it.

Your dear little note made me shed many tears. When you left I felt as if you had left me *really* only *now*.

But we must not dwell on that; but on the work *to do* before us – and to try to bear up against the trials which beset us in this world, which is only a preparation for the *next*....

Your dear photographs are a great pleasure and comfort as well as your dear hair, and I will get a crystal locket to put a small photo into it of you which I will *wear* daily till D.V. we meet again.... Dear Beatrice sends you much love. The good Child loves you much....

(721)

The Queen preferred to part earlier at Balmoral rather than see Louise and Lorne off from Liverpool on 14 November.

THE QUEEN TO LORD LORNE BALMORAL, 21 SEPTEMBER 1878

Royal advice:

Dear Lorne, I had meant to say a few general words to you while you were here but I could not manage it, so I will write them. But first I must say what a terrible parting it was from my dear Louise; – so far off, and for *so* long! But the thought she may come back to see me is a consolation.

What I would principally wish to advise and impress on you, is to be very cautious and do nothing in a hurry; – not to be rash – or *act* on the spur of the moment. But always to *reflect* well, and delay any answer or action for a day or two. I know from experience how difficult it is not to put pen to paper, or to speak when one feels strongly, especially if one is irritated. But also, how, when one pauses and waits for a day and a night, one calms down and is able to take a different and more impartial view of things.

Good Lord Dufferin with the best intentions has not made it easier for either of you, by making people perhaps expect so very much. Still what he said was very pretty....

(722)

The appointment was for three years minimum, with leave each year and an extension to five years if Louise liked it.

PRINCESS ALICE TO PRINCESS LOUISE DARMSTADT, 2 NOVEMBER 1878

A farewell letter:
Dearest Louise, Only two words as I am again laid up, to send you the enclosed paper from a Frau Thörber, agent for the emigration of Germans to Canada. Please read it and beg Lorne to do so. I shall see the lady probably again before she leaves for Canada, and she has begged me to give her a letter of introduction to you. She is not prepossessing but does good work and it would be *very* useful if you both would lend your attention to it.

How is dear Leopold? Arrived all right? His visit was such a *great great* pleasure to me, to us all, and he is so nice to have in the house dear boy!

Tell him I will write as soon as I can. Please let me know beforehand the day of your departure. How much we shall all think of you when you leave and during your passage and be so anxious for news – there have been such storms. I do hope you will have fine weather. Goodbye once more and God bless you ever your loving sister Alice.

(723)

Louise was never to see Alice again.

JAMES MCNEILL WHISTLER TO PRINCESS LOUISE 8 NOVEMBER 1878

Nature painted without fog – a present from the artist:
Madam – I feel it incumbent upon myself, as your Painter – by devotion, if not by office – to right myself, if it be possible, in the eyes of my Royal Mistress.

You may have forgotten a right suggestion of General Fog in the methods of the one, who, if indifferent absolutely to the judgment of all others, has the ambition to be seriously considered by the Artist Princess whose high opinion he has made it his duty to acquire.

It saddens him to think that she, who has been so often most gracious and indulgent in her protection, should at all accept the popular belief of meretricious and wilful eccentricity in the work of the painter she has been so kind to!

May I venture to offer Your Royal Highness as a tribute of devotion and gratitude, a favourite picture of my own – which has successfully resisted the danger of sale on more than one occasion – and which I send herewith?

In it, I would timidly hint that, while I recognise nature's masterly use of fairy fog – 'when the evening mist clothes the riverside with poetry, as with a veil' – I still do love to look at her when she is beautiful without it.... If in my impulse, I may have been presumptuous, I entreat Your Royal Highness to forgive – and not to refuse my offering.

(1993)

THE PRINCE OF WALES TO PRINCESS LOUISE
SANDRINGHAM, 13 NOVEMBER 1878

Another farewell letter:

Dearest Louise, these few lines are to wish you once more goodbye, and God speed! I could not bear wishing you goodbye on Monday but live in hopes that in less than a year you will be back and only trust that you will have a prosperous and speedy passage, and like your life in Canada more than you expect. Both you and Lorne have a great future before you, and I feel convinced will make the most of the great opportunities which are afforded you.

I hope that you and Lorne will write to me from time to time, and remember if I can be of any use to either of you, in any way, you have only to let me know. I wish I was at Liverpool tomorrow to see you off, but as it is impossible you know I shall be with you in thought. Will you give the enclosed letter to Affie, and send me a telegram that you have received these lines. Once more goodbye and God bless you, darling Louise. Alix sends you her best love, and the children many kisses. Give Lorne many kind messages from us. Ever your devoted brother Bertie.

(724)

PRINCE ARTHUR TO PRINCESS LOUISE
WINDSOR CASTLE, 23 NOVEMBER 1878

Dearest Louise, How kind of you still writing me a line from Loch Foyle – Leo and I felt so sad going home without you but it was a great pleasure to us having seen the last of you on this side of the Atlantic. I do hope you have had a fine passage and auspicious weather for your arrival at Halifax. How well I remember my arrival there on a fine summer's morning nearly ten years ago. Almost the first thing that will have greeted your arrival in Halifax will be the sad news of poor little May's death [Alice's baby daughter, from diphtheria], and the serious illness of all the others. Thank God they are getting much better, but imagine the frightful anxiety Alice has had to go through. At the very time of the funeral of her little darling she had to go into the room of Louis [her husband] and the others with a smiling face as if nothing had happened. We have all felt so much for her and I am sure that you will do so too.

24 November

We have just heard of your safe arrival but alas after a stormy passage which I am so sorry to hear. I do hope you will soon have shaken off the effects of your journey across. I feel so much for you having had such a tossing, for I know how bad a sailor you are. I find Mama and Beatrice looking very flourishing; I have just come from breakfast, where we talked a great deal about you.

I leave tomorrow night for Berlin and am overjoyed at the prospect of seeing dear Louischen so soon. I am longing to hear an account of your reception in Canada and how everything goes off. I hear that they have gone to a great deal of trouble and expense to do you honour – you know what a Canadian I am in feeling so you can imagine the interest I take in all that will be going on there now.

Arthur continues with domestic news about ladies-in-waiting and also the Afghan War.

I am afraid that I have quite exhausted all I had to say – With my humble duty to His Excellency the Governor-General. I embrace you and remain ever your most affectionate brother Arthur.

(725)

Alice was to die of diphtheria at Darmstadt on 14 December, the date on which her father, whom she had nursed so devotedly seventeen years before, had died.

THE QUEEN TO LORD LORNE
BUCKINGHAM PALACE, 19 FEBRUARY 1880

Louise's sleigh accident in Ottawa, 14 February (see pages 97–8):

Dear Lorne, What an awful accident and *how* alarmed you *must* have been! I can't say how *terrible* it is to be away and so far away at such a moment! I feel *very anxious* still and fear my poor Darling must suffer much from her poor head, this coming so soon after her bad voyage. I wish I could be near her, but I doubt not how tenderly she will be cared for by you....

I must end, hoping that my Darling Loosy will be nearly or quite well, when this reaches you. Ever your devoted Mama V.R.I.

(1706)

The Queen came to feel that Loosy was never 'quite well' again, at least in regard to her relations with her husband. Others have believed that Louise used the accident as an excuse for escaping for months on end from a husband – and country? – she disliked. Certainly the marriage began to go wrong in the early 1880s. But Louise did not dislike Canada – quite the opposite. Nor was she malingering, an idea which arose as the result of suppression of the facts by her misguided staff. No one realized how serious her condition had been.

LORD LORNE TO THE QUEEN
GOVERNMENT HOUSE, OTTAWA, 23 FEBRUARY 1880

Nine days after the accident:
Madam and dearest Mama, Louise will herself write to you today and tell you how she has moved to the sofa. I know you will approve of the change, for you do not like too much lying in bed, but she must be kept very quiet for some time, as any excitement makes the place where she received the blow ache much. The hearing, which was affected, owing to the blow affecting the 'auditory nerve', on one side, is much improved, although not yet perfect. My chief anxiety now is that she may for some time feel the effects of fatigue undergone at any place in the form of severe headache at the injured part, but we must hope for the best. The lying quiet is very wearisome to her, and she is always inclined to do more than she ought to do. We have every reason to be most thankful that such good progress has been made, constant applications of cold cloths to the head have had good effect, and it is the only thing she asks for. Last night for instance she called me in four times to change the cloth. It was the first night on which she had *not taken* a teaspoonful of Bromide to make her sleep, and although her sleep was intermittent, she had a good deal.... I shall regularly let you know what the doctor says of her, and what are my own impressions.

(1796)

THE QUEEN TO LORD LORNE
BUCKINGHAM PALACE, 13 MARCH 1880

Dear Lorne, Many thanks for your 2 kind letters of the 16th and 23rd Feb: – the first of which crossed mine. I thank God! my darling Child has been mercifully preserved, as well as you too from death, for *that in fact* is the *truth*! Dear Louise of course was in much greater danger from the fact of the severity of the injuries, which *you* telegraphed to me the 1st day were *not serious*! how could you say that, when the injuries were SO serious? ... I am disappointed at having no telegram for a week and only one medical report. Dr. Grant should write once a week. Whenever any of my children are ill the doctor always writes to me. I was pleased to get 2 letters written by her. When one has lost one dear child far away one becomes terribly anxious. Young Bagot and the groom seem to have shewn such presence of mind. I hope you will never use a covered sleigh again; they are said to be so dangerous....

Olive Campbell, Lorne's sister-in-law, was also bad news.

I *must* tell you that *'Olive's' style* of dressing is really dreadful. So painted and so decoletée that she does not *look* respectable, and I hear *no one* would think, to see her driving in the Park, that she belonged to society!! *Can* you not get Walter [Olive's husband] to keep her in order and stop this!

I am in a great hurry to start for Windsor and so can't write more. Hoping that this will find dear Louise quite strong again. Ever your very affectionate Mama V.R.I.

(1707)

LORD LORNE TO THE QUEEN
SS *DRUID*, GASPÉ, PROVINCE OF QUEBEC
6 AUGUST 1880

After Louise departed for home, Lorne went on tour.

Madam and dearest Mama, I have received your beautiful present, for which pray accept my loving thanks; and 2 telegrams ... and the second message, which had waited 3 days at Gaspé. These messages are most cheering, and when one is in low spirits are especially so. Of course after Louise's departure my spirits are not at flood tide. I wish I could think it would be right to go over to England for a visit, but the effect would be bad here, and I should stick to my post. The [people] are ridiculously sensitive about everything that looks as if their country were disagreeable to Englishmen, and they have besides a very proper opinion that an official should remain at his office, as long as their country pays him to remain there.

About Louise, I must make up my mind that she should have a good long time at home. If she came back before spring, she would very probably get into a weak state again, and only have to return. If she remains till the spring I think there is good hope that the quiet and rest and home-surroundings may give her back such strength that she may really enjoy the spring and summer season of next year here, and not be too much fatigued with the work which is inseparable from the position. No real rest can be got in Canada, for people expect one to appear everywhere, and are angrily disappointed if the appearance be not made. I told them in a speech lately at Quebec that they must consider her to have been injured in their service just as much as any soldier might be on duty.

They can be got to understand illness but they don't understand anyone in apparently good health not doing all that their own hardy constitutions make them think mere trifles. Louise has almost always the appearance of being well, even when she feels great weakness, and is up to doing nothing, and a retired residence among them they would not understand, and attribute it to ill will and dislike of themselves. So on all accounts it is wisest, however painful, that she should come back with the Birds in the spring, and able I trust to sing as strongly and happily as they.

I was very glad that before going I was able to arrange a ceremonial for her in the laying of a memorial stone in the great Dock Works undertaken at Quebec, and which are to bear her name. Next year I hope to get a new province in our 'North West' named after her [Alberta, her third name], which shall have a population equal to that of Greece and Denmark together, for we have room for four or five such Provinces there....

It would be so very good of you dearest Mama if you would let me hear how you think Louise is in health during the winter. I am ever with the greatest devotion and love your devoted Lorne.

(1797)

LORD LORNE TO PRINCESS LOUISE
QUEBEC, 13 SEPTEMBER 1880

Dearest One, vast wood fires are going on everywhere in the Ottawa valley, and in Bagot country, where at a place called Upton over 30 miles of country have been laid waste. They say that the scenes have been terrible, for the fire came on so quickly, blown by a strong wind that people saved themselves with great difficulty. Several were lost and much property has been destroyed. The Priests are making appeals for assistance. I should like to subscribe but am about 5,000 dollars in debt, and have not yet paid a vast coal bill, so I refrain, especially as the fires have been so widespread, and have hurt so many Districts that there would be no end to the claims if one once began sending subscriptions. The whole air here has been full of fog smoke and the smell of wood....

She [Mme Bierstadt] is so delicate now that she has kept her room entirely since she has been here, and subsists wholly on sugar biscuit and ices, varied by very hot sips of coffee. [Albert] Bierstadt looks benignant and gentlemanlike about it all, and paints away all day long in the most philosophic manner.... We had M. Bosset, and Miss de Salaberry, O'Brien P.R.C.A.! [president of the Royal Canadian Academy] to meet him at dinner. Mad. Bosset has made another small Bosset and could not appear. There is talk of getting up a General Art Union Society at New York like the English one. Agnew, the great picture dealer, is to have a house to sell pictures at, in New York.... Bierstadt's account of the manner in which Americans are now buying European paintings and the immense sums they give for them, and their inability to know what to buy, or where to put it when bought, is sometimes amusing. For instance he says that one New Yorker lately bought an immense anatomical study of a dead man, with plenty of blood about it, and highly shadowed pale muscles, and then stuck it up in his dining-room, where several friends when they were asked what they would like to eat, pointed to the 'cold meat' on the side wall, and said, 'A slice of that please?' 'Well you must be hungry', another man said 'to feed your appetite on a dead Caesar.'

Lorne continues with an account of the painter's activities and of his womenfolk:

... his wife and sister-in-law creep out of their rooms for dinner, and sip their iced water, and then creep back again, all tinyness, twang and toggery....

Perhaps you are now at Salzburg. Mozart's house is there. I wish I could see all these places again with you. It is very hard not to be able to do so. Your own L.

(1811)

JAMES MCNEILL WHISTLER TO CAPTAIN ARTHUR COLLINS, PRINCESS LOUISE'S COMPTROLLER, INCORPORATED SOCIETY OF BRITISH ARTISTS SUFFOLK STREET, PALL MALL EAST 188... (DATE INCOMPLETE)

An invitation from the famous painter to Princess Louise to 'touch a cup of tea':

Do my dear Collins listen to me for an instant in the midst of things!

You perceive from the printed business at the side here [the address], or top rather, qu'il s'agit of matters that I have at heart.

I do so want the most charming of Princesses to be gracious and kindly intentioned to this most respectable and hitherto dreary dank and moss grown body of British artists whose wisdom was in their despair – when they called upon me to join them!

I mean to bring upon them and into their very midst the unknown success and joy of whose very existence they doubt themselves not! You know that this we cannot fail in if we tarry with the dear old things – and at present we *mean* to abide! and so have created a tabernacle of 'sharp bright gaiety' in Suffolk Street to which I venture to entreat the Princess to give her gentle countenance.

Do my dear Collins say things nicely for me to H.R.H. She has been so good and indulgent that I really have not the hardihood to trouble her with a note to answer.

Tell her that you know how dainty and pretty are our Sunday afternoons – and say that if she would only pass through the galleries next Sunday at about five o'clock or so and touch a cup of tea in the place our triumph would be complete!

It would seem impossible that I should think further! – and yet do you know I really believe that perhaps the Princess would come also to my little 'Arrangement in Gold and Brown' in Bond Steet.

Dare you ask?

Mon cher je vous laisse! – with all this! Forgive me, and merci mille fois d'avance.

Always J.

(1995)

The next letter suggests that Collins did his work well, though he probably had little difficulty in persuading Princess Louise to visit an art gallery equipped with so many 'dainty' attractions.

JAMES MCNEILL WHISTLER TO PRINCESS LOUISE NO ADDRESS OR DATE EXCEPT '188 . . .'

Madam – I cannot tell you how charmed and delighted I am to know that you are coming tomorrow. From what you said at first, I suppose that four o'clock would be the hour at which to expect you, also I hope that this would be your choice, because in the afternoon the light is so much better. Therefore if I do not receive an intimation to the contrary at Tite Street tomorrow by 12 o'clock, I shall be at the gallery in Suffolk Street to receive Your Royal Highness at four o'clock.

I hope also that perhaps Mr. Boehm may be able to come at about half past four – and he would be far better able to point out the pictures than I should unaided! I have Madam the honour to be your most devoted and obedient servant. J. A. McNeill Whistler.

(1994)

This is possibly the first of the letters to Louise from artists. They were not very good at dating their letters. Edgar Boehm was the Queen's sculptor-in-ordinary and Princess Louise's instructor.

THE CROWN PRINCESS OF PRUSSIA TO LORD LORNE
WIESBADEN, 26 NOVEMBER 1880

... How very lonely you must feel in Canada all by yourself.... I pity you very much, – a Home is only half a Home when the mistress of the House is absent....

Charlotte and Bernhard have been staying with us for a fortnight, the dear little Baby begins to run and to talk and is a merry lively forward little thing though diminutively small!

My other girlies send you their best love, and often ask after you! Victoria is taller than I am now. I think she will hardly grow any more! She reminds me of Louise very often, and I hope she will be like her when she grows up!...

(1719)

Victoria was known as Young Vicky or Moretta.

THE QUEEN TO LORD LORNE
WINDSOR CASTLE, 9 DECEMBER 1880

After seasonal wishes and notes about her present to him, the Queen continues:
As for our dear Louise, I cannot honestly say I think her looking well. She suffers so much from her head, and any fatigue or excitement brings it on. She is grown so thin too. It is very distressing that this terrible accident should have shaken her *so much.*

We must hope that time and continued quiet will restore her shattered nerves. She has been staying with Leopold, and is coming to us on the 13th and will go with us to Osborne where I hope she will stay some time, and be very quiet.

(1708)

SAME TO SAME
2 JULY 1881

Should Louise return to Canada now?
... I have not yet seen her since I got your second letter. But I sent it her. She is so afraid that people in Canada will think she is not doing her duty – that she would rather risk her health than not to go back.

But I say that is *not* wise; that it was *in doing her duty* that she met with her dreadful accident and that she would be of no use to you if she returned quite weak and broke down again. She is *looking* decidedly better but I fear it *is* not as much as we could wish yet....

Louise is in despair at not making this long and interesting journey with you [to Western Canada], but even if she were not delicate as she is now, it would be far too fatiguing for her who requires often days of complete rest and even comfort.... Still I can understand her being disappointed.

(731)

SAME TO SAME
OSBORNE, 10 JANUARY 1882

Lorne returns to Canada alone.

Dearest Lorne, One more loving word to wish you God speed – and every possible blessing. I don't think I thanked you half enough for the lovely little Poem you sent me which brought tears to my eyes – especially the combining my sweet, good, faithful child's and companion's name with mine, pleased me so much. You should print them.

It is very wild and very blowy tonight and I trust the packet will delay if it blows hard.... Louise will now know what we have twice gone through: the long and anxious waiting. God bless you! Surely *that* comprises all. Beatrice sends many many loves. Ever your devoted Mama V.R.I.

(733)

LORD LORNE TO PRINCESS LOUISE
LETTER WRITTEN AT SEA TRAVELLING TO CANADA
JANUARY 1882

Letter ends:

... I forgot I think to mention Du Maurier as a man who might be asked to dine. He is a very nice man as well as a good artist – married, I think.

Now my little one you must entertain yourself well, for health much depends on good spirits – WALK EVERY DAY – God bless you. Your L.

(1814)

JAMES MCNEILL WHISTLER TO PRINCESS LOUISE WEDNESDAY, 8 NOVEMBER 1882

Madam, I have never forgotten the flattering visit to Chelsea, and indulgent sympathy evinced by Your Royal Highness in my work, – and so venture to beg that you would come and see the decorations I am now completing at no. 49 Prince's Gate, where I should be ready to receive Your Royal Highness tomorrow at any hour, or on any other day you would kindly appoint. I have the honour to be, Madam, your very faithful servant J. A. McNeill Whistler.

(1996)

PRINCE ARTHUR TO PRINCESS LOUISE BUCKINGHAM PALACE, 1 JUNE 1883

News from home:
... There is a great deal to see in London this year and what with duty at Aldershot I have a deal of running about.... The new Water Colour exhibition is charming in every respect, the rooms admirable and the shows of pictures quite excellent, I think better than the Academy....

Poor Leo is very much cut up at his not being able to get out to Canada as Governor-General. I am very sorry for him, but 'entre nous' I don't think he quite set about it the right way, having neither asked Mama or the Ministers in time. Poor Mama has been terribly upset by Brown's death – and her knee has given her so much trouble, she is still very lame.

(737)

Louise and Lorne were in their last year in Canada. John Brown died of erysipelas caused by alcoholism on 29 March 1883.

PRINCESS LOUISE TO THE QUEEN KENSINGTON PALACE, 25 MARCH 1884

Anniversary of John Brown's death:
Dearest Mama, I know that tomorrow will be a trying day to you all, the sad recollections of last year coming back to you, accept my warmest sympathy dear Mama, the loss of a friend no other can replace though they may be as devoted and true, yet of course they are not the same. Yet I trust with time you may find comfort from those around you, who think but of your happiness and good. Ever your dutiful and devoted daughter Louise.

(Z211/85)

PRINCE ARTHUR TO PRINCESS LOUISE MEERUT, 5 APRIL 1884

Death of Leopold:
Dearest Louise, I feel I must write to you about dear Leo – What a loss we have all had and how fond we were of the dear boy with all his whims and his brightness of intellect. His life has not always been a happy one and he has been at death's door on so many occasions. I had so hoped that he had really got stronger and that now his life was so much happier and that he had got such a nice home at Claremont he would worry himself less about things and that he would be happy and contented. I have heard of no particulars and am longing to know what really happened and what brought on his end.

The terrible news fairly broke me down and with the great heat and the immense amount of writing I have had to do this week I feel quite knocked up.

How are you dearest Louise and how do you feel now you are once more in England again. The papers are full of reports of Lorne's coming out here to succeed Lord Ripon, is there any truth in it; I never believe anything I see in an Indian paper.

(744)

Nor in a British one. Lorne longed for the rumours to be true, but Lord Dufferin got the plum job.

DUCHESS OF CONNAUGHT (LOUISCHEN) TO PRINCESS LOUISE MUSSOORIE, 24 APRIL 1884

Leopold's dream:
His strange and touching dream and presentiments must have warned him of his approaching end and he must, I feel sure, have been prepared for it.

What your grief must be I can well imagine, you, dear Louise were so devoted to that beloved brother, and I feel for you with all my heart. Since I have known darling Leo, I have always been so fond of him, he was so kind and dear and such a delightful companion....

(745)

An extremely well-written letter and more legible than most of the English family. We do not know what Leopold's dream was.

PRINCE ARTHUR TO PRINCESS LOUISE
BALMORAL, 24 OCTOBER 1885

Put out by Mama:
Dearest Louise, Many thanks for your letter received this morning. I was afraid you would be rather taken aback at my telegram and all the time feared that you might not be able to manage to come out to India this winter, much as we regret to hear that you cannot come, we understand your reasons fully and cannot help thinking that you are right in your decision.

It is now very likely that we may not go out to India till next spring, as since yesterday Mama *positively refuses* to let us go so soon as next month, partly on account of the elections and possible consequences and partly because she thinks it wrong in Louischen taking so long a journey so close to her confinement. As long as we did not go later than the end of next month it would do Louischen no harm and she was most anxious to go out with me then. Of course everything would be much more convenient if Louischen could be confined here, but then she does not like to separate herself from me for so long when so far away and she does not wish to interfere with my military projects. We were quite prepared to go out and are very much put out at Mama's having *now* refused to let us go. It is not *settled* of course but the authorities have been asked if they could not allow Sir Biddulph to remain another six months at Pindi so as to prevent my going out till next spring, and after Louischen's confinement. The chopping and changing that has been going on about our movements has been something fearful and we have been nearly worried to death about it.

It was only two days ago that I heard finally that the Indian authorities refused to give me the Bombay government on political grounds; this question has been going on since July with endless ups and downs, hopes and disappointments. I really don't know how the whole thing is going to end.

Mama made such stipulations about the children coming back in April that we most reluctantly decided not to take them with us. If we went out in the spring we *could not* take them *out with us*, as the climate would be too trying for them at that time of the year. They might perhaps follow out in the autumn.

I have now given you all the ins and outs of our present and past position. I do hope that you might really be able to come out next autumn for the winter. We don't know when we come south yet; to add to our complications Buckingham Palace is closed till the beginning of December on account of all the drains being up and we don't know where to go to, as Bagshot of course is still shut up. *All* our things are at Buckingham

Palace and we could not even go out for a walk without going there to get our clothes from there. It is very cold here and I should like very much to get away and take the children with us. You will agree with me that we are met with difficulties on every side and that we are and have really been rather sorely tried. Louischen, who keeps well sends you her best love and I remain your most affectionate brother Arthur.

(759)

SAME TO SAME
BALMORAL, 2 NOVEMBER 1885

Dearest Louise, It was most kind of you offering to take us in, in answer to my telegram.... Although we are not coming to stay with you I hope we shall see something of you. We bring the chidren with us which is a great thing. You will have heard by now, and I think I mentioned it in my letter, that we do not go out to India till next spring when we got to Rawalpindi. Now we shall have time to make our arrangements, which would have been impossible had we to have gone out end of this or beginning of next month.

We are looking forward to leave this as it is awfully dull here. All the trees have lost their leaves and everything presents a very wintry appearance.

Mama is wonderfully well and can walk a mile at a time now and also rides her pony again – the 'young couple' [Beatrice and 'Liko', Prince Henry of Battenberg] are very flourishing and Mama more taken with him than ever. It is very nice having Georgy [the future George v] here, he is such a good boy.

(760)

SAME TO SAME
BAGSHOT PARK, SURREY, 28 NOVEMBER 1885

Lorne defeated:
I am afraid that Lorne must have been very much disappointed at losing his election, although my feelings are more conservative than anything, I am very sorry for him.

(761)

THE QUEEN TO LORD LORNE
BALMORAL, 3 JUNE 1886

Lorne under siege:
Dear Lorne, I am *most* anxious that you should come forward *now* and stand for the *Unionist* and *Imperial* cause, and stand for some good place! I know how useful you would be, *not* as a *party* man, but as a *true patriot*, and as everyone else *must* (and all *do* who are not blinded by Mr. Gladstone's words and name) – put your shoulder to the wheel and strive to help our country.

Mr. Goschen would I am sure give you the best and wisest advice and *now* is the right moment. I spoke to your Father about it and he agreed with me.

Hoping to hear soon from you and that your party tomorrow will go off well, believe me always your affectionate Mama V.R.I.

The country is looking beautiful.

(771)

SAME TO SAME
BALMORAL, 16 JUNE 1886

Lorne's career:
Dear Lorne, I am anxiously hoping to hear that you are coming forward to put your shoulder to the wheel. If not in Scotland, where it may be more difficult, I hope it may be found feasible in some other place. You would be of so much use, that I write to press you again. This is a moment when every true and loyal subject should put his shoulder to the wheel and come forward to try and defeat the most wild and dangerous plans ever proposed. Ever your very affectionate Mama VRI.

(772)

PRINCE ARTHUR TO PRINCESS LOUISE
RAWALPINDI, 18 NOVEMBER 1886

He is very disappointed that she has decided she can't come to India this winter. He then goes on to the birth of Beatrice's baby.
Were you in time for the great event at Windsor; it surely came off long before it was expected, what a fluster there must have been at the Castle – our wet nurse was to have been Beatrice's nurse but I don't think that Patsy was yet weaned. Now that Beatrice has got a baby we feel more than ever that our children would be much better away as they must be '*de trop*'.

(777)

THE PRINCE OF WALES TO PRINCESS LOUISE
SANDRINGHAM, 27 DECEMBER 1886

We *quite* understand that Lorne prefers *not* coming [to stay]. The resignation of R. Churchill is a severe blow to the Government and in my humble opinion will cause its downfall. The suddenness of it indeed took me greatly by surprise. Who is to fill his place? and be Leader of the House of Commons? I cannot say. It is indeed a serious 'impasse' and will greatly weaken our position in the Council of Nations. Well indeed can poor Mama be put out about it....

(778)

PRINCE ARTHUR TO PRINCESS LOUISE
POONA, 30 DECEMBER 1886

... How sorry I have been for you at all this disgraceful *Colin* divorce case, there has never been anything so bad before and I am amazed that the Duke, Lorne and all the family ever permitted the matter going before a public court. One is quite ashamed to talk about it and I should think that Colin will be unable to show his face for some time to come.

(779)

Lord Colin Campbell was Lorne's youngest brother and his notorious divorce case a major Victorian scandal that bankrupted him, causing him to be ostracized. It involved accusations of syphilis.

SAME TO SAME
THE RESIDENCY, ADEN, 18 FEBRUARY 1887

... I have not heard much news from home and get a *little exasperated* when Mama enlarges on the affection of our children for 'Auntie B. and Uncle Liko' – It is hard enough to be separated from the children but then to be told *how fond* they are of other people is a little *too much*. We would give anything to bring them or have them sent out to us this autumn but I fear the opposition in high quarters 'on medical grounds' will be something fearful.

(781)

PRINCE GEORGE TO PRINCESS LOUISE
RÉUNION DE CANNES, 4 APRIL 1887

My darling Aunt Louise, I am writing you these few lines to Naples where I hope you will get them. I was dreadfully sorry to say goodbye to you the other day at Malta, but still the few days we spent together were better than none at all. I hope you had some fun after we left and went for some rides. Now I suppose you are in the 'Alexandra' on your way to Naples. I hope you will have a good passage and that you will not be ill. I miss you very much, my dear, you are always so kind to me. We must look forward to our next meeting in June, which I am glad to say is not so very far off now....

(784)

SAME TO SAME
SAN ANTONIO PALACE, MALTA, 24 APRIL 1887

My darling Aunt Louise – Here we are back at Malta again and everything is much the same as when you left. I miss you very much my dear and wish you were here now, I have nobody to ride with or joke with now that you are gone, and I miss our little talks we used to have.

Uncle Alfred, Aunt Marie and cousins are all very flourishing, Aunt Marie and cousins leave for Coburg in the 'Surprise' on the 30th, Lady Mary [Fitzwilliam, Marie's lady-in-waiting] goes with them, she is just the same, but I am always very good friends with her, she has not mentioned your name, except she told me you had been to Rome with Fortescue and Marsh, it amused me very much the way she said it, as much as to say that you ought not to have gone with them and that she did not like it. The first night these two came back they were asked to dinner, but they were not cross-examined about Rome as I expected they would have been, I was dining that night. Fortescue and Bourke dine continually to Lady Mary's delight, it is very amusing the way she goes on with them....

Fortescue, Marsh and Bourke were officers on Affie's ship, Bourke being the commander of Surprise. *Georgie was reporting implied criticism of Louise's unconventional behaviour.*

Uncle Alfred wishes me to ask you what you have done with the caricature you did of the Governor as he can't find it anywhere, and he has looked in all his books, so he imagines you have taken it away, but he wants to know....

We shall all be here for Grandmama's birthday and on the 27th we start on our summer cruise, but it is not quite settled where we are going yet;

but Uncle Alfred and I will leave Marseilles on the 15th or 16th of June for England whatever happens, so I suppose we shall be home by 17th or 18th; how delighted I shall be to see them all again, I am going to have a month in England I believe which will be too delightful, it will be nearly a year and a half since I was in England and I think that is quite long enough, don't you.... I hope you spent a pleasant time at Rome and Aix. Have you met Liko anywhere yet? I hope Lorne is very flourishing, give him my love.... Now I must close this stupid letter which I hope you will burn. With very best love.

(785)

There is a postscript on the back of this letter saying that it is all right: they have just found the caricature of the Governor and have stuck it safely in the caricature book.

SAME TO SAME
HMS *DREADNOUGHT*, SUDA BAY, CRETE, MONDAY 9 MAY 1887

My darling old Aunt, I was delighted to get your charming long letter of the 29th from Kensington, I thank you a thousand times for it, and feel very touched at your thinking about poor me. I hope you have got the letter I wrote you from Malta, it ought to have arrived the day you wrote. I am so glad you have seen Papa and that he is very flourishing, so Neilson was just as clumsy and stupid as ever, I should have gone into fits of laughter too, but still I like him, he is a very good creature but certainly not gifted with too much common sense.

This was possibly Soren Neilsen, a page in the Wales's household, who seems to have come from Denmark with Princess Alexandra in 1863.

I am so sorry you are so dull out at Kensington and that you are in bed with a knock on your chest, poor thing, how did it happen, I shan't say anything about it. I wish I was in London, I would come and see you and read to you and try cheer you up [*sic*], but that I can't do unfortunately, so I hope you will soon be all right again and get more lively.

I am very glad you spent a pleasant time in Rome.... So Liko arrived before you left and began abusing your clothes, you certainly ought to have snubbed him well and told him you had not so much money as Beatrice has to spend on your clothes, *damn* his impertinence, he has nothing else to do I suppose but look at people's clothes, poor creature.

There has been another awful row about the uniforms at Malta, this time the old Governor was certainly wrong, I have tried to stop Uncle Alfred doing anything, because it is such a pity always having rows, don't say a word about it, will you? I must say I think the Governor is a *damned old fool* about lots of things, don't you, and it is such a pity always fighting when you are in such a small place as Malta.... I miss you my dear, very much and all our nice rides and talks and jokes etc. etc. but I hope we shall very soon meet again now....

(786)

PRINCESS LOUISE TO THE QUEEN KENSINGTON PALACE, 22 MAY 1887

Queen Victoria's birthday in Golden Jubilee Year:
Dearest Mama, Let me wish you all that's good and blessed on your dear birthday, my thoughts will be much with you on the dear day when I wish I could be near you to kiss your dear hands.

I send you a silk shawl which I got at Aix the other day, it will I think be useful when driving in the summer or sitting out just round your shoulders.

The fan I painted is my first attempt on gauze so it's not very good, and a china cup which seemed to me to be appropriate for this year, it is a copy of an old one – and I join with Beatrice in giving you the present for the Osborne church room, which we partly gave you at Xmas time. Many thanks for sending me the flowers they were a great pleasure. Also for asking dear Janie Ely and Harriet [Phipps] to call. I am better though feel washed out, and depressed; after Tuesday or Wednesday I hope to be allowed to move about like other mortals....

(F46/31)

THE QUEEN TO THE DUKE OF ARGYLL BALMORAL, 4 JUNE 1887

My dear Duke, I am so overwhelmed with letters, questions, telegrams arrangements etc. about my birthday and the Jubilee that I have got quite behindhand with my correspondence and therefore have not been able to thank you for your very kind letter with your very affectionate congratulations.

My feelings, as you will easily understand are very mixed – on this occasion – great gratitude to our Heavenly Father, for His protection and help – thankfulness for the extraordinary and unusual display of loyalty and devotion from high and low from all parts of the world – and deep sorrow at the *absence* of my beloved husband and children and many dear friends who would so warmly have shared *all*, and who are 'gone before'.

This beloved country never looked lovelier or brighter than in this very early spring here.... But I am tired *already* and dread the exertions which I shall have to undergo.

We remain here till the 16th. There is *no* cause for alarm about the dear Crown Prince's throat. He is to be treated by Dr. M. Mackenzie and is coming over soon.

Mackenzie raised false hopes about Fritz's cancer.

I hope some day you will come here again to see the many memorials to those who are in a happier world.... With kind remembrances to the Duchess, believe me always yours affectionately V.R.I.

(791)

PRINCE ARTHUR TO PRINCESS LOUISE
POONA, 17 NOVEMBER 1887

... What dreadful accounts these are of Fritz, we feel so anxious about him, as the telegrams sent out here sound so very bad, I do hope they are exaggerations.

What you tell me about Inverary [*sic*] and non-payment of rents is very sad; it is such a nice place and I know you are fond of it.

(793)

THE EMPRESS FREDERICK TO PRINCESS LOUISE
24 JUNE 1888

Fritz died of throat cancer 100 days after he and Vicky succeeded as Emperor and Empress.

Darling Louise, Lorne saw me in all the misery which is now my lot! He will tell you what he saw and heard! Let me only add TENDER and loving thanks for your *dear kind letter*, full of soothing affection for your afflicted sister! O dearest Louise, if ever life seems hard or difficult, think of me, think of the tortures I have endured! Heaven indeed gave me much!! It is *all* taken away! The kindest and best of husbands – my protector and help!

You knew and *loved* him. He was very fond of you, very fond of Lorne! You will *not* forget him I know! You will remember the kind smile with which he ever greeted you, the *pleasure* your presence always gave him! He was indeed a Brother to you all, and never happier than when he could give you pleasure...!

Poor Vicky goes on for another three pages in this vein, finally begging Louise to forgive her for not writing more.

When I begin to write, the flood of tears runs and blinds my eyes and the grief I feel seems to rob me of my senses and my memory! Goodbye – God bless you, your devoted and unhappy sister Vicky.

(801)

PRINCE ARTHUR TO PRINCESS LOUISE
MAHABALESHWAR, INDIA, 14 NOVEMBER 1888

Louise as a go-between for the Connaughts:
Dearest Louise I was so glad to get your letter of the 25th from Inverary [*sic*] – I am very much obliged to you for telling me all you have done about the dear children. All along I have felt that morally it was not the best thing for them to be with Mama and I was quite sure that the Battenberg children would be made no. 1. But great pressure has been put upon us and Mama is not at all pleased that they are coming out to us this winter and quite looks upon it as a condescension on her part.

It is very difficult to know what to do for the future as there is no chance of my returning home before the summer of '90 and Mama expects them back next spring. Daisy is rather old to remain out for the hot weather and I fear she might feel the heat.

Of course I know as well as you do that neither Mama nor Beatrice understand children and I fear ours have rather high spirits. Poor Arthur, like all boys, is occasionally naughty, but he is a good dispositioned child and I have always found him very intelligent and even thoughtful, of course he is not 6 years old yet and it is difficult to expect a child to be always obedient at that age. It is quite ridiculous Beatrice saying that he is 'slow and wanting', I do not believe a word of it – the difficulty of knowing where to send them to and 'Her Majesty's commands' may oblige us to send them home next spring, but we will consider the whole thing thoroughly before then. However, whatever happens we both feel very grateful to you for letting us know how things are – I will not show you up and no one shall know what you have written.

It is most unfortunate Colin Campbell's coming out to Bombay. . . .

We cannot of course receive him or be civil to him and we hope not to be forced to cut him publicly and I hope he will have the sense to keep clear of us as much as he can. If he is clever and hard-working he will get on as the natives are sure to employ him on account of his being the son of the Duke of Argyll.

(807)

SIR HENRY PONSONBY TO PRINCESS LOUISE
OSBORNE, 9 FEBRUARY 1889

A home of her own?
Madam, Your Royal Highness is perfectly correct in your recollection of the conversation which took place about two years ago. Of course I do not know what sum the Queen would be prepared to advance to Your Royal Highness but I should think that as no place of any size could be purchased for less than £20,000 Her Majesty would probably agree to this amount. Still as I have not spoken to Her Majesty I cannot of course speak with any authority.

I am very sorry to hear that Your Royal Highness is suffering from this bitterly cold weather.

I have the honour to be, Madam, Your Royal Highness's obedient humble servant Henry Ponsonby.

(810)

Sir Henry wrote again on 14 February saying that he was to make arrangements with Sir Arnold White to have £20,000 at Her Royal Highness's disposal under the conditions already mentioned.

'TED' TO PRINCESS LOUISE
THURSDAY, 4 JULY 1889 A.D., NO ADDRESS

My dearest Angel, I beg most respectfully to transmit these beautiful cards for your gracious acceptance.

Ever thine most humbly,

Ted.

(821)

The interest of this note is that it gives the flavour – colourful but not impolite – of the Bohemian society in which Princess Louise now moved. More than one of her artistic friends could in theory have had their first names shortened to 'Ted': Edward Çorbould, Edgar Boehm, Edwin Lutyens, Edwin Landseer, Edward Godwin, not to mention the grandees Edward Burne-Jones and Edward Poynter. But in fact all must be eliminated. Landseer and Godwin were dead and the handwriting of all the rest was quite unlike.

SIR EDGAR BOEHM TO PRINCESS LOUISE
THE AVENUE, 76 FULHAM ROAD, 8 DECEMBER 1890

Louise's advice:
Madam, Your Royal Highness's kind letter only came into my hands today as I was not here on Saturday nor yesterday.

I am more sorry than I can say not to have been in and I hope that Wednesday or Thursday will be equally convenient to Your Royal Highness to honour me with a call in the afternoon and to give me your valuable advice on the design I am just preparing.

I may be obliged to go to Windsor on Wednesday as I believe the statue of the Emperor Frederick is then to be unveiled, but I trust to be able to return and be here by 5 o'clock latest. I have the honour to be Your Royal Highness's ever most faithful servant J. E. Boehm. This and tomorrow afternoon I have to go to the R. Academy.

(1773)

Sir Edgar Boehm RA evidently led a rushed life. He was to die that very week while moving forward a bust of Lord Dufferin and other heavy pieces, at the time when Louise was with him in his studio, giving him her 'valuable advice' (see pages 60–1). It was probably his overwork on the statue of Fritz, the late German Emperor, that affected his delicate health and indirectly killed him.

PRINCESS LOUISE TO THE QUEEN
MONDAY EVENING, 15 DECEMBER 1890

Boehm for St. Paul's?

Dearest Mama, I telegraphed to you the feeling there was in favour of good Sir E. Boehm being buried at St. Paul's. Frank Holl the painter was, and young Caldecott, the man who drew those charming illustrations of children's books, a very clever young fellow. I think you ought to express your desire that he should be buried there, as he did more for modern art, than any one of the day. If you remember 22 years ago it was dull heavy and bad classic, he was the first almost to introduce life and action into his work, also it is very important that those who want to try and ignore him, should be shown by *you*, the Queen, what you thought. It is *not* asking an unusual thing, as you see these two artists who died so lately were buried there. Please communicate *direct* with *me*, it will save time, and is better.

Poor little Mr Gilbert [Alfred Gilbert, the sculptor] is so touching, his thoughtfulness and devotion to the memory of his friend and master. Fancy he sits in the room where he lays, he helped to dress him just as he was that afternoon he died and does all he can.

One person has not shown much generosity, or feeling! so do not communicate with the R. Academy on the subject there is no necessity.

Sir Frederic (later Lord) Leighton was president of the Royal Academy, 1878–96.

Sir E. Millais, Richmond etc., all have been most kind.

Excuse my writing at such length but it is best to let you know. And I feel sure you wish all done to show honour to Sir E. Boehm's memory, and his great talent as much as you appreciated his works in his lifetime.

(F39/65)

The Queen agreed, writing to Vicky on 20 December: 'Today good and ever-to-be-regretted Sir E. Boehm will be laid to rest in St. Paul's, where many others are. He will rest near Landseer, Reynolds, Turner, etc., and many others are there besides, Wellington and Nelson.' (A. Ramm [ed.]), Beloved and Darling Child, *p. 119)*

EDWARD BURNE-JONES TO LORD LORNE
THE GRANGE, NORTH END ROAD, NO DATE (1890S)

A royal visit manqué!

My dear Lord Lorne, I was very vexed not to be here to receive the Princess and yourself when you called on Friday – missed you by one minute only, and indeed saw you driving away, but felt it impious to run after the carriage and stop it.

But please express my real regret to Her Royal Highness and accept my thanks for the visit and for your kind message and believe me faithfully yours Edward Burne-Jones.

(1981)

SAME TO PRINCESS LOUISE
NO DATE

Madam, I send all the drawings I can find – but fear they will not be of much service.

Nor will I forget the head in gold – even if delay in sending it happens I shall not have forgotten.

If it might be explained to that High Lady that an inroad of babies is not an inevitable incident of seeing my pictures – and that their osculations were unpremeditated and in ignorance – if one day you would say this. Always your very faithful servant and friend Edward Burne-Jones.

(1982)

Another note (1983) states that he has done 'a little golden head' for Louise, which he will send to her or keep till she returns.

EDGAR C. BOEHM TO PRINCESS LOUISE
THE AVENUE, 76 FULHAM ROAD, 17 JANUARY 1891

Eddie was son of the late sculptor.
Madam, I venture to write to Your Royal Highness to beg your gracious acceptance of some of the implements which I have learnt ... were most used by my Father; as well as a book containing a number of his most interesting sketches. I also beg to assure Your Royal Highness how deeply sensible I am of the kindness which you have shewn to my sisters and to me.

In the book which I have sent to Your Royal Highness, there is a sketch of my mother, and I did not like to touch it, without first knowing whether Your Royal Highness would like it, but if not I thought I might venture to ask for it, as it is the only portrait I have of my mother done by him, excepting those which Your Royal Highness did, which I would always regard above everything. I have the honour, Madam, to be Your Royal Highness's loyal and obedient servant Eddie C. Boehm.

(1999)

SAME TO SAME
SPA, 26 JULY 1891

Madame, I am unable to explain my great pleasure and feelings which I had on receiving Your Royal Highness's kind letter accepting the things in the studio, and saying that you would make me a present of the sketch of my dear mother in a frame: it is a thing which I and all of us will reverence very very much. I venture to add with great humbleness, that if there is anything that Your Royal Highness knows of and would like, as well as the other things, or anything that Your Royal Highness is associated with or would like done, I should like, and consider it a very great honour, to be able to do it.

I was in London for four or five days, and Mr. Grass pointed out to me the things that Your Royal Highness was pleased to choose. I am abroad very much now as London seems so different without one's parents.

(2000)

This time he signs it Edgar C. Boehm.

THE PRINCE OF WALES TO PRINCESS LOUISE
MARLBOROUGH HOUSE, 15 NOVEMBER 1891

Georgie has typhoid:
Dearest Louise, Your dear and kind letter has touched me very much –

and I knew how deeply you would sympathize with me about poor dear Georgie. Alas! the spots have shown themselves today and the Doctors' fears that it would be typhoid are now realized. Fortunately he has it in a very mild form – the temperature is not very high and he is doing as well as can be expected. He is kept perfectly quiet and nobody is allowed to see him excepting the Doctors, Nurses and myself. Nothing can be done beyond careful nursing and watching. In Doctors Broadhurst and Laking he has the best advice and the two Nurses seem excellent. Both are from St. Mary's Hospital. Our local Doctor (Manby) advised me to bring him up here, which I am glad to have done, as if he had been ill at Sandringham with the house still damp and uncomfortable and workmen in it I should have been doubly anxious in Alix's absence. I have heard from her that she is leaving Livadia as soon as she can, and I hope may be here by the end of the week at latest.

Alix had temporarily left Bertie, sickened at last by his infidelities. Georgie's illness brought her hurrying home.

So sorry you are laid up again just now, but I fear if you were well you would not be allowed to see Georgie at present, though it is very kind of you to offer to be of any use, and I shall be delighted to see you when you are able to get about again.

(842)

PRINCE ALBERT VICTOR OF WALES (EDDY) TO PRINCESS LOUISE
WINDSOR CASTLE, 11 DECEMBER 1891

Dearest Aunt Louise, I was so pleased with your nice letter for which many thanks, and also Uncle Lorne for having wished me so many good things. I wonder if you were surprised when you saw that I was engaged? I daresay you were, for I must say I made up my mind rather suddenly, which I think however was the best thing after all, and it is really time that I thought of getting married, if I ever am to be. Anyway it is now settled at last, and I think I have done well in my choice, for I feel certain May [Princess Mary of Teck; the future Queen Mary] will make an excellent wife, and you may be certain I shall do my best to make her a good husband, and I am naturally looking forward to many happy years to come. I hope we shall meet again before very long. Ever your affectionate old nephew Eddy.

(843)

Eddy's hoped for 'many happy years' were to be reduced by pneumonia to less than two months.

THE QUEEN TO LORD LORNE
OSBORNE, 6 JANUARY 1892

Modest promotion for Lorne:
Dear Lorne, I was just going to write to you to make you the formal offer of the office of Governor of Windsor Castle and Constable of the Round Tower when I received your kind letter. It gives me great pleasure that you should accept this offer and thus have another connection with Windsor where you so often are. The slight duties can I am sure be made of more importance even than they are now. The Bishop of Rochester (former Dean) can tell you all about it. Ever your very affectionate Mama V.R.I.

(844)

SAME TO SAME
OSBORNE, 11 JANUARY 1892

How very kind to write these *lovely lines*, and so quickly and so beautifully and gracefully. Thousand thanks. They will be most gratefully treasured and placed beneath any representation of the brilliant scene which there will be. With renewed thanks. Ever your very affectionate Mama V.R.I.

(845)

THE EMPRESS FREDERICK TO LORD LORNE
SCHLOSS HOMBURG, 21 AUGUST 1892

My dear Lorne, I hope you will not think me very ungrateful not to have written yet to thank you for your kind letter of congratulations for my daughter Margaret's engagement! To my thanks you must let me add my best wishes for your birthday the day after tomorrow. You once spent that day *here* at Homburg with us, and with a bitter sigh ... I think of all that then still was mine! You can imagine what it will be to have to part from my little Mossy, my Benjamin who is so precious to me, the *last* dear child to brighten my saddened and lonely existence! The idea of being *quite* alone for the rest of my days is one which seems very bitter, and yet of course I am intensely thankful that my darling is happy and that she will have a good and kind Husband, and not have to live *far* away! But it can never be the same thing, and it is a parting which I shall feel dreadfully.

Vicky's reaction to a daughter's marriage was surprisingly like Queen Victoria's.

You must be quite engrossed with the political situation which is so fraught with anxiety! Can Mr. Gladstone carry out the measures he has bound himself to – and which seem to me full of evils and dangers – or can he not?... I am very sorry you were not returned and I am sure it was a disappointment to you....

(851)

Gladstone had lost the remaining allegiance of the royal family.

SIR FREDERIC LEIGHTON TO PRINCESS LOUISE
2 HOLLAND PARK ROAD, KENSINGTON, 16 MARCH 1893

Leighton was still leader of the artistic establishment, but now a friend of Louise's. She sensibly kept in with all sides.

Madam, In obedience to the request of your Royal Highness I note down a few of the minor towns in Central Italy which on artistic grounds would offer special attraction to Your Royal Highness. It is no doubt needless specially to allude to Prato, Pistoya and Lucca, all three so easily accessible from Florence, in Prato the Donatello outer pulpit and the cathedral and the Lippi frescoes would more than repay the journey; in Pistoya there is, in one of the churches, a very fine carved pulpit by (I think) Giov. Pisano, and in Lucca the...

He goes on for page after page of wonderful suggestions, and ends:

I trust these brief notes may be of some little use to Your Royal Highness. Although I gather that there is little hope of my having the honour of seeing you next week at my studio I must inform Your Royal Highness in conclusion that the Empress Frederick and the Prince of Wales have altered to *Friday* at 4.30 the time of their visit. Permit me to remain Madam, Your Royal Highness' obedient servant, Frederic Leighton.
P.S. I must throw myself on the indulgence of Your Royal Highness for some incoherence in this letter written as it is under no little stress of occupation.

(1774)

Leighton was said to be a mixture of the Olympian Jove and a head waiter, which this letter seems to bear out.

SIR ARTHUR SULLIVAN TO PRINCESS LOUISE VILLA MATHILDE, ST JEAN DE VILLEFRANCHE, FRIDAY NIGHT (BETWEEN 1894 AND 1900), VERY PRIVATE

Sullivan, the composer, is famous for the 'Gilbert and Sullivan' operas; the tragedy of Prince Alfred was drink, and an unhappy marriage to the Russian Emperor's daughter Marie.

Madam, I cannot really find words to tell Your Royal Highness how grateful I am for your kind, *dear* letter (forgive this bold phrase, Madam, but it is heartfelt) which I received this evening. Ever since I wrote to Your Royal Highness, I have been worrying over the matter you spoke to me about, and now your letter has lifted a great weight off me, and I feel happier and more at rest than I have been for a long time. Not only Your Royal Highness's reassuring words have relieved me, but the kind tone, and the true womanly sympathy evident in every line have touched me deeply. To say more now, would be distasteful to Your Royal Highness, but some day perhaps I may take courage, and open my heart on a subject connected with this. Yes, indeed, all my life I have tried to influence him whom we were speaking of, in the right way. Years ago even, before he was married, I have tried to check the evil tendency which was manifesting itself. The difference of position compelled me of course to use all possible tact and discretion, but I never allowed timidity to prevent me from saying what I thought was right, and I have often neglected important work – I take no credit for this because it was a real pleasure to me – to be with him by night or by day, when I thought that my companionship would be beneficial to him. To keep him at home – to prevent his going out into society injurious to his health and reputation, I have over and over again gone to him late at night, taking little pieces I had especially written or arranged for him, and then once having got him interested would remain playing accompaniments till two o'clock in the morning. But after his marriage I naturally saw less of him, and dared not attempt to resume the relative position I occupied before; because I saw there was a distinctly *hostile element* risen up against me, which made me feel very uncomfortable, and always embarrassed. I saw that in any effort I made even to hint or indicate what I thought was judicious or discreet, *I got no help* whatever from one to whom I desired to be a faithful servant and ally [Marie]. Madam, I am writing in *sacred confidence* to you, because I know you love him so much, and I know that you are his favourite sister. *He never had any support or help in his home life.* Don't be angry with me for being so bold, but it is the truth. I have seen things – witnessed little scenes – heard words which have pained me dreadfully. And yet withal he was so sweet and gentle – so patient and forebearing that I could not help admiring and respecting him more than ever, and could hardly blame him if he sought a little 'soulagement' in a resource which was neither right nor healthy. I hardly know whether I ought to send this letter – so free and outspoken. But after all it is my unshaken affection and devotion, which makes me speak out, and I am sure Your Royal Highness will understand and forgive me. He has so many fine qualities both of head and heart, and it makes me boil with indignation, to see him, through his own fault alas! so misunderstood, and talked about even by a lot of ignorant fools who don't even know him personally.

But I am quite helpless. To do him good – to practically influence him for good – one ought always to be with him. Being with him for an hour or two now and then is of no use. I wish he had one of his children with him to save him from the loneliness of that big house – from the solitude of his life.

Or if he could stay quietly with one of his family that he likes, he could be influenced in the right way. But, failing one of these means, I don't see what is to be done. I shall go over on Sunday and see him, and if he will let me, I will stay with him all the afternoon, and longer.

I am so very very sorry I missed seeing Your Royal Highness again before you left. I had no idea you were going away so soon, and as I knew Your Royal Highness had many friends and acquaintances at Cannes, and were also in constant communication with Her Majesty, I did not like to press myself unduly upon you. And then the strong desire [to] see Your Royal Highness again, coming upon me, I wrote to propose myself for this week. I shall not read this letter through again, or my courage might fail me, and I might destroy it, and write one more formal. But I have said what I felt, and to no one else *could* I say it. So I let it go, trusting for forgiveness to that sweet womanly sympathy I gratefully appreciate.

I am, Madam, Your Royal Highness's ever faithful and devoted servant Arthur Sullivan.

(868)

Marie of Edinburgh was bitterly disappointed by her prestigious marriage and regarded everything English, including her husband, with increasing sourness. Meanwhile, the once handsome, musical Alfred (he had a moderate talent for the violin) was drowning his sorrows in the traditional way.

THE QUEEN TO PRINCESS LOUISE
OSBORNE, 6 AUGUST 1894

Darling Loosy, Many thanks for your dear letter received yesterday and which made me so sad. I do feel so deeply for you. The loss of a dear, faithful darling dog is that of a devoted friend – almost of a Child!

(1711)

2ND LORD TENNYSON TO PRINCESS LOUISE FARRINGFORD, FRESHWATER, ISLE OF WIGHT 6 NOVEMBER 1894

There is no beginning to this letter.
How can I thank you enough for all your kindness to my wife. She has not returned and is not returning yet. She is with our children and her brother at Wimbledon: but she writes that she was very heavy-hearted at leaving Your Royal Highness. If I may venture to say so, you have certainly inspired a romantic and devoted affection in her.

May I also humbly offer my loyal thanks to Her Majesty. I do not think that Your Royal Highness ever saw these lines which I enclose, and which my Father never thought worthy enough of the occasion [the death of Leopold] and so may I ask you to keep them private for the Queen and yourself.

I believe that he never wrote them out himself, but I took them down as he made them.

My mother joins with me in dutiful and affectionate gratitude and remembrance. I am ever Your Royal Highness' grateful servant, Tennyson.

On reading the lines over again after this lapse of years, they seem to me to be so beautiful that I think that I must publish them in my Memoir of my Father.

(871)

Prince Leopold, Duke of Albany – an epitaph:

Early-wise, and pure, and true –
Prince, whose Father lived in you.

If you could speak, would you not say –
'I seem but am not far away,

Wherefore should your eyes be dim?
I am here again with *him*.

O Mother-Queen, and weeping wife,
The death, for which you mourn, is life.'

(872)

TELEGRAM FROM QUEEN VICTORIA
BALMORAL, 20 JULY 1895

Anniversary of the coronation:
Princess Louise Kensington Palace. Many loving thanks You are the only one of my children who remembers this day quite mild today V.R.I.

(876)

SIR ARTHUR SULLIVAN TO PRINCESS LOUISE
BERLIN, 26 NOVEMBER 1895

A 'thank you' letter:
Madam, I have received letters from home which tell me of the splendid gift which Your Royal Highness has sent me. How shall I thank Your Royal Highness sufficiently for your kind and gracious thought of me – kindness which has taken such a valuable form? For nothing could be of greater value to me – nothing give me more real and lasting pleasure than to possess something done with your own hands and head – a part of yourself, I may say. Pray, Madam, accept my warmest and most heartfelt thanks. I am longing to get back to London and see 'My Queen'!

I am also longing for this evening to be over, for tonight sees, at last, the production of 'Ivanhoe' at the opera house here. I have been here a fortnight, and have had nothing but work and worry all the time. For ten days I rehearsed without either Rebecca or Rowena, Rebecca sprained her knee, and Rowena lay in bed with lumbago.... The Emperor and Empress are coming, and oh! shan't I catch it in the press tomorrow! I hear they have all made up their minds about it, and they are furious also that so much money should be spent upon the work of a foreigner....

(2018)

THE PRINCE OF WALES TO PRINCESS LOUISE
MARLBOROUGH HOUSE, 11 JANUARY 1896

The Jameson Raid was a disastrous attempt by Cecil Rhodes and his friend Dr Jameson to 'support' a rising in Johannesburg against the Boers. The rising was a fiasco, the raiders were captured and the British Colonial Secretary, Joseph Chamberlain, was widely suspected of collusion with Rhodes.
Dearest Louise, I am so sorry to hear from your letter how unwell you have been since I saw you a fortnight ago, but I am glad to know that you are better. I should be delighted to come and see you at 5 either on Monday or Tuesday whichever would suit you best.

This year indeed brought great troubles upon us in S. Africa but I trust the worst is now over. Mr Chamberlain has indeed proved himself a strong man! William's Telegram was most uncalled for, and has made him *very* unpopular over here and I should strongly advise him *not* to come to England this year.

The Kaiser congratulated Kruger, the Boer leader, on defeating Jameson's attempt.

It is certainly unfortunate poor Liko's being prevented from going to 'the front' owing to an attack of fever! I always said, 'Que Diable allait il faire dans cette guerre?'

The news of Prince Henry of Battenberg's [Liko] death in the Ashanti War was to arrive in eleven days. He died of fever.

I am in town to go through a course of electricity for rheumatism. I was much interested in seeing Lowther which is a fine and interesting place – and everything is well kept and arranged, my host did not attempt to defend the conduct of his Imperial Friend! From your devoted brother Bertie.

(881)

SAME TO SAME
NICE, 29 MARCH 1898

Affie's illness was 'a developed rectal inflammation', according to Sir James Reid.

Dearest Louise, Though I know you have been kept informed about dear Affie and the operation which had to be performed on 26th you may like to hear that I went to Villefranche today – and paid him a long visit on board 'Surprise'. He was of course in bed, and though he looks pulled down was wonderfully cheerful under the circumstances. Though he thought the sulphur baths, at Heluan, were much too strong and he hated the place, still the eczema is almost gone which shows they did good. He feels so much better.

He looks so much better in mind and body since the operation, which I trust may be the end of his troubles. The doctor on hand seems quite excellent, though looks very young. Affie likes him very much, and he has great influence over him, so we all hope he may remain some time with him after he is convalescent!...

(916)

PRINCE ARTHUR TO PRINCESS LOUISE
BAGSHOT PARK, 31 MARCH 1898

Many thanks for your two letters and for sending me that of Beatrice which I return. Till I heard from you I had not the least idea how ill Affie had been nor in what a poor state of health generally he is in – I had hoped that the cure at Heluan had done him good but this appears not to have been the case.

I think you are very wise in going off into the country and making up your mind to lead an invalid life for a month or five weeks, I do hope it will set you quite right. I believe Victoria of Wales is quite a different person since she has adhered to [Dr] Laking's instructions. We are so sorry you will not be able to come and see us here but possibly you may be able to come to Aldershot....

(917)

THE PRINCE OF WALES TO PRINCESS LOUISE
NICE, 2 APRIL 1898

Bertie is evidently the one in charge of his brother Affie and of giving the news to Louise.

... The wound is healing satisfactorily but he is not to be allowed to sit up till it has quite healed. He quite agreed to a Diet chart which the doctors have suggested for him.... The difficulty may be to keep him quiet when he gets better....

(918)

Bertie also said that it had never entered Marie's head to visit her husband.

LADY BURNE-JONES TO PRINCESS LOUISE
25 JUNE 1898

Death of Sir Edward Burne-Jones, the painter:

Dear Princess, They gave me your note and I thanked you for it then as I do now. You knew something of him and what he was to those who lived near him. But still I thank God that no infirmity fell upon him, body or mind, and that before he left us he had done so splendid a day's work. Respectfully and gratefully yours, dear Princess, Georgiana Burne-Jones.

(1985)

Georgiana Burne-Jones was one of the five attractive Macdonald sisters, two others being Lady Poynter, wife of a president of the Royal Academy, and Mrs John Kipling, mother of the poet and writer, Rudyard Kipling.

PRINCESS LOUISE TO THE QUEEN
NO DATE (1890s)

Dearest Mama, A little weakness Lorne just wrote I thought you might like to have. Louise.

(1807)

The 'little weakness' was enclosed, a poem of five verses by Lorne in praise of Queen Victoria on her birthday. The tone of Louise's note is unmistakably maternal and indulgent, as if written by one mother to another. She would call Lorne her 'darling boy', while Lorne was to call Queen Victoria his 'second mother'.

LORD LORNE TO PRINCESS LOUISE
TOURS, 21 AUGUST 1898

Frank Hird was the protégé of Ronald Gower, Lorne's uncle.

Hird is bathing in the Loire. Ronald and I have had a tub each in our rooms – and I write with nothing on! Clothes are altogether a mistake. I anoint myself with eau de cologne after bathing, and remain horizontal till dinner.

(1827)

ANOTHER NOTE ON THE SAME DATE

I am very glad to know that you are not overdoing the water drinking. The great thing is to get fat and thereby blood and strength – which can't be done by washing oneself out, getting nervous, and having 'crises'.

The Princess was at a German spa.

These are all nonsense except for the very strongest. If one is an Elephant one can amuse the doctors by playing their games but not otherwise.

(1828)

YET ANOTHER NOTE ON THE SAME DATE

Dt. [Dearest] Alba, Thanks for No. 2 letter. I don't want you to fatigue yourself by writing. A line to say you are well and content is all that is necessary, though I am very glad to know details and to be able to picture to myself what you are doing. The heat was greater than ever today, so much so that a walk to the Cathedral in the morning made one feel giddy....

(1829)

It is not known why Lorne called Louise by the nickname 'Alba'. It may have had something to do with her third name Alberta, or with the Spanish and Italian meaning of Alba – Dawn.

SAME TO SAME
TOURS, 25 AUGUST 1898

The account you give of the effect of the waters being strengthening and blood-making is satisfactory, and I trust they will do you good. The mountain air at all events ought to be bracing....

(1833)

Ever since her sleigh accident Louise had paid visits to foreign watering-places, to seek a cure for neuralgic pains in her head and also for her rheumatic knee.

SAME TO SAME
TOURS, 30 AUGUST 1898

Dt. Alba. Thanks for yours about the bignonia plants. I will try to get some plants sent straight from here. There is no end to the amount of it planted in all the gardens, and the blossom is in great beauty this year.

I like to talk about additions to houses or new things long before one can do them, to settle what is best with least expense, so you need not think if I talk of stair towers that I want to build one now. But I have come to the conclusion that these round or angled towers are charming to look at, but are only comfortable for W.C.s or toilette places. As stairs they are dangerous.

(1834)

The letter includes a sketch of a mansion with two towers and plans. But Lorne reassures his 'Dt' Louise that she need not fear that he wants to build one.

PRINCE ALFRED TO PRINCESS LOUISE 21 FEBRUARY 1899

Death of young Alfred:
My dear Louise, Heartfelt thanks for your dear sympathy in my terrible grief. You knew my dear boy so well and have almost seen him grow up and know how lovable he was so that you will appreciate what a fearful blow his loss is to me. Doubly cruel coming so immediately after receiving so many congratulations [on his son's twenty-first birthday]. You remind me of Eastwell and all those happy days and how all my hopes are gone and crushed. It is awfully hard to bear. I do not know if you have left for Cannes yet so I will send these lines to London. Ever your affectionate brother Alfred.

(938)

Young Alfred's great-uncle Ernest of Saxe-Coburg had been his undoing. As heir after his father to the dukedom, Alfred had been brought up at the scandalous court and caught a venereal disease. He was forced to leave the army and died alone at Meran in the Austrian Tyrol.

L. ALMA TADEMA TO MAJOR COLLINS, PRINCESS LOUISE'S PRIVATE SECRETARY 17 GROVE END ROAD, ST JOHN'S WOOD, 19 JULY 1899

The 'Greenery Yalleries' are abandoned by the 'oldfashioned'.
My dear Collins, I ought to say Messrs. Macniel [*sic*] Whistler & Co. find, it appears, that their art does not possess sufficient attraction to fill their galleries. I may be mistaken but I dislike that kind of advertising an Art Exhibition by means of teas music and displays which have nothing to do with the pictures exhibited. Burne-Jones and I've left the Grosvenor Gallery for that very reason. In any case they might have approached Her Royal Highness with a properly *written* letter, but I am so oldfashioned.

Yours always sincerely, L. Alma Tadema.

(2006)

There was a certain amount of rivalry between the older and younger artists for Princess Louise's favours. She was mainly on the side of Whistler and the 'moderns'. What would Alma Tadema have thought of today's shops in art galleries and museums?

PRINCE ARTHUR TO PRINCESS LOUISE
COWES, 1 AUGUST 1899

... We sold all your charmingly painted matchboxes but I don't know of any more being asked for so I won't trouble you any more. Thanks to relations and friends and our working very hard at the Bazaar we took £2300 and will I hope have almost over £1800 which I think is very good. – You will I suppose have heard that, through most unwise and heavy speculations, Affie is in great monetary difficulties. Mama and Bertie are in an awful state over it.

(945)

THE PRINCE OF WALES TO PRINCESS LOUISE
MARLBOROUGH HOUSE, 25 JANUARY 1900

Bertie is very interested in
... Mr Chamberlain's wish that you and Lorne should go out to Australia....

Bertie thinks it would be an excellent thing politically.

(952)

Louise had already turned down the suggestion in 1884 and did not enjoy either long sea-voyages or Lorne's undiluted company.

JOAN RUSKIN SEVERN TO PRINCESS LOUISE
BRANTWOOD, 26 JANUARY 1900

John Ruskin's burial, described to Louise by his niece. Joan Severn had already answered Louise's letter of condolence, saying,
My darling was so loyally devoted to you – and all the Royal Family – but especially to Prince Leopold – and your words would have gratified him....

(2026)

SAME TO SAME

Your beautiful wreath was laid on my darling's coffin while he rested in the church [at Coniston], and was lowered into his grave with one sent by G. F. Watts RA (a victor's crown cut from Grecian laurel – of which one was cut for Tennyson, Leighton and Burne-Jones) and to-day I placed yours on his grave – at his head, then lilies and violets (by my daughters

Lily and Violet) then *my* cross of roses – all colours! – then the Watts laurel wreath! (as requested at his feet).

(2027)

Ruskin died at Brantwood on 20 January 1900. He had met Leopold while the Prince was up at Oxford and Louise through her brother. He had given postal drawing lessons to Louise's sister, Princess Alice.

THE EMPRESS FREDERICK TO PRINCESS LOUISE
LERICI, GULF OF SPEZIA, 18 MARCH 1900

The Boer War:
. . . Now the relief of Mafeking seems to me to be the *one thing* to be prayed for! It *would* be terrible if the patient heroic endurance of the garrison and townspeople were not to have its reward, – and be obliged to surrender – to those horrid Boers! . . . How is your father-in-law the Duke? I hear he has been very ill?

(956)

THE PRINCE OF WALES TO PRINCESS LOUISE
COPENHAGEN, 12 APRIL 1900

Dearest Louise, Many thanks for your dear letter of sympathy on the occasion of the unpleasant incident which occurred to us at Brussels. It was certainly a most unexpected surprise that a man should fire a pistol at my head into the railway carriage at 2 yards distance. However he fortunately proved to be a very bad shot, so no harm was done. Alix was most courageous and none the worse. . . . The sympathy manifested towards us from all parts of the world by the shoals of letters and telegrams that we have received has been most gratifying but entails a considerable labour in answering them. . . . We found my Father-in-law wonderfully well, more like 62 than 82 and marvellously active. All of the rest of the Family are well.

What a sad state the poor Duke of Argyll seems to be in and one can hardly wish his life prolonged. Lorne must really 'bury the hatchet' now and I sincerely hope that he will not think of calling himself in the future anything else than the fine historic title to which he must succeed. Hoping you will enjoy your stay at Roseneath [*sic*] and with Alix's best love, ever your devoted brother Bertie.

(959)

Since the Duke's third marriage he and Lorne had not been on speaking terms. He had married Miss Ina McNeill in 1895, after his second wife died the year before. Ina was half the Duke's age and had been on Louise's staff in Canada. Lorne at first refused to take the Argyll title, which he felt his father had disgraced.

III

Duchess of Argyll

1900–14

THE QUEEN TO PRINCESS LOUISE DUCHESS OF ARGYLL, VICE-REGAL LODGE, PHOENIX PARK, DUBLIN, CONFIDENTIAL, 25 APRIL 1900

The funeral of the 8th Duke of Argyll – family trouble (see pages 68–9)
Darling Loosy, I must tell you *how* miserable I am at all this sad trouble and sorrow and at *what* you must be suffering! It is simply incredible that Lorne should behave as he does. I am really grieved as well as shocked and I shall not write as I could not pass over his *unfilial* and unChristian conduct in silence. You are truly forgiving to unfortunate Ina [the Duke's widow], who I fear is in a very bitter state also! People of course remark with astonishment on L's absence from his Father's deathbed; the only people who know and grieve about it are Gerald and Betty Balfour. She has been unwell the last three or four days, but he is much better and able to come out to dine . . . only not to stand. He is distressed beyond measure at L's behaviour and feels sure he will lament it later on.

Now comes the funeral. I have telegraphed to ask you – and also to Frances B. [Lady Frances Balfour, Lorne's sister] to ask her if she knows – as I wish naturally to send someone of rank – what would you wish? . . . How I wish I could help but I can't do so at present. . . . The Duke upheld his Church and L. and you must do so too. There Ina did what was right. I wrote to her a few words yesterday and to Frances today. She had written about her dear Father. I shall ever cherish his memory as he was a kind old friend of upward of fifty years and so agreeable and intellectual. I know how attached to him you were and he to you and so was L's dear mother. We all feel for you so much. How kind and pleasant Gerald and Betty Balfour are. Archie is and has been at Inverary [*sic*] but where is George? Can the Bishop do nothing with L? I don't like to speak of these things. . . .

(960)

Lorne was still not on speaking terms with Ina, his stepmother. Archie and George were two of the Campbell brothers and the Bishop was Edward Glyn, Lorne's brother-in-law. Lorne refused to attend the funeral.

THE EMPRESS FREDERICK TO PRINCESS LOUISE SCHLOSS FRIEDRICSHOF, CRONBERG, 25 APRIL 1900

Death of Lorne's father; Lorne succeeds as 9th Duke of Argyll.
Darling Louise, dear Mama has telegraphed the news to me of your poor

Father-in-law's death! I know how sincere your regret will be – as I remember you used to be much attached to him and he was very fond of you! What a gifted and amiable man he was!

How many new duties and new interests and occupations will come into your life, and I shall be very anxious to hear what changes will take place, and where your principal home will be.

I hope matters will all go smoothly – which in so large a family is not easy. My thoughts are so much with you and Lorne! I hope he is well again – and will be careful of his chest after this nasty Influenza. I hear that you are both at Roseneath [*sic*] and it must be a comfort to have been with the poor Duke at the last! A few weeks ago when his state was so precarious you and Lorne could not leave Kensington.

I am rather better, up – and on my legs again but am rolled in a bath chair in the garden, and still have to spend most of the day on the sofa, which is a most terrible bore, and have to keep very quiet! The pain in my back is still very bad when I move.

She had cancer of the spine.

I shall be very thankful for a line – to hear how you are getting on etc. and how your health is just now. Excuse this dreadful writing but I am still in bed. Ever your devoted old sister Vicky.

(961)

AN ODD SHEET WITH NO BEGINNING OR END, FROM THE PRINCE OF WALES TO PRINCESS LOUISE AFTER 24 APRIL 1900

Lorne's succession:

... calling myself Duke of Brunswick! You will always be called Princess Louise but Duchess of Argyll afterwards instead of Marchioness of Lorne. It is perfectly simple and what is the use of making a fuss which will only raise ridicule and I am sure Lorne would not like that. I hope Archie and his children may have a calming influence over Lorne and I think you and Archie get on very well together.... Now all is over I hope you and Lorne will be kind too [end of sheet]

(962)

THE QUEEN TO PRINCESS LOUISE
WINDSOR CASTLE, 3 MAY 1900

The Queen is still distressed over the 'great trouble and difficulty' about the funeral.
You ought certainly to go to the Funeral. I know that you are doing all you can to *soften* bitterness but it must be very trying. I do hope you will come south before I go to Scotland....

(963)

THE PRINCE OF WALES TO PRINCESS LOUISE
MARLBOROUGH HOUSE, 13 MAY 1900

Dearest Louise, Many thanks for your letter just received.... I was glad that you attended the Duke's Funeral, but it is much to be regretted that Lorne did not do so as it has produced universal and most unfavourable comment at his absence! Whatever the differences there may have been, it is at least one's duty to go to one's Father's Funeral! However, I know how obstinate and self-willed he is – that I don't suppose he cares about public opinion! Well can I understand how worried and upset you have been, and quite ill in consequence – but trust you may soon be coming to London and you must let me know when you arrive....

(964)

Bertie criticizes Lorne quite openly to Louise, the marriage having long been unhappy, though less so in recent years.

TELEGRAM FROM THE DUKE AND DUCHESS OF CUMBERLAND TO PRINCESS LOUISE
GMUNDEN, 5 AUGUST 1900

Death of Prince Alfred from cancer of the throat:
We feel deeply with you dear Louise at the sudden death of your dear brother Alfred. Ernest Augustus. Thyra.

(965)

PRINCE LOUIS OF BATTENBERG TO PRINCESS LOUISE
HMS *DRAKE*, 2ND CRUISER SQUADRON, HALIFAX, 23 OCTOBER 1900

A favour of Louise?
My dear Louise, When you have read this formidable looking letter you will say to yourself: 'He only writes when he wants something.' Well I admit that I want something very badly and you can help me. To begin

at the beginning. As I dare say you know there is a great spirit of emulation in the Fleet over the Target Practice. Quite lately – only a year or two back – we have begun to realise (strengthened enormously by the late war) that we must practise our guns' crews, as they would be in battle, by firing all together at a fairly large target and at long ranges, six to 7000 yards. This ship has just done some wonderful firing under these severe conditions, which delight me very much, as a Flag Ship should always be a model to the other ships. From experience I know that, however people may sneer at 'pothunting', nothing causes so much keenness as the competition once a year for some trophy. As the shooting of my other ships requires improving a good bit to bring it up to the 'Drake's' standard, I intend to present to this squadron for all times a trophy to be competed for at the annual long-range firing ... to be held by the ship for a year.

There are a number of these trophies in the different fleets: silver shields, silver cups etc. I want to give them something really fine, artistic and appropriate. As I hoisted my flag in the year of the Nelson centenary, I should like to give them a lifesize bust or a small statue of Nelson, in bronze, which could stand on the quarter deck, as a standing example to be emulated by all....

Now for the execution of this scheme – and that is where I turn to you. Before I sailed you once asked (and I am sure you meant it) whether there was not a figurehead or something you could model for me. I could not, stupidly enough, think of anything. Now I have had this brilliant idea. Will you help me?

This is what I thought might be possible. There is a very fine bust of Nelson at the United Services Club. Perhaps they [the committee] would allow a plaster cast to be taken from which a bronze might be cast. There is also a bust (but not so good) at the Royal United Service Institution, which might be treated in the same way.... Then there is a very good silver statuette, also in the banqueting Hall of the Royal United Service Institution in Whitehall.

Will you in the first instance give me your advice and perhaps be so very kind next time you are in London, and go and look at the 2 busts and the statuette I mention and say which you consider most suitable from an artistic point of view....

I am sure you will be pleased to hear how much people in Canada still remember you and Lorne. They were always glad to speak about you and asked me much about you. I assured them that you loved Canada and had never forgotten your time out here.... Ever your affectionate and devoted Louis.

(1037)

Louis and Louise were great friends. Ponsonby described him as: 'Handsome, tall and with enormous ears'. The bust of Nelson does not seem to have been modelled by Louise, perhaps because of her new duties as Duchess. Louis had got Louise's housekeeper at Kent House to show him her memorial to Liko in 1897, destined for Whippingham church. He said he greatly admired it. Louise was to give Kent House to the Battenbergs after Lorne's death in 1914 and Prince Louis's tragic resignation as Admiral of the Fleet, which also lost him his home. He was forced to resign on account of his German birth.

PRINCE ARTHUR TO PRINCESS LOUISE
OSBORNE, 23 DECEMBER 1900

Queen Victoria's last Christmas

Dearest Louise, Many thanks for your dear letter and for the list of the presents which I will carefully unpack myself. Our presents for you are Sheffield plated dishes and a little Irish school of art table cover of Celtic design for a small table or a chest of drawers. For Lorne we send two old Delft pottery beer jugs; I hope these will reach you all right. I find Mama very feeble and unable to do anything, she comes to no meals and goes out at odd hours, she is better today and had a good night, but I very much doubt her being able to come to the Christmas tree tomorrow – this throws quite a gloom over our already sad Xmas. You are very right in what you say about Lenchen and Beatrice not reading out any of the sad accounts of poor Vicky's sufferings to Mama, it is very bad for her in her present state; I will do all I can to prevent it. There is so much that is sad just now that I feel it very difficult to make even a semblance of being cheery at Christmas time. I enclose a card for Lorne. We leave this on the 2nd and expect to be in London for six days before returning to Ireland. With Louischen's and the children's best love to you ever your most affectionate brother Arthur.

(970)

TELEGRAM FROM PRINCESS BEATRICE TO PRINCESS LOUISE
OSBORNE, 25 DECEMBER 1900

Death of Lady (Jane) Churchill, the Queen's lady for over fifty years. Louise was at Sandringham.

Mama now knows could [not] be kept from her any longer as she began to suspect it but through gradual preparation has so far borne the shock well though deeply affected her first thought was the grief it will be to you she wishes me to tell you this. Beatrice.

(971)

Lady Churchill had always been a great friend and champion of Louise.

SIR JAMES REID, THE QUEEN'S DOCTOR, TO PRINCESS LOUISE
OSBORNE, 25 DECEMBER 1900

Death of Lady Churchill:
Madam, I know well how Your Royal Highness must have been shocked by my telegram this morning; but I felt that, as one of Lady Churchill's best friends, Your Royal Highness ought to be one of the first to know.

I was called to her at 7.20 this morning. The Housemaid who took in her tea at 7.15 could not rouse her and called her maid, who, seeing that something serious was amiss, called me at once. I found her quite dead, having apparently been so for some time, as she was nearly cold. She looked quite placid, and I have no doubt she passed away in her sleep.

Her maid tells me she had been feeling better than usual since coming here. She was quite bright yesterday, and dined with the Royal party, who all say she was looking well and happy.

Personally it was no surprise to me: but it is most unfortunate it should have happened *here* and *now*. The Queen does not know yet more than that she is ill and that her son has been sent for. I rather dread the effect on Her Majesty when she knows, and it is impossible to conceal it long from her.

The Queen has been eating and sleeping better the last few days and is really better again; and it is all the more sad and unfortunate that she should have this fresh shock to bear.

I am writing in great haste but have I think mentioned everything. I have the honour to be Your Royal Highness's most humble and obedient servant, James Reid.

(972)

THE QUEEN TO PRINCESS LOUISE
OSBORNE, 10 JANUARY 1901

Dictated by the Queen, this is said to be her very last letter. The Queen merely suggests that Jane Churchill, who had died at Osborne on Christmas Eve, should be replaced in a month's time by Jane's daughter-in-law Verena. But in a month's time

the Queen herself was dead. She was asking Louise to copy this letter for Bertie and Alix,
as I am too tired to write to them too.

(981)

PRINCESS IRENE, WIFE OF PRINCE HENRY OF PRUSSIA, TO PRINCESS LOUISE CRONBERG, 23 JANUARY 1901

This letter shows the impact of Queen Victoria's death the day before on her family.
My Dear Aunt Louise, From the depth of our heart Henry and I feel for you in your great grief, which is also so real to us alas! Now suddenly it has all come and how deeply you must have suffered from the shock poor Aunt! Poor Aunt Vicky, so helpless in her suffering here,. lies there and cries her heart out not to be able to see beloved Grandmama's face once more – and how I too long to fly and have one last look – but how dare one leave her [Vicky] at such a moment. God help us all. Many and many a kiss from your loving niece, Irene.

(983)

THE EMPRESS FREDERICK TO PRINCESS LOUISE CRONBERG, 22 FEBRUARY 1901

Vicky has already dictated one letter of thanks to Louise for sending her 'the sad details'. Now comes another:
... I am so sorry that I cannot write to you myself, but with my stiff hand it is so very difficult. I know you will not mind my dictating to my Sophie [daughter]. I cannot imagine a heavier trial than having to be separated [from] you all at this sad time and being so useless and feeling so ill. Of course it would be an immense pleasure to [me to see] you but just now I do not see how it could be managed perhaps you will let me tell you later on when it would do. I have received the fans and pictures all right by messenger many thanks it makes one terribly sad to look at them all how they bring back times and things now alas belonging to the past. I cannot bear to think about dear old Windsor – what it must be like now without beloved Mama it does not seem possible!

Today it is a month that she was taken from us but I cannot realise the sad fact. How does the statue [of Queen Victoria] look in the Mausoleum on the sarcophagus? I would not mind its being a little stained and think the crude whiteness being a little toned down the effect is much more harmonious and effective.

Goodby darling Loo once more affectionate thanks best love to Lorne from [the next words are pencilled by Vicky] Your devoted but sorrowing and suffering sister, Vicky.

(987)

PRINCE GEORGE DUKE OF YORK (LATER GEORGE V TO PRINCESS LOUISE YORK HOUSE, 1 MARCH 1901

Thank you so much for sending me that chain which dearest Grandmama always used to wear, I value it very much, it was so kind of you sending it to me. I was so sorry to hear that you had been laid up. I will try and call on you to-morrow afternoon, in the hopes of your being able to see me. I have been so busy that I have not had a minute to myself. Thanks I am now really quite well, but have still a little weight to put on which I had lost. I quite agree with what you say about Papa, and will speak to [Dr] Laking, he returns Sunday evening. How is Lorne getting on with the book [about Queen Victoria], I see he has gone to Scotland, I suppose to have more leisure and quiet for writing.

With best love, Ever dear Aunt Louise, Your loving nephew, Georgie.

(988)

THE EMPRESS FREDERICK TO PRINCESS LOUISE CRONBERG, 18 MARCH 1901

A pencilled birthday letter from Vicky (present will follow), written 'in bed'.

... *How sad* this day will be without beloved Mama's telegram and letter and present, if you were not with her at Windsor. Oh how you will *miss* her and her *love* and kindness! But let me express every manner of *good* wish for you, and trust you may yet have many a happy day and hour fraught with hope and interest and usefulness. What *I* wish for you most ardently is that you may ever be spared sufferings such as mine – the untold misery of a long lingering illness, bearing only the *name* of Life – but cutting one off from all and everything! I will not complain more.... Your devoted and very miserable sister, Victoria.

(991)

PRINCE GEORGE, FORMERLY DUKE OF YORK, TO PRINCESS LOUISE WINDSOR, 12 NOVEMBER 1901

He has been made Prince of Wales.

Darling Aunt Louise, Many thanks for your dear letter. It does seem funny at first having this dear old name, which dear Papa bore for upwards of 59 years. Of course I am very proud to have it, and only hope that I am worthy of this great honour. We are staying here for a few days shooting, I mean Papa and I, this house Frogmore is really very comfortable....

(1002)

EDWIN ABBEY TO PRINCESS LOUISE CHELSEA LODGE, 42 TITE STREET, 11 JULY 1903

Coronation painting; Louise's sculpture:

Madam, You were so very good as to say I might have your train and the corsage of your dress for a few days. I wonder if I might have them for tomorrow? There is a prospect of a visit from His Majesty on Monday and I would like to have the Royal Box in a rather more presentable condition. I have sketched in the Royal ladies in accordance with your Royal Highness's most helpful suggestions, and if I might have the train and corsage I think I might get the figures fairly right by Monday....

I add the address of a tall, thin model – a restless person, to whom repose, unfortunately, means sleep. In the pose you require, however, Madam, this failing may not be a drawback. His hand is rather good, too. His name is Arthur Dickinson, Wenlock, Thornhill Road, Thames Ditton.... Edwin A. Abbey.

(1770a)

Many of the London models were Italians so Thames Ditton sounded much safer. Perhaps it was the sleepy Arthur Dickinson who modelled for the male head and torso in the Boer War memorial. The model for the angel was a Mrs Lloyd, found for Louise by the painter William Blake Richmond and guaranteed 'really refined'.

LORD LORNE (DUKE OF ARGYLL SINCE 1900) TO PRINCESS LOUISE INVERARAY, 20 SEPTEMBER 1906

Dt. Alba, You say nothing against my plans telegraphed, so I leave on Monday for London arriving there Tuesday. It will be heaven for me to see you again. But I do hope you won't tire yourself in Lancashire....

Louise Talbot is your godchild, so she is my child too, and says she always wants to ask advice about her own life, so I suppose I shall have to choose a husband for her. She is a good nice child, and as we have no daughter, I am very glad to have a nice god-daughter. Her brother says she is schwärmerisch [gushing] but it is nice to be pleased with things instead of bored, or chaffing everything as so many young things are nowadays.

(1842)

THE EMPEROR WILLIAM II TO PRINCESS LOUISE NEUES PALAIS, 27 DECEMBER 1906

Willy the peacemaker:
Dearest Aunty, How kind and thoughtful of you to send me those nice gifts for my Xmas! They were on my table under the tree and gave me great pleasure. They recalled to me the many happy times of my childhood spent in dear *Osborne*!!! Windsor, Balmoral! All the scenes so vividly before my eyes! Then the last solemn time in Osborne! The passing away of that great Queen and kind grandmother when you were so kind to me! Osborne, what became of this heavenly, holy quiet spot so dear to me!!

Of course Willy knew perfectly well that his much disliked uncle Bertie had presented Osborne as a home for convalescent officers.

And to think that, I, who have looked upon my task to draw the two nations closer together, to teach them to know each other better, and to slowly learn to honour and cherish each other's traditions, I the grandson of Britain's greatest Queen, should year by year be hooted, jeered at, cavilled and slandered, and held up to ridicule by the British press and literature mercilessly and endlessly. To have every event which does not turn out according [to] British expectations in any corner of the globe invariably saddled on me quite as a matter of course as one of my usual intrigues!

That is very hard! For it hinders me from coming over as often as I wished to visit my friends and the places where I once was a happy child! May Providence grant that 1907 may show us the beginning of better feeling among nations who are threatened by a common danger! With best love your affectionate nephew Willy.

(1040)

LORD LORNE TO PRINCESS LOUISE
ROSNEATH, 9 MARCH 1908, INCOMPLETE

Lorne's scrapbook (see page 71):
Dt. Alba, I have found 17 more useful letters today for 'the Book', and have sent them in registered cover to Mrs Culver to be typed. In case she is away I have put an interior cover with a memo on it to send one copy here, and one to Sanders to put them with the rest....

(1846)

PRINCE ARTHUR TO PRINCESS LOUISE
THE PALACE, MALTA, 8 MAY 1908

Another grievance:
So many thanks for your dear letter of congratulations on my birthday, written on the 1st but which only reached me this morning. I have to thank you too in advance for the old military caricature of Napoleon's time which you are giving me for my birthday which I will look forward to receiving on our return. I don't know why you imagined that I would be home for the 1st, I never intended coming home before the end of the month and I am afraid that I shall not be very welcome to some people then, as Bertie has written to me to express 'his *very great surprise*!!' at my coming home so soon after my taking over the command (it will be six months by the time I get home) – I hope to reach home on the 20th – I have finished all there is possibly to be done here for the present....

(1050)

SAME TO SAME
3 JUNE 1908

On Arthur's return he writes to thank Louise for her letter of welcome and adds,
I found Bertie and all looking very well and he has been very nice to us.

(1052)

SAME TO SAME
MALTA, 8 APRIL 1909, PRIVATE

Louise as go-between for Arthur and Bertie:
Dearest Louise, Many thanks for your letter of the 1st from Kent House received this morning. As Bertie is expected here on the 21st and *you* write that 'there is something you want to say to me *quite privately*', I answer your letter at once in case you would wish to write to me before Bertie's

visit. Your letter shall be kept *strictly private* and *nobody* shall see it. I can't imagine what you want to write to me about; during the last six months I have been out I have never said anything about this command to Bertie, though I may be obliged to ultimately speak to him as I am not satisfied with it on military grounds – this view of mine is also *very strongly* held by both Sir John Maxwell (my late chief of the staff) and by General Hamilton (my present staff officer). Dull as this place is, *I* have no *personal* objections to this command, but with the best will in the world I am convinced that on military grounds it *can't work well in peace and would be fatal in time of war* ... you must not say anything about it to *ANYONE* and I am trusting you *alone* in this matter. So far all letters between Bertie and myself have been most amicable. Of course one is quite out of the world here and I therefore don't know anything that is going on at home both politically and socially....

(1067)

Arthur was dissatisfied with the Mediterranean command.

LAWRENCE ALMA TADEMA TO PRINCESS LOUISE 28 JANUARY 1910

Madam, Today I lost a very bright spot in my room, for the time had come to eat the beautiful red apple brought me from Kensington Palace at Christmas. I never saw a more beautiful red and I never tasted a better apple and I trust that Your Royal Highness will not mind my saying how grateful I feel for the kind thought of sending me that joy to behold and to eat and the charming pot that accompanied it. Believe me, Madam, your most devoted L. Alma Tadema.

(2007)

Tadema's highly decorative house in Grove End Road was a rival to Leighton House in Kensington. As establishment artists, neither Tadema nor Leighton belonged to Louise's Bohemian set, which is perhaps why Tadema only got an apple for Christmas. Louise generally made or painted something for her particular friends.

TELEGRAM FROM PRINCE ARTHUR TO PRINCESS LOUISE ROME, 11 MAY 1910

Death of King Edward VII:
Thanks kind letters and telegram your sympathy so acceptable also first account have heard dear Bertie's end arrive Friday afternoon. Arthur.

(1076)

QUEEN ALEXANDRA TO PRINCESS LOUISE
SANDRINGHAM, 31 JANUARY 1911

My beloved Louise, You do not know! nor can you *ever* believe what *real* pleasure your very dear and kind letter gave me after your first stay at Windsor without *us*! Dear kind Lorne's too touched me so very much that I was quite overcome by reading them. . . .

(1086)

PRINCE ARTHUR TO PRINCESS LOUISE
5 JULY 1911

Dearest Louise, So many thanks for your dear letters and the prescription of the wonderful 'pick me up'; I *will take care only* to take it under *exceptional* circumstances. I am *too* sorry for you being laid up with a sharp attack of laryngitis, both annoying and painful; I do hope you are already better today.

(1090)

LORD LORNE TO PRINCESS LOUISE
16 AUGUST 1911, INCOMPLETE

Louise's new country retreat – Ribsden in Surrey:
Dt. L. Many thanks for [your] letter. It is delightful to know that you have fixed upon a haven of rest, and have enjoyed the time at Bagshot. Arthur should have some peace and quiet before the Canadian autumn and winter when there will be a good deal of 'Representation', and he will be expected to return any amount of affection.

(1870)

Arthur was about to go out as Governor-General of Canada, as Lorne had done thirty-three years before.

LORD STAMFORDHAM TO PRINCESS LOUISE
BUCKINGHAM PALACE, 1 NOVEMBER 1911

The letter is headed 'Please return' and concerns George V's visit to India.
Madam, It is so nice of you to address me by my old name [Arthur Bigge, Private Secretary to three consecutive monarchs]! I sent on Lord Lamington's letter to the King who quite realises the point upon which he dwells.

Boons which will cost upwards of *£700,000* are to be granted in honour of the King's visit: but His Majesty quite sees that *some* at all events, of these should be made to appear as personal gifts from His Majesty and *not from Government* – on Your Royal Highness' initiation we suggested that a special Famine Trust bearing the name of King George v should be founded and to which he should be the first contributor. The idea was telegraphed to India, but the Viceroy would not have it – I am going to see Lord Crewe, by the King's wish this evening, and try to carry out what you propose –

Your humble and obedient servant Stamfordham.
May I keep Lord Lamington's letter?

(1093)

PRINCE ARTHUR TO PRINCESS LOUISE
GOVERNMENT HOUSE, OTTAWA, 8 NOVEMBER 1911

Arthur as Governor-General of Canada:
Dearest Louise, It was very kind of you to write to me again and I was very much interested in all you say. Personally I think Winston Churchill will do....

(1095)

SAME TO SAME
OTTAWA, 21 JANUARY 1912

I am glad that Lorne is better but I feel so much for you at the anxiety and responsibility I know you must feel.

I have positively no news to give you, everything is running well and smoothly and I think people are beginning quite to get accustomed to us. I like them, they are easy to get on with – and have plenty to say for themselves and are easily pleased. We try to make our parties as little stiff as possible and to put people at their ease and I think they like coming here. We have instituted dining at small round tables which they much prefer....

(1096)

Since 1911 Lorne's health had deteriorated.

SAME TO SAME
10 FEBRUARY 1912

... I am glad that Lorne continues better, but I have no doubt that you must constantly feel anxious about him and I grieve to think of this for you....

Will you send your picture (the pendant to Lorne's) here to Government House?

I am enquiring about the Duke of Kent's picture, it is naturally not here (where there are only those of governor-generals) nor have I seen it at the picture gallery. So many thanks for sending me the standard which you frequently used here. Since Bertie's time the Royal Standard is *never flown* by *anyone except* the *Sovereign* and the different members of the Family have their own distinctive Standards, I fly my own here or wherever I am in residence. I will take the greatest care of the Standard you sent and I will be ready to send it back to you whenever you like....

(1097)

This is probably the standard that Louise incorporated in her St Paul's memorial to the 'Colonial Soldiers' who fell in the Boer War.

SAME TO SAME
18 MARCH 1912

A gloomy birthday letter:

... I have sent you a Canadian woollen rug which I got for you at the Canadian handicraft school, it has been worked by French Canadians.... I hope you will like it and that it will find a place in your room.

Loving thanks for your letter of the 6th, this moment received, full of details of this disastrous coal strike, of the outrageous conduct of the suffragettes – really affairs have come to a nice pass in the Old Country; people here are astounded at what is allowed to happen at home.

I look upon the Asquith government, and especially Lloyd George, as entirely responsible for this unrest and all these conflicts between labour and capital. His violent and indefensible Limehouse speech two years ago whetted the appetite of the workmen and the trouble dates from then.

I should imagine these great labour troubles and their attendant great losses to the country will shake the government if anything ever will. It was their business to look ahead and to take timely measures to prevent this colossal strike. All these strikes we have been having these last two years have done indescribable harm to the country and have caused *enormous* losses and unknown want and suffering. *What* an expensive government this has been for England....

(1101)

SAME TO SAME
3 MAY 1912

The Titanic *disaster:*
... I am sorry to say that one of our mails went down in the 'Titanic' and I believe a letter of yours in it. *What* an awful catastrophe that was, and to my mind there was no need for it had only proper precautions been taken as soon as news had been received of icebergs – the ship was never slowed down, nor was the lookout ever doubled nor was the captain on the bridge and this huge ship, with her enormous speed crashes into the iceberg of which always 2/3rds are below water. Had it been blowing hard I don't suppose a soul would have been saved, as the hurricane deck where the boats are stored is such an enormous height above the water that the boats were bound to be either smashed or swamped before they touched the water.

I am grateful to say that very few Canadians lost their lives and those belonged almost entirely to Montreal....

(1105)

KING GEORGE V TO PRINCESS LOUISE
BUCKINGHAM PALACE, 4 JUNE 1912

Georgie on the 'strange and troublous times' they live in:
Dearest Aunt Louise, Loving thanks for your dear letter and for all your good wishes for my birthday, and for the beautiful old box which you have so kindly sent me. I think it very dear of you to have remembered me. I shall put it with my collection either here or at Windsor.

Yes, we live in strange and troublous times, but I shall go on working and doing my best for the people of this great Empire. Some day they will see they are making a mistake. I am convinced as you say of the loyalty and devotion to the Crown which exists and very strongly too, in the Country at this moment. I see it wherever I go and get letters every day from all kinds of people wishing me well. The unrest is mostly produced and kept alive by a few agitators who live on strikes. But I feel soon the people will see how they are being taken in by them and then there will be a reaction....

Excuse this scrawl, but I am very sleepy and must go to bed. With renewed thanks and love to Lorne, Ever dearest Aunt your devoted nephew Georgie.

(1108)

At least 'this scrawl' is absolutely legible though extraordinarily immature.

QUEEN ALEXANDRA TO PRINCESS LOUISE
MARLBOROUGH HOUSE, SUNDAY

... It is all *dreadfully* sad coming back here now in this for ever beloved happy house now so sad and desolate without him my beloved Bertie. I miss him more and more and the house is in a dreadful state nothing arranged yet!! ... Ever your most affectionate old sister-in-law Alix.

I hope dear Lorne is better.

(1112)

Despite his infidelities, Alix had spent happy years with Bertie as Prince and Princess of Wales, leaders of the dashing 'Marlborough House set'.

PRINCE ARTHUR TO PRINCESS LOUISE
GOVERNMENT HOUSE, OTTAWA, 29 NOVEMBER 1912

Laying an old ghost in Canadian politics:

Dearest Louise, Thank you for your answer to my cable which I sent in cypher through Clarence House. I am so glad you have allowed your letter to Sir John M[acdonald] and his answer to you to be published. This will show everyone how erroneous is the statement made by Sir Richard Cartwright (who died a few months ago) in his memoirs just published, that you and Sir John were on bad terms owing to his having insulted you at a ball here.

I felt certain that there was no truth in this statement as I know that you had a great regard for the old Prime Minister. Sir Joseph Pope, now Deputy Minister of External Affairs, was Sir John's Private Secretary and he ... was naturally much shocked at this statement concerning you and his former chief and the more so as every Canadian paper has been writing about this stated behaviour of Sir John towards you which naturally puts him in a very bad light to the public.

Sir Joseph Pope sent privately to Colonel Lowther your letter to Sir John and the copy of his answer to you and asked Lowther whether he would show them to me, and ask me whether it would be possible for them to be published so that an end might once and for all be put to the statements made by Sir Richard Cartwright.

Of course I said that *I* could not dream of authorising this, but that I would wire to you to see if you had any objection to these letters being published. I felt sure that you would not wish the memory of old Sir John to be maligned in the way it had been done. Both are very nice letters and show conclusively on what good terms of friendship you and Sir John were.

In his letter to you he referred in rather strong terms to the American

Press and as I thought this might offend them I suggested this particular part of the letter might be expunged. I hope you will understand and approve of my action.

I believe that Sir Richard Cartwright was a very strong and bitter partisan and he may have put this statement into his memoirs with a view to damaging Sir John's memory in the eyes of the Canadian public. I have been told that someone was impertinent to you at some ball and that this person was some Senator or M.P. from somewhere in British Columbia. Have you any recollections of the incident?

People's manners have much improved since your days out here.

Occasionally people do still get drunk on official occasions – at my State Dinner the night of the opening of Parliament last week the Private Secretary of the Lieutenant-Governor of New Brunswick got drunk and had to be got out of the dining room by one of my A.D.C.s who then handed him on to one of the orderlies who drove him back in a cab to his hotel. Of course I received a letter of apology afterwards from the Lieutenant-Governor. I had the matter kept very dark and I hope very few people know of the occurrence.

(1122)

THE LETTER REFERRED TO ABOVE FROM PRINCESS LOUISE TO SIR JOHN MACDONALD HMS *DIDO*, 25 JANUARY 1883

Dear Sir John, I have been wanting to write to you ever since I saw those ill-natured articles in the papers against Lady Macdonald and myself, but His Excellency thought, as they were such preposterous inventions, that I should leave it alone. Now that you have written to Col. de Winton, I cannot help sending you a few lines, having received so much kindness from you and Lady Macdonald ever since I first came to Canada and I have learnt to look upon you both as friends that I made out there. It is, therefore, most annoying to me that such stories should have been circulated.... To invent that I have had a misunderstanding with your wife vexes me beyond measure....

You must know in how many ways I admire Lady Macdonald and think her a worthy example to every wife.

I hope your health is quite restored. Believe me, with kind remembrances to Lady Macdonald, yours very sincerely, Louise.

(1126, copy)

The passage omitted from Louise's letter, in which she rounded on the (American) press, ran as follows:

That the press should write me down, I do not mind; it has been amusing itself for some time past cutting me to pieces in the most uncalled for way, knowing that I am defenceless, and in no ways deserving of their attacks, but to invent that I have had a misunderstanding with your wife, vexes me beyond measure, as it is making use of her name as a pretext for attacking me. etc. Signed, Yours very sincerely, Louise.

TWO LETTERS FROM ALICE, PRINCESS ANDREW OF GREECE, TO HER MOTHER, PRINCESS LOUIS OF BATTENBERG FROM HER FIELD HOSPITAL DURING THE BALKAN WAR, ONE DATED 26 OCTOBER 1912 – SERVIA, MACEDONIA; AND THE OTHER VERRIA, 2 NOVEMBER 1912

The family were most touched and excited by these letters, Louise receiving her copy and sending copies to Arthur in Canada, who was tremendously struck by them and showed them to his family and also to his family doctor. Alice was mother of Prince Philip.

An extract from the end of letter 1:

Meantime our 4th Division had already marched 24 hours from beyond Elassona, twelve hours fighting and another twenty-two hours to get round the mountains and cut off the retreat of the Turks at the Servia end of the Pass, and fired on the Turks, with mountain guns, as they were breaking up camp to retreat in orderly fashion; then a [Turkish] panic ensued, the camps and guns were left, they cut off the traces, mounted their horses and galloped off anyhow; 400 Turkish prisoners were taken, but many Turks were killed because the mountain batteries followed them all the way almost into the town, and when Tino [of Greece] rode down into the Pass this morning, the bodies of the Turks were piled up all down the road, ten deep, high as a wall. Awful! Awful!

As I passed I saw all the guns, the camps, the uniforms, the officers' trunks and camp beds. It was extraordinary, for the Turks are rarely given to panics and they had a strong position, so there was not the slightest excuse for a panic; but oh! the splendid revenge, owing to the extraordinary courage of our troops. Ours was a severer battle than the Servians and the Bulgarians have had and we came quicker and further than they did, thanks to Tino's plan of advancing with great speed. Goodbye. Alice.

(1129)

GRAND DUCHESS OF MECKLENBURG-STRELITZ TO PRINCESS LOUISE, STRELITZ, 27 JULY 1913

My dearest Louise, I was indeed glad receiving your dear letter for my old 89th and that you thought of me, though so very old!... It is a pleasure to know not to be forgotten, in England too, where I have not appeared for eight years. David's [later Edward VIII] staying here is such a pleasure to us; to me he seems to like to listen when I tell him of the *Past*, me being about the very last of olden times, with a good memory still, besides it is a good thing for olden times not to be forgotten....

(1141)

KING GEORGE V TO PRINCESS LOUISE YORK COTTAGE, 26 OCTOBER 1913

Dearest Aunt Louise, Thanks for sending me Russell Stephenson's letter which interested me very much. From letters I have seen and from everything I have heard concerning the feelings of the Protestants in Ulster entirely bears out what he says.

I am indeed very anxious and worried by the state of affairs in Ireland caused by the Home Rule Bill. Please God a solution may be found before it is too late.

As soon as you send the papers to Bigge with regard to the 'Regimental Agency' I will consider whether it is possible for me to give my Patronage to the Bazaar which is to be held in aid of it. As a rule I never give my patronage to Bazaars.

I am sorry Lorne was not looking well the other day when you left for Roseneath [*sic*] but I hope he is all right. We have had glorious weather here last week, it is raining this evening. The Connaughts arrived safely at Quebec yesterday they were delayed by gales and fog, but she was well. With much love ever your very affectionate nephew Georgie.

(1142)

Stephenson described himself as 'a devoted loyalist'.

SAME TO SAME BUCKINGHAM PALACE, 18 MARCH 1914

A birthday letter:

Dearest Aunt Louise, Many thanks for your kind letter. I was so distressed to hear that you were laid up with that horrible influenza and have suffered so much pain, but am glad to hear that you are now on the mend and trust that you will soon be up and all right again. I know it takes some time to get over these attacks. Today being your birthday I send you all my loving good wishes and congratulations and am only sorry that you should have to spend it in bed.

I am sure your thoughts are with me during this critical time, I confess I am greatly worried and very anxious with regard to the grave situation and it is difficult to see how civil war [in Ireland] is to be avoided at the present moment, but I have not given up all hopes yet, that reason and common sense on both sides may prevail in the end. I am very busy and have a great deal to do and many people to see. I hope Lorne is well. With love from May and hoping that you will soon have recovered . . . Georgie.

(1161)

PRINCE ARTHUR TO PRINCESS LOUISE
GOVERNMENT HOUSE, OTTAWA, 30 MARCH 1914

. . . I am terribly upset by all that is going on at home and am longing to receive some authentic news as to the exact state of affairs. Here the wildest rumours have been published in the local and thoroughly untrustworthy press on this side of the Atlantic – only extracts from the most radical and socialistic papers at home have been published here and these were pleasant reading I can assure you!! with the abuse of Georgy, the Army, the aristocracy and the Unionist party. The whole tone was more worthy of the yellow press of the United States or of the Red press of France than of anything English.

Being so far away and not receiving any authentic news till 12 days afterwards makes me very desperate. There is one thing I can see however quite clearly, and that is, that the seed so sedulously sown by that *scoundrel* Lloyd George is bearing fruit and that the socialist and unEnglish party are dominating the government. It was *their intention* for *party purposes* to *coerce Ulster* at the point of the bayonet, and it was the refusal of the officers of the Army (and *I have no doubt* of the men too) to shed the blood of loyal men that has exasperated the party of Lloyd George and Co: and allies. They have shown it by their wild shrieks of abuse of the King and of the Army; anything more disgusting or more unEnglish I have never heard, but then *none* of them care *one rap* about their country, about truth, honesty or fairness, SELF is all they care for.

The general election can't be staved off very long now and, unless *all honest* Englishmen rally round the Throne, on the side of order, the disruptionalists will come in with even a larger majority than now.

Poor Georgy, I *am so sorry* for him, his position is indeed a *hard one*, I wish I was there to help him. . . .

(1163)

Arthur's account of the officers' 'refusal' is a reference to the 'Curragh Mutiny'.

QUEEN ALEXANDRA TO PRINCESS LOUISE MARLBOROUGH HOUSE, 30 APRIL 1914

Lorne's last illness – double pneumonia:
My darling Louise, I was so more than touched by your turning to *me* in your agony and anxiety about your beloved Lorne – I do indeed feel and share all your anguish and misery with you and only wish I could be with you now to help and comfort you.

Poor darling *what* you must be going through now and how it must remind you of our days of anguish for beloved Bertie. I do pray to God night and day for you both that the dear one may be spared. It must all have come upon you suddenly as I thought he was well during your horrible spell of influenza, and he took you down to Kent House [in the Isle of Wight]. I do hope the warm mild weather may still do good – all you tell me about the dear patient touches me so much – and I am sure he is an excellent patient full of kind thoughts for others.

I fear the night was bad and restless which naturally is weakening, but if only his strength can keep up he may suddenly take a turn for the good.

Poor darling Louise I *do feel* so intensely with you and in your own weak state of health this fearful strain night and day is so bad for you. I am glad you have got his sister Lady Frances and young Niall Campbell with you they will be a comfort and help to you *both*. So touching to think of him looking out of the window to see how lovely the country is in this glorious spring and brightness, and also that he should have thought of the 6th May and wishes to go there with us all to Windsor! Oh it is all as you say too heartbreaking to think of – oh my poor darling Louise indeed to me you have *always* been the dearest sister and I too think of all former happy times when we were young together and saw so much of each other. Life has so many ups and downs but I have never changed to any [rest of letter lost]

(1164)

This letter is one of the many that shows that Louise's and Lorne's serious estrangement of the 1880s was past.

IV

Widowhood

1914–39

PRINCE ARTHUR TO PRINCESS LOUISE
GOVERNMENT HOUSE, OTTAWA, 3 MAY 1914

Death of Lorne, 9th Duke of Argyll, on 2 May 1914:
Dearest Louise, No words can adequately express to you *how much* I feel for you in the sad loss you have sustained. I know how anxious you have for some time been on Lorne's account and how carefully you have looked after him and nursed him. I own, when I received your first cable to say that he was seriously ill with pneumonia, I felt very anxious and feared that he would be a very bad subject for so serious and trying an illness.

Every day I have been fearing for the worst, but when I received your cable this morning giving me the sad news that all was over it gave me a great shock. We have always been such good friends for so many years now that I know that I shall miss him very much. I know that life has not been easy for you and that you have passed through many trials, but still I know how much you will be feeling it at the present moment, left all alone in that little house [Kent House]. If only I had been at home and could have hurried down to the Isle of Wight to be of some use to you and to comfort you. It makes me miserable to think of you in Kent House with no one to help you – My heart goes out to you beloved sister and I can think of nothing else today but you. It is sad to be separated so far away at this moment and I feel that words can't convey to you all my feelings. You have always been such a dear affectionate sister to me that it makes me miserable not to be able to do anything for you, when I might have done so had I not been out here.

Canada will sympathise with you and many will be the kindly thoughts of you in this loyal Dominion at this moment.

You and Lorne have always been remembered here with the sincerest affection, and with gratitude for the kindly interest you have taken in all Canadians when they visited England. I cabled to you the sympathy of the government and the Canadian people....

(1166)

KING GEORGE V TO PRINCESS LOUISE
BUCKINGHAM PALACE, 3 MAY 1914

Dearest aunt Louise, It is impossible for me to find words to tell you how deeply I feel for you in your overwhelming sorrow. You know how devoted I have been to dear Lorne ever since I was a child and he was always so kind to me. I feel that I have lost one of my oldest and best friends.

He rendered great services to his Country as Governor-General in Canada and in always working for the Empire since then, he was a great Imperialist and everyone was fond of him. I well know the terrible time you have been through and all you have suffered in your anxiety during these last days. My heart goes out to you in sympathy as I know how devoted you were to him and all you have lost. He simply worshipped the ground you trod on. I know that God will protect you and give you strength to bear your great sorrow....

(1168)

QUEEN ALEXANDRA TO PRINCESS LOUISE
MARLBOROUGH HOUSE, 5 MAY 1914

My poor darling Louise! My heart bleeds indeed for you in this awful calamity and the deep and great sorrow which has befallen you! I did so hope against hope! and prayed so hard to God to spare *you* dearest! from this greatest of all sorrows and trials. To see your beloved life's companion taken from you! And *I* having had to go through all the *agony* of seeing the beloved one taken from me and *left* behind *alone*! *I* can indeed feel more than many others all the misery you must be suffering now. There is no early comfort for a broken heart. My thoughts have never left you for a single moment in all those terrible 6 days and nights – and I feel sure HE knew and felt your care when you watched by his side and was glad and grateful to you for all your tender care of him during his last and fatal illness.

Dear Victoria B[attenberg] I know has been a great comfort and help to you in your loneliness and anguish and now she will do all she can for you in these terrible days still before you. My poor darling Louise how I wish I could have been near you and helped you to bear it all – I do hope you will let me come to you either on the Thursday you come up or Friday after the last heartbreaking ceremony at Westminster. A telephone message will bring me to you at once. God help and give you the strength to bear all this crushing ordeal ever your most devoted old sister Alix.

(1173)

SAME TO SAME
MAY 1914

Darling Louise, Here is my old [widow's] bonnet as a pattern which I hope you may like and copy. I wore it always but I had another older one with a shorter lighter veil behind. I was so pleased and DREADFULLY touched to see you poor darling Louise and I thank you so much for sending for me. God help and comfort you – your loving Alix.

(1174)

PRINCESS HENRY OF PRUSSIA TO PRINCESS LOUIS (VICTORIA) OF BATTENBERG
6 MAY 1914

... poor dear Aunt Louise she must have gone through terrible days till the end came and will miss him sadly I fear in spite of all, after such a long married life – and being so poorly it will have been a great shock I fear.

I felt sure you would be near her in her grief and worry as you have always understood her *so* well, poor dear. Should she like a change, something completely different, I am at any moment ready to go and fetch her and ask her to make a stay with us at Hemmelmark, where perhaps the quiet, and even my dullness might at such a moment be a relief to her – middle of July from 10th or 12th July would be the quietest time for her and August with us, and I could ask Bäuerlein to come too [the beloved German governess], or any one else of Uncle's [Lorne's] nieces she might like to bring, or the like – you know best what would suit her – it is only a suggestion because one longs to cheer her and be of help to her somehow. ...

Russia seems more restless again. Many a kiss from your ever loving sister Irene.

(1179)

THE EMPRESS OF RUSSIA TO PRINCESS LOUISE
LIVADIA, 17/30 MAY 1914

My darling Auntie, I just received your letter forwarded to me by Victoria, and thank you for it with all my loving heart. It is a comfort to know that at least one of dear Mama's [Alice's] daughters [Victoria] was near you during the first trying days. You know how especially dear you have always been to us and how tenderly Papa [Louis of Hesse] and we loved you. More than ever are my thoughts near you, and the home-coming to the empty house will be bitterly trying.

But you are brave, darling, and God is sure to give you strength and comfort. You are right in saying that one must ever turn to Him and trust that all is for the best. I too have ever found that in prayer alone one can gain strength to bear one's crosses.... He soothes and enlightens one. Being myself such an invalid these last eight years, I have learned to look upon Him every moment of my life. Our Church-services and prayers are most beautiful and consoling – and to partake oftener of Holy Communion brings such peace and resignation....

You kindly asked after the children, so I enclose their last photos to give you an idea what they look like. Thank God Alexei has been keeping in much better health and has grown very much. He will be ten this summer. I think you would love him, you always loved boys so much. He has such a tender heart – and bears pains so patiently – is very merry and clever. We return to Zarskoe in two weeks, and regret having to leave this lovely place. You cannot imagine what quantities of roses we have – of every colour and sort and so immense – one longs to be an artist to paint from morn to night.

But I must end. Baby [Alexei] is waiting to say his evening prayers with me. Nicky [the Emperor], the children and I kiss you very affectionately. Goodbye and God bless and help you, beloved Aunt Louise, ever your devoted Alix.

(1186)

The Empress of Russia was Princess Alix of Hesse, daughter of Princess Alice.

PRINCESS VICTORIA OF WALES TO PRINCESS LOUISE MARLBOROUGH HOUSE, 19 MAY 1914

... Oh! how you must miss that beloved husband who simply adored you – and he was loved and reverenced by all who knew him....

(1194)

KING GEORGE V TO PRINCESS LOUISE BUCKINGHAM PALACE, 6 JUNE 1914

My dearest Aunt Louise, It was dear of you writing to me, in the midst of all your sorrow, for my old birthday, I send you my loving thanks for all your good wishes. We live in difficult times and one is anxious for the future, but I trust in God to guide me and to help me to do my duty. I am sorry that you have been obliged to return to London so as to see your old lawyer. I hope all your affairs will soon be satisfactorily settled, but all these things take time....

The suffragettes are behaving worse than ever again, it is impossible to know what to do with them, they must be mad and are not responsible for their actions.

With renewed thanks for your kind letter and I trust you will not feel too sad at Kensington. With love from May Ever dear Aunt Louise your devoted nephew Georgie.

(1197)

MARIE, DOWAGER DUCHESS OF SAXE-COBURG-GOTHA TO PRINCESS LOUISE COBURG, 11 JUNE 1914

Dear Louise ... Now that I hope to see you soon and tell you myself what I feel for you, I implore you not to trouble about answering. You know how fond I was of your dear husband, we were always good friends and I cannot think without a pang of real sadness of seeing Kensington Palace without him! We used to talk through the window when I was walking in the garden and I always see his kind face and hear his jokes. How you must miss him, dear Louise and *how* lonely you must feel now in your empty home where you spent together over forty years.... Your affectionate sister Marie.

(1198)

Marie was Affie's widow. Did she and Lorne talk through the famous French window that Louise later had bricked up?

PRINCE ALBERT ('BERTIE' – GEORGE VI) TO PRINCESS LOUISE HMS *COLLINGWOOD*, FIRST BATTLE SQUADRON 14 JUNE 1914

Dearest Aunt Louise, I am writing to thank you so very much for the excellent day's fishing you gave Sir Stanley Colville and me on Saturday. We both enjoyed ourselves immensely, and the weather was lovely. We caught 7 trout, I caught 5 and the Admiral 2.... Again thanking you very much indeed for your kindness, I remain your devoted great-nephew Bertie.

(1199)

AUSTEN CHAMBERLAIN TO PRINCESS LOUISE HIGHBURY, MOOR GREEN, 6 JULY 1914

Death of Joseph Chamberlain, in the same year as Lorne:
... That Your Royal Highness in the midst of your own great sorrow should have thought of us and ours moves us all and we value your testimony to my Father's greatness. I am, Madame, Your Royal Highness's obedient servant, Austen Chamberlain.

(1945)

THE PRINCE OF WALES (EDWARD VIII) TO PRINCESS LOUISE BUCKINGHAM PALACE, 9 AUGUST 1914

My dear Aunt Louise, Thank you a thousand times for your dear letter enclosing £1000 for the National Fund. How good and kind of you to send such a magnificent sum in response to my appeal, and I am most deeply grateful to you for this great help.

Also I have to thank you for your congratulations to me on receiving a commission. I join the 1st battalion of the Grenadiers at Warley tomorrow morning. I am so pleased to be taking some part in the defence of the country.... I remain ever, your most affectionate [great] nephew, David.

(1203)

PRINCE ARTHUR TO PRINCESS LOUISE GOVERNMENT HOUSE, OTTAWA, 9 AUGUST 1914

War spirit in Canada:
... The enthusiasm throughout the length and breadth of the Dominion is splendid, but I expect it is the same everywhere else – I don't think our enemies will know us again....

(1204)

SAME TO SAME GOVERNMENT HOUSE, OTTAWA, 25 OCTOBER 1914

... I *never* read anything like William's [German Emperor and Arthur's nephew] order to his troops, for want of dignity, fine feeling and personal animosity; he *must* be *mad.* I was so sorry to see that poor Mossy's son Max had been killed, in the papers I read that he had been buried with 3 English officers....

(1210)

Mossy was Vicky's youngest child and the Emperor William's sister.

QUEEN ALEXANDRA TO PRINCESS LOUISE
20 APRIL 1915

Louise's grief for Lorne:
Excuse this selfishness talking only of my self when you poor darling Louise were so sad and lonely! With a fit of the blues as you call it. While reading through poor dear Lorne's verses and looking at his various drawings. How well I understand your poor feelings! Those little things are just the *very* things which bring everything back to one's poor sad mind and open afresh the awful PAIN OF PARTING and all the horror of those last sad hours! No wonder you quite broke down. My poor dear Louise, I am so awfully sorry for you in your terrible loneliness which at times must be almost too great a burden to bear! As soon as I am better I will come. God help us all! We *all* want His help! Ever your most devoted sister Alix.

(1229)

THE PRINCE OF WALES TO PRINCESS LOUISE
HEADQUARTERS 1ST CORPS PRINCE OF WALES
25 JUNE 1915

Dear Aunt Louise, Very many thanks for your kind letter of good wishes for my birthday. It was a sad day this year with this ghastly war on, and so many of one's friends killed. I am having an interesting time out here but of course life gets rather dull and monotonous when there is no fighting as at the present moment. But we are rather short of shells as you know, and so shall have to wait till we get enough to enable us to resume the offensive. The weather is lovely and hot out here now, which is nice for the troops.

How splendid it is of you having had all those wounded officers in your house; what a real rest and change it must be after the trenches. I suppose some of them have been pretty bad. I fear I have absolutely no news as all is so very quiet just now.

Again my most sincere thanks dear Aunt Louise for your kind letter and all the nice things you said in it!!

With my best love, I remain, your affectionate great nephew David.

(1236)

KING GEORGE V TO PRINCESS LOUISE BUCKINGHAM PALACE, 13 MARCH 1916

Many thanks for your very kind letter and enclosures which I have read with much interest.

It was very dear of you to suggest a message to my people and I am touched by all you say. But as you know anything of the sort can only be done after consultation with my Ministers.

Yes, I agree with you that the Unity of the Empire and faith in God will bring us Victory. The Dominions are supporting the Old Country splendidly and every day we, as a Nation are more and more determined to see the War to a successful end.

But the time for any appeal to the people is I think not ripe, and I am sure you will realise that one must carefully choose the 'psychological moment', as they say! for such a communication.

Every one is doing their best to win this war from the highest to the lowest and I am doing all in my power to help them, in spite of the criticisms of the press and many people who are ignorant of what is being done and the difficulties which have to be overcome. I am ever your devoted nephew Georgie.

(1248)

PRINCE ARTHUR TO PRINCESS LOUISE OTTAWA, 29 MAY 1916

I so much agree with you about politics etc. – the English are an odd people, politics, fads and prejudices come before patriotism. I attribute it entirely to false and viciously radical education. Patriotism has by order of the authorities been carefully kept out of all the national schools with the painful results that we unfortunately see – no respect and love for the national flag has ever been inculcated into the minds and lives of the young.

(1251)

THE EMPRESS OF RUSSIA TO PRINCESS LOUISE HEADQUARTERS, 2 DECEMBER 1916

My darling Auntie, I was so touched and happy to receive your dear letter and thank you ever so tenderly for it. It was indeed dear of you thinking of me....

I come down here every month for a week's rest and to see my two darlings. It is hard not being together at such trying times and he is very lonely, therefore I have left my Boy with him for 6 months. I miss them awfully, but they are happy together – sleep in one room, go out and take meals together etc. Alexei has grown very much and developed in every sense of the word – being only amongst men has been good for him and he has heard much that is interesting.

(1268)

A letter from Nicky to Alix on 6 October 1915 describes how the plan for 'the Little One's' visits to HQ began:

My precious little Bird.... It is very cosy sleeping side by side. I say my prayers with him every night ... he says his prayers too fast, and it is difficult to stop him. He was tremendously pleased with the review.... [Alexei] begged hard to be allowed to lunch with all of us.

(C. E. Vulliamy [ed.], *Letters of the Tsar to the Tsaritsa*, 1929)

ARTHUR JAMES BALFOUR TO PRINCESS LOUISE 4 CARLTON GARDENS, PALL MALL, WEDNESDAY

Probably c. 1916, when Balfour lived in Carlton Gardens as Foreign Secretary.

Madam, Please accept my grateful thanks for Ovaltine. We live in strenuous times, and even if our vocal chords hold out (which is very doubtful) our general system will require special sustenance and support! I speak for politicians in general, and for myself in particular.... I shall certainly make use of 'Ovaltine', with many kind thoughts of the donor.

(1952)

In another undated letter, this time from Whittinghame, Balfour thanks Princess Louise for her presents, 'literary and hygienic'.

KING GEORGE V TO PRINCESS LOUISE WINDSOR CASTLE, 9 SEPTEMBER 1917

Dearest Aunt Louise, Thank you for your kind letter and for the article which I will certainly try and find time to read and which I am sure will interest me very much, but you have no idea of the mass of papers I have to read every day and I think they increase each week. I am glad to say Bertie is much better now, although he will not be fit to go to sea for some time.... How sad that your Vicar died and I fear in him you have lost an old and valued friend. I hope you are well in spite of this damp weather.... This terrible war drags on and there is no prospect of it coming to an end yet, but from all accounts the Central Powers will have a real bad time of it this winter and I can't say that I am sorry for them, as they continue to behave worse than brute beasts. We still hope to remain on here for a little, but I don't get much rest. Thanking you again for your letter with love from May ever your devoted nephew Georgie.

(1280)

W. B. RICHMOND TO PRINCESS LOUISE BEAVOR, C. 1917

My dear Madam, When I have made a friend, if I may call you that? I believe!! And nothing would move me from perfect faith. I know how busy you are and indeed rightly. That you feel a lack of nerve power who can wonder but reserve of strength and blessed sleep will restore that. You could never *bore* me.

Thank you I am quite well again as long as I continue to remember that 75 is not 35.

(2010)

He suggests coming to pay his respects to her on Sunday morning – his only free time. Louise and Leopold had known him as a young painter.

PRINCE ARTHUR TO PRINCESS LOUISE ALDERSHOT, 8 JUNE 1918

Louise's honour; Georgie's silver wedding present:

Dearest Louise, I must send you a line to tell you *how* pleased I was to see your *splendid* and *untiring* services, in connection with the war and especially with *all you have done* at Kensington recognised by your appointment of D.B.E. I am *sure* that *everyone will rejoice* to see you thus honoured.

With regard to our combined silver wedding present to George and May I have found a very interesting and cleverly painted *war picture* by Sir John Lavery which I am sure they will like; it has been very difficult to find a good modern picture by a wellknown English artist at a moderate price and I think you will like it. As you 3 sisters deputed me to choose one, without further bothering you I have [made] my choice and I must hope that you will all agree. The *price* is *75 guineas* and to this I hope you will send me £10.

(1292)

LORD LOUIS (DICKIE) MOUNTBATTEN TO PRINCESS LOUISE LUTON HOO, 4 JANUARY 1919

Louise kept in close touch with the younger generation.

Dear Aunt Louise, Thank you a thousand times for the lovely Russian cushion you sent me for Xmas. It will look quite lovely in my cabin if I go in the 'Renown' with David [Prince of Wales] to Australia, as I hope to do. I live in hopes of his taking me on his staff as he promised he would.... It was too good of you to offer to put me up and if I am coming up to London in the future I'd love to come to you. The next time I come however I must go to Zia's [Wernher] as I have left most of my clothes there.

I hunted yesterday, which was great fun. The other night we had a small dinner party at the Ritz to which Lady Loughborough came, who is so pretty, I think. Audrey James, Mrs. Brinton's youngest girl, also came, and she is if possible even more lovely [Dickie's first love].

I also went to the Albert Hall with the Ludlows, Georgie and Nada [his brother and sister-in-law], Zia and her husband Harold Wernher, and lots of others. That was also great fun....

Much love from ever your devoted own nephew Dick.

(1296)

JOHN MURRAY TO PRINCESS LOUISE
50 ALBEMARLE STREET, 21 JANUARY 1920

The gift of a picture by Princess Louise:

Madam, Your very beautiful picture has just arrived, and I hasten to offer my very warm thanks for it, and also for the kind letter which preceded it. If I, a mere inexpert, may venture to comment on the picture I would say that I am at a loss which to admire most, the composition, the treatment of the subject, or the colouring.... It is especially refreshing after a recent visit to the Cubist deformities in Burlington House.

(2034)

The painting cannot be traced among the famous publisher's archives.

PRINCE ARTHUR TO PRINCESS LOUISE
NICE, 3 DECEMBER 1920

The headstrong Prince:

... I am sorry about Sidney Greville having left David; I am very fond of him, but believe me he was not *strong* enough to have any influence with a headstrong character like David's, I have recognised this for some time, and was sure that there would have to be a change.

(1316)

SAME TO SAME
15 DECEMBER 1920

Dearest Louise, I have only time to write you a few lines in answer to your little letter of the 9th. What a splendid description you give me of David's speech at the Mansion House. It is wonderful how he has come on and it is a great thing that he should speak so well.

(1318)

SAME TO SAME
GOVERNMENT HOUSE, CALCUTTA, 2 FEBRUARY 1921

... Many natives had come to the three large dinners there have been, and several of them brought their wives with them and they appeared to be quite at their ease in society; this is a great advance on what I have hitherto known. There is no doubt that the natives are getting more and more emancipated, and some are going in for games, lawn tennis and golf, one sees natives too playing cricket, and I am told that some of them are quite good at football....

(1327)

Arthur had been opening the various legislatures.

SAME TO SAME
VICEREGAL LODGE, DELHI, 10 FEBRUARY 1921

... You are probably aware that the unfortunate proceedings at Amritsar, where General Dyer behaved with such severity, has unfortunately called forth throughout India a nasty racial feeling against the English, the English government and all Indian officials. In some of the big cities like Calcutta, Bombay, Madras etc., agitators led by a certain Gandhi have urged the people to boycott anything English, any institutions and *even my visits* and they have used considerable intimidation and have not hesitated to misrepresent facts in the most shameful manner. The agitators have had a certain amount of success, the Indian, like the Irishman, is easily led, and especially youths. The agitation has so far not spread into the country, and is confined to the towns, but I have been of course up 'against it' in many towns I have been to.... Yesterday, after opening the United Indian Chambers, I made a reference to this regrettable state [of] affairs and assured them how George and I both felt deeply about what had occurred (which was as you know not without considerable and indefensible provocation) and I *urged* them to forgive and forget....

(1328)

Arthur's many speeches in India made a deep impression on him, at least, and he wrote long letters to Louise, both from India and on the voyage home. His theme was 'forgive and unite' for the sake of India. His son Arthur writes to Louise from Government House, Cape Town, on 6 April saying, 'I am so glad that dear Papa's mission was such a tremendous success and he is none the worse for his exertions.'

SAME TO SAME
BAGSHOT PARK, 25 SEPTEMBER 1921

Death of Sir Ernest Cassel:
... Poor Cassell's [*sic*] sudden death was very sad; ... he had been a very true and loyal friend to Bertie, and he was wonderful in his generosity; which was done without any idea of getting anything for it! ...

(1339)

Some people believed he was closely related to the royal family or at any rate had adopted two illegitimate children of Bertie's (Edward VII).

KING GEORGE V TO PRINCESS LOUISE
BUCKINGHAM PALACE, 2 MARCH 1922

Marriage of the Princess Royal to Lord Lascelles:
Dearest Aunt Louise, How dear of you to write me those kind words of sympathy. I was proud of my dear child on Tuesday and she looked happy and I *know* is happy. But it was a terribly sad day for me. I can't tell you how I miss her and fear I always shall, she is my only daughter and had never been away from us except for a few days – since she was born. The blank she has left in the house is awful and I still feel miserable. But I mustn't be selfish.

(1346)

There is a remarkable family likeness between the reactions of George V and George VI when their only, or elder, daughter married.

PRINCE ARTHUR TO PRINCESS LOUISE
CAP FERRAT, 18 MARCH 1922

... I also heard from Dickie [Mountbatten], who wrote to announce his engagement; *I* think it is a very good thing; she has plenty of money and is very attractive and sensible; her father is not a Jew and I think the mother was not either, and Sir Ernest Cassel [her grandfather] had been a Roman Catholic half his life. Dickie is so far removed in relationship from Georgy, that I don't think the connection with Cassel matters much.

I am sure that his marrying money will be a great relief to Victoria [his mother].

(1347)

ARTHUR, SON OF PRINCE ARTHUR, DUKE OF CONNAUGHT, TO PRINCESS LOUISE 24 MAY 1923

The younger generation was beginning to realize the drawbacks of being royal.

I suppose poor [unmarried] Maudie is leading the same shut-up experience. What a waste of life!

(1366)

SAME TO SAME 14 JULY 1923

Two months later young Arthur was again writing on the subject.

We were thrilled at the news about Maudie and much surprised. Alix knew nothing about it, and neither of us know the young man. However I am very delighted for her sake and to think she will have a life of her own at last.

(1369)

'Maudie' was Princess Maud, the second daughter of King Edward VII*'s eldest daughter, Princess Louise, Duchess of Fife. When the Duchess was made Princess Royal in 1905, King Edward declared that both her daughters, Lady Alexandra Duff and Lady Maud Duff, should bear the title of Princess. Princess Alexandra (Alix) had married Prince Arthur of Connaught, the writer of this letter, in 1913; Princess Maud married Lord Carnegie, later the 11th Earl of Southesk, on 12 November 1923. The 14 July letter refers to their engagement earlier that year.*

PRINCE ARTHUR TO PRINCESS LOUISE 8 DECEMBER 1923

I am very distressed at the result of the election; the reduced majority of the Government and the increase of Labour? (socialists) party. I won't begin writing what I think about the whole matter as I might write pages to you. There are really now only two parties, the *labour* and the *anti-labour*.

(1378)

SAME TO SAME
13 DECEMBER 1923

The result of the election was a great disappointment and I can't help having the feeling that the Conservatives did not have a fair chance against the lies and intimidation organised by their opponents. The terrible thing is the large increase in the number of the Labour members. I don't envy Georgy being placed in the very difficult and trying position he is in at the present moment – I can't bear the very *idea even* of his possibly being obliged to send for Ramsay MacDonald to form a labour government.

(6379)

In fact Prince Arthur's nephew, George V, coped effectively in his own way with the post-war changes in politics.

SAME TO SAME
20 DECEMBER 1923

I do hope that you will spend a Happy Xmas, but I own that at our age it is difficult to do so.

(1380)

They were aged seventy-five and seventy-three respectively.

KING GEORGE V TO PRINCESS LOUISE
BUCKINGHAM PALACE, 20 DECEMBER 1923

My dear aunt Louise, How too kind of you to send me that interesting autograph letter of the Electress Sophia of Hanover [mother of the first of the British Georges], which I shall add to the collection at Windsor. I don't know if there is a letter of hers there. I am also delighted with that lovely big magnifying glass which will be most useful for looking at my stamps with, when I am arranging them.

Thanks also for your kind letter and enquiries about my health, I am glad to say I am getting on capitally and practically have no pain now.

(1381)

The long-lasting pain was due to the King's accident during the late war, when his horse reared and fell on him while he was reviewing troops.

PRINCE GEORGE, DUKE OF KENT, TO PRINCESS LOUISE
YORK COTTAGE, MONDAY, DECEMBER 1923

The letter is written in a good 'modern' hand.

Thank you so much for those handkerchiefs you sent me which was very kind of you. Well here we are all spending Xmas together and it isn't very thrilling and I'm not enjoying it *too* much. You would laugh if you were here!

(1382)

Louise was particularly devoted to 'little Georgie', and bequeathed him some of her personal treasures. His artistic interests and temperament appealed to her.

KING GEORGE V TO PRINCESS LOUISE BUCKINGHAM PALACE, 30 MARCH 1924

These strikes are giving me a lot of anxiety. The Labour Government can do no more than any other Government to stop them and I am glad they should be now in office and have the responsibility and feel what it is like.

(1389)

PRINCE ARTHUR TO PRINCESS LOUISE CAP FERRAT, 8 NOVEMBER 1924

She has been laid up with another very bad cold.
Don't forget what I have so often told you, that you ought not to DO any outdoor function in the winter; it is folly to go into an open tent, especially if it is wet – you really must chuck such functions, it really is a great risk at your age, I know that I could not do them, and you are both a woman and are older than me.

(1395)

In fact both were exceptionally tough, each living to over ninety-one.

LORD ROSEBERY TO PRINCESS LOUISE DICTATED TO A TYPIST, THE DURDANS, EPSOM 9 FEBRUARY 1925

An insult to Queen Victoria:
Dear Princess Louise, I was overjoyed to get your letter, for, though I did not doubt your sympathy with my view I was glad to get its expression. The fact is, my letter was much milder than I could have wished it; but I desired to avoid controversy, and so drew it very mild. But when I thought of the forgetfulness of a nation which adored your mother till it became a sort of worship, assenting in silence to the scrapping of her statue to a landing on a staircase in Parliament, I could have burst.

Anyhow, I am glad to say that the thing is now put an end to by the action of the King.

Pray forgive my dictating this, as I can do no other. I am, Your Royal Highness' obedient and devoted Servant, R. [almost illegible]

(1944)

THE PRINCE OF WALES TO PRINCESS LOUISE WINDSOR, OCTOBER 1925

Dearest Aunt Louise, How sweet of you to write to me and send me those lozenges although as a matter of fact I have kept fairly well considering how much I feel the cold on my return from hot climates.... Poor Aunt Beatrice has had a bad time while we have been away and then it's terrible for Ena and Alfonso [King and Queen of Spain, divorced, Ena being Princess Beatrice's daughter] both of whom I have seen. She has taken it all very much to heart but is wonderfully brave and chic about the whole thing as I expected and then Papa has been seedy so altogether I don't return to anything to cheer one up. But I shall do my best to follow up what I have learnt in South America by offering some ideas to British Industry.

(1403)

KING GEORGE V TO PRINCESS LOUISE BUCKINGHAM PALACE, 3 NOVEMBER 1925

I am sorry to hear Duchess Ina of Argyll is so ill, I won't mention it. I am glad you have been to see her and that she was pleased to see you and that you ignored the past, as I suppose you had not seen her for some years.

The Borough elections yesterday were not satisfactory as Labour gained seats in many places. The right people are always too lazy to go and vote....

(1404)

Duchess Ina was Lorne's stepmother, with whom he died unreconciled.

PRINCE ALBERT, DUKE OF YORK, TO PRINCESS LOUISE 17 BRUTON STREET, 23 APRIL 1926

Birth of Princess Elizabeth:

It was too nice of you to have written to me and I do thank you so much for congratulating us on our little girl. She is too delicious and is such a great joy to us both. Elizabeth is progressing wonderfully well and the baby is flourishing. I do hope you will come in later and see your new niece, a great great niece.

(1426)

The Duke had happily picked up one of his wife's favourite adjectives, 'delicious'.

PRINCE ARTHUR TO PRINCESS LOUISE
CAP FERRAT, 2 MAY 1926

An extreme view of the General Strike:
It now appears to me that miners' leaders (all agitators paid by the Bolshevists through their Paymaster the Soviet Minister in London)!! have all along intended to have [a] strike whatever it might cost the country!! As long as they (the agitators) make money, that is all they want: *they* don't care a *hang* for the miners nor any other English workmen!!

(1428)

SAME TO SAME
CAP FERRAT, 25 NOVEMBER 1927

I think with you that our mutual friend 'Jinx' [William Joynson-Hicks, the Conservative Home Secretary, generally known as 'Jix' not 'Jinx'] is very foolish on some subjects, viz: 'the flapper' bill and the 'Prayer Book Revision'; I can't understand it, and the only thing to explain it to me would appear that he is suffering from 'swollen head'.

(1456)

Joynson-Hicks defeated the attempt at revision of the Prayer Book, but brought in the popular votes for women at twenty-one, known as the flapper vote.

If her brother was right, Princess Louise must have changed her mind on the subject of full women's suffrage, made law in 1928.

SAME TO SAME
CAP FERRAT, 23 APRIL 1928

A tragedy of haemophilia – the death of Rupert, only son of the Earl and Countess of Athlone (Princess Alice, daughter of Prince Leopold), after a car accident in Africa:
I am so grateful to you for giving me all the details of poor Rupert's death and illness. How strange that that nightmare should have brought on his haemorrhage through shock. How nice of Cambridge [his cousin], Seymour and his former Governor having gone out to him and having remained with him to the end. I almost wonder at May [the Queen] not having rushed out incog: to have seen her brother's only boy after his ghastly accident; however I am happy to think that his cousin, his own doctors and two friends were with him to the last. I am sorry that [young] Arthur's cough prevented him going to the funeral. I am also surprised at Patsy [his daughter, Lady Patricia Ramsay] not having motored down

with Alec; his leaving on Monday ought not to have prevented their both running down to Windsor for the short service there!!

(1462)

Prince Arthur, like his mother Queen Victoria, was a stickler for funeral attendance.

SAME TO SAME
BAGSHOT PARK, 27 MAY 1928

The lunch on Friday in honour of May's birthday was very cheery, all four boys were there – little Elizabeth was delightful running about and beating time with both hands to the music of the band, and then going up to shake hands with the Bandmaster, whom she had seen at Windsor.

(1468)

Princess Elizabeth was just two.

SAME TO SAME
HOVE, 1928

I was so pleased to hear how well everything had gone off at Kensington on the occasion of your being presented with the freedom of the Borough, the first woman to have been so honoured. I am sure you appreciated their wish to show you the esteem in which you are held by the inhabitants of that part of London in which you have lived for so long, and where Mama was born. I can't understand the Clergy being so little represented, beyond the Vicar.

(1469)

Princess Louise was created the first Honorary Freeman of the Royal Borough of Kensington on 31 July 1928.

ALFRED GILBERT TO PRINCESS LOUISE
THE STUDIO, KENSINGTON PALACE AVENUE
20 MARCH 1933

Ripening Fruits, betoken vigorous life of the plants that bear them, as the best of hearts is set pulsating by memories remaining ever young. I send Your Royal Highness the accompanying token of Homage from the studio where Time is at a discount in the tending of the Flowers of Experience. Alfred Gilbert.

(1988)

The sculptor of Eros, Gilbert had a beloved master in the urbane Boehm, and both were gifted exponents of the New Sculpture, to which Louise was ardently devoted.

Sculptors had always been imagined as craggy and uncouth, but Gilbert was pleasantly plump, and florid in appearance and prose style.

PRINCE ARTHUR TO PRINCESS LOUISE
SIDMOUTH, 8 NOVEMBER 1934

... Now let me tell you how *sorry* I am at your natural grief at the rather sudden death of Sir A. Gilbert who you knew so well and admired so much; I only met him once, and then only for a few minutes. I am so sorry there is trouble about his ashes being given a place in the crypt of St. Paul's; I hope that it may be ultimately arranged as *you* and so many artists would wish. Arthur Ponsonby is a 'mauvais coucheur' if anyone ever was!! *I despise* the man, he is no *Englishman*! only a low '*internationalist*' and a *communist*; he is a disgrace to the 'House of Lords'!!

(1555)

Arthur Ponsonby came of the famous court family and Prince Arthur saw his defection to Labour as gross betrayal. As grandson of Sir Henry Ponsonby and son of Sir Frederick Ponsonby (Lord Sysonby) Arthur had been a page at Edward VII*'s coronation. Arthur's grandson, Tom, was to become Labour Chief Whip in the House of Lords.*

SAME TO SAME
BOURNEMOUTH, 8 MARCH 1935

Deciding on a Jubilee present:

Dearest Louise, So many thanks for your writing again so soon and for telling me that you had been to 'How's' and had seen there the 'Wine Coolers' (I had heard about) and that you liked them, and thought them genuine (as I am sure they were). Oddly enough I have this very moment learnt that May had sent to 'How' to say that she had heard of the *Wine Coolers* and would like to buy them (as they were just what she and George liked) – 'How' very rightly let May know that he *thought* that they were *bespoken* for a Jubilee present and that she had said that under these circumstances she would look forward with pleasure to George and her receiving them. Now that we have heard this, *I* feel that we *ought* to close with 'How', and buy them.

It is a bit of luck hearing that they would like to have them; George is generally satisfied with May's taste, and *he* also particularly likes to buy back old pieces of family plate, especially when they have the arms of their former owners on them.

It is very dear of you telling me of other things that you think might do. I think you will however agree with me that now we know what May and George would like we ought at once to get the wine coolers *then, if we get more money* than they will cost? we might think of adding to our present. I will get some younger members of the family to collect the money; it is very tiresome and worrying work. I hope that you however will allow me to receive your subscription and of course I am sure that we shall all be delighted to receive whatever sum you may like to give; I think the amount given by subscribers ought to be kept private, the only proviso being that it should not be *below five pounds*.

(1570)

Louise had seen the wine coolers in the Connoisseur *magazine. They cost £80.*

SAME TO SAME
BAGSHOT PARK, 20 SEPTEMBER 1935

War comes nearer.

... Mussolini has *evidently decided* on *going* to war with *Abyssinia*! Whatever the remainder of the world may say. There will *never have been a more unprovoked war*, nor one which will have *cost so much* as the attacking country; I should think that the expenses will about *ruin* Italy. I fear that it may end in antagonising the whole of the black population of Africa!!

(1580)

SAME TO SAME
PULTENEY HOTEL, BATH, 20 JANUARY 1936

Illness of King George V*:*

... I can't tell you how anxious I am about Georgie's illness; it is too sad and I fear *very serious*. I have heard *little* or *nothing* from any of the *Family* and my news is derived chiefly from the bulletins and the papers and what I get over the wireless. I gather however that the Household at Sandringham are very pessimistic and fear the worst. I have hopes as long as he is able to keep his strength up; the last news in the papers said that there had been no change for the worse and that he was maintaining his strength and was having some quiet sleep.

I own that the last two times I saw him before leaving London I thought he was coughing and seemed to me rather listless and his deafness much increased. *God grant* that he may pull through.... I was so grieved at the death of Rudyard Kipling who I knew very well and liked so much; he is a great loss ... He was the most loyal of Englishmen and a very strong Imperialist and he was kindness itself and especially with children.

(1589)

SAME TO SAME
PULTENEY HOTEL, BATH, 23 JANUARY 1936

King George V *died on 20 January.*
... The wonderful display of loyalty, and sympathy for his loss, and of affection for May and for the whole family is most touching. Throughout the whole world too, have *all* countries joined in the sorrows of the British Empire. We ought all of us to be proud of what George has done for his country.

I feel confident that dear David will do his utmost to follow in the footsteps of his dear father. He starts with the great advantage of having visited every part of the Empire and of being personally known by all its inhabitants. He is, too, very well known by most of the people of the kingdom and [seems] to be very popular with them. He must never forget what an old and experienced country we are, and how much we treasure our past and honourable history. He must of course look forward to the future, with all its never ceasing changes, but we must never forget the great deeds of our past.

It is *so dear* of you wanting to come down here for a few hours on Tuesday, the day of dear George's funeral; but *I do* think that it would be ABSOLUTELY FOLLY on *your part*; and *I must entreat* you *not* to *run* the *great risk* of taking this *long and cold journey* in this very *trying* and changeable weather and in this, the *coldest month* of the whole winter. I am happy to say that *I* am quite all right, and had arranged to attend a memorial service in the abbey here [Bath] at noon on Tuesday, accompanied by the Lord Lieutenant and the Mayor of Bath....

Thanking you again so very much for all you wrote in your dear letter and with my warmest love ever your devoted brother Arthur.

(1590)

THE EARL OF ATHLONE TO PRINCESS LOUISE
KENSINGTON PALACE, 27 JANUARY 1936

Dearest Aunt Louise, It is too sweet of you to have written in the way you have done and I *do* thank you from my heart.

Before I married he [George V] gave me rooms at St. James's and Marlborough House and I was treated as a younger brother. He was the kindest of brothers-in-law to me.

I have just returned from dining at Buckingham Palace with the Kings and representatives and I must say that David was wonderful as a host. He spoke German and French and was at his ease with the guests. God grant that he may be a great King.

Thank you again for your great kindness. Your most affectionate nephew Alge.

(1592)

Alge Athlone was Queen Mary's brother.

PRINCE ARTHUR TO PRINCESS LOUISE
BOURNEMOUTH, 4 MARCH 1936

... I did hear David's admirably worded address to his people, on my wireless, and did not miss a word of it. I thought that I had never heard his voice clearer and stronger; at times it reminded me so much of his father.

(1594)

SAME TO SAME
BOURNEMOUTH, 9 APRIL 1936

Easter wishes:
... How I wish that holy Easter might have brought us happier times even to *look forward to*!! There is *too much dictating* and *interfering* with half the powers of Europe, who alas are all *suspicious* of *one another*, besides having two *dictators,* like Mussolini and Hitler to reckon with, and also the *French*, who are the most *suspicious* of all, besides the Russians who are *always* on the *lookout* for *disturbing* the *world*!!

We *must all pray* for *real* peace and Christian Unity!!

I hope that you are pretty well, and with heartfelt love Ever your devoted brother Arthur.

(1601)

KING EDWARD VIII TO PRINCESS LOUISE
SUNDAY

Dearest Aunt Louise, Thank you so much for your sweet letter and for the carnations for buttonholes! I appreciated your kind thought of me *so* much. I was so pleased to find you at the Tottenham hospital the other day and you were marvellous as you always are. Nobody works as hard at charitable and healing instructions as you do and you are a great example and inspiration to all of us of our generation who are trying to emulate all that you have done.

I had not read the article you sent me but I feel that von Papen's dictatorship is the best thing for Germany at the present time as political government has proved to be a failure there. With my love and thanking you again always your very devoted affectionate David.

(1599)

Arthur's letters to Louise had narrow black margins after George V*'s death; not so David's. His were on blue paper with the address (The Fort, Sunningdale, Ascot) in scarlet.*

PRINCE ARTHUR TO PRINCESS LOUISE
BAGSHOT PARK, 9 AUGUST 1936

King Edward VIII *was cruising with Mrs Simpson.*
I am *very sorry* that David has gone abroad at the present moment, I regret that he should be going away; I can't help feeling that the government should not have allowed their Sovereign to be absent when the slightest spark might produce war in Europe!! ...

(1608)

SAME TO SAME
29 SEPTEMBER 1936

First direct mention of the Wallis Simpson affair in this correspondence:
... I too was *very* distressed at the party staying at the Castle [Balmoral], what a pity! I wonder what the Scotch people thought of it; of course *I never refer to the subject*; it is *not my business*, and he is *over 40 years old now*. Wishing you again a comfortable journey and not too *fatiguing* and a pleasant stay at Roseneath [*sic*] with good weather, Ever your devoted brother Arthur.

(1615)

SAME TO SAME
PULTENEY HOTEL, BATH, 10 NOVEMBER 1936

The Spanish Civil War – General Franco's right-wing dictatorship against the left-wing Republic:
How kind of you letting me know what Ena [ex-Queen of Spain] wanted *one* or all of us to do. The idea of getting one of us to become President of a Committee that she is getting up, for sending comforts and clothes to the poor suffering Spanish people is a very natural one, and she may be able to get her immediate friends in England to subscribe.

But *you* are *so right* in *pointing out* to her and Beatrice and B.B. ['Baby Beatrice', the Edinburghs' daughter] that it *would never do* for any of us to be *mixed up* even with such a scheme. It would be *very unwise* and would, to *my mind* be *quite impossible*, with *present* very sad state of feeling that unfortunately exists amongst many of the British public. If you had asked me to do what Ena wanted, I could not have done otherwise than point out to you how *impossible* it *appeared to me* for *any* of *us* to *join even* in such a scheme. How *wise* you were in consulting others you know and trusted before giving any answer to B.B. and the others. I was so much relieved when I read your 2nd letter, to know that you had got them to see the *impossibility* of what they wanted. Now I understand that *you* have *settled the whole thing* and I need not think any more about it.

(1618)

Louise understood politics better than her younger royal relations.

SAME TO SAME
BATH, 6 DECEMBER 1936

The royal crisis – the family point of view:

... I am so distressed to hear that you have been suffering so much pain with the carbuncle that had developed itself on the nerves of your temple; I have always heard how painful it is, but I am so relieved to hear that owing to your doctor's good treatment, it is now at last becoming better. ...

Now about this dreadful crisis that David has suddenly brought upon us all. It came as an *awful shock* upon me, as I had never heard *anything definite* about what was going on, as I am always away from London and did not know of the gossip that *everybody* seems to have been talking about and that suddenly came to a head when a certain Bishop made an outrageous speech which was quoted by all the papers.

Naturally the Prime Minister became alarmed and felt himself obliged to speak to D. [David] on the subject and very pleasant for both of them it must have been. Alas D. is very headstrong and *is determined* to have his *own* way, and won't listen to *anyone*.

I never knew that the King could marry anybody he chose and had only to announce it to Parliament as a 'fait accompli'; but surely D. must have known that, once he was Sovereign he was no longer a *private individual* who could do as [he] liked, during every week and during his annual holidays.

Now he has been rudely reminded of the oaths he took when he became king; these were at complete variance with the life he had been living when off duty. Evidently he resented being reminded of this. Oh dear, oh dear! *what* a position he has got himself into! and how on earth will he extricate himself without either being obliged to resign or causing the government to fall and producing a most serious state of affairs.

I can't bear the whole thing and much as I like D. and would like to help and look up to him as our Sovereign, I feel, to my great regret, that I find it difficult now to have the same respect for him now that I had. I am awfully sorry for him, for I feel that he must be having a terrible time of it just now. But what about all of us?

Has he, I wonder, ever thought what we must be feeling at 'the Queen'!! he is going to introduce into our family?

I know that he is much beloved by the working people, for the great interest he has taken in their trials and sorrows and has seen for himself the dreadful state in which they have been living in 'the distressed areas' in South Wales and elsewhere, and has been moving government to do their duty. For this we ought to be very grateful, and I think the country recognise this and many will not *hear of his abdicating*. A pleasant position he is placing himself and the government of the whole Empire in! From what I have written you will see *what my feelings are* and *how unhappy* I am at the state of affairs that D. *alone* has brought the country into. God help us all to do what we can to find a solution to the most difficult position in which this country as [*sic*] ever found themselves.

Bless you dearest sister and believe me in my deep sympathy with poor May and all of us of the Family. Ever your devoted brother Arthur.

(1622)

STANLEY BALDWIN TO PRINCESS LOUISE
10 DOWNING STREET, 8 DECEMBER 1936

She must have written to sympathize with him over the stress and strain of the Abdication.

Madam, Your most kind letter has touched and pleased me. Your sympathetic realisation of the gravity and difficulty of the situation is indeed a help.

I thank you most sincerely.

I have the honour to be Madam, Your Royal Highness' obedient servant, Stanley Baldwin.

(1937)

PRINCE ARTHUR TO PRINCESS LOUISE
BATH, 14 DECEMBER 1936

The Abdication:

As you justly say, *I* am very relieved at the end of this terribly regrettable climax, that our Empire has just been through. But *how sad* is the sudden end of poor David's short reign of a little over 10 months, and who we all hoped would make a model though rather too modern King. He meant well and was, I know, deeply interested in making the poorer and more unfortunately placed working men happier and more helped than they had been, by *his* Government and by Parliament. Wrong-headed as I think he was in his friendships, and in his loves, we must always remember that he *was but human.*

That he should have given his love to a woman who had been *twice* through the divorce court and who was still the wife of her 2nd husband was a *perfect tragedy*, but alas he was too weak to give up this undesirable woman. Poor man he has to pay for his obstinacy and one must feel sorry for him though we feel that he should have stuck to the proud position that he held and to which he succeeded a well beloved Sovereign. *I* can't help feeling deeply for him, for he must have gone through agonising days, and he was always so dear and considerate to me and I will always retain most pleasant recollections of him, especially ever since he became King.

I wrote him a nice farewell [*rest of letter missing*]

(1623)

LORD WIGRAM TO PRINCESS LOUISE
NORMAN TOWER, WINDSOR CASTLE, 19 DECEMBER 1936

Private Secretary to George V, *he stayed on for the usual six months with a new sovereign (Edward* VIII), *then resigned, and was asked by George* VI *to stand in for three months while Alexander Hardinge took sick leave.*

Madam, Your Royal Highness' letter has given me great pleasure and I am truly grateful for these words of encouragement. I will do my best to help the King and Queen not only from feelings of loyalty but from pure love and affection for Their Majesties.

The last ten months have been an absolute nightmare to me but the clouds have cleared away and I am confident that we now have a King who will be exactly like his Father.

(1624)

PRINCE ARTHUR TO PRINCESS LOUISE
BATH, 28 JANUARY 1937

David leaves a muddle for Bertie.

I hear that David rings Bertie up once or twice a day. I hear that he [Bertie] is working very hard trying to read up all that he has not hitherto known, so as to understand all the many questions that come up to him daily for decision. I gather that now the Sovereign is the *direct king* of *all* the *dependencies* of the Crown, everything comes direct to him and not through the Colonial Office as it used to do. I believe that the Private Secretary's work has enormously increased.

It must be very trying for Bertie to find himself suddenly plunged into this new unexpected work. David never did it, and when he abdicated Bertie found all the Sovereign's work in a frightful muddle; Clive Wigram who is acting for Hardinge (during his absence on sick leave) is working hard to get things in order again, as they were when George died. *I* don't think that official affairs can possibly be put in *proper order* till after all the Coronation functions are over....

(1631)

SAME TO SAME
BRANKSOME TOWER HOTEL, BOURNEMOUTH
21 FEBRUARY 1937

Problems for the future – the family point of view:
Harry Harewood came here for a few hours last week on urgent Masonic business. He had just come back from accompanying Mary [his wife, the Princess Royal] to Austria; he said that he found David well and in very good spirits; but at times he would talk about the month of April, when he hoped to marry, when the time would be up for Mrs. [S.] to get her divorce. Harry could not make out *where* it was proposed that the wedding should take place, nor anything on the subject. *I* have *no idea* if the King is *bound* to *give* his *consent* to the marriage or not? and if he does, whether *she* automatically becomes a Royal Highness? How awful this would be!! and *what* a position the whole family would find themselves in. Harry H. told me also that *he* thought that David would give Bertie a very nasty time of it if the Sovereign did [not] give his consent to the marriage.

I can't find out that *anyone knows what* is likely to happen. I wonder whether it is very wise on the part of the Kents going to *Munich just now*, which is so close to Vienna? and I can't help thinking that David will *expect* Georgy [Kent] and Marina to pay him a visit? when D. would be sure to talk about his marriage and the hereafter. However, it *is not* my business, and I *don't know anything* about what is going to happen. H.H. also told me that he gathered that David quite expected to be coming back to England some time this year!! This Harry Harewood said would be quite *impossible* and *most disastrous*.

Altogether I am very worried about the future and have no idea how it will be possible to overcome all these difficulties, especially as alas David does not seem to take in his position and *what* he has *wantonly done*. However

I am not going to write any more on this disagreeable subject; matters will unravel themselves in time, and I only hope that *everyone* will support poor Bertie. . . .

(1632)

SAME TO SAME
4 MARCH 1937

What may be in store for us all? What on earth will Bertie do? I can't imagine, and what will the country say?

He is probably referring to the Windsors' wedding.

The possible events of the future quite sadden my life, and I can't bear to think what must be May's feelings. However I suppose that there is nothing for us all to do, but to wait and see what is going to happen. I believe that there is a case of *libel* being brought against (a lady) (I don't know who), by Mrs. Simpson's sister, over some remarks she made at a lunch, (by the lady) not knowing in the least that one of the ladies at lunch was Simpson's sister. It may be very awkward!!

(1633)

SAME TO SAME
BOURNEMOUTH, 25 MARCH 1937

. . . Your American joke about Mrs. S. and the only *throne* that she would ever sit on, is very funny and *very strong*. . . .

(1636)

SAME TO SAME
BOURNEMOUTH, 29 MARCH 1937

. . . It is really incredible that David should for a moment be thinking that May and the brothers could *possibly* attend his wedding!! (whenever that may be). I am [afraid] he will be terribly upset but what else could he expect! apart from the impossibility of their leaving England during the Coronation festivities.

(1637)

PRINCE HENRY OF GLOUCESTER TO PRINCESS LOUISE YORK HOUSE, ST JAMES'S PALACE, 17 MARCH 1938

My dearest Aunt Louise, We send you our best wishes on your 90th birthday and congratulate you on being the first member of our family to attain this age.

(1662)

One of very many congratulatory messages. Princess Louise was the first but not the last. She was to be followed by Prince Arthur, Princess Alice Countess Athlone (ninety-seven) and HM Queen Elizabeth the Queen Mother (ninety on 4 August 1990).

VICTORIA, MARCHIONESS OF MILFORD HAVEN TO PRINCESS LOUISE

Victoria is trying to arrange, apparently, a Christmas lunch with her in 1938.
I suppose it would be too late for the turkey if we came on Sunday? and please do not trouble about asking anybody else, if Sunday should happen to suit you; if William's son ['Little Willy'] is free and you like to ask him I will be pleased to meet him, as I know him already, but generally he has a lot of engagements. I think if you wrote a line to Wil. as you did in old days, to thank him for the book he sent you, it would touch him very much. He has grown much gentler and kinder during his long exile and that dreadful war ended 20 years ago now. Ever, with much love your devoted Victoria.

(1906)

PRINCESS BEATRICE TO PRINCESS LOUISE KENSINGTON PALACE, CLOCK COURT, 9 MARCH 1939

Dearest Louise, Thank you so much for the dear messages you gave to 'Jamie' for me, and I am so touched at your thinking of me. I can assure you I am doing so of you morning noon and night, and feel it terribly not being able to go over and see you, if you cared for me to come. But my tiresome bronchial asthma has been very troublesome of late, I suppose owing to the cold winds, and I am at times so breathless, I can hardly talk, and the least exertion brings it on. I am so grieved that your foot and ankle cause you so much pain and can throughly sympathise with you, as mine are much the same. All my best love and wishes for your improvement your loving sister Beatrice.

(1693)

SAME TO SAME
KENSINGTON PALACE, 22 SEPTEMBER 1939

I must send you a little line to say that I am off to the country [Sharpthorne in Sussex] as it has been thought better for me to go away for a little while, my bronchial asthma having been so very troublesome of late. I hate not being able to wish you goodbye but my breathlessness is so bad every exertion and agitation easily brings on an attack which makes me speeechless and choky, so I could not dare venture to come for fear of upsetting you.

(1698)

On 3 October, exactly two months before Louise's death, came a letter with a melancholy ring from Bessie Bulteel, Princess Beatrice's lady-in-waiting:

... we are leading a very quiet life, and have seen nobody, so there is nothing to tell you.

(1699)

The three last surviving members of the old royal family – two sisters and a brother – were drifting out on the same quiet tide. Louise went first, aged ninety-one years, eight months and fifteen days. Arthur followed at ninety-one years, eight months and twenty-six days; Beatrice at eighty-seven years, six months and twelve days. The world they knew had already ebbed away.

INDEX

Index